Caught in the Web of Words

James A. H. Murray
and the
Oxford English Dictionary

K. M. ELISABETH MURRAY
with a Preface by
R. W. Burchfield

Oxford   New York   Melbourne
OXFORD UNIVERSITY PRESS
1979

Oxford University Press, Walton Street, Oxford OX2 6DP

OXFORD   LONDON   GLASGOW
NEW YORK   TORONTO   MELBOURNE   WELLINGTON
KUALA LUMPUR   SINGAPORE   JAKARTA   HONG KONG   TOKYO
DELHI   BOMBAY   CALCUTTA   MADRAS   KARACHI
IBADAN   DAR ES SALAAM   CAPE TOWN

British Library Cataloguing in Publication Data

Murray, K. M. Elisabeth
  Caught in the web of words.
  1. Murray, *Sir* James Augustus Henry
  2. Lexicographers – Great Britain – Biography
  I. Title
423'.092'4   PE64.M8   79-40275

ISBN 0-19-28265-3

Printed in Great Britain by Hazell Watson & Viney Ltd,
Aylesbury, Bucks

CONTENTS

Contents

ILLUSTRATIONS

PREFACE

THIS is a biography of a lexicographer greater by far than Dr Johnson, though he lacks the lustre and legend associated with Johnson, and greater perhaps than any lexicographer of his own time or since in Britain, the United States, or Europe.

James Murray's beginnings were spectacularly unpromising. It is natural to think that young James Murray, as the son of a village tailor and of the daughter of 'the only man in Hawick who could produce the finest table linen at that time', might perhaps in due course have become a draper. Instead the 'tall, strong, healthy, good-looking boy', who wore his hair to shoulder length in the fashionable way of his time, left school at fourteen and a half and took casual work on neighbouring farms while continuing to educate himself. The young Borderer of Teviotdale studied the geological structure of his district and mastered the classification of plants. He showed precocious interest in the dialectal varieties of the Border area, and while still at Minto school, his second parish school, he acquired some knowledge of four languages, French, Italian, German, and Greek. 'Knowledge is power' he declared on the flyleaf of the first issue of John Cassell's serial publication, *Popular Educator*, which appeared in 1852, and the omnivorous young reader added 'Nihil est melius quam vita diligentissima'. At the age of seventeen he became an assistant master at Hawick United School. During the next few years the pursuit of the *vita diligentissima* knew no bounds: he was a founder of the Hawick Archaeological Society, he 'discovered' Anglo-Saxon and was excited by King Alfred's translation of Orosius, and he embarked on a life-long study of phonetics, at first by means of Alexander Melville Bell's system of 'visible speech'. He acquired a knowledge of the written form of many languages, and he enthusiastically explored the various branches of natural science. Fortunately Miss Murray, grand-daughter of Sir James, has been able to uncover all the details of this early great learning period.

Marriage took Murray away from Scotland. He left Hawick and

took employment as a bank clerk in London in a vain attempt to find a healthier climate for his moribund wife. She died in 1865 and Murray remained in London. Two years later he remarried and the book provides an account of this long and happy second marriage, with brief glimpses of the later lives of some of the eleven children born to James and Ada.

He remained a bank clerk until 1870 and he must have been the most learned bank clerk of the century. He met A. J. Ellis, the greatest English authority of the time on pronunciation, and through him Henry Sweet, Richard Morris, and other philologists and scholars. Incredibly, in view of his lack of professional qualifications, he was invited to read some papers to the Philological Society himself in 1867 and 1869 on the dialects of the southern counties of Scotland (later the subject of one of his books), and he edited a volume for the Early English Text Society.

In 1870 he returned to schoolmastering, this time at Mill Hill School. From this base he continued his philological and dialectal work outside teaching hours. It was while he was at Mill Hill School that the invitation came to edit the *New English Dictionary* (later known as the *Oxford English Dictionary*).

First at this school and later in the back garden of his house in Oxford he built a Scriptorium, and from these most improbable workshops came the greatest dictionary of modern times. The treasure chests of letters and documents kept lovingly by the Murray family, and now opened with skill by Miss Elisabeth Murray, and numerous documents and minute books preserved by the Oxford University Press and generously made available to the biographer, have enabled the compilation of an extraordinarily detailed account of the frustrations that attended the making of the Dictionary. There are glimpses of the mercurial Frederick J. Furnivall, and shafts of wisdom and of impatience in turn from those who had to deal with Murray—the Delegates of the O.U.P., the Vice-Chancellor of Oxford University, and others. Faced with exasperatingly lengthening forecasts of the date of completion and of the size of the Dictionary, and confronted with a desperately inadequate financial return from their heavy investment, the Delegates of the O.U.P. would have been justified, one feels, in abandoning the project altogether. It is to their eternal credit that they did not. James Murray was allowed to go on. Distinctions were conferred on him as the work proceeded and he was knighted in 1908. Oxford University at last recognized the magnitude of his achievement by bestowing an LL.D. on him in 1914.

He did not live long enough to edit the last pages of the Dictionary. He laid the lines of the Dictionary and drew the plan, and edited more than half of it himself, with the help of a handful of devoted assistants. More than any of his celebrated colleagues, Henry Bradley, Sir William Craigie, and Dr C. T. Onions, and of his analogues in Europe in the nineteenth and early part of the twentieth century, he will be remembered as the founder of the art of historical lexicography, and his name will always be synonymous with 'the long and efficient working of the great engine of research by which the Dictionary [was] produced'.

R. W. Burchfield
June 1977

ACKNOWLEDGEMENTS

I N WRITING this life of my grandfather I have had the advantage of a trunk full of letters and other material in manuscript and in print which was collected by my father, Harold J. R. Murray, in the twenties. My grandmother kept every letter, but unfortunately, when the Scriptorium at Oxford ceased to be used for Dictionary purposes it was no longer heated, and my father found that many of the papers stored there had rotted from damp. Even so, the number of family, personal and official letters which survive is very great and covers all periods and activities of my grandfather's long life. The Murray papers, which will eventually be presented to the Bodleian Library, are my principal source. They include also information collected by my father from people who had known James Murray, such as his pupils at Hawick and Mill Hill, and, most important, his brother Charles O. Murray.

For the information about James Murray's ancestors I am again indebted to my father, who with his brother Aelfric did extensive genealogical research, covering not only the Murray direct line, but also the trees of the families with which they were allied. The pedigree in typescript with many letters and photographs is also in my possession.

Next in importance to the foregoing material is the information from James Murray's children. Many of the family stories I heard from my father and uncles and aunts from childhood. Harold and Wilfrid both wrote biographies of their father, Wilfrid's privately published in South Africa and Harold's in typescript in my possession. These include a good deal of information from their own experience, especially of the Mill Hill period. Wilfrid drew largely on the letters of his father to Aelfric, and these, covering the period 1902 to 1913, still survive and together with a collection of James Murray's sermons were lent to me by my cousin Mrs Manning. Information from Oswyn is included in his life by his widow, Lady Murray. For the Oxford period I collected much oral information from my Aunt Rosfrith before her death in 1973, and also from my Uncle Jowett, who kindly lent me his collection of letters from his father, 1909 to 1914, and his own delightful account of his childhood, which he wrote down when in internment in China during World War II. Some information was also given to me by Gwyneth Logan, the youngest of the Murray family.

The great bulk of these primary sources poses problems in providing the reader with references. The Murray papers are unindexed and arranged only in date order, and are likely to remain so. Hence it is necessary to do more than refer to the collection generally if the document or letter is to be traced by another student. Yet to give an exact reference to every fact used would unduly burden the text. I have therefore made a compromise. Where the writer, the date or the subject is of importance, a full reference is given, but statements of anecdotal character without a footnote are taken either from the Murray papers, from other letters belonging to members of the family, or from family oral tradition.

My thanks are due to the following: the Delegates of the Oxford University Press, Oxford, for allowing me to use the Order Books of the Delegates and some correspondence: to R. W. Burchfield, Editor of the four volume *Supplement to the Oxford English Dictionary*, for making available to me letters and papers removed from the Old Ashmolean on completion of the Dictionary and other letters since acquired, especially those of James Murray to Fitzedward Hall: to Professor R. H. Robins, Secretary to the Philological Society, for a loan of the Minute Books of the Society: to the Headmaster and D. M. Hall, archivist, of Mill Hill School for showing me the school and the archives and arranging with the present occupants of 'Sunnyside' for me to visit their home: to the following who answered my appeal in *The Times Literary Supplement* and kindly gave me information about letters in their collections: R. W. Pound, Deputy Librarian, King's College, London (Furnivall Papers): D. W. Evans, Rare Book Librarian, Birmingham University: and Miss E. D. Yeo, Assistant Keeper, National Library of Scotland. Vincent Quinn, Librarian of Balliol College, told me of the important Hucks Gibbs correspondence in the Guildhall Library, London.

I received much kindness and help when I visited Denholm and Hawick, and my special thanks are due to the Editor of the *Hawick Express* for arranging for me to use the early files of the *Hawick Advertiser* and to T. Inglis Storie, Secretary of the Hawick Archaeological Society, who lent me its first Minute books.

Acknowledgements

Finally, my very great thanks are due to Dr Robert Gittings, who gave me his valuable advice on improving my first draft and on finding a publisher. My long-suffering friends Alice M. Burnet and Janet S. A. Macaulay gave criticism, secretarial aid and encouragement, while Agnes Sibley patiently typed and retyped the text and footnotes and persuaded me to continue when, like my grandfather wrestling with the Dictionary, I felt near to despair.

Prologue

I AM three and a half years old and I am walking with my father and my brother down Bateman Street, Cambridge, where we live. We seem to have walked a very long way, and I think I am tired and am trying to induce someone to carry me. 'Walk as far as that flowering tree,' they say, 'and then we might carry you.' And when we get to the tree my brother says, 'Now see if you can walk as far as that man.' And when we get to the man I find we have reached our gate, and that the man with a long white beard is my grandfather. I know he is a very important man because I went with my nurse to the picture sellers in a little shop in King's Parade and asked him to allow us to sit in his upstairs window so that we could watch the procession when Grandfather was given an honorary degree because he is writing the great *New English Dictionary*. I liked the procession and although there was a long line of men in red robes, it was easy to pick out Grandfather because of his beard. No one told me to notice whom he was walking with, which is a pity as it was Thomas Hardy.

The only other time I remember seeing Grandfather Dictionary was when I was five and this was at his home in Oxford. He was sitting with a great number of my aunts and uncles round a very large dining table. I think we must have arrived just as they were finishing tea. I was made to go all round the table and kiss each in turn, and Grandfather's beard tickled. I did not like kissing people much, and I hated that long journey round the dining table. It seemed only a few minutes later when they said it was my bed time, and I must kiss them all goodnight. That tickly beard again so soon, and all those uncles and aunts! I rebelled and stood firm, and they all began to coax me: 'Don't be shy. Be a good girl!' The youngest, kind Uncle Jowett, suggested that perhaps I was afraid that he had a pigtail as he had just come home from China. I gratefully accepted the excuse and was allowed to go to bed.

A few months later, back at home, my father came into the nursery to get his top hat out of its leather box in the cupboard, and I was told he was going to Grandfather's funeral.

Now, sitting down to write my grandfather's life, I feel it is almost an impertinence for me to attempt to interpret this remote patriarchal figure belonging to a pre-World War I age which I can only just remember, even though I have a mass of his letters to help me and am constantly surprised to recognise in his character and interests traits which I had thought peculiar to myself but now find to be inherited. I am further intimidated by his own strongly expressed views on biography:

> It is one of the hateful characteristics of a degenerate age, that the idle world will not let the worker alone, accept his offering of work, & appraise it for itself, but must insist upon turning *him* inside out, and knowing all about him, and really troubling itself a great deal more about his little peculiarities & personal pursuits, than his abiding work.[1]

> I wish we knew nothing of Carlyle but his writings; I am thankful we know so little of Chaucer & Shakspere . . . I have persistently refused to answer the whole buzzing swarm of biographers, saying simply 'I am a nobody — if you have anything to say about the Dictionary, there it is at your will — but treat me as a solar myth, or an echo, or an irrational quantity, or ignore me altogether.' It was unfortunately not practicable to edit the dictionary anonymously, else I should certainly have done so . . . it is extremely annoying to me to see the Dictionary referred to as *Murray's English Dictionary*.[2]

He did, however, in later life reveal that he had always intended to write out a narrative of his life and memories when he had completed the Dictionary and leave it to his family 'to suppress or publish it, or such parts of it, as their wisdom should choose'.[3] This intent was never fulfilled, but certainly his children had no doubt that their father's life story should be made known despite his views, and I can only hope that he might have felt differently about a biography written sixty years after his death.

CHAPTER I

'Round O and Crooked S':
The Formative Years

It was in Teviotdale, a fine open hill country of wide skies and a
peculiar clarity of atmosphere, that James Murray spent the first
twenty-seven years of his life and where one must seek the influences
which shaped his character and determined his career. He was proud
to be a Borderer, a member of a tough and independent stock, born, as
he said

> within three hours walk of English ground, & within sight of
> mountain peaks that rise under English laws . . . My native parish
> was very near to that nondescript tract which in older times was
> known as the Debateable Ground—because it was claimed by both
> England & Scotland & whose inhabitants were neither English nor
> Scotch but simply Borderers.[1]

In spite of recent afforestation the country has not changed much in
the past 130 years, and Denholm, James' birthplace, is not greatly
enlarged. It is an unusual village for Scotland, being built round an
oblong green. At one end is an early nineteenth-century church,
looking as though it were constructed with toy building blocks, and in
the centre of the green an ornate steeple, like a miniature Albert
Memorial, commemorating the local poet, John Leyden. The small
neat houses, some of them old, built close together, have a pleasing
diversity of roof line and effectively screen modern development
behind, while above them one sees the surrounding hills. All his life,
James Murray was only really happy when he was in sight of rising
ground and where he could experience the exhilaration of scrambling
up steep slopes and breathing keen mountain air.

The Teviot Valley here is fairly wide and the river flows through
flat pastures below the village. As a boy James often crossed the bridge

3

to Hassendean and Minto on the far bank. Here are the two detached, rounded, grassy Minto hills, smooth as a chalk down and softly reflecting the changing lights as sun and cloud chase across them. Just beyond, down stream, is the contrasting wooded cliff of Minto Crag, a happy hunting ground for James in search of rare ferns and flowers, while in the village below is the school in which he finished his education.

Behind Denholm in the other direction the land rises steeply to the south to a ridge now crowned with a fir wood. Beyond, over fields of red earth, is the striking Ruberslaw, a hill only 1500 ft high, which seems much more because of its isolation, standing up from a distance as a prominent feature of the landscape and seen from Denholm as a challenge to be climbed. It is also notable for its colour. In the generally green country Ruberslaw, rocky and heather-covered, lowers darkly. James got to know every inch of the hill and to his inquiring mind the contrast between the green Minto Hills, the sandy red soil on the lower slopes of Ruberslaw and the grey rocks above, posed questions to be satisfied by a study of geology.

Ruberslaw lies between two tributaries of the Teviot—Rulewater, in a beautiful valley running up towards the English border, is on the Jedburgh side; and closer to Denholm is the Dean Burn, winding its way through woods in a deep sandstone cleft. Up the Burn and west of it is Cavers, the estate of which Denholm is a part and to the Laird of which, James Douglas, the village owed its neat lay-out. In 1835 he cleared the green by giving his sixty tenants, or feuars, land behind their cottages to store their wood and keep their pigs and geese, and showed interest in their culture by presenting them also with a library and the instruments for a brass band.[2]

This year of change was that in which Thomas Murray, James' father, a young bachelor of twenty-four, decided to settle in Denholm to ply his craft of tailoring.[3] Thomas had good reasons for taking this decision to live in Denholm when the idea was suggested to him by a friend while on holiday there, for Thomas' ancestors came from Rulewater and had farmed land on the Cavers estate at Spittal Tower on the shoulder of Ruberslaw. His grandfather, Andrew, had moved across the Teviot to rent farms on the Hassendean estate, and Thomas' father, an earlier James, left farming for tailoring. After learning the trade in Denholm he set up in business in the High street of the neighbouring town of Hawick. There he married a widow, Christina Wintrope, grand-daughter of a former Town Clerk. The grandchildren were often told the story of this match. Before her first marriage Christina had a vivid dream that she was walking in her father's garden and met a man there. Later the East Bank Secession church was built on the site, and in her widowhood Christina attended it. There one day she recognised in an Elder of the church the man in her dream—and they later married. Christina and James had seven children, of whom Thomas was the third.

After learning his father's trade in Hawick, Thomas became a journeyman tailor in the north of England; but when he began to think of settling down he found Hawick overstocked with tailors and generally very overcrowded. Denholm, by contrast was much more attractive and seemed likely to develop. Stone quarries established in 1818 were flourishing, employing up to 200 men and with an output of sixty cart-loads a day, while in almost every cottage knitting frames were set up and every week a cart-load of finished stockings went into Hawick and came back with the yarn for more. The needs of the prosperous inhabitants were supplied by joiners, millwrights and blacksmiths, grocers, bakers, butchers, shoemakers and drapers. There were at one time nine tailors,[4] which perhaps explains why Thomas Murray later regretted his choice of profession and was disappointed in his career and anxious to see his sons do better. Trade for him never boomed and he earned only about twelve shillings a week. He came from a family noted for honesty and religious principles but he was not a good business man and he was apt to make bad debts by letting men better off than himself owe him money. In any case the demand for good suits was very limited. Thomas found that his best customers were the 'courting' young men: after they settled down to married life, money was scarce, clothes had a way of redoubling their life, and a good suit of black for Sundays and funerals might easily last a lifetime.

Another factor in Thomas' decision to settle in Denholm was that he found his wife there. Mary Scott, seven years his senior, was a Hawick girl, sixth child of a linen manufacturer, auld Charlie o' the Crescent. Hers was a well known family, claiming to descend from the Scotts of Bunraw, a claim which was thought to be supported by a small silver vinaigrette handed down for generations and treasured by Mary. Her uncle James, surprisingly, was a dancing master, first in Edinburgh and then at St James's Square, London, where he taught members of the royal family. Mary was named after his wife, who was a niece of the painter Thomas Gainsborough. Her father, auld

2. James Murray's birthplace, Denholm, near Hawick, Roxburghshire. The Murrays' lodging was in the last house on the right.

Charlie, was the only man in Hawick who could produce the finest table linen at that time, and he employed six or eight weavers in his own house as well as a number of women working in their homes. He was on his way to becoming a wealthy man when unfortunately, soon after 1830 he was prevailed upon to stand surety for a bond by a gentleman of the county who became bankrupt, and Charlie Scott had to repay the bond. It therefore became necessary for his children to find employment and Mary took a post as a servant at Deanburn Cottage, Denholm, the residence of the Independent Minister.

Thomas Murray and Mary Scott were married on 19 December 1835. Houses were scarce and they rented two rooms on the first floor of the Crown Inn on the south side of the Green in the main street of Denholm. It was the principal inn and the stopping place for the stage coaches, but it faced competition from five or six drinking shops in the short length of street so it also sold drapery and grocery. The house is still standing, now roofed in slate instead of thatched, no longer an inn but still a shop. A plaque over the door records that James Murray was born there on 7 February 1837 in the last months of the reign of William IV.[5]

6

Four other children were born to Thomas and Mary Murray—Charles, born in 1838 who died in 1842; Alexander Davidson, born in 1840; Charles Oliver, and Margaret Scott, born at two-year intervals. The Murrays lived in various cottages in the village, always small, humble dwellings in which the children looked forward to the time of year when the roof space was emptied of the fuel stored there and they had room to play.

The family was a united one and the religious and moral influence of his home persisted in James Murray throughout his life. He learned there by example, the duties of parents towards their children, the reciprocal obligations of sons and daughters and the value of strong parental support. Family ties were sacred ties and the family something tangible and enduring, rooted in pride in ancestry and manifest in the shared glory in present achievement.

Although their means were very limited and it was a hard struggle to rear and educate four children, the Murrays did not indulge in self pity, but were thankful for opportunities available to them which had not been given to earlier generations. They did not think of themselves as poor—that would have been so had they been in receipt of the parish dole, which they never were. On the contrary, they were conscious of belonging to good families and having 'good blood'. This in Scotland was very important, those so privileged might be suitably respectful to their own aristocracy but would adopt a very different attitude to members of other families, however exalted their rank, holding themselves as good as any man of them if these families were not adjudged to be of 'good blood'.[6] Hence Thomas Murray, although not one of the hereditary feuars of Denholm, was none the less a highly regarded member of the community. When he left Denholm in 1858 he was presented with a Family Bible in recognition of the part he had played for twenty years as an active and efficient member of the Congregational Church, a promoter of the Total Abstinence and Horticultural Societies, of the Reading Room Club and other institutions concerned with the welfare of the village.[7] He also acted as almoner and adviser to Douglas of Cavers with regard to the annual distribution of alms to the poor.

Thomas had a special link with the Douglas family through his religion, for the Douglases and the Murrays were alike descended from men who had been ready to suffer for their faith in the seventeenth century. From early years Thomas' children would hear of the stirring events of those times.

The Reformation in Scotland, taking a rather different course from that in England, was at first mainly directed to the practical issue of introducing control by the laity to restore pastoral care to the people, and doctrine was not in question. It was Charles I who, completely out of touch with reality, precipitated a crisis by trying to force the Scottish church to follow English usage, after the introduction of a new prayer book. This led in 1638 to the uniting of nobility and common people, royalists and non-royalists, in a protest embodied in the National Covenant. When the King treated all the signatories as rebels the result was a General Assembly which abolished Bishops because they were now identified with the royal cause. Under Charles II, when the Bishops were restored, but the Puritan forms of worship were tolerated, the Covenanters were split, some accepting the compromise, but others, particularly in the central Borders, continuing resistance.[8] Amongst those remaining true to the Covenanting cause were the Douglas family: they supported ministers ejected for refusing to recognise the Bishops, and resisted the induction of a curate sent to replace the minister in their own church at Cavers, withholding the church door key while local women pelted their opponents with stones and abused them as 'soul murderers and the devil's servants'. Secret conventicles were held on the Cavers estate, hidden in the Dean Valley or on the summit of Ruberslaw. In 1690, when the Presbyterian Church was recognised as the Established Church of Scotland, the Douglas family remained true to their old beliefs and loyalties and the persecuted remnant of the Covenanters formed a congregation of the Cameronian Church in Denholm on a site given by the Laird.

The Murrays in Hawick had been members of the Secession Church but later joined one of the first Congregational churches in the south of Scotland and when Thomas arrived in Denholm he found the Congregationalists also established in the former Cameronian chapel. Thomas became an elder and at one time Precentor of this church and his son liked to say that he belonged to a congregation which, through the Cameronians, was a direct descendant of the Covenanters. Just as he later delighted to trace back the history and form of a modern word to its remote origin in an unbroken record, so James early developed his appreciation of being part of a present which has its roots in the past.

Religion was a powerful, binding force in the Murray family. Their strong faith, forged by their ancestors under persecution, was allied to patriotism. In his thirties James boasted that his forefathers had declared for the Commonwealth and stood shoulder to shoulder with the Ironsides at Naseby and Marston Moor. 'Seven generations ago,' he said, his ancestors 'endured suffering & tribulation & persecution & loss of worldly all for their puritanism—and puritans we are still.'[9] In his home he was brought up to see the hand of God in all that befell them and to give thanks, and as an old man he looked back and felt that his successes in life were due to the family practice of daily prayer.[10]

Religion was an important influence in the Murray home in another sense. John Knox, greatly honoured in that family for his influence on moral life and political freedom, was convinced of the importance of education and introduced a scheme to provide education for the poor by appointing a schoolmaster to every church. His writings continued strongly to influence the Covenanting stock of the Border country, giving the people an ingrained respect for sobriety, industriousness and the fulfilment of a social role: they believed in the need to work systematically for a positive purpose. Even in the seventeenth century it was normal for a parish to provide five years schooling for children before they moved on to a bigger school in the town and there are numerous examples of able boys from humble homes who achieved a university degree.[11] The Murrays were therefore quite justified in being ambitious for their sons.

Thomas himself regretted very much that his own education had been neglected and had not given him more than a basic knowledge of the three *R*'s. He had a good mind and his children felt that he would have made a lawyer because of his enjoyment of a discussion in which he would weigh up the pros and cons, looking at the proposition all round without ever getting overheated and drawn into dispute. After work he would sit and talk with his cronies, keeping the children awake but also often giving them something to think about.

One of the conversations James overheard stuck in his memory. A group of villagers were listening to one of the party who had been away for some years 'up England' and was recounting his adventures. Amongst them was a visit to a Quakers' meeting and his audience burst into loud guffaws when he described how he had sat for an hour or more and 'never a word was said'. To his audience, going to church was 'going to the preaching' and the idea of sitting in silence hearing nothing seemed quite ludicrous. But when the laughter had subsided, Thomas Murray looked up and said sternly that he could conceive of nothing better for some people than to have to sit and think in silence for an hour. He knew people who, he dared say, had never sat quiet for one half hour in their whole lives: had they done so they would have been better men. James also had been ready to laugh at waiting for a sermon which never came, but his father's earnest speech struck him as a new and revealing idea which evoked in him a sympathy he always retained towards the Society of Friends.[12] From his father's talk James gained an early and lasting interest in public affairs. He remembered especially later discussions about slavery in the United States when Thomas quietly, but very tenaciously put the case for the North at a time when nearly all his friends were supporters of the Southern States.

Although a less forceful character than his wife, Thomas could be firm and independent in the family too. Mary did her best to get him to give up smoking, claiming he had promised to do so before they married. When she twitted him sharply about his pipe he would smile sheepishly, but he stuck to it all the same. She had more influence over her sons: James never smoked, Charles only broke away after he was forty. But because Thomas was on the whole a man of few words, when he asserted himself his teaching was remembered and his favourite maxim, 'Can do's easy carried', was perhaps the foundation of James' abnormally wide interests and varied skills.

James certainly had every encouragement at home to make the most of his talents, but yet one is still left with no explanation of why there was a sudden flowering of genius in this simple family in which no one hitherto had made any special mark. In the direct line of descent there were farmers and shepherds and a variety of artisans, stocking-makers, tailors and the like. The only scholar in the immediate family circle was Robert, Thomas' first cousin who achieved a local reputation as an antiquarian and historian of Hawick; on Mary's side, her nephew Adam Scott, a joiner living in Hawick, showed some inventive ability.

Of James' unusual intelligence there was no doubt. From the first he was a precocious child. He said that he was always interested in language, especially in its written forms, since before he could remember anything. He was given a primer 'reading made easy' known as a 'tippenny' and he is reported to have known his letters by the time he was eighteen months old. His desire to communicate his knowledge was also shown very early, and the first time he saw his baby brother, born in 1838, he at once brought his primer, saying, 'I will show little brudder round O and crooked S', as the greatest treat he could offer the baby.

Before he was seven James had begun to hunt out strange words such as Latin and Greek in any books he could lay his hands on, and he copied them out on scraps of paper without knowing their meaning. A big family Bible borrowed from a neighbour fascinated him when he found in it the Hebrew alphabet and the names of the letters marking the sections of the 119th Psalm. At seven he made an exciting discovery, a page of the Gospel of St John in Chinese reproduced in the *Juvenile Missionary Magazine* for 1844, a periodical taken by his parents. He copied this many times in a scrawly hand until he had identified the characters for such words as beginning, God, word, light, life, witness, man and so on, by observing their recurrence in the columns and comparing them with the English text.[13] Years afterwards he could still write these characters from memory, and this method of learning a foreign language by acquiring a Bible, and if possible a grammar, was the one he always followed.

Lack of transport meant that it was an adventure to go outside the village, but occasional excursions were made, travelling by cart to see relations in Hawick. His maternal grandparents lived in the Crescent, on the banks of the turbulent river Slitrig, and here at twenty months James' curiosity nearly lost him his life: straying from his parents he fell into the water and was carried downstream till he was fished out just before he was swept into the Teviot. These rivers can be formidable in spate: Grandmother Scott would tell stories of the great flood of 1767, and one of James' treasured possessions was a book which bears the mark of water unmistakably upon it and belonged to his great great grandfather, whose bed had floated out of his house with the cat still asleep on it. As a lad James himself witnessed the devastation wrought at Denholm by a night of violent storms when sheds and hedges were swept away and hay, wool, sheep and pigs were carried far downstream.[14] These stories and experiences of the forces of nature awakened James' interest in freaks of weather and their meteorological causes.

Another visit to Hawick to his father's family introduced him to his great grandmother Isabella, born about 1760, who died when he was five years old. She told a story James never forgot, to illustrate the virtue of honesty and the standards expected of a Murray. Once, when his great grandfather was ploughing on a rented farm at Westerhouse he came excitedly into the house to show his wife a pot of gold coins he had turned up. 'Eh Andrew!' Isabella exclaimed, 'but what will you do with it?' Unhesitatingly Andrew replied, 'I am just going to shave and then take it down to the Burn', the residence of his landlord. The landlord kept the valuable find, but rewarded Andrew by remitting the rent of the farm for a year.

To a child thirsting for information and with few books, the stories of parents and grandparents were treasured as history—an important aid to seeing himself as a link in the chain of events. From boyhood he began collecting and creating direct links. He himself met an old man who had known an eye witness of events at the proclamation of William and Mary in 1689, and his mother had known a very old woman who again knew someone who was taken as a child through the camp of the Young Pretender in 1745 and remembered his long yellow hair. More directly his mother would tell him how she heard the news of the victory of Waterloo. Groups of people had gone out to various points along the road to meet the stage coach and the shouts of jubilation were passed over the hills from one group to another, so that by the time the coach arrived in Hawick everyone was already out in the streets.[15] Later James created similar links for his own sons, taking the two eldest to sit on the knees of an old naval officer who was present when Napoleon surrendered in 1815.

Concerned to place himself in time, James was also very early concerned with problems of geography. A rare family holiday, which took place before he was five, was south over the hills to the Liddel Valley where some cousins lived. Here the family stayed at Deadwater where there was a mineral spring from which there had at one time been an idea of creating a spa. James was disappointed on revisiting the spot years later to find they had stayed in a rather dingy shepherd's cottage amid peat stacks in a wide stretching reed-grown swampy waste. But in memory everything about this visit to a new environment was full of charm and romance. The highlight of the holiday was being taken just up the road where a little stream in a deep ditch marks the boundary between Scotland and England. Here he was told to straddle the ditch and that then he stood with one foot in Scotland and another in England. The little boy was extremely puzzled and thought this must be wrong. He had seen a map on which the two countries were painted in contrasting colours, making a very distinct boundary where they met. But here, looking to right and left he could detect no difference at all in the rather barren and dark moorland. Thinking this over, he next looked carefully at the people he met on either side of this alleged boundary and could see no difference in them either, nor, listening to their speech, could he understand why one should be called English and another Scotch. Finally, after an exhaustive examination of the master of a farm house which he was told was in England, he decided that the only way he differed from the farmers he knew round Denholm was that this man wore knee breeches and wooden clogs with bright brass mountings. Thereafter for a long time he always pictured Englishmen in that dress.[16] This experience remained in his mind, to be recalled years later when he was studying the local dialect and found, to his delight, that his own Border language was in fact identical with the language of Northumberland and that the boundary had no linguistic significance.

Clearly James at seven was ready for school and he was sent to one kept by a distant connection, Mrs Jane Telfer, widow of a Denholm baker. She was helped by her daughters and a young niece, Catherine Rutherford, who lived to a great age and used to recall James Murray as a fair, slightly red-haired little boy. The school was held in the old church at Cavers, which meant a walk of three miles each way. It was a walk full of interest. It started by a footpath up the Dean Burn, crossing and recrossing the stream as it cut its way over and through sandstone rocks, the cliffs overhung with trees and the banks full of beautiful wild flowers at all seasons. Here in spring were celandine, marsh marigold, wind-flower, primrose, cowslip and dog's violet. James learned to chew the wood sorrel for its acid flavour, to watch for its flowers closing on approach of rain, and found where the rare bird's-nest orchid grew. Every season brought fresh discoveries: in July, when they came out of school, the children would collect bladder campion and sitting down 'burst its air distended calyx and wondered at the unco noise sic wee things as the Cow-crackers could make'.[17] Possibly this walk awakened James' life-long interest in botany.

Cavers church was an unusual schoolroom. It is probably a pre-reformation building and stands in a graveyard filled with interesting old tombs. This was the scene of the stoning of the new minister by the women in the days of the Covenanters, and the Misses Douglas, living in the big house close by, who took an interest in the school, could tell other stories of the past. James probably saw the family treasures, which included a little pair of gloves embroidered with pearls and the device of a lion, a lady's favour, said to have been taken from Harry Hotspur before the battle of Otterburn in 1388. James remembered that the Misses Douglas brought flowers and illustrated books to show the school children and felt he owed a great deal to them for early lessons in taste and refinement.[18]

The school room church also had its history and its ghosts, most of them connected with the pranks of the locally famous Dr John Leyden, now almost unknown but still honoured in his native village of Denholm, where his birthplace in 1775 — a little thatched cottage — is shown to visitors.[19] Young James Murray was clearly influenced by Leyden, whose career and interests showed many parallels with his own. Leyden, whose father was a shepherd, came like the Murrays of farming stock long settled on the Cavers estate and sharing the Douglas' traditions of independence. Like James Murray, John Leyden showed an insatiable thirst for knowledge and a wonderful memory for all he read or heard. His education was rudimentary, but enough to enable him to teach himself, and the fact that he was able to work his way to college at Edinburgh was a stimulus to the ambitions of young James. At college Leyden was supposed to be studying theology for the ministry, but he also attended all the other lectures he could, particularly those in medicine, Italian, German, Old Icelandic, Hebrew, Arabic and Persian. Inevitably James' early interest in language would lead his parents and neighbours in Denholm to draw parallels, and James' wish to learn as many languages as possible may well have been fired by the desire to out-Leyden Leyden.

During his time at College Leyden also acquired a working knowledge of mathematics and a smattering of natural philosophy, natural history, chemistry, botany and mineralogy, deliberately bringing each subject to the point at which he could pick it up again if needed, saying, 'If you have the scaffolding ready, you can run up the masonry when you please.' James Murray seemed to echo this when much later he wrote, 'I was always learning, always collecting knowledge, always fitting myself for better things and for higher work when it should come to me.'[20] Many places in Denholm were associated with Leyden's activities; he was said to have conducted chemical experiments in a sort of furnace he built in Dean Burn glen and a tree, familiar to the children, was known as Leyden's tree. Cavers old church was his favourite place of study in vacations, and he maintained his privacy there by trading on the local superstitious fears of the place. James Murray with wide-eyed interest would drink in tales of how curious visitors peering in at the windows and seeing the dead adders and toads Leyden used in his studies, would take them for the stock-in-trade of a witch, and how Leyden would scare them away by various pranks which confirmed the belief that the place was haunted. One can imagine with what eagerness James sought more information about the life of this remarkable man who had achieved such fame.

James did not stay long at Cavers, and in 1845 he started attending Denholm school, which stood on the village green near the spot now occupied by the Leyden Memorial. James' younger brothers wrote vivid accounts of this school, which they both attended, and of the schoolmaster George Scott, known in the village as 'the Maister'.[21] He was a good natured, easy going man, making no pretensions to be better spoken or more refined in manners or dress than those amongst whom he moved. He lived over the school, a square house with large windows and white shutters, overhung with ivy and honeysuckle and with a playground in front. In spite of the large windows, the school room, entered by a blue door hung on rickety hinges, was ill ventilated owing to the low ceiling. The six foot Maister, nicknamed 'Long Legs', could hook his roll of maps up to the beams without difficulty.

It was an all-range school, taking children from infancy until they were big enough to go out to work. Those who had not yet mastered the Primer were drilled single file, the others were divided into classes, taught in turn by the Maister and the rest of the time learning by themselves. The first impression on entering the school room was one of confusion and noise, but Scott did not notice the din and in it his pupils must have acquired great powers of concentration. An English class might be in progress in a semicircle around the Maister who, sitting in front, corrected their reading from the First Collection (the reading book for those who had mastered the Primer): at the same time Scott would be pointing out *A B C* in a Primer open on his knee, to the newest infant entrant and from time to time giving attention to a slate covered by sums thrust under his eyes by a boy from the arithmetic class. This class, seated with slates before them, emitted a sort of humming sound, for the whole calculation was conducted audibly. This background hum, however, was hardly noticed, as it was drowned by the transition class, next above the infants. They would be seated on a form along one wall, learning a double verse of a metrical psalm. Each child put his arms round the shoulders of his neighbour and the row swung pendulum-wise back and forward on their seats, half whining, half singing in concert the lines they were learning.

An early exercise book belonging to James survives. It is neatly written and contains mnemonic rhymes for the parts of speech and the measures:

> Three little words, we often see,
>   Are *Articles*, a, an and the.
> A *Noun*'s the name of any thing,
> As school, Garden, Hoop or Swing.

> 12 lines are an inch
>   The length of a thumb
> 12 inches a foot
>   Rather longer than some.

The rhymes are followed by the story of Whittington and his Cat.

In another corner of the school room there was a clatter like a fencing match from the geography class. Scott was a good geographer and drew many maps himself for the school (a practice imitated in later years by James Murray). These maps were let down from a beam near the door and the older boys would gather round, each with a pointer. The leader would call out the name of a town, cape or island, and there was at once a competition to get one's pointer on the right spot, the slower judging that this was most likely to be where the greatest number of pointers were already gathered. The maps must often have been punctured in the process. The children were also taught to draw maps for themselves and James was reminded of his early efforts when he found the lichen *Rhizocarpon Geographicum* on rocks on Ruberslaw. He was himself a born teacher, never throughout his life able to resist passing on information. He remembered coming back from school to instruct his younger brothers, selecting a newly whitewashed wall on which to demonstrate his map drawing—a lesson which ended suddenly in a beating by an enraged parent.[22]

Luckily George Scott was a good teacher. The noise in the school room was not of idleness but the busy hum of a hive of industry, and the children acquired self reliance. There was no marking time and Scott would push a child on to more advanced work as soon as he was ready. Scott quickly recognised a pupil of unusual ability in James Murray and he allocated the lad a desk to the right of his own seat, where he could pay him special attention. James spent four years in the school, and George Scott gave him a good grounding in mathematics, including algebra to conic and cubic equations. Seeing the boy's keen interest in language he also taught him Latin, although he was the only pupil studying the subject at the time.

At home too, and in the village, James took every opportunity of practising and adding to his knowledge. His mother did not hold with men doing women's work in the house, and she scorned to ask help in what she considered to belong to her sphere. She had no use for a neighbour who sat looking on while her son did the dish washing. On the other hand, she expected James as the eldest to show some responsibility for his younger brothers and he took this seriously. He was always seeking to educate them and they looked up to him in awe, although they lacked his perseverance. His long-suffering brother recalled that

> Now it was rocks and stones and the mysteries of strata and formations with long nebbed names, jaw-breaking—that Geology is full of—anon it was the flowers of the field, and the insects, and James's wonderful memory hugged and remembered all the Latin names so easily. Then there was all the mystery of the Linnaean system and the Natural system to rack young brains.[23]

Denholm was a small enough village for most people to know of any bright and inquiring lad, and young James found others ready to help him. He was interested in the stars and the solar system, and someone, probably a school friend, Robert Moodie, son of a prosperous mill owner, lent him a globe. His brother Charles remembered as a very young child being woken from his first sleep to be carried to the stair top to watch for Sirius the dog star, which James had calculated would be visible that evening, and the excitement when he proved to be right. Old friends of his father recalled how they used to sit taking their snuff and enjoying the fun of questioning the serious little boy about the sun and moon and stars.[24]

A very influential person in his life at this time was a retired minister, the Rev. James Duncan. Mr Duncan, son of a minister of Denholm Cameronian Chapel, had been over-persuaded to follow his father's vocation in spite of the fact that he was an extremely shy man to whom public preaching was an agony. This led to a breakdown and he left the church to devote himself to his real interest—the study of geology and botany and the formation of a complete flora for Teviotdale.[25] James was only too happy to join him scrambling over the Minto Crags, tramping the surrounding moors or searching along the valleys for specimens of rare flowers and ferns. Before 1849 he had fully mastered the classification of plants and for many years botany was his principal hobby, and he won many prizes at school for making the best collection of identified wild flowers. Mr Duncan kindly lent him books, and when he died James continued his work on the Teviotdale flora, contributing a number of articles on the subject to the Hawick Archaeological Society.[26] Most of his nine-volume herbarium of pressed specimens survives, beautifully arranged and inscribed.[27]

In spite of his unusual interests and scholarly tastes James Murray was neither priggish nor solitary. He had a lively sense of humour and enjoyed the normal interests of a healthy youngster. True, he came in for some teasing about his strange hobbies and he learned as a very small boy to take this. At four or five he was the butt of the bigger boys because of his inability to pronounce 'ch' and he found that the best defence was to hold his tongue: this stood him in good stead in later years. Organised games such as football or cricket were unknown in Denholm, but he was very imaginative and joined in improvised amusements. Being tall for his age, long legged and thin, he was a good runner—barefoot of course—and he excelled at long jump. With the other boys he climbed trees and fished in the Dean Burn and as he grew older he went on long walks with his brothers and their friends. He records their reception on coming into someone's house on one occasion, very muddy. They were met at the door with the injunction, 'Nuw screape yer feits weil, an' pyt off aa o' yer schuins i' the passage.' With ears already alert to strange word forms James made some remark on the word 'schuins'. Misunderstood, he was told testily, 'Gin ye had them tui clean, ye wad ken the difference atween ae bodie's schuin an' aa o' yer schuins.' He did not argue further, but was set thinking about double plurals, for example in such words as *children* and *brethren*, the original plurals of which were *childer* and *brether*.[28]

In 1849 disaster befell Denholm and interrupted James' schooling for a year when the dreaded cholera struck the village.[29] Cholera, spreading over Europe from Asia, first hit Hawick in 1832—a mild epidemic with only four deaths; but there was another outbreak in 1847, and these two experiences of the suddenness with which strong men and women could die was sufficient to cause near panic at a third outbreak which proved much more serious. In 1849 in Hawick and the immediate neighbourhood there were over 550 cases, and the normal annual death rate of about thirty people was doubled. A whole gang of Irish labourers was wiped out (not surprisingly as they took their drinking water from an open drain). Soon the infection spread to Denholm. It was an alarming time to be in the village when the question every day was, 'Who has it now?' and many coffins, soaked in pitch as a disinfectant, would be carried up the hill to Cavers churchyard to be buried in a pit on the northwest side of the church. The Murray boys remembered with a shudder the gruesome sight and smell of a bonfire by the wayside and the half consumed mattress and blanket of a cholera victim.

Young people and children were particularly susceptible to the disease and Thomas and Mary Murray soon took the decision to remove their family from danger. They went temporarily to Innerleithen which had escaped the scourge. This gave young James another example to add to his collection of links with the past. He was taken to see a Mrs Penn, then 92, who was to live to 107. She had known Sir Walter Scott and was reputed to be the model for Lady Pennefeather in his novel *St Ronan's Well*.[30]

As the Denholm school remained closed because of the cholera, it was arranged for James to spend six months as a cow-herd on a friend's farm on the slopes of Ruberslaw. It was thought good for a boy to spend a time amongst strangers, and James, with the promise of twelve shillings and his keep for his six months' work, was supremely happy. He remembered lying amongst the heather 'hammering away at my Latin grammar and *Lectiones Selectae*'. He had as usual to stand up to a good deal of teasing from his fellow farm hands. He was careful to hide his books from them in the evenings when they would taunt him, asking whether he had taught the cows to understand Latin and to listen to Latin shouts.[31] Mr Barrie, the farmer, commented dryly that James Murray would never make a farmer: he had always a book in his pocket, a warning to his own sons for whom farming was to be a serious employment for life, and not a pleasant interlude. Nevertheless James did not neglect his job: his brothers often came to visit him, and Charles remembered the 'close and loving intimacy' between James and his herd, especially a favourite Jersey cow.

Up there on Ruberslaw James revelled in the fresh air, plunging up the hill knee deep in heather or jumping from tussock to tussock over a patch of bog, watching with joy the changing patterns of sunshine and cloud and the storms of rain in the valley below. He had also much to think about. As he climbed up through the golden gorse he would look for orchids amongst the commoner cotton grass, bog asphodel and butterwort, and try to detect the exact point at which the sandstone gave way to the hard grey rock which Mr Duncan had taught him to identify with the ancient greenstone or trap, proving that Ruberslaw must once have stood up as an island in the remote past when the surrounding country was covered by sea. On the rocky summit James not only admired the wide view from the blue Cheviots round to the three summits of the Eildon hills and the sparkling water of the Teviot, but also identified the site of an ancient hill fort. Here too he would imagine himself one of a secret conventicle listening to a sermon from the famous Covenanter Alexander Peden. He would picture the sudden approach of a troop of cavaliers and recall the story of how, when the minister's voice rang out, 'O Lord, lap the skirts of thy cloak ower puir auld Sandy', preacher and congregation were saved by a thick mist which hid them from their enemies.[32]

Down below in the valley of the Rulewater James found in the churchyard of Bedrule the gravestones of many Murrays, his own ancestors who had been identified with the Covenanters and were tenants long ago of the farm on which he was now working—Spittal Tower. His interest was awakened in his descent from Andrew, 'the Hazel dog o' the Tower' whose red hair he inherited. He carried on investigation into his pedigree for many years, helped initially by a distant cousin, Robert Kerr, a tailor who every year performed the feat of walking in one day from Newcastleton in Liddesdale to Edinburgh to see the latest fashions, a distance of rather over seventy miles. He started before daybreak to cover twenty-one miles to Hawick in time to breakfast there and call on Thomas and his family at Denholm, before going on another thirty miles to Dalkeith, where he took his lunch. It is a reminder of how isolated the Borders were at that time.

With the aid of Robert Kerr, who said his mother had often heard her grandfather, who died in 1749, tell the tale, James worked out a romantic story of the family origins. They sprang, according to this version, from three sons of Andrew Murray, an anti-Jacobite and Protestant farming near Aberdeen on the estates of the earl of Mar. When the Earl tried to force them to join a rising in support of the Pretender in 1715, Andrew and his brother, sacrificing their land and property for their principles, fled south to Teviotdale. James liked to think proudly of the six generations since the Hazel Dog Andrew had so suffered, and to boast that his descendants down to the present had continued faithful to their religious and political beliefs.[33] Small matter that later research by his sons proved the story a myth.[34] Its impact on James left a lasting impression: once again he felt himself a link in the long chain of history—in this case the chain of his own ancestry in which he had the responsibility of carrying on a family tradition of sacrifice, even martyrdom, for duty and for principle. It was the basis of his whole code of conduct.

When the summer was over, the cholera had spent itself in Denholm, families returned, the school reopened and it was time for James to leave his Arcadian life on Ruberslaw and to renew his education. But he did not go back to Denholm parish school. Instead, with his two brothers, he was now moved to Minto school, held in a better designed and healthier building on the other side of the river. The headmaster's wife remembered the three Murray boys walking the one and a half miles from Denholm to Minto barefoot. Shoes were not worn by village children in summer and it was considered something of a hardship to have to don stockings and boots when the colder weather set in.

Many boys, like the Murrays, transferred to Minto school, which was under a notable schoolmaster, John Rankin Hamilton, who had built up its reputation and attracted to it boarders as well as day boys from a wide area. Hamilton's methods were more modern than those of George Scott at Denholm, and his discipline was considered superior. Not that George Scott's school was lacking in rudimentary order, but he was criticised for paying no attention to the manners of his pupils. The Murray boys were expected to 'behave yourself before strangers' and no doubt the refining influence of the Misses Douglas on James at Cavers was wearing thin and he could now do with some polish.

In his new school James found he had a certain amount to re-learn. Hamilton laid stress on fluent reading and correct English pronunciation. For a boy like James, fascinated by language, the different ways in which a vowel could be pronounced and the different words which could be used to convey the same idea was a source of much interest. Hamilton cast some ridicule on the teaching of George Scott, and when James read out for 'it is a man' 'eet ees ay maan' as he had heard his former master say it, Hamilton was at pains to point out that this was neither Scotch nor English. In fact Hamilton's own speech, and the English generally heard in pulpit and schoolroom in the Borders at that time, was about as far removed from the English of the educated Londoner as the French of Stratford atte Bowe was from that of Paris in Chaucer's day. No one in Hawick and its district would have had much chance of hearing standard English spoken. In Latin also James had some unlearning to do. Hamilton insisted on the English way of pronunciation while Scott had followed the Continental practice. When James went to London later he found the Continental pronunciation used there and he had it all to relearn once more. All this was irritating, but it drew James' attention to phonetic problems and some of his observations were to be of value to him in the future.

Hamilton was an able and inspiring teacher, and like George Scott he quickly recognised that James Murray was a boy deserving of individual attention. James responded eagerly. He was a most painstaking and persevering pupil, and if he was in doubt about the lesson to be prepared for the next day he would sometimes return to Minto in the evening to make sure. Hamilton proposed to start him on algebra but was surprised to find how far he had already gone in this subject. Again, when he took the school out for nature rambles he found that James already, with Mr Duncan's help, surpassed his own rather rudimentary knowledge of rocks and flowers. He was able, however, to teach James some chemistry: Hamilton used to devise interesting experiments to demonstrate to his older pupils after school, such as putting them under laughing gas. One of the few books owned by the Murrays was a bound volume of a magazine published by the Religious Tract Society, *The Visitor or Monthly Instructor* for 1837, containing a series of articles on electricity and botany, which were carefully annotated by James. One of his early exercise books from Minto school also survives: it is entitled *Notes on the Steam Engine* and contains very neat diagrams, but at the other end of the book are rules for Latin grammar, written mainly in Latin.

In his two years at Minto school James acquired some knowledge of four languages. In April 1850 he began to learn French and one of his first books was Surrennes' *New Pronouncing French Primer*, 1847. By the next winter he was spending every evening poring over the work of Théodore Agrippa d'Aubigné on the French Reformation by the light of a little oil lamp, with a tiny cistern the size of an orange and no chimney, held upright by a spike driven into a candlestick. A little later this was replaced by a new-fangled naphtha lamp made by a local tinsmith which gave a better light but emitted an evil smell. While James read volubly, translating as he went, the family, from parents to young brothers, gathered round listening, partly in admiration for the reader, partly taking an intelligent interest. The children later re-enacted some of the incidents, like the valiant Vaudois defending a mountain pass, in their attic playroom.

It was probably Mr Hamilton who introduced James to Mrs Selby, wife of the factor on the Minto Estate. When he was thirteen she began to teach him Italian and German out of school hours: given a start he could teach himself, and taking a cue again from John Leyden, like him he would follow the lesson at family prayers in a German bible and when his turn came he read his verse in translation. Finally, in his last year, Hamilton started teaching him Greek, and James followed this up by acquiring a Greek testament.

He was now fourteen, and it was time to leave school and to think what work he should take up. There seems never to have been any question of sending him on to the Grammar school at Melrose. There were two more boys to be educated—no schooling was free—and his parents and James himself seem to have been confident that with the start already made he could teach himself. With Leyden's example ever before him, the next step must be to gain entry to a University and to work for a degree. Determination and perseverance would get him there, but at fourteen that must lie ahead. Meanwhile, what to do? Mr Duncan was naturally consulted. A slightly older boy, Johnnie Scott, who later became foreman propagator at the Botanic Gardens, Edinburgh, had recently taken a post as gardener to the County Sheriff, and James asked Mr Duncan about the possibility of finding a similar opening. But Duncan was discouraging, explaining that systematic botany was no qualification and had little to do with horticulture, and he suggested that teaching would be more in James' line.[35] This was an attractive idea, offering the opportunity for further study, and his parents made some inquiries about the openings. At once they came up against a difficulty. The appointments to the Parish schools in which a boy would have to make a start were in the hands of the Parish Ministers and went almost invariably to members of the Established Church of Scotland. None of the Murray family would think for a moment of changing his church for the sake of a career, so this was a serious obstacle.

The next idea was probably that of Mr Hamilton. Why should not James, like Leyden, aim at becoming a doctor of medicine? Leyden, though at heart a linguist, had qualified as a doctor with apparent ease, in order to obtain a post in India, where he hoped to be able to study languages. There was a vacancy in a chemist's shop, run by James Walker, in Melrose, and it was decided that James should go there, in the hope that this would enable him to add to his scientific knowledge and eventually to qualify for college entrance. What happened is not known, but James did not stay long. It was said that he was not well, but this was probably only an excuse to cover some disagreement between apprentice and master. Probably James was disappointed in not finding the opportunity and encouragement for further study for which he had hoped.

At this stage John Leyden had been more fortunate: in the vacations he had had the run of the good library at Cavers House. For James, seeking self-education, books were a problem. There were few at home and Thomas, not being a feuar, was not entitled to use the village library, but among some religious books, placed in charge of the Minister by one of the Douglases, James found a copy of Borrow's *Bible in Spain*. This interested him because of the many Romany phrases, these he memorised and could quote with spirit. The family possessed in addition to the Bible, a copy of Milton's *Paradise Lost* and *Samson Agonistes* and the works of Cowper. James and his brothers greatly enjoyed poetry, and they borrowed and learnt by heart the poems of John Leyden, James Hogg the Ettrick Shepherd, Walter Scott and the Border Minstrels. James and Alexander tried their hands at writing their own verse on these models. The works of more recent poets, such as Keats and Wordsworth, seem to have been unknown to them. Novels, though not forbidden, were deprecated by their parents, and James under their influence claimed to have no use for them. He boasted at that time that the only 'novel' he had ever read was *Pilgrim's Progress*. He held all his life to the opinion that novel reading was a waste of time, and was disgusted to find his sons reading Kipling's *Stalky & Co*. This probably became something of a pose: he did read Anstey's *Vice Versa* with enjoyment on its first publication and also James Barrie's stories. When in Edinburgh with his family in 1884 he read them Scott's *Heart of Midlothian* aloud, and on a much later visit abroad he confessed 'having nothing better to do, I wasted my time over the first story in George Eliot's *Scenes of Clerical Life*—perhaps not wasted for it touched my heart and brought tears to my eyes.'[36]

James still had the use of Mr Duncan's scientific books; and

George Scott, bearing no ill will against the pupils who had left him, was also willing to lend what he had. The greatest help, however, was the publication in 1852 of John Cassell's *Popular Educator* as a cheap serial. This was the first publication of its kind and James bought it from the start. He wrote on the fly leaf, 'Knowledge is power', 'Docendo didiscimus' and 'Nihil est melius quam vita diligentissima' although he certainly needed no reminders to spur him on to study. He worked steadily through all the exercises in Cassell in German and Greek. Pushing on with his mathematics, he acquired an elementary knowledge of mechanics and learnt to survey. He made a map of the Cavers Estate which was still in use in 1920; and later, in Hawick, he surveyed the Muir and made the first plan for the new Wellogate Cemetery for the Town Council.[37] At the same time he was gaining some manual skills. Someone taught him to bind books and he bound the *Popular Educator* and other books and taught his brothers too. Mr Hamilton was quite a good draughtsman, and it was probably at Minto that James became adept at penmanship and painting. Certainly it was Mr Hamilton who first noticed that the Murray boys were colour blind.[38] James developed a tiny but very regular and legible handwriting and he could embellish the transcript of a poem with beautiful borders and flourishes, or copy an engraving with delicacy and accuracy.

While at home waiting for an opening to some permanent employment, James earned a little money towards his keep in days of haymaking and harvest time helping local farmers at Ashybank and Whitrigs. He also at this time learned his father's trade. Thomas Murray, little satisfied with his prospects, wished for something better for his clever eldest son, but he had normally employed an apprentice and now, with his boys growing up, there was no longer a spare room and the work could be done by James. Thomas had already taught all the boys to sew—he was a great believer in the value of any skill which enabled a man to help himself. James made his own trousers until he left Scotland for London. He also learned a good deal about the quality of cloth, the technical terms used and listened with interest to the dialect of his father's customers.

Although he was studying and adding to his skills during these years after leaving school at fourteen and a half and until he was seventeen, they must have been years of frustration. James continued to look hopefully about him and to scan the local papers for possible openings. Then one day in 1854 his chance came. The Hawick United

School was advertising for an assistant master. James applied, and, to his delight and surprise, there was no religious test and he was appointed.[39] At last he had got his foot onto the bottom rung of the ladder.

He was a tall, strong, healthy, good-looking boy, asserting his independence and sense of manhood by following the height of fashion in dress and refusing to shave. Already he was encouraging the growth of the red beard which, turning to snow white in later years, was to contribute to his striking and patriarchal appearance. He was very susceptible to feminine charm and had a keen sense of fun, but he also had already a strong sense of duty and accepted completely the standards and discipline of his home. He had developed the powers of memory, concentration, perseverance and determination and had the energy needed to make a success of anything on which he set his mind. At seventeen he felt that he was already a man, with a man's responsibilities, and from the day when he left home in 1854 to board with his uncle in Hawick he never needed to ask his father for further financial help.

CHAPTER II

The Great Learning Period:
Schoolmaster and Citizen

HAWICK is only four miles from Denholm, higher up the Teviot where the valley is narrower and the land rises steeply on either side to hills of seven or eight hundred feet. Although a very ancient settlement, it is a plain little town today and the traces of its early origins are not immediately apparent. Already in 1854 it had lost its medieval character, and many of its older buildings had been torn down to make room for the knitting mills which were turning the town into a thriving industrial centre.

James Murray was no stranger to Hawick; his visits to his relations and the stories his mother told him had made him familiar with its personalities and history, and when he left home to work there he said it was like returning to a place in which he had spent his childhood.[1] It had indeed a special fascination for him because of its song or war cry, thought to be pre-Christian:

> Tyribus ye Tyr ye Odin
> Tyr haab us ye Tyr ye Odin!
> Tyr keep us both Tyr and Odin!

It was sung from the top of the oldest house in the burgh every June at the Common riding, which served both for a perambulation of the bounds of the common pastures or Haughs and to commemorate the young men of Hawick, who after the defeat and death of James IV at Flodden in 1513 ambushed the booty laden victors near the town and returned triumphant with the colours.[2]

James' grandparents were now dead, but it was arranged that he should lodge with his uncle, Charles Scott, who, through his wife, owned a substantial house, 5 Bourtree Place, off the north end of the High Street. Of his eleven children, only four were now at home and

3. The Murray family. About 1860. Left to right, seated: Thomas Murray, Mary Murray (née Scott); their children standing: Margaret, James, Alexander, Charles.

there was plenty of room for James. He paid his uncle one shilling and six pence for his room and catered for himself. His food bill for three months was only two pounds, eleven shillings and four pence. His diet, probably what he was used to at home, consisted of bread (usually three loaves a week), meat (for ten pence a week), potatoes, oatmeal, milk, tea and broth. He did not buy sugar and butter every week, and fish (at a penny three farthings) only once.[3] He usually walked home to Denholm at the weekends. This arrangement lasted until 1858, when his brothers having joined him in Hawick, his parents also left Denholm and made a new home for the family next door to Charles Scott at 4 Bourtree Place.

James, ambitious and idealistic, flung himself into his new work and life with enthusiasm and determination. On the face of it, his position as an untrained assistant teacher in a small Border town in the throes of the Industrial Revolution did not look a particularly promising one for a young man with academic aims. The town was in a transition stage. Still semi-rural, many of the burgesses kept cattle which they had the right to pasture on the Haughs, and in the centre of the town piggeries and cowhouses abounded, with manure piled up beside them so that some streets were little better than dung hills. On the other hand, wool mills and warehouses had been built and the

28

population doubled between 1850 and 1860. There had been no corresponding extension of the town boundaries, and houses had been squeezed onto every vacant corner; old smithies and out-houses were converted into dwellings of some sort in which large families lived, often 12 to 14 in a single room.[4] A special commission in 1860 noted that 'intemperance, sabbath profanation and daylight wickedness' made Hawick stand before the eyes of the surrounding towns and villages 'as a Saul among the sinners of this generation'.[5] Under fourteen per cent of the children went to school, and while this was only a little below the average for the country, illiteracy was greater in Hawick than elsewhere.[6]

The United School, a union of an old Grammar school founded in 1711 and a Parish School to which it had been joined in 1825, was good compared to the many private schools in the town; but the Rector, Mr Dodds, was very old fashioned compared to Mr Hamilton at Minto. James found the only apparatus was a blackboard and a map stand and it was said that when an infant teacher a few years later purchased some pictures from Edinburgh, Mr Dodds, who had to provide equipment from his pupils' fees, exclaimed, 'You'll ruin me!'[7] Over 120 children were crowded into a small school room built thirty years before, with James sharing with a third member of staff responsibility for about eighty of the younger ones. James had only his experience at Denholm and Minto and his own wits to guide him, but in a very short time an improvement in the standards reached by his pupils was noted.[8] Although he had taken the post more because it would give him opportunity to pursue his own studies towards a University degree than from any sense of vocation, he found that he had a natural ability as a teacher, he had a genuine liking for children and he thoroughly enjoyed the work.

He went out of his way to see children, and one of his pupils remembered how he would visit her home, bringing presents such as an alphabet book for her younger brother, illustrated, written and bound by himself:

> F was a Frog that from slimy pool crawled
> And over his pictures most wickedly sprawled

and a set of *Happy Families* (or Quartettes) drawn by hand on pink cards. Like his own teachers he was always ready to take pains with a promising pupil, to give individual teaching after school, to stay behind to answer questions of those in difficulties and soon, with the parents' approval, to coach some of them in the evenings.[9] He was able then to use more enlightened methods than those of Mr Dodds in the United School.

As a result, after three years, and at the age of only twenty, James was approached by some of the leading townsmen whose sons he had been teaching, inviting him to come as Head Master to the Hawick Academy, a private school for paying pupils. He accepted the offer at a guaranteed salary of £150 p.a. It meant putting off the hope of a University course, but he was attracted by the chance of having his own school in which he could give the boys and girls the kind of education he believed in. In order to get a qualification he began studying at once for the Fellowship of the Educational Institute of Scotland, taking the first examination in February 1858, and the Final Examination five years later.[10] At the age of twenty-six he had for the first time some proof of the standard of education he had reached.

At the Hawick Academy the Head Master was the only teacher and the announcement James placed in the *Advertiser* on 12 September 1857 that classes were now being formed indicates the demands this made upon him:

> In addition to the usual elements of education comprising English Reading, Writing, Grammar, and Composition, Arithmetic, Mathematics, Geography, Drawing, Ancient and Modern Languages, Mr M. will make it his endeavour, to impart to his Pupils, both Male and Female, the leading principles of Moral Science, Political Economy, History, Natural Science, Human Physiology, and the other Branches of Knowledge which must form an important part of every Enlightened System of Education.[11]

Not content with this programme James also, a year later, started evening classes, beginning with free lessons in German to his brother Charles and three or four friends, and a few years later offering instruction, especially in architectural and mechanical drawing, at three shillings a month to young men engaged in professional occupations.[12]

Once again, as at the United School, the success of James Murray's teaching was quickly recognised.[13] The school started in the gallery of the Evangelical Union chapel but soon outgrowing that space moved to the Congregational Chapel and in 1859 to a disused Friends' Meeting House in Buccleuch Street, where there was a spacious single room which, after the example of George Scott at Denholm,

James partitioned by large maps drawn by himself let down from the beams.[14]

In most Scottish schools learning was beaten into the children, but while James Murray might punish a late comer by a stroke on the palm of the hand, the children found his lessons so interesting that he had no need to resort to the 'tawse', the traditional leather strap, that descended on the shoulders of Mr Dodds' pupils at the United school. At the Academy the children remembered their master with affection and looked back on their school days with him as the happiest and most fruitful period of their education, contrasting it sadly with later years when under another teacher they reverted to the old learning by rote. One pupil, who later became Town Clerk of Edinburgh, said that in such an unlikely place he had received an education superior to that given in many of the famous public schools.[15]

To us who have never experienced the mechanical teaching usual in the 1850s, James Murray's methods do not seem very revolutionary and he himself acknowledged in 1906 that though he did his 'enthusiastic best', the school was by later standards neither satisfactory in its accommodation nor efficient in its methods, but he was certainly ahead of his time.[16] Treating the children as individuals and adapting the curriculum to their needs, he kept detailed monthly records of the progress of each pupil in every subject. He wrote plays for them to act, drawing on local history for his topic: he did not believe in grammar books, holding that all that was necessary could be learned from the study of great writers, and he printed his own comprehensive outline of English literature showing his personal interests by beginning with the 'four antecedent literatures'—Celtic (i.e. Gaelic, Cymric or British), Latin, Anglo-Saxon, and Norman— and continuing down to 1859 with lists of the chief writers of each period.[17] He did not limit geography to the then usual lists of principal towns and rivers, but linked these facts to the history of the country. On the lines of modern environmental studies he developed Mr Hamilton's practice of leading nature rambles and on day excursions he studied everything of interest with the children. He was 'in his glory', they said, talking about ancient earthworks and ruins: then he would send one group over the hills looking for plants and flowers and another to bring back all the insects they could lay their hands upon, while at the end of the day those interested could stay on at school to identify what they had found.[18] Each year the work of the school was publicly examined by a group of leading townsmen, and in

1859 they noted that Mr Murray aimed 'not merely at drilling his pupils well . . . but in drawing out and cultivating their powers, which will make them in future years enlightened and useful citizens, and will fit them for enjoying the wonders of nature and art . . .'[19]

For James Murray, the future lexicographer, the importance of this period of his life was that it was his own great learning period. Words continued to fascinate him. He had, he wrote later

> a sort of mania for learning languages; every new language was a new delight, no matter what it was, Hebrew or Tongan, Russian or Caffre, I swallowed them all, at least so as to master grammar & structure, but rarely did enough at the vocabulary. Still I at one time or another could read in a sort of way 25 or more languages.[20]

His brother Charles remembered hearing the most alarming sounds coming from James' bedroom on one of his weekends at home. He opened the door to ask if he were ill and found James still in bed, with a book, practising Arabic vowels, while on another occasion he startled his companions by pensively bursting out with Hottentot 'clucks' which he was trying to produce with the aid of instructions in a book. If any foreigners happened to come to the town he always got into touch with them and he used to bring these strangers into his school, paying them for their trouble if they proved useful. On one occasion he unrolled the map so that members of a German band could point out where their homes were, and on another he introduced a Hindu and questioned him about the grammar of his language. He had always been interested in Hindi since he learned his first word *cuddy* from an Anglo Indian. His informant suggested that the word might somehow be connected with the Scottish word *cuddie* and to have been introduced by the Gypsies. James was disappointed when years later he came to *cuddy* in the Dictionary and had reluctantly to dismiss the suggestion as having 'no basis in fact'.[21]

He was always alert, storing odd little bits of information in his excellent memory until they fell into place, and in 1856 he was able to use his slight knowledge of Hungarian with effect in the following circumstances. Hawick prided itself on having a national reputation as a champion of liberty and James Murray joined his fellow citizens in following the struggles for independence on the Continent with keen sympathy. A few years before his arrival in Hawick, Hungary had broken loose from the Austrian Empire, but, after six months independence, had been defeated and a number of refugees, including the patriot leader Louis Kossuth, had come to England. In 1856 a move was made in Hawick to get Kossuth to visit the town and deliver two addresses. Led by the town band, Kossuth was driven from the station to the Town Hall in a carriage with four horses through crowded streets hung with thirty-eight welcoming banners. Amid those saying 'Welcome Kossuth', 'Liberty', 'There's a Good time coming', the patriot noted with pleasure one in Bourtree Place in Magyar, 'Jöjjön-el a te országod!' (Thy Kingdom come.) James' practice of learning languages from a study of the New Testament explains his choice of phrase.[22]

As a lexicographer James Murray was to find it an immense advantage that he was no narrow linguistic specialist but had a wide general knowledge. This was essential to him as the sole teacher in his school, where he must meet the varying needs of his pupils, but he owed his success as a teacher to the fact that every new bit of information was also a joy to him. In a sermon later to school boys at Mill Hill he spoke of every increase of knowledge as 'an absolute increase to our pleasure' and told the boys how scholars will 'sacrifice *time* & *money* & *health* & LIFE even, for knowledge, & find their reward in the knowledge itself & nothing more. And not in one solitary direction, alone, does thirsting mind thus expand & yearn—[but] in every direction, in every field, in every corner, and bye path & alley of the great field of knowledge.'[23] He was here clearly drawing on his own experience and in Hawick he was still keeping up his study of the sciences, botany, geology, entomology (he lectured to a Hawick society on British moths, illustrated by specimens and 'magnificent' drawings of their various organs), anatomy, chemistry, mechanics, archaeology and electricity.[24]

Of these, geology was a major interest and he gave help to the professional geologists making the first full survey of the country, especially in helping to determine the dividing line between the old red sandstone and the greywacke rocks to the south of Hawick on the watershed between the Slitrig and the Liddle and the stratification of the beds of peat and boulder clay in the same area. This led to a friendship with Sir Archibald Geikie and his brother and Geikie encouraged him to continue his research in this field.[25] James' confidence led to an amusing situation: when on holiday in Oban he was in a shop which had some fossils for sale. An innocent tourist seemed to be being imposed upon and persuaded to buy a fossil of a fox which, James intervened to point out, showed 'the utter absence of any organic structure' and was in his opinion a forgery. He was highly embarrassed to discover that he had presumed to instruct none other than the leading geologist of the time, Sir Roderick Murchison, then Director General of the Geological Survey.[26]

At this time he gathered geological specimens for himself as well as continuing to add to his pressed ferns and flowers. He was a compulsive collector of natural specimens and he also collected stamps at a time when philately was still in its infancy and the Hawick police were suspicious that he was collecting in order to remove the postmarks and re-use the stamps. Whatever he acquired he carefully identified and classified, and the discipline of closely observing and analysing the likenesses and differences of similar objects and deciding how to arrange them he found valuable when later he had to trace the complex history of the various senses of a word.

As a schoolmaster he at last had a regular income. With what he saved James began to accumulate a library, and on his rare visits to Edinburgh he used to comb the second-hand book stalls. Amongst books he bought in 1854 and 1855 were a German grammar, a Bible in Italian, Arabic and Syriac readers, a Dutch Bible, an Entomologists' Annual, a book on *Our Domestic Fowls and song birds* published by the Religious Tract Society, an illustrated handbook of British ferns, C. M. Mitchell's *Planetary and Stellar Worlds*, H. Johnson's *Catechism of Agricultural Chemistry and Geology*, the *Works* of Terence, Humboldt's *Travels* and George Buchanan's *Paraphrasis Psalmorum Davidis Poetica*.[27]

James could only get through his programme of study by a careful use of his time. He claimed that he learned at least two languages on his way to school. He had only, in early years, to come the length of the High street and by the Sandbed to the United school in Orrock Place, or later a little further on to Buccleuch Street and neither journey could have taken much more than five minutes. He was described by his former pupils as hurrying up the street, never a moment to spare, bearded chin in air and the cape of his Highland cloak (which he wore all his life on holidays) flapping behind him, open book in hand which he glanced at from time to time as he memorized the contents.[28] Already he had formed the habit of studying late and rising early. He existed on a minimum of sleep, but was fortunate when he did go to bed in sleeping quickly and deeply.

'When I was your age,' he wrote fifty years later to a son whom he suspected of idleness

I was deeply conscious of how little I knew, and I employed all my leisure time from my daily work which I had to do for a scanty living, in learning everything that I could, learning as far as I could something about everything that I did not know, while also trying to learn everything that could be known about some things. I had no time and no desire to have changes in my surroundings . . . I was always . . . sharpening my mental and intellectual tools in faith that they would be useful.[29]

It would be wrong, however, to think of James Murray the schoolmaster as only interested in study. One reason why he was so popular with his pupils was that he gave them plenty of evidence of youthful high spirits and tastes. He liked the company of pretty girls: with his cousin Adam Scott he attended the evenings arranged by the town's dancing master.[30] Adam sometimes led James into a scrape, and once persuaded him to try out a velocipede which he had constructed. Coming down one of the steep hills into Hawick the machine got out of control and, swerving to avoid a heavy farm dray, James shot through the hedge and down a thirty-foot drop into a midden, from whence he emerged with no bones broken, but covered with smelly mud, having wrecked the machine. It was the first of many adventures on bicycles.

He was a fashionable young man, wearing his hair to shoulder length, and on one occasion he owed his life to the latest style of neck tie. This happened one hot day in June 1855, when having gone home for the weekend his brothers suggested they should go swimming with a friend in the Teviot. This was strictly forbidden as unsafe. There are deep pools in the river, known as hutch pools because they are formed by hutches—breakwaters—built out from the bank. The hutches were believed to create whirlpools which could suck a man down to his death. But one day a boy who was new to the district exploded the myth by diving in off the end of a hutch and swimming round mocking those who had been so gullible as to believe old wives' tales. After that the taboo was ignored and now Alexander and Charles Murray, who were learning to swim, were eager to persuade their older brother to come with them so that they could show off. James could not swim, but he was full of scientific theories about the specific gravity of water and of the human body. He had recently read a book which argued that as the gravities were nearly equal, a small float hung about the body would keep the head above water (on the

35

principle of the modern water wings or inflatable arm bands). The book further suggested that the leaves of many waterside plants would serve the purpose. So on the way the boys gathered the thick cellular leaves of the water iris and tied them together with bits of string into bundles which James fastened on each side below the arm pits. Confident in his invention, James went in off the end of the hutch into deep water. Presently he disappeared near the centre of the pool and his brothers thought he was just having a joke when, to their horror, they saw his hand emerge from the bubbling water desperately clutching at nothing, and they realised he was drowning. The boys knew that they were incapable of swimming out to James, but recently the papers had reported a case of drowning and said a few feet of rope would have saved the victim. Charles bethought him of this and rushed to their heaps of clothes with the notion of fastening their braces together, but before he could begin struggling with the buttons he saw, neatly on top of the pile, James' new black silk tie. It was the latest fashion, described by *Punch*:

> The bow must extend from shoulder to shoulder
> If it be a little longer it will make you look the bolder.

It was nearly five feet long. The tie saved James— and the future Dictionary—and James was hauled out, anxious to impress his brothers with the fact that his theory was correct, the floats did work but had unfortunately slipped to his haunches and turned him upside down.[31]

Like many young men of his generation, James was also trying his hand at poetry, in the tradition and style of John Leyden. A long and sentimental poem addressed to a young lady and entitled 'Think on Me' appeared in the *Hawick Advertiser* of 19 July 1856 and was later reprinted in an anthology of Hawick poetry published by his father's cousin, Robert Murray. An 'Address to a skeleton discovered in a stone cist in this vicinity' written in 1858 reflected his current interest in archaeology.[32] At this time he may have been thinking of journalism, and under various *noms de plume* he wrote several articles in a flowery style. On 3 February 1855, the *Hawick Advertiser*, which had started publication in 1854, printed 'An account of a visit to Ruberslaw' by 'Surgere Tento' followed in September of the same year by 'A Ramble in the vale of Jed'. Later James looked at these early efforts with amusement, pointing out that the half a dozen companions he describes—botanist, geologist, archaeologist and so on—were all in fact aspects of himself and that the quotations of poetry were of his own composition—to provide an opportunity to display his learning.[33] Botanical articles of a more serious kind followed, beginning with 'A Glimpse of our native ferns'[34] and continuing with a series on the wild flowers of the month, under the pen name 'Chrysanthenum Leukanthenum'.* These compositions he used furtively to slip into the letter box of the *Advertiser* under cover of dark, but after the Editor, James Haining, inserted a notice saying that anonymous contributions were unacceptable, he revealed his identity and his final article under his pen-name was also signed J. A. H. Murray.[35] He and the Editor shared many interests and became close friends. When James left Hawick, Haining acknowledged in the paper his debt to the younger man for many anonymous contributions.[36] The friendship was a help to Alexander Murray for whom James obtained an apprenticeship on the staff of the paper to learn compositing, which led eventually to his becoming editor of the *Newcastle Daily Journal*.[37]

At the same time James had quite a reputation as an artist: in 1858 his drawings of Hermitage Castle in Liddesdale and of Leyden's birthplace in Denholm were included in an edition of Leyden's *Poems and Ballads* published at Kelso.[38] Again, although James never developed this skill, a brother did. Charles had first been inspired by tracings which James made from a volume of line drawing reproductions of the Elgin marbles which he borrowed from someone. Later, rescuing Charles from apprenticeship as a clerk in a Hawick wool mill, James helped him to go to Edinburgh to train at the Scottish Royal Academy, and he became an etcher.[39]

The chief source of information about James Murray's early activities is the *Hawick Advertiser*, but until 1855 it is difficult to be certain of the identity of 'James Murray'. There were several of that name in the town; one was a foreman at Watson and Sons Mill, a second a teacher in another school, and a third was a banker. This was inconvenient, and early in 1855 James, who had only been christened James, adopted the initials A. H. to save his letters from going astray. This of course excited curiosity amongst his cronies. What did those letters stand for? James apparently had not given this a thought, and when his friends began to taunt him, suggesting all sorts of impossible and improbable Christian names, he adopted his customary way of

---

* Ox-eye daisy.

dealing with teasing and held his tongue. It is said to have been the suggestion of William Norman Kennedy, the Poor-law Officer, which stuck. He threw out 'Augustus Henry' as a little jibe at James' ambitious ideas and omniscience—grand names that would take some living up to for a lad of eighteen in a junior post. His brother Charles used to ask coldly, 'Do you mean my brother James?' But James himself quietly accepted them and by July he was writing his full name in a book of Syriac Reading Lessons and Jacobus Augustus Henricus Murraeus in his commonplace book. James Augustus Henry he became and remained, and J. A. H. Murray is easy to pick out from the newspaper reports.

Although very fluent on paper, he was at first shy and halting in speech. He had a slight stammer, which he said was inherited from his father. This he was successful in overcoming, although close friends noted his habit of sometimes hesitating over a word and substituting another for it, and he was left with a rather unusual and self-conscious enunciation.[40] He used to tell of how he had followed Demosthenes' example and rehearsed his speeches in the open air by a waterfall up the Slitrig valley. He was very embarrassed one day to find a stranger standing listening to him, who called out, 'Very good—go on.'

With this practice James soon acquired fluency both in public speaking, in the flowery style of the time, and in giving humorous recitations.[41] For the latter he usually chose poems connected with the Border: a favourite was 'The Fate of Macgregor' by James Hogg the Ettrick shepherd poet—a stirring ghost story ending with Macgregor's brother Malcolm rushing to his rescue:

> 'Macgregor Macgregor' he bitterly cried:
> 'Macgregor Macgregor' the echoes replied.

In rendering this James showed his natural high spirits, sense of humour and dramatic talent, and all through his life Macgregor never failed to create a profound impression on his hearers, but he was equally moving on more serious occasions.

The *Hawick Advertiser*, recording his various activities in nearly every issue, shows James Murray to have been a young man of remarkable energy, interested and involved in everything going on in the town, pouring forth words in support of every good cause and on every occasion which required an uplifting address.

One of the exciting things about moving from Denholm to Hawick was the discovery there of a number of like-minded friends, some rather older than himself, who shared his interests. James was no longer misunderstood or looked upon as an eccentric by his contemporaries. 'Self improvement' was an accepted ideal, and the appalling slum conditions in Hawick and incidence of drunkenness in the streets stirred James and his friends to lead in movements for reform.

As a schoolmaster James was naturally concerned to raise the intellectual and moral standards of children and young people. He had been a Sunday school teacher at Denholm and continued to go to the annual New Year party to supplement the 'service of bun' with an edifying address on some subject such as 'The Mariner's Compass and the Compass of Faith' illustrated by a pocket compass. On another occasion he lent support to a crowded public meeting to call attention to the 'unprosperous state' of Denholm's library.[42]

This was the great age of the 'Soirée', first introduced in 1836 in Edinburgh. These were evening meetings providing the public with a mixed diet of entertainment, enlightenment and refreshments—all for one shilling or less. Around Christmas and the New Year every factory or organisation had its soirée, and James Murray was much in demand as a speaker. On one occasion, at Wilson's Mill, when he gave a peroration on 'Labour is nobility, perseverance is genius' (a call to young people to show themselves worthy of their forbears), he was preceded by the Chairman giving a résumé of the year's progress and an 'energetic speech' on Duty. There followed an attack on the Duke of Buccleuch for causing delay in executing orders by refusing to release land for an extension of the factory, and a 'thrilling and eloquent speech on the crusade against intemperance', songs and recitations. The proceedings began at 5.30 and ended on the sixth stroke of midnight.[43]

Sometimes his desire to instruct led James to put this before the cause he was supposed to be supporting: in an address to the Total Abstinence Society he had to acknowledge that his subject, 'The wonders of the earth on which we tread', had no direct bearing on the work of the society, but he justified his choice by claiming it to be a duty to encourage a study of geology in order to provide a substitute for the bottle they were asking men to abandon![44]

His speeches have some interest in revealing his philosophy. Most of the views he formed at this period remained unchanged throughout his life.

His reading on scientific subjects and especially his interest in geology inevitably forced him to consider the effect of recent discoveries on religious beliefs, but he seems to have found no real difficulty in reconciling the two. He had his own explanation of evolution and believed that the extinct animals and plants were doomed to disappear before the coming of a higher type 'in accordance with the grand provision of Nature, that those beasts which cannot be turned to the profit or use of Man, shall only "occupy till he come".'

He had complete confidence in a divine power which would in the fulness of time bring the earth and its inhabitants to a state of heavenly blessedness. Men's gifts, he held, are given to them only to enable them to carry out the purposes of God.

> We cannot doubt the evidence . . ., that man was created with his noble faculties to be exercised in discovering Nature's laws, and by possessing himself of her secrets to possess himself of her powers, and finally to attain through intelligent obedience and responsible action, to a state better for himself, the universe & his Maker, than he ever enjoyed in primeval days.[45]

James Murray put his beliefs into practice, seeking in daily prayer for himself, and later for his family, to know what God's purpose was. This gave him in all his work a strong sense of vocation which sustained him in the difficult and often discouraging task he undertook as Editor of the Dictionary.

His optimism was also founded on the Victorian faith in human progress. He felt he was living in a golden age of promise. Its learning was symbolised by the *Encyclopaedia Britannica*, a set of which he presented to a retiring Minister on behalf of the townsfolk, saying,

> These [past] ages in true excellence, were all little and poor: there is no age but the present which could erect such a tablet to its literary and scientific lore—its moral and sacred progress as we behold in these volumes. [Cheers] This earnest of the true greatness of the age, and key to all its knowledge . . .[46]

Hope for the future he saw, surprisingly, amid the slums of Hawick, in the Industrial Revolution and the invention of steam. A lecture which he gave on two occasions took the form of a prophetic vision of the history of Hawick past and future. The Spirit of Steam, rising from a caldron, cries, 'Schaw! spirits of evil begone make way for the spirits of good', and James continued 'I perceived . . . that the spirit of the pot spake truth. For from many a tall chimney in dense fumes, the smoke of his nostrils came bursting forth and the redoubled energy of the flashing wheels told that he was working there.' After imagining the building of railways to connect Hawick with the outer world, he concluded by a vision of the future:

> Methinks . . . I see in that far-coming land, scenes more glorious, and enchanting than ever have painted the past. I can see that the monsters of Intemperance and War have left the shores of Old Earth, that Labour reigns in royal dignity, that Peace and Plenty dispense their blessings on Young and Old, that rich and poor, strong and weak are bound together by happy laws of indissoluble love, that Earth clothed in living glory has glided into the Majesty and beauty of Heaven. And looking up I heard a voice which said unto me 'From past experience, learn present Duty, and trust in Heaven for the future'.[47]

Present duty was something James Murray was always conscious of and he supported his Hawick friends in their efforts to bring about the future that Heaven planned for their town, being, as he said 'always on the side of freedom and equality'.[48] Brought up in the Hawick tradition that the Tories were the embodiment of all evil,[49] he was now, as he remained, an ardent supporter of the Liberal Party. The pages of the *Advertiser* show him increasingly to the fore in public affairs.

In 1858 he moved a resolution in a densely packed public meeting to petition Parliament against the Conspiracy to Murder Bill of Lord Palmerston, which he criticised as a concession to Continental despotism and 'altogether unworthy of the support of the British people'. The motion was carried unanimously and, joined to similar expressions of opinion on all sides, led to the defeat of the government and resignation of Palmerston. Young James Murray felt that he had helped to make history.[50] He supported Italian emancipation and subscribed to Hawick funds in aid of those fighting for freedom. On a motion which he seconded, he forwarded a resolution to the Earl of Derby urging neutrality and non-intervention in Italian affairs. He heard an Italian, Signor Saffi, give an address in the East Bank Chapel and was much disappointed when Garibaldi, 'the greatest of Patriots, the grandest of heroes'—refused an invitation to visit the burgh. He preserved a letter with Garibaldi's signature amongst his treasured possessions.[51]

In Hawick the 1850s and 60s were stirring times. The first five years that James Murray was teaching there were years of controversy over the route to be taken by a railway proposed to connect the town with Carlisle.[52] Two rival companies were in competition. The Caledonian company, supported by the Duke of Buccleuch, whose collieries would be served by it, wanted a line via Langholm, while the North British Company offered a route slightly further east by Liddesdale. The Langholm scheme involved the acquisition of a considerable part of the Common Haugh. There was no guarantee that the Duke would implement a vague promise to make other land available to the burgesses for their pasture and to their wives for their bleaching and drying grounds. He owned almost all the countryside around the town and was blamed for hemming it in 'most tyrannically',[53] causing the overcrowded conditions and preventing the expansion of the wool mills. The issue of the railway divided both the town and the Town Council into rival camps and numerous public meetings were called, some lasting for four hours and drawing such large crowds that they had to be held in the open air. The telegraph system had just been established and when the Bills of both companies were before Parliament in 1858, every night reports on progress in London were read from the steps of the Town Hall to crowds listening with breathless interest.[54]

James Murray was soon drawn into the controversy, as a staunch supporter of the Liddesdale route and the Common Haugh. In May 1858 when all were ready to celebrate a Liddesdale victory there was consternation at the news that the Bill had not been approved. James Murray was a principal speaker at a mass meeting of 1500 people addressed from the steps of the Town Hall, as proposer of a resolution demanding that the House of Commons should be asked for its reasons for the rejection, and it was he who drew up a petition to their Member of Parliament.[55] He was active in the subsequent campaign organising opposition to the bill of the rival company still before the House of Lords, which in June was also thrown out.[56] There was bell ringing, with band playing and fireworks and the burning of an effigy of the chairman of the House of Commons committee,[57] but both companies were determined to go to Parliament again, and all through the summer and late autumn rival meetings and a good deal of mutual mud-throwing continued.[58] Only in 1859 did the Liddesdale scheme triumph. When the first train from Carlisle arrived (an hour late) at 9 *a.m.* on 1 July 1862, James Murray again felt that he had helped to determine an historic issue.

The Railway controversy was linked to the much more important matter of the reform of the Burgh constitution.[59] The town, still governed by a self-elected body of thirty-one members under a Charter of 1537, was described as 'the closest and most rotten borough in Scotland'.[60] The Burgesses, numbering 400 in 1770, were now reduced to 127, in spite of the great increase in the total population; there was much evidence of general maladministration,[61] and the railway issue had made it abundantly clear that the Council no longer represented the views of the majority of the inhabitants. Once again James Murray was to the fore in a series of exciting meetings, speaking and moving resolutions in favour of extending the franchise and taking a lead in securing the reduction of the Burgess entrance fee from £4 to five shillings.[62] Although he depended for his livelihood upon his standing with the ruling class of the burgh whose children he was educating, he showed no fear in being outspoken in condemnation of any whom he regarded as the enemies of freedom.

At a public meeting in October 1859 he argued that it was the bounden duty of everyone to support the few Councillors who favoured reform in their efforts to extend the franchise and to take advantage of the reduced fee to enroll as Burgesses.[63] He set the example by becoming a Burgess himself and inducing his father to do the same.[64] In the case of Thomas Murray this was important, as it made him eligible to represent his trade and as a result he was elected Quartermaster for the Tailors and in 1860 took his seat on the Town Council for the last year of its life under the old constitution.[65] Later James praised his father for his public spirit in 'voting himself off the Council' by supporting reform, but of course old Thomas well knew what was expected of him when he yielded to his son's persuasion to become a Burgess.[66] Meanwhile the battle continued, with James still to the fore and the issue in doubt up to the last moment. Victory was finally won in November 1861 and at the first election under a new constitution James and his cousin Adam Scott were registered among the 364 voters.[67] It was a triumph, albeit only a partial one, since the qualification to vote was fixed at ownership of a property worth £10 and this left the majority of the working class still disfranchised.

None the less it was an exciting outcome for James Murray who had been privileged at under twenty-five to be one of the leaders, working with older men, having the thrill of addressing and holding the attention of big crowds and seeing his motions passed and influencing the course of public events. Nothing in the future changed the principles which had inspired him then. He had achieved much in the seven years since he had moved from Denholm to Hawick, a village boy of seventeen and a half. Now it seemed as though it would be open to him to become a politician, a member of the Town Council, a journalist, a minister of the church, or a distinguished teacher, according to which of his many interests he chose to follow. Unexpectedly the way forward was to be through yet another sphere of activity, the Hawick Archaeological Society. But for this body, he later recognised, he would never have become Editor of the *Oxford English Dictionary*.[68]

CHAPTER III

The Discovery of Anglo-Saxon

THE GROUP of men with whom James Murray was associated in Hawick shared his wide interests and his ideals. Like him, they were excited by everything around them and like him they wanted to use their knowledge to improve the moral and intellectual character of their fellow townsmen.

James and his brother Alexander belonged to a 'Mutual Improvement Institute'[1] and supported a series of public subscription lectures on learned topics arranged every winter. James also joined a Literary and Scientific Society as soon as he came to Hawick, and in December 1854 at its Soirée he gave what was probably his first public lecture on 'Reading, its pleasures and advantages'. The members of this society used to meet to read and discuss essays and poems and to help each other by mutual criticism. On various occasions James read papers, including at the Society's final Banquet in January 1856 a 'very learned and critical essay' on Language. It seems to have been a rather exclusive group, accused of being self opinionated and too censorious, and it was brought to an end with the idea of forming instead a popular society which would provide instruction and entertainment 'tending to improve youth, and to lead them to a more profitable way of spending their leisure hours, than hanging at street corners, or frequenting the dram shop'.[2]

On 25 August 1856 a public meeting was called at which it was agreed to form a Society

for the Collection, preservation & elucidation of the Antiquities & Natural productions of the district: & also, connected therewith a Museum, for the preservation of such remains of Antiquity, as may be procured by the Society: as also, Specimens illustrative of the

Zoology, Botany, Geology, Manufactures, & General Resources of the district: as also, whatever objects of Curiosity, Natural, Historic or Artistic Interest may be obtained by the Society.[3]

The scientific study of archaeology was then just beginning to be taken seriously and the 1840s and 50s saw the foundation of many county archaeological, architectural and historical associations, several of which were of a rather hybrid character. It was first suggested that this new Hawick group should be the Antiquarian Society, but James, who was a member of the steering committee, persuaded the others that it should be named the Hawick Archaeological Society, which he felt widened its scope.[4] The objectives reflect the varied interests of the founders, and at first James' contribution was mainly in the fields of geology and botany. At the second public meeting at which the rules were approved and the officers elected, with James Murray as Secretary, his exhibits were a five-foot-long geological map of Scotland and his collection of pressed plants. His friends showed a magpie collection of flint arrow heads, celts and stone axes, Roman querns, fragments of British canoes, bronze axes, 'ancient, modern, and curious' iron spears, swords and fire-arms, together with a large assortment of Roman, British and foreign coins; and the inaugural lecture stressed the value of archaeological study in increasing general knowledge of 'old world lore' and stimulating self improvement in almost every other branch of information.[5]

As Secretary, a post into which he threw himself with customary enthusiasm and energy, James soon widened his knowledge of archaeology and was able to make a contribution. He kept the Minute books meticulously, recording in detail the contents of the papers read at the monthly meetings, and often illustrating them with drawings and diagrams. At each meeting gifts flowed in for the Museum, and James made a practice of commenting on the more unusual or important of these, which often necessitated some research on his part. At first he was also responsible for cataloguing the accessions. From an original twenty-seven members the Society grew to fifty-five by the end of its first year of existence and it was largely due to the efforts of the Secretary that it prospered. He himself contributed an original paper to nearly every meeting, his choice of subject illustrating his wide interests; and although he sometimes did little more than summarise whatever book he happened to be reading at the time, often he had done some independent work.

For the first meeting in October 1856 he prepared a large map of Scotland under the Romans and after pointing out the main features he led a lively discussion on whether the Roman Gadenica could be identified with Hawick. At the next meeting he was back on a geological topic illustrated by maps, diagrams and specimens, and the following year he spoke on 'The Noachian Deluge, universal with regard to man, but very restricted with regard to the earth', the geology of the Slitrig valley, the discovery of America by the Norsemen (illustrated by a large chart), the religion and remains of the Druids (illustrated by models of Stonehenge and Avebury), and the history of Denholm and recent archaeological finds there.

His growing interest in archaeology was developed in lively argument with his friends and expeditions with them. He used his eyes and he thought about what he saw and because he never compartmentalised his interests, he never missed seeing something because he had allowed himself to become preoccupied with another line of research. Visiting Liddesdale again, he recalled his childhood wonderment that the boundary between England and Scotland was marked by no visible change in the land or in the inhabitants. Now, standing on a British fort on Caerby Hill and looking south over a sterile tract of moorland (today afforested) thinly clad here and there with natural birch and stretching away as far as his eye could see, he realised that he was looking into England and that the brook below him was the boundary.

> How often does man hairsplit, and sever, and part asunder what Heaven has made a whole! [he reflected] ... Man is fond to classify, to separate, to discriminate, to set apart in little cells of memory the mass of facts he gathers from the field of nature. But nature has no such isolating method—her facts and laws are a continuous, all-connecting network.

So, when he visited a hill fort he noticed the rare fern growing between its stones: walking up the Slitrig valley, on the look out for geological changes in the ground, he would also glance up and pick out on the skyline the silhouette of an ancient earthwork on one side and on the other the deep cutting made for the new railway, and would speculate on the possibility that the time would come when both alike would be included in the archaeology of Britain.[6] This happened sooner than he would have dreamed, for the railway, so much desired and achieved with so much difficulty in 1862, is now abandoned and a fit subject for industrial archaeology.

In his archaeological activities as in other things James was sometimes the serious scholar, sometimes the high-spirited youth but always exhibited his great vitality, his zest for living and his keen interest and wonder at everything around him. Leading a society expedition to Hermitage Castle, at one moment he would be risking his neck scrambling into a deep dungeon and the next delivering a learned discourse to the company on the castle's history.[7] Riding in a two-horse carriage with a party of fellow archaeologists, some inside and some on top, he would join with them in chanting a ballad about the Society, with the refrain,

> The Hawick Archaeologists I trow ye dinna ken!

then dismounting make a serious investigation of an earth work on Rink Hill, trespass through a field as a protest against a farmer who had ploughed out an ancient ditch, and end by collecting objects for the museum. Bad weather never deterred him and on one occasion, setting out for a long tramp in driving rain and mist, he told a friend who pointed out that the barometer was still falling, that he was determined to have 'no official information' as to the weather. His bursting energy was sometimes difficult to restrain: leaving by a 7 *a.m.* train for a meeting at Galashiels he described feeling 'too big for the interior of a railway carriage with a brace of fellow-travellers monotonously discussing the prospects of hosiery, the comparative merits of Hawick and Galashiels and the water-power of the Teviot and Slitrig' and how he impulsively leapt out of the train at the next stop in order to rush up the Eildon Hills, long familiar to him in the distance viewed from Ruberslaw.[8]

At the same time he was deepening his knowledge of archaeology and archaeological techniques. In 1863 he persuaded Henry McLauchlan of the British Archaeological Institute, who had been surveying Watling Street, the Roman wall and sites in Northumberland, to join him in a three-day expedition. They examined the Catrail, a lineal earthwork in the then wild and almost inaccessible region between Roberts Lynn and Peel Fell and from Riccarton to the Knot o' the Gate and the Roman roads known as the Maiden and the Wheel Causeways. A fragment of James' report on the Catrail survives which is extremely detailed. It satisfied him that earlier accounts were full of errors and taught him the dangers of copying what others have said and repeating them as if the results of one's own investigations.[9] In his future work for the Dictionary he frequently found wrong definitions and even non-existent words which had been blindly copied from one dictionary to another, and he was never satisfied until he got back to the source for himself. He saw some early excavations in Northumberland and came back to make a full and accurate survey of one of the local forts—Kirkton Hill just outside Hawick—which he hoped to get permission to dig.[10] He realised that the Society's museum was a confusion, since they accepted anything from Indian objects sent by the brother of one of the committee, to a stuffed tame rabbit that had belonged to the local hairdresser, or a ticket for the Lord Mayor of London's ball in 1806. Tactfully, so as not to offend members who had spent much time in arranging the museum, James suggested separating the local from the general collection and classifying the objects in different groups.[11]

In 1858 the records of the Society show that James Murray was developing a new interest, this time in philology, and he lectured that autumn on 'The Contributions of philology to the History of Western Europe' and in the following April on 'The Origin and History of the Scottish Language'. This new study rose from various causes. As a teacher James faced the problem he had already met as a pupil at Minto school, of teaching English pronunciation to those whose natural tongue was the broad Scotch of the Border. He was very particular about this and would insist on his pupils repeating their reading after him until they got the sound right, and it was probably to acquire some knowledge which would help him in teaching, as much as to perfect his own speech, that he decided in the summer of 1857 to attend a vacation course at Edinburgh on elocution, given by Alexander Melville Bell, Professor of Elocution and Vocal Physiology.[12] This course proved an unexpectedly rich experience. Professor Bell was one of the first men in this country to make a scientific study of phonetics and was the inventor of Visible Speech — an alphabet of symbols which, he claimed, made it possible to record with complete accuracy the pronunciation of every sound used in human speech. This was exactly what James had been looking for, and from his own experience he knew the help it would be in attempting to learn languages from books. 'Visible Speech' did more than this for him. It opened a door revealing phonetics as an exact science applicable to the comparative study of languages. His hitherto compulsive but rather aimless picking up of foreign tongues suddenly became purposeful and he developed an interest in the history of the whole Germanic group.

Melville Bell could not fail to notice this unusually keen young student. He was surprised to discover the depth of his knowledge of the English language and acquaintance with the roots and history of words, his quickness to appreciate and apply basic principles and above all his delight and enthusiasm in study. He invited him to his house and introduced him to his family, and this was the start of a long and fruitful friendship, particularly with Professor Bell's youngest son, Alexander Graham, then a boy in his teens. One afternoon, sitting in the garden at the Bells' house at Trinity, Edinburgh, Graham, talking to James, said he would very much like to learn something about electricity. James of course was only too glad to teach him. He made for Graham an electric battery and a voltaic pile out of halfpennies and disks of zinc. Graham, who later became famous as the inventor of the telephone, used to say that James Murray was the 'grandfather of the telephone'.[13] Later it was Melville Bell who introduced James Murray to the Philological Society in London, so he might have claimed to be the grandfather of the Dictionary. For a young man educating himself in a provincial town this contact with the outside world of scholarship was invaluable.

Another chance happening at this stage of his career also pointed in the direction of philology.

There was in the second half of the nineteenth century a growing interest in England in the history of language and in the value of surviving dialects (already threatened with extinction) in throwing light on the origin of words and their forms. Hitherto Britain had lagged behind the Germans in philological study, but now several scholars and amateurs were at work in this field. Amongst them a leading figure was Prince Louis-Lucien Bonaparte, the nephew of Napoleon. The Prince was collecting examples of dialect and wrote to Henry Scott Riddell, then Minister of Teviothead, author of poems and songs in Border dialect.[14] At the Prince's request Riddell put the gospel of St Matthew and the book of Psalms into Lowland Scotch. An extract from his translation of the Sermon on the Mount was read one evening to the Archaeological Society by the President, W. N. Kennedy and immediately excited James Murray's interest. He got hold of a fuller version from a London literary magazine and included a criticism of it in his lecture to the Society on 'The Origin and History of the Scottish Language' in April 1859. He put his finger on the unscientific quality of Riddell's work.

> It is an attempted *restoration*, and not the Scotch of any particular time or district . . . Thus, though interesting, the work has not to posterity the scientific value that would attach to the rendering of any passage into the precise spoken language . . . which would then appear before the world, not as an opinion but as a testimony — not a picture from memory or from fancy, but an actual photograph of the very tones in the middle of the nineteenth century.[15]

He had evidently already realised the possibilities of doing a study of this kind on his own dialect, using Bell's Visible Speech to make an accurate record. In a few years this work was to put him amongst the leading philologists of his time. He began experimenting at once, following Riddell's example in attempting a translation of Matthew, but using phonetic symbols which could be recognised by those who had never heard the speech of Teviotdale. He found Matthew not very suitable for his purpose, and abandoning this, next translated half of Acts, and still was not satisfied. Finally, he found the books of Jonah and of Ruth gave the best opportunity of demonstrating the Border speech and construction and completed these. He did not venture to send his version to the Prince, but he was able to publish his *Ruth* years later in his *Dialect of the Southern Counties of Scotland*. That was, however, far ahead: his immediate task was to continue his new study by planning a phonetic key to Jamieson's *Etymological Dictionary of the Scottish Language*. He only partly completed this, but it was a valuable preparation for his later work as a lexicographer. His attempted translations had called his attention to structure and to grammar, and he realised that the constructions he had been scolded for at school and which he was now criticising in his own pupils' work as 'bad grammar' by English standards were in fact 'good grammar' in Scotch, and for his own satisfaction he wrote a Scotch Grammar demonstrating this.[16] He learned Gaelic and was amused when travelling in the north of Scotland to overhear two young men commenting disparagingly in Gaelic on the dress of himself and his companion, and to be able to discomfit them by addressing them in their own language.

James was still building up his library, and poking round a second-hand book stall in Leith he picked up by chance a copy of Bohn's edition of Pauli's *Life of Alfred the Great*, with the text of Alfred's translation into Anglo-Saxon of Orosius' *Historiarum adversum Paganos*. The difficulty of self education is that it may leave gaps, and it is surprising that James Murray had got so far in his studies before for the first time seeing Anglo-Saxon written. He carried his find back to Hawick in a high state of excitement, and the more he read the more excited he became. This was another new world, and he says, 'I simply bathed and basked in it.'[17] The excitement was that he now realised that the Border dialect of his childhood speech was not something local but belonged in fact to the Anglo-Saxon root and he began working at Scotch with renewed vigour in the light of Anglo-Saxon. The Highland speech he could trace to Gaelic origins and in the Strathclyde area he found words akin to Welsh, but the Border and the east owed their speech to the Anglian invaders, with some added Norse elements.

Increasingly he noticed words, observing that in Hawick the processes and tools used in preparing flax were mostly pure Anglo-Saxon, with a few borrowings from Danish: that in Orkney many more words of Norse origin were used; he noticed that there was a difference between the speech of people in Teviotdale and those in Liddesdale, where already he could detect a 'trilling of r' which east and south became the Northumberland burr. He began to pay attention to the evidence of place-names, and lectured to the Society on the origin of the name Hawick and on personal names.[18]

But he was still working in a vacuum, worrying things out for himself, but cut off from the world of scholarship, although he was encouraged in 1860 by Melville Bell's opinion that his conclusions on the derivation of the name 'Hawick' were 'incontrovertible'.[19] From his isolation it was his connection with the Hawick Archaeological Society which rescued him.

The Society was flourishing. By 1859 the Secretary could report that 'the solid progress, and enlightened researches of the Society, have wherever he has gone won for it a high and respected position; . . . everywhere, throughout the Border Land it is found to be looked up to as an intelligent & trustworthy authority in matters of Archaic importance.'[20] By the end of 1861 numbers had risen to 100 and the Society reached a much wider public through the Museum, now installed in the old United school building in Orrock Place and drawing nearly a thousand visitors a year, and through the monthly reports supplied by the Secretary to the local press, the *Border* as well as the *Hawick Advertiser*. From 1863 the Transactions were published in an annual volume—the start of a series which has been continued to the present day. The Society had gained a reputation for looking after local antiquities and rescuing them from destruction and loss. Led by their energetic Secretary, they had collected the scattered stones of the ruined abbey of Melrose: they had watched the rebuilding of Hawick Parish church and rescued several carved stones from the foundations:[21] a muster of stalwarts had removed a fragment of the town Cross from where it had lain for twenty years, upside down embedded in the pavement.[22] They had fought, unsuccessfully it is true, but with considerable publicity, to retain in Hawick a Bronze Age spear-head found in making the railway tunnel, first against a claim that it was Treasure Trove, and then that in Scotland what belongs to no one belongs to the Crown, and therefore in this case should go to the National Museum.[23]

As a result of all this activity, the Secretary began to receive invitations to attend the meetings of other local societies, notably the well-established Berwickshire Naturalists' Club, which he soon joined. Here in June 1861 he met for the first time the literary and scientific elite from both sides of the Tweed, whom he had known before only by name and repute. He was impressed particularly by a member of the Berwickshire Club who thrilled his audience by a paper on the place-names of the locality and his explanations of names of farms and streams which he derived from many different languages, including Persian, American Indian and Arabic. A few months later James was at a larger meeting of the united Berwickshire and Tyneside Clubs at Alnwick where about 150 members were gathered. This was an epoch-making occasion for him. The place-name expert, looked upon as a man of prodigious learning, was again present and this time James ventured to express to him his surprise at his vast linguistic knowledge. He was even more surprised at the reply. The man frankly confessed that he really did not know these languages, but had a considerable stock of dictionaries. His experience was that an explanation of British place-names could usually be found in some language if only one had a sufficiency of dictionaries. This was the first time that James had met with one of the bogus etymologists common at that period, who believed that the derivation of a word could be solved by finding any foreign word that sounded something like it. When, on this occasion, the confident 'expert' on place-names began to hold forth and attributed a name near Alnwick to Persian origin, one of the company, Canon Greenwell of Durham, asked dryly would the speaker give them any idea of when the Persians lived in Northumberland or had been there to teach the inhabitants their words? This led to a lively discussion in which the speaker argued that these were 'words of the original human speech which had floated down through the ages & like fern seeds had taken root alike in Persia & in England.' James contributed eagerly to the debate, in which derivations from Anglo-Saxon were suggested as a likelier explanation.[24] Afterwards Canon Greenwell came up and introduced himself, asking how James had come by his evidently unusually wide knowledge. James explained that he had picked up his Anglo-Saxon on his own, but feared that his information was still only elementary owing to the great difficulty he had in getting hold of books. Canon Greenwell was impressed and on returning home generously despatched to Hawick a box full of volumes from his own and the Cathedral Library on loan. James described his excitement: 'there were Hooker and Lye & Thorpe & Thwaites, & the Heptateuch, & Durham Gospels — it was glorious!'[25] He set to work, and actually made copies of several complete books. Some of these copies he continued to use, and at Oxford found it convenient to keep them at hand for reference to save visits to the Bodleian Library. More important, by copying them he gained an exceptionally detailed knowledge of some of the texts, which he stored in his retentive memory.

In his enthusiasm, Anglo-Saxon was included in the curriculum of his school, and he dreamed of popularising its study by writing a Grammar and reading book, which he got as far as submitting to a London publisher. The manuscript was returned with the cutting comment that this was merely a hobby for antiquarians and his intention of publishing the books to sell at a few shillings was sheer lunacy. He kept the manuscripts but never did any more about publication.

Next he discovered Gothic from one of Canon Greenwell's loans and began working at this. Help came from a new source. James Douglas of Cavers, a man renowned for his kindness, and who had become a life member of the Archaeological Society, probably through its Secretary, began to take an interest in the young man from Denholm of whom he must have known in a general way since James' childhood and whose thirst for knowledge could not fail to impress him. James Murray had often thought enviously of John Leyden's luck in being allowed to use the extensive library at Cavers. Now

Douglas began to lend him books from it, and generously presented him with Rask's *Anglo-Saxon Grammar* and a splendid reprint of the *Codex Argenteus* which was what he needed for his Gothic. Following his usual practice in tackling a new language, he worked his way through this version of the Gospels, preparing his own grammar and a set of examples as he went along. This time he did not attempt publication: he was quite happy to work as a scholar for the sheer enjoyment of the research.[26]

Through his reading elsewhere than in the local papers James was beginning to improve his own literary style. In speech he still indulged in flights of rhetoric, but in prose he used fewer hackneyed phrases and purple patches. He may have taken to heart a cutting but not quite unfair comment on his first published book, a little one reprinting his account of a week's holiday in Orkney in 1860, which he had read to the Archaeological Society and printed in the *Advertiser*. Writing from London in a Caithness & Sutherland local newspaper, the reviewer made merciless fun of what he referred to as

> gross ignorance or the entire neglect of the first principles of the language he uses . . . penny-a-lining love of redundancy and empty phrases . . . Oh! my young poetic fledgling, where were you put to school? . . . I have perhaps made a mistake in assuming that the writer has reached that period of life when it is considered necessary to send young gentlemen to school.[27]

In spite of the reviewer, however, James felt pleased enough with his work to present a copy later with his 'most affectionate regards' to his second wife. Perhaps he also gave one to the girl he was in love with in 1861 — Maggie Scott. She was an infant school mistress, daughter of a Hawick clerk, and sister-in-law of one of the pillars of the Temperance movement, George Easton the barber, through whom James met her. Maggie was his senior by three years and he described her as a very 'refined and talented' young lady. She was musical, she sketched a little, was intelligent and spoke well. She was also very devout. The only drawback to the match was that Maggie was extremely delicate. During her three or four years' service in a primary school near Manchester she had had one long period of sick leave and her testimonial on leaving referred to the badly ventilated classroom and the fact that she had sacrificed her health 'to advance our noble cause'.[28]

In 1862 she was resident in Ireland and she was married to James

4. James Murray and his first
wife, Margaret Scott. 1862.

Murray on 12 August at Fisherwick Presbyterian Church, Belfast.

James had applied for a post as headmaster of the Parish school at Ashkirk, a small village between Hawick and Selkirk,[29] but he was again balked by the religious question as the school managers would only consider a member of the Established church. The move would have provided him with a school house, but influential friends in Hawick, anxious to retain his services at the Academy, helped him to obtain a south-facing house in Wilton Terrace, newly built in the suburb across the river.

When term started, Mrs Murray joined her husband at the Academy and introduced music—almost the only subject which James felt incompetent to teach himself.[30]

At first all went well with the marriage, but it was to be the cause of James leaving Hawick and Scotland for London. In January 1864 the young couple rejoiced in the birth of a daughter, but unhappily both mother and child were weak and ailing, and the doctor warned James that Maggie's health was now a matter of grave concern. She was suffering from consumption in an advanced stage, and the only hope of her survival lay in taking her as far south as he could. Wintering in the south of France was of course out of the question for a man of James' limited means. He was in despair, faced with both the problem of finding somewhere to go at once in order to save his wife's life and of obtaining employment if he left Hawick. One branch of his father's family and also one of his mother's brothers had emigrated to Australia, and they all seemed to be prospering there, so James wrote off to his cousin Margaret Scott (Mrs Miller) to inquire whether there would be any opening for a teacher near her. Time was short, and before Mrs Miller's encouraging reply reached him he had already been forced to take a decision in order to be settled before the onset of winter.[31] Had he heard sooner, his future career would not have included editing the Dictionary.

In 1858 James had paid his first and only visit to England, when he had seen London and stayed with another cousin, John Somerville, who was manager of the Maidstone Gas Works. Now, as soon as the summer term ended, he took Maggie to Maidstone and she seemed somewhat better for the change. Maggie's brother had a connection with the Chartered Bank of India, Australia and China in Threadneedle Street, London, and he told James they were looking out for a clerk with a knowledge of foreign languages. This seemed a possibility, and James had an interview with the Directors on 26 July 1864. He returned with Maggie to Hawick still uncertain and reluctant to give up his teaching. He then sought advice from Mr Douglas of Cavers, who thought he was wise to move to London but could not make any suggestions as to employment; he did, however, send a draft for £10 so that when they moved they might travel first class with the comfort desirable for an invalid.[32]

Then, while James still hesitated, another blow fell on the harassed couple. On 15 August the baby died, and this finally decided James to take his brother-in-law's urgent advice and accept the post at the Bank. It must have been a bitter blow to him. It meant leaving the work he enjoyed in his flourishing school; the Archaeological Society where, he said, he was 'up to the waist' in work; plans to excavate; his research on the Catrail;[33] a series of descriptions of Border castles, only two of which were completed; an investigation of the original site of Hawick; his handbook to the flora of Teviotdale, and a scheme to extend the Society to cover the whole county.[34] There was also his involvement in local politics and public life, his home and his many friends. He was, however, quite clear where his duty lay and must have warned the School Committee that he would have to resign, as they released him so as to be free to take the bank post in September.

He was in London at the end of August house hunting, and returned to Hawick to make final arrangements for his departure, before he received a letter from the bank confirming his appointment at £150 *p.a.* to start work at the head office on Monday 12 September.[35] On Thursday 1 September fifty members of the Archaeological Society and friends honoured him with a dinner at the Museum in the room in which he had started his career as an assistant master ten years before. Many tributes were paid to his efficiency as Secretary, and James for his part took a last opportunity to appeal to the young men present to cultivate and improve their minds by acquiring useful knowledge. A special meeting of the Society was held on the following Tuesday, when James gave a farewell address on his researches into the origin and purpose of the Catrail and listed the many projects he had been unable to complete.[36]

There was no time to collect money for a presentation before he left, but on 24 September the *Advertiser* announced that the testimonial to Mr J. A. H. Murray had reached the handsome total of £50. More money must have come in subsequently as the presentation consisted of an 'elegant time piece and a purse of sovereigns'. The elegant time piece, in a weighty setting of polished black marble with an inscription, still exists in working order; the purse of sovereigns was presumably spent at once. In any case it did not reach James in that form, since on 2 November the organisers sent a cheque for just over £42, the balance after the purchase of the clock.[37]

The effect on the Archaeological Society of the loss of its Secretary was immediate. Four months after his departure it was proposed that monthly meetings should be replaced by quarterly ones, and although this was negatived there were no meetings in May, June or July. Miraculously, and perhaps largely because of the Museum, the Society survived and recovered and has had a continuous existence down to the present time. While his parents were alive (Thomas died in 1873 and Mary in 1888) James paid fairly regular visits to Hawick and whenever possible the Society persuaded him to read them a paper on whatever subject he happened to be working at the time.[38] In 1906 the Society celebrated its jubilee and had the happy idea of making James Murray, sole survivor of the founder members, President, and inviting him to be present at the Jubilee Dinner. In spite of having been absent from Hawick for over forty years he still held the record for the number of papers contributed to the Society's

Transactions—sixty. The Town Council rose to the occasion and gave him the Freedom of the Burgh and the scroll in a casket of Hawick bog oak with silver mountings. On the same day the Edinburgh Border Counties Association presented an address of congratulations and welcome.[39]

On his part James Murray never felt that he really belonged to England and he remained a Borderer at heart. His family remembered how on any train journey which took him beyond the Midlands he would lean out of the window, saying with immense satisfaction, 'I smell the northern air!' drawing in great breaths of it.[40] He looked back on those ten years in Hawick between the ages of seventeen and twenty-seven as one of the most satisfying and fruitful periods of his life when, although he had still not settled on a real vocation, he revelled in the pursuit of knowledge for knowledge's sake.

CHAPTER IV

New Life in London

FACED with the task of finding a house at short notice in London, James had looked south of the river, probably wanting to be in a suburb and not too shut in, both out of consideration for his wife's health and because of his own preference for a district where the country would not be far away. He may have noticed this part of London on his visits to the city from Maidstone. Camberwell and Peckham were then rapidly growing, and he found what he wanted in a newly built terrace with a sunny aspect on the north side of Nunhead Lane. Beaufort Terrace, no longer standing, consisted of ten houses and James rented number 6 for £24 *p.a.* It was conveniently situated: Nunhead was a self-contained community with its own small green and the necessary shops, Beaufort Terrace was at the end of the lane where it leads into Peckham Rye, a fifty acre open space. The surrounding low hills, Denmark Hill, Telegraph Hill, Honour Oak and Forest Hill were not yet built over and Dulwich Park was quite near. Cannon Street station was approaching completion and rail communications with the City were adequate.

Adjusting to their new life was not easy for the young couple. Maggie was of necessity left alone all day, while James got little satisfaction from his work. He had been teased in Scotland for his immense learning and bookish ways: in London, he must have seemed a very odd character to his fellow clerks in the bank, with his Scotticisms and his rather prim views on religion and morals. He came in for some jibes and it took a little time for his sterling qualities of generous good humour, diligence and accuracy to be appreciated, but eventually he made good and lasting friendships. The work itself bore no comparison with that of teaching: it was dull in the extreme, and although James took pains to master the technicalities of banking, the

whole business world was alien to him and he referred disparagingly
to the 'Mammon-worship of Threadneedle Street' and said he found
the work 'adverse to my tastes, and the course of my studies'.[1]

He had a hope that he might find more congenial occupation in the
library of the British Museum in which he could use his linguistic
gifts to better advantage, but was disappointed to learn that there was
an age limit of twenty-six for applicants and he was too late by
eighteen months. So far as he could, he continued his hobbies. The
bank correspondence, dull as it was, at least enabled him to increase
his collection of foreign stamps and practise his modern languages.
He studied local history and he continued to add pressed flowers and
grasses to his herbarium. Many of these he spotted from the train
window, growing on the embankments. In England, as in Scotland,
he was an inveterate trespasser and years later, at Oxford, used to lead
his large family along the railway line, ordering the children to throw
themselves into cover in the ditch if a train approached—not because
of danger of being struck, but to avoid prosecution. The lawn at
Hampton Court and the river bank at Kew yielded other specimens.
He sent further articles to Hawick to complete his work on the flora of
Teviotdale and in one of these he gave his impressions of the English
countryside:

> in the immediate neighbourhood of London, the observer may
> walk for mile upon mile without meeting with a stream, a burn, or
> rill of running water, and, in consequence, it is necessary to provide
> in the corner of almost every field a pond, or tank . . . as the only
> available drinking place for the cattle. These stagnant holes,
> overhung by a few melancholy pollard willows . . . are favourite
> haunts of many species of plants obnoxious to the agriculturist . . .
> the streams themselves, winding sluggishly along their level
> course, and spreading into shallow oozy marshes, provide similar
> conditions, and . . . afford numerous plants unknown to . . . Upper
> Teviotdale, where sparkling perennial rills are found in every
> ravine, and where the streams rush in lively glee down the valleys.[2]

He was obviously very homesick for the Border country and his
exhilarating tramps over the moors.

Unexpectedly he found that he was not cut off from his study of the
dialects of Scotland. The London police force was at that time largely
recruited from the north—200 came from Caithness alone—and he
used every opportunity to get into conversation with them, testing

and recording their grammar and their pronunciation. This became so characteristic an occupation that later it impressed his family and I remember my father in the 1920s asking for direction from a policeman outside Richmond Park. 'You must be from very far in the north of Scotland', he observed. 'Yes,' was the reply, 'from John o'Groats!'

The daily train journey gave time for reading and the continued study of languages: he mentions Hindustani and Achaemenian inscriptions. In listening to the conversation of his fellow travellers, he noted great contrasts with Scotland and was not a little shocked. He found, for instance, that church membership was taken very casually: most young men went to a Free church because their parents went there, or drifted into an Anglican church because they liked the music or preferred the *Book of Common Prayer* to extempore prayers. To James this was a betrayal of principle which roused his anger: he was proud to be a Dissenter, these men seemed shamefaced and apologetic.[3] Again, he found England very backward in support of the temperance movement and that even the clergy seemed lukewarm. He said he was

> first startled & then grieved to see the extent to which the habitual use of alcoholic drinks pervades the community . . . I actually meet with men on the train, who in sad solemn earnest believe . . . wine to be a panacea or universal remedy for any ailment . . . with a credulousness & gullibility which no follower of Holloway or Morrison's pills ever attain to.
>
> To me such things are perfectly wonderful. I listen to them with the wonder I should experience in hearing them discuss whether 2 + 2 make 3 or 5.[4]

The argumentative, earnest, naïve young Scotchman was soon well known. He was at that time much interested in the works of the German natural philosopher Humboldt and one day a middle-aged traveller commented on his reading matter, saying that he was also an admirer of this writer. They exchanged names and James learned that George Ruthven was a near neighbour. George was an interesting man, then a draughtsman working in the London office of the Great Indian Peninsular Railway and he had considerable artistic ability as a portrait painter. He was a native of Kendal and second son of a shoemaker who was an amateur geologist and prepared the first geological map of the Lake District, the basis of all later surveys.[5]

James and Maggie were invited to the Ruthven home and got to know the family.

Mrs Ruthven claimed to have been educated with Charlotte Brontë at the school at Cowan Bridge described in *Jane Eyre*—but could say little about it beyond the fact that they were taught to sew beautifully. She had lost four children in infancy, the last as recently as December 1862, and in this could sympathise with Maggie in her tragedy and perhaps give her hope in that she had two surviving sons and three daughters. Ada, the eldest daughter, was only just nineteen and Maggie found a link with her in her love of music.

James entertained Maggie by devoting a good deal of time to her autograph album, many of the contents of which were his work and illustrate his interests.[6] One humorous contribution was

> Literary and Fine English Version. The Domiciliary Structure Erected by John (Recognised in the Uncultivated, Plebeian Nomenclature of the Illiterate under the Appelation of the House that Jack Built).
> Behold the Mansion reared by Dædal Jack!
> See the Malt stored in many a plethoric sack,
> In the proud cirque of Juan's bivouac!

and so on, with illustrations. His serious researches were represented by a facsimile transcript, on paper carefully coloured to simulate parchment, of a page from a 1630 copy-book of a Selkirk schoolboy which James had been lucky enough to find in the binding of a seventeenth-century Greek grammar which he had picked up on an Edinburgh book stall.[7] Two more pages recorded 'The Lord's Prayer from Age to Age Showing Growth of the English Tongue'. Starting from Aelfric's Anglo-Saxon Gospels, he gave examples which he described as Later-Saxon, Dano-Saxon, Semi-Saxon, Old English, Early English, Middle English—down to the Modern English of the Geneva Bible and the authorised version of 1860.

Together James and Maggie attended the Congregational church at Camberwell, and James was soon invited to preach, to address temperance meetings, and to join in the educational work of the church. A surviving advertisement from the Congregational Church, Luton, states that

> The second lecture of the course will (D.V.) be delivered . . . on Tuesday evening, October 30th, 1866, by J. A. Murray Esq.,

THE DOMICILIARY STRUCTURE ERECTED BY JOHN.

[Recognised in the Uncultivated, Plebeian Nomenclature of the Illiterate under the Appellation of THE HOUSE THAT JACK BUILT.]

Behold the Mansion reared by Dædal Jack !

See the Malt stored in many a plethoric sack,
In the proud cirque of Juan's bivouac !

Mark how the Rat's felonious fangs invade
The golden stores in John's Pavillion laid !

Anon with velvet foot and Tarquin strides,
Subtil Grimalkin to her quarry glides ;
Grimalkin grim that slew the fierce Rodent
Whose tooth insidious Johannis sacket'lh rent.

5. Parody of *The House that Jack Built*, written and illustrated by James Murray for his first wife's autograph album. About 1864.

FEIS* Member of the Society of Meteorologists of Scotland, of the Berwickshire & Northumbrian Naturalists' Society, of the Hawick Archaeological Society, etc. Subject:—The House we dwell in: or the body and its Architecture. Illustrated by beautiful diagrams etc.

In this lecture there is a reference to the diseases of the respiratory organs as 'the scourge of modern England' and he was evidently thinking of his own wife. By the time he spoke at Luton poor Maggie had died. James had nursed and cosseted her through the winter of 1864/5, and together they went north and were at Silloth in August, where James picked a scarlet pimpernel to press for her album; but she did not recover her strength. On their return to Peckham she became desperately ill. James nursed her, noting with interest, in spite of his distress, that when in delirium she dropped the refined speech he had so much admired and reverted to the broad Scotch of her childhood.[8] She died at the end of September. Twenty-three years later, when he was again happily married and the father of eleven healthy children, James used the opportunity of commissioning a tombstone to his parents in Wellogate Cemetery, Hawick, to commemorate also

<blockquote>
Maggie Isa Sarah Scott
(The beloved wife of James A. H. Murray)
Who died at Peckham Rye in the county
of Surrey 29 Sept. 1865
aged 31 years
and lies interred
in Nunhead Cemetery London S.E.
</blockquote>

<blockquote>
and of
</blockquote>

<blockquote>
Anna Maria Gretchen Murray
their only child who died at Wilton Place
Hawick 15 August 1864
aged 7 months
and is buried in this place.
</blockquote>

Writing in 1903 he recalled his sense of desolation—'a marriage, a birth, two deaths, all in three short years! . . . and I was left alone in London, doing uncongenial work.'[9]

*Fellow of the Educational Institute of Scotland.

For once his optimism and strong religious faith were momentarily shaken, and a scrap written by him on the back of a print of Hawick High Street seems to refer to the crisis through which he passed,

> The anchor of hope given way, the straining eye [is] unable to catch one gleam of light in the great void, till the soul in very dispair [sic] cries 'Oh God! if there is a God, why hast thou forsaken me?' . . . I am prone to doubt—My besetting sin—one of them at least, is to exalt & unduly deify the province of *reason*. I become impatient at times of the deep & mighty mysteries with which an all-wise providence has enveloped the problems of the Universe . . .

But private sorrow and temporary doubts did not influence his public pronouncements. In an address given at this time he referred to the Utilitarians, attributing the general feebleness of faith he noted, to the way in which the human mind had become partly materialised through scientific and philosophical speculation. Faith, he conceded, was more difficult now than in the days when men could ascribe every event to the direct intervention of God, but it must grow in step with the development of man's mental powers. For himself, while he accepted the natural laws, he was secure in his belief that they were framed by the Creator and worked in accordance with His will and pleasure. James had perhaps lost something of the youthful excitement which saw mankind advancing steadily to a new heaven upon earth, but he concluded confidently, 'I do not often indulge in the future—except in faith—faith that God who has so blessed the past will far more amply & gloriously bless the future.'[10]

At first he kept house for himself after Maggie's death, but in the summer of 1866 his father suggested that a change would be good for James' sister—another Maggie—and she, replaced for a time by their cousin Christine Hood, kept house for him for a year.[11]

In spite of their company James was still very lonely and not unnaturally his mind turned to a second marriage. The Ruthven family continued to befriend him and while on earlier visits he had been engrossed in his discussions with George Ruthven and had hardly noticed the women and children, now for the first time he became aware of Ada and in the family Annals which he later compiled, he records November 1865 as the date of his first meeting with her. The family tradition was that Ada was completely taken by surprise when that Christmas he kissed her under the mistletoe. She was just twenty and rather imagined herself to be in love with her music master and had not thought of James Murray in this light. James however was very much in earnest and in the following September they were engaged.

He knew that a second marriage, so soon after his first wife's death would not be approved at home, and for a time the engagement was kept secret. A letter to his future mother-in-law, with a hand illuminated border, to congratulate her on her wedding anniversary on 3 February 1867 reflects his renewed optimism without revealing the cause

> All our anniversaries come to us freighted with mingled feelings, and if life seemed in some things brighter three-and-twenty years ago than it does this morning, yet its course since then has been strewed with many blessings . . . If we feel less faith in men, less trust in ourselves, we see reason to feel more in God.[12]

At last towards the end of February he plucked up courage to write rather guardedly to tell his parents of his intention, supported by his sister's recommendation and enclosing Ada's photograph. His mother was ill with influenza when the letter arrived and they kept James waiting for what must have seemed a very long time before Thomas wrote on 11 March and Mary a fortnight later. Mary once said that none of her children had ever done anything to make her 'take a red face' and now the parents gave their cautious approval 'of what you allude to if you think so, after a prudent time'. His mother wrote

> I must say the last [letter] rather took us by surprise, altho it did not displease us to hear of your being engaged to again marry as your letter implied so far as I can understand it . . . I think you are quite right to marry again if you think you have found a congenial companion which I hope you have . . . The only thing I would like is if you would wait till nearly two years after Maggie's death before you again Marrie and then nobody could say you had soon forgot them thats gone, altho' I do not think that, theres plenty to say tho' you made a great work and so soon to take another in her place I cannot think to hear you reprotched in that strain . . . Father liked her appearance very well, he says if she's as good otherwise as she looks, thats the main point. Maggie is very high in her praise, and that she knows the Truth which makes us glad, without that great important knowledge all other accomplishments, are of small value and I hope you have considered that and are satisfied.[13]

James had considered and was pleased to learn that Ada's grandmother had been a Quaker before her marriage, remembering his father's approval of the Quaker practice of sitting in silent thought.

George Ruthven exacted an undertaking that James would include Ruthven in the names given to any children they might have, and this they did for the first nine born to them. Whether by their own wish, or out of consideration for the views expressed by James' mother, they also waited about six months longer before they married on 17 August 1867 by special licence at the Congregational Chapel, Camberwell Green. Graham Bell, by this time at College in London, was best man, rushing out of the British Museum to buy a pair of white gloves.[14] The honeymoon began with a week at Kew, then they went to Hawick, visiting also Dumfries and Galloway, and on to Kendal, the first of many visits to the Lakes, where James climbed a precipice on Loughrigg as an introduction to the Westmorland mountains.

He had had thoughts of looking for a house nearer to the City, but for the time being they returned to Beaufort Terrace and there on 24 June 1868 was born their eldest son, Harold James Ruthven—Harold after Ada's dead infant brother. Thirty-seven years later James looked back sentimentally to the occasion, remembering how he had carried the baby out into the little back garden on the hot summer morning to see the sun and smell the air, before he left for Threadneedle Street at 9 o'clock. 'That was a great day . . . big with hopes, & wishes & prayers! Mother not 23, only a child herself, but such a sweet mother! I, 31, still looking upon myself as a mere youth, who had all the world in front of me, and was just entering on its solemn privileges.'[15]

It is said that at first Ada found James not very easy to live with. She was disconcerted by his changes of mood, normally so serious, scholarly and high minded, but at times just a mischievous boy, teasing and tickling her. When intent on some line of study he could be exasperatingly absent minded, losing his belongings and forgetting important engagements and Ada soon found that for all his Scotch ways he was like his father, naïve in dealing with money matters. Nevertheless they soon settled down together and the marriage proved an exceptionally happy one. Ada had an unbounded admiration for James and devoted herself to his welfare: she was intelligent enough to be able to share his interests to some extent, and in early years even to help him in his literary work. She was practical and business-like and he became increasingly dependent upon her to run the household and manage his affairs.[16]

In 1869 James' younger brother, Charles, the artist, also married and settled in London. The brothers found terrace houses next door to each other, newly built in Denman Road, Camberwell, on the south side of Peckham High Street. The houses are still there: the road runs up hill and number 5 in which James lived is near the top on the west side. There, in January 1870 the second son, Ethelbert Thomas Ruthven, was born. 'I do not say he is as pretty a baby as Harold was', James later recalled Ada saying, 'but still a fine boy!'[17]

Meanwhile his life was becoming again a busy one, and although the reason for settling in the south was removed when Maggie died, he never had any idea of returning to Scotland. Maggie's death had left him free to devote himself to his studies once more. Soon after coming to London he had started to work at Russian and this led to friendship with another commuter, Robert Giffen. Giffen was also a Scot, came from the Glasgow area and was almost an exact contemporary of James. Like Alexander Murray he had started his career as a journalist and was now sub-editor of the *Globe*, living near the Congregational church in Camberwell. Later he became chief of the Statistical Department of the Board of Trade. At this early stage in his career he was keen to learn Russian and he and James studied together, James going two evenings a week to Giffen's house for the purpose. James kept just ahead of Robert in Russian, partly because he was only interested in the linguistic aspects and was not aiming at proficiency in speaking the language.

At that same time James resumed his self education in earnest. He had taken out a ticket for the British Museum Reading Room as soon as he came south and as a widower he had formed the habit of going there every Saturday afternoon as soon as the bank closed. Robert Giffen was able to help him by introducing him to one of the sub-librarians, William Ralston, a Slavonic scholar. This was a fresh stimulus to James' interest in comparative philology, and it seemed as though this would be the field, particularly in Semitic, Aryan and African languages, in which his main interest would lie.[18]

William Ralston had also revived the idea that James might obtain a post in the British Museum Library, as there had been a recent extension of the age limit for applicants to 30. 'You have a very fair chance,' was Ralston's opinion 'but you must *keep shoving*.'[19] So from November 1866 until January 1867 James busied himself writing round seeking supporters. It was necessary to be nominated by one of the three principal Trustees, the Archbishop of Canterbury, the Speaker of the House of Commons, or the Lord Chancellor.[20] James' brother Alexander enlisted the support of William Ewart, M.P. for Dumfries, who was an old friend and schoolfellow of the Speaker. Ewart received two very encouraging letters. 'Indeed,' Ewart wrote to James, 'did I not dread being too sanguine, I sh^d say that they encourage us, not only to *hope*, but to *expect*, success.'[21] The draft of James' letter of application to Thomas Watts, Keeper of Printed Books, to whom Ralston gave an introduction, illustrates both the remarkable range of James' knowledge and also his ingenuousness. Referring to his qualifications he wrote

> I have to state that Philology, both Comparative and special, has been my favourite pursuit during the whole of my life, and that I possess a general acquaintance with the languages & literature of the Aryan and Syro-Arabic classes—not indeed to say that I am familiar with all or nearly all of these, but that I possess that general lexical & structural knowledge which makes the intimate knowledge only a matter of a little application. With several I have a more intimate acquaintance as with the Romance tongues, Italian, French, Catalan, Spanish, Latin & in a less degree Portuguese, Vaudois, Provençal & various dialects. In the Teutonic branch, I am tolerably familiar with Dutch (having at my place of business correspondence to read in Dutch, German, French & occasionally other languages) Flemish, German, Danish. In Anglo-Saxon and Moeso-Gothic my studies have been much closer, I having prepared some works for publication upon these languages. I know a little of the Celtic, and am at present engaged with the Sclavonic, having obtained a useful knowledge of Russian. In the Persian, Achaemenian Cuneiform, & Sanscrit branches, I know for the purposes of Comparative Philology. I have sufficient knowledge of Hebrew & Syriac to read at sight the *O.T.* and *Peshito*; to a less degree I know Aramaic Arabic, Coptic and Phenician to the point where it was left by Gesenius.[22]

Reading this letter one is not surprised at the comment of one of those whose support was sought, 'He must be a natural curiosity'.[23]

But after all this effort and letter writing and raising of hopes, disappointment followed. On 9 January 1867 Mr Ewart wrote enclosing a letter from the Speaker in which he explained that he had been inadvertently misleading as to Mr Murray's prospects. He had had a letter from the Principal Librarian speaking in high terms of Mr Murray and saying that the Archbishop of Canterbury was anxious for his success. It now turned out that this was another Mr Murray and not Mr James A. H. Murray of Beaufort Terrace.[24] James had already ascertained that, supposing he did not obtain this particular appointment the only vacancies for candidates over thirty were ones requiring a knowledge of Sanskrit, Chinese and other Oriental languages and although it was not until May that he finally heard the result of his application, his hopes were at an end.[25]

Ada tied the letters relating to the British Museum post together and labelled them. She was born a hoarder and throughout her married life every document which came into her hands, from sale catalogues to letters refusing or accepting invitations, were carefully bundled together and marked with the contents.

As things turned out, James did not long regret his failure to obtain the British Museum post and in September 1868 he told Canon Greenwell that he was satisfied that he would not have been so well placed there.[26] His remarriage made him glad not to have a drop in salary and other avenues quickly opened up with prospects of more interesting activity. In fact the vacancy had occurred too soon. In 1867 James was still almost unknown in the world of literary and linguistic studies: his lack of recognised qualifications, particularly a university degree and the very extent of his claimed knowledge of foreign and ancient languages made him appear suspect. The Hawick Archaeological Society, which had seemed such an influential body in the Borders, meant nothing in London and no one there had read his many contributions to its *Transactions*. Five years later in Philological circles in London he had surpassed the reputation he had previously enjoyed in the Borders.

He arrived in London at a strategic time for the history of English studies. In the 1860s and 70s the curriculum of the schools and universities was still largely classical and the study of English language and literature was not ranked as an academic discipline.[27] At Eton the teacher of English had less seniority than the teacher of French and on the staff at Marlborough the English master brought up the rear, behind even the dancing master. Oxford had a Professor of Anglo-Saxon, but at Cambridge there were only two lecturers in English.[28] Henry Sweet, speaking from his experience of Oxford, observed as late as 1877 that

71

Most of us — indeed, nearly all of us — are by force of circumstances compelled to work in a dilettante style; we cannot expect much from a philologist whose whole working day consists, perhaps, of an hour snatched from other labours. Where, again, are we to get our training? We are left to pick it up at random, often quite late in life.[29]

Only in London were things different: at University College a Professorship of English Language and Literature had been established in 1828 and in 1835 the first Professor of English Literature and History was appointed at King's College. In the country too, English studies were developing as 'the poor man's classics'. The spread of literacy and the philanthropic movement to provide adult education for the working classes were fostering a study of literature in a belief in its humanising and moral influence. In 1855 English language and literature was included in the examination for entrance to the Indian Civil Service; by 1858 English was required for the Oxford and Cambridge Local Examinations and a year later the first B.A. examination in English at London University was held.[30]

The significance of this for James Murray was that London was a centre where all the excitement and enthusiasm of a renaissance atmosphere existed for the studies in which he was now most interested, and where the fact that he had no qualifications on paper did not matter. The scholars with whom he soon came into contact were university men certainly, but their degrees were in Classics or Mathematics and in the study of English and Philology they were as much amateurs as James himself. In some directions indeed he found that his knowledge was superior to theirs and he was in a position to help and even correct them: he met them on equal terms and without diffidence.

The first of this group of enthusiasts whom he came across was Alexander John Ellis. Ellis, a mathematical scholar of Trinity College Cambridge, was a Fellow of the Royal Society and author of numerous very abstruse mathematical papers, but he was also interested in the scientific study of music, musical pitch and voice training and wrote on these subjects. This in turn led him to a consideration of phonetics and at this time Ellis was engaged on a monumental work on the history of English pronunciation which involved him in the study of dialects and the light they throw on local differences of pronunciation and the history of the vernacular in its various branches.[31] Melville Bell, of whose Visible Speech Ellis had made use, had come to London in 1865 to a post at London University which he held until he went to America in 1870. He had kept in touch with James Murray ever since James had impressed him as a student at his Edinburgh vacation course. When James described to him the research he was doing on the Border dialects Bell realised that this would be of great interest to A. J. Ellis. In 1868 he introduced the two men and as a result James was invited to hear an instalment of Ellis' research on pronunciation delivered in a lengthy paper to the Philological Society. This led to a close friendship which lasted until Ellis' death in 1890.[32]

Ellis, like James, was a man with many irons in the fire, and he kept up all his interests simultaneously. At one time he said that he was correcting the proofs of nine different publications and he complained that he could not get on with dialects because he was so busy visiting organ builders and looking for organs with ancient pitch.[33] Unlike James he was not in good health: in 1849 he had suffered a serious breakdown lasting about three years, and although he was still only in his early fifties he seemed a much older man. He fussed about his health and used to fuss—quite unnecessarily—about James' health too. He was attracted to the younger man not only because of their common interests, but also because he found James' energy and enthusiasm of practical assistance.

Ellis had the habit, which James shared, of learning from anyone he came across who spoke an unusual dialect or language. He bemoaned the fact that he had just missed meeting an Icelander, and was excited when Professor Trumbull, an American, sent him a note of the words used in counting by Wowenoc Indians in Maine, which seemed to provide an analogy with sheep counting words used in Yorkshire.[34] On being introduced to James Murray he immediately asked him to provide him with all the different pronunciations of certain vowels which he knew in Scotland, Cumberland or Westmorland, or indeed any place in England, writing them down in Visible Speech or phonetic symbols and to come back with his list so that Ellis could hear the words spoken.[35] James performed this task quickly and competently. 'I shall be glad to be of any assistance to you,' Ellis told him. 'You have been of the greatest assistance to me.'[36] Ellis lived in Kensington and James became a welcome visitor, coming on a Saturday early in the afternoon, staying to dine with the family at 6.30 *p.m.*, and remaining for as long after as he had time. Soon he was busy correcting the proofs of Ellis' book on pronunciation and helping him with his research.[37] For his part James was overjoyed to find a scholar who shared his enthusiasm and recognised that colloquial, so-called illiterate forms of speech were as important to the science of comparative historical philology as the study of dead and existing literate languages on which the science had hitherto been built. He was particularly pleased to find in Ellis one who had recognised the possibility of using a phonetic system to record dialect accurately.

Since the 1840s Ellis had been working, at first with Isaac Pitman, to evolve a system of phonetics which would use existing letter types and so avoid the use of special symbols and accents. Ellis called his system Palæotype, and Melville Bell said that it was so complex that it needed an Ellis to use it.[38] He was now experimenting with an even more complex system, devised particularly for the accurate recording of English dialects and capable of being used concurrently with present orthography in order to remedy its defects. He enlisted James' help to try out this so-called Glossotype and report on its usefulness.[39]

In the 1860s the immediate practical importance for James of these experiments lay in their use as a basis for scientific linguistic observation. When he first met Melville Bell in Edinburgh he had at once recognised that phonetics could make the vague and un-satisfactory study of dialects precise. In his historical introduction to his book on Scottish Dialects he wrote:

> It cannot too often or too loudly be repeated that words are combinations of *sounds*, not strings of *letters*, and that to attempt to describe an unknown language or an unknown dialect by spelling its words in such and such a manner, without rigidly defining the values attached to the letters, is as futile as it would be to represent to us a landscape with its various parts not only uncoloured, but labelled with the names of their diverse hues and shades in an unknown tongue.

James was still a great believer in Bell's Visible Speech with its symbols indicating the exact position of the lips and tongue in making every sound, and in his book he adopted a very elaborate system. He wrote out the words in Ellis' Glossotype, but a key related these phonetic equivalents to the symbols used in Visible Speech so that the student could identify each sound and also see how each was to be produced.[40]

Using these new methods of recording speech, Alexander Ellis and James Murray energetically pursued their research in the decade 1868–78. James at forty was as happy and excited tracking down local speech in unusual places as he had been at twenty striding over the Border hills in search of the Catrail. He had recovered all his old *joie de vivre*. Both men used every opportunity to listen to and record the speech of any strangers, just as James, when in Hawick, had seized on any foreigners to help him in mastering the pronunciation and grammar of their languages. Now it was the speech of a Mr Gregg of Ledbury that Ellis was studying,[41] getting him to push up his moustache so that he could observe his lips, or he wrote, 'I have had two *lessons* today; a poor one from a non-native Gloucestershire resident, an excellent one from a Devonshire servant.'[42] 'Hearing from a peasant's mouth is always safer than from a gentleman's & far better than from a lady's',[43] he observed, and servants were a great source of information. Ellis got his cook to talk to him, James his Norfolk gardener.[44] 'My nursery maid is come', James wrote'. . . Hambürgerin, who only left Germany some few months ago. She speaks Platt-Deutsch as her native tongue & also Hoch Deutsch as the result of education—(the latter with my children) . . . I shall learn Platt Deutsch sounds from her: *g* is clear hard (*g*) not (*gh*).'[45] Ellis on another occasion hoped to catch some working men he was 'trawling for',[46] and wished he could hear the Nottinghamshire booking clerk James had found at St Pancras station.[47] Stations were a fruitful hunting ground: standing in the booking hall at Euston Square James heard a soldier at the barrier when asked where he was for, stammer 'till . . . till . . .' and the inspector say 'Oh yes—till Scotland—all right?', and James compared Shakespeare's 'shipped me intil the land' in *Hamlet*.[48]

Ellis had no time or energy to travel,[49] but James did. When he went to Matlock for Ada's health he was able to examine characteristics of the north western group of dialects spoken in Lancashire, Cheshire and Staffordshire and he described the speech of the charwomen washing the hotel stairs and gave lists of words collected from the bathmen.[50] On another occasion he was found in a small fishing village on the east coast 'smacking his lips over what he called a great discovery . . . A fishwife had greeted him with the phrase "It's a cauld and yagach morning sir." He repeated "yagach" (which means raw and shivery) over and over again, and said it was worth travelling so far north to obtain such a treasure.'[51]

When James went north for a holiday in 1875 he promised Ellis to make 'a vigorous attack on both the phonetics & grammar of the speech' and later reported on conversations with dialect speakers who were interested in the study at Kendal, Penrith and Appleby. He complained that except from these observers it was difficult to hear dialect.

> One *can't* get into conversation with dialect speakers—they *will* try to speak Cockney to me—even the little boys near the rural schools cannot be tempted to repeat the numerals for a penny. They only 'gurn' & look ashamed, or if they try, begin with w*u*n, t*u*u, in Westmoreland English—valuable in its way, but not the thing.

He envied his children, who heard much more dialect than he did and came in quoting children in the street. He referred to 'much difference of opinion' and hours spent trying to phoneticise vowel sounds: sometimes the local speakers heard distinctions James could not, sometimes he recognised two sounds where Kendal folk could 'neither hear nor feel' any difference, e.g. between 'done' and 'dun'. 'So *t'aad dun horse* is either the Old Dun Horse a "pub" in Kendal or "the old done horse" (only fit to be shot).' He chatted to the Italians working on the geological survey finding they had 'splendid phonetic feeling', and he concluded his letter with an elaborate account of his research likened to his climbing experiences:

> We shall finally get at the summit, but it's like climbing Fairfield— peak after peak, each believed to be *the* peak, till it is surmounted & lo! another, & then another & yet another [he draws them], but there *is* a true summit at last, $7\frac{1}{2}$ miles off the starting point, & those who persevere reach it, & peep over into the abyss of Deepdale beyond, & can try accoustic effects in hurling stones 2,600 feet down if they like. I think we have nearly surmounted the Northern ù, but the route has had many experiences & shows that the Visible Speech railway stopped at the first apparent summit . . . Yet *without* it . . . we should have looked with helplessness on those inaccessible & undescribable sounds which to be understood must be heard & remembered.[52]

Stimulating as this work was, James might have remained a keen amateur but for the fact that the friendship with Ellis led to introductions to other workers in this field. There was, for example, the brilliant young Henry Sweet. Sweet, still in his twenties, was at this time a student at Balliol, where he took a fourth class in *Literae Humaniores* in 1873. He was already engaged in research in comparative philology and had studied in Heidelberg before coming to Oxford. Germany was then far in advance of England in this field and this experience gave Sweet, young as he was, a standing amongst the English philologists. Before taking his degree he published an edition of Alfred's version of the *Cura Pastoralis* and entered into the debate on phonetics with a system of his own which he called Romic. He was to gain international repute as a phonetician and some notoriety as the original of Bernard Shaw's Professor Higgins. James Murray never became a close friend; indeed Sweet had few friends, for he was a most difficult, cross-grained man. He was often, it was said, 'splendidly right, but nobody could be more deplorably and pigheadedly wrong', and his rudeness was at times colossal.[53] He had a chip on his shoulder, increased over the years by Oxford University's failure to recognise him until 1901 when, having been an unsuccessful applicant on various occasions for higher academic appointments, he was given a sort of consolation prize of a readership. Before this solution James, discussing Sweet's persecution mania, said that although a professorship or readership might restore him to sound mindedness 'many people would rather that it were not in Oxford, where they fear many troublesome collisions may occur, through his faculty of running his head against stone walls'.[54] Sweet was however a worthy opponent to argue with and a useful man to know, and James, accustomed to the stimulating discussions among members of the Hawick Archaeological Society, was thoroughly at home in this atmosphere of scholarly debate.

In arguments on dialects and phonetics James usually found himself in agreement with Ellis and opposed to Henry Sweet and Henry's cousin Henry Nicol, who, unlike Sweet, was what is known in Scotland as a 'bonny fighter'.[55] Nicol was very well disposed towards James Murray, because, like Ellis, he found him useful. Nicol was working on borrowings from the French in various European languages and thanked James for his trouble and thoughtfulness in assisting him, particularly in the matter of French elements in Scottish dialects. In return, Nicol helped James from his wider knowledge of comparative philology in Germany, corrected some of his mistakes, and kindly read his book on Scottish dialects in proof.[56]

Another friendship formed through Ellis was with a Somersetshire antiquarian, Fred Elworthy, who was making a study of local speech

6. Fred Elworthy.

and gave some lectures to the Philological Society. Ellis was worried that while Elworthy's word lists were valuable, his phonetics were 'in an alarming state'.[57] Ellis and Sweet, finding it impossible, without hearing the words actually spoken, to agree on corrections to the word lists on which they were collaborating, were to send James in the spring of 1877 down to Somerset. Staying with Elworthy, he listened to dialect speakers daily until he could settle the points which had baffled them in London.[58] This was to be the first of many holidays in Wellington. The two men found that they and their wives had much in common. Mrs Elworthy became a voluntary reader for the Dictionary, their children exchanged visits, and James enjoyed walking and exploring the country with Fred, who shared his interest in local antiquities, folklore, botany and gardening. Elworthy often visited Oxford and was a great support to James later on when problems connected with the Dictionary plunged him into despair.

Fred Elworthy's scholarship was not great, and it was James who helped him to improve his book; but Richard Morris, to whom Ellis also introduced him, gave an important impetus to his own studies. Morris, a few years James' senior, was like him largely self taught. He was a schoolmaster, studying for ordination. As an editor for the Early English Text Society, which he invited James to join, he introduced

him for the first time to a number of the works published by the
Society in conjunction with the Philological Society. These included
Richard Rolle de Hampole's *Pricke of Conscience* and *Prose Works* in
northern Middle English. James wrote later 'What a revelation! Here
in 14th C. Eng. of Yorkshire, I found my Southern Scotch in full
bloom in an earlier form as a literary language, with its own grammar,
precisely as I had made it out for Southern Scotch!'[59] So close was
this identity between Rolle's language and that of the Border that
James amused himself by reading passages from Rolle to English and
Scotch friends in order to hear them all decide that the language was
old Scotch, and when he told them it was written in Yorkshire, hear
them protest that then the writer must have been a Scotchman settled
there.[60]

Morris' own researches were also of the greatest interest to James,
who wrote that his classification of the Early English dialects into
Southern, Midland and Northern, with the careful discrimination of
their grammatical forms, had introduced order and precision into a
region of research which had been all but *terra incognita*.[61]

Under Morris' influence the study of dialects took on a new
significance. The objective now was to use the still surviving dialects,
together with the early literary sources, to determine the geographical
limits of the various branches of early English and if possible to
further subdivide the roots of the language. It was the first time that
the literary sources and local speech had been used to illustrate each
other, and it was important that the work was attempted at a time
when a good deal of dialect survived.

It was also important that in a field which had been in the hands of
amateurs James insisted on applying standards of exact scholarship.
How he formed these standards is something of a mystery. He had
had no training in research, and until he came to London, very little
contact with those who had. As a boy and a young man he had shown
the ability to absorb any knowledge which came his way. Now, for the
first time brought into the centre of an academic circle, where he had
hitherto been only an outsider, picking up what he could on the
fringes, and from books, he obviously learned rapidly from his new
friends. But even before these new contacts had time to influence him,
James showed intuitive grasp of essential criteria. In an unpublished
letter of 19 April 1869 to the *Athenaeum* (a journal to which he was a
regular contributor from 1868), he cautioned students of dialect
against accepting an isolated piece of negative evidence as to a word or

form being obsolete. He said that it required the united testimony of every local observer, and often even more than that, to prove such a thing, and in the state of dialect study at the time, so absolute a pronouncement was not possible. He warned against local observers who regarded their own dialect as typical of a whole region through failure to recognise the minute variations of pronunciation, form and vocabulary which existed.[62] As Editor of the Dictionary James was relentlessly to pursue statements back to their origin, and already he showed this scrupulous thoroughness. Ellis, for example, used a map of the territorial divisions of England in the seventh century given by Professor Freeman in his *Old English History for Children* and copied by J. R. Green in his *History of the English People*. This was not good enough for James, who challenged the speaker, asking 'What authority is there for these boundaries? are they not mere hypothesis?' When no one seemed able to say, he wrote off to Freeman himself and learned that the map was 'entirely theoretical'. This meant that an accurate one would have to be constructed from the evidence of the dialects, instead of the boundaries being taken as known.[63]

James was already cautious about stating as fact anything which he could not prove conclusively. Describing the talk of country people he had overheard in a third class market train in Lincolnshire as sounding familiar and homely to his northern ear, he said, 'I have a *feeling*, I can't say a distinct *conviction*, but a strong feeling that a lot of Lincolnshire . . . will eventually have to be annexed to the Northern family.'[64] He was indignant when what he had said was distorted, protesting 'I did not advocate removal of the N.E. dialect *bodily* into the Northern Branch . . . I only expressed a *doubt* . . . that further examination might cause us to make important changes there, to what extent I could not say.'[65] His opponent here was none other than Prince Louis-Lucien Bonaparte, the man who had fired James' interest in dialects long ago by his inquiry about a version of the gospel of St Matthew in lowland Scottish.[66] Once again Ellis was the person responsible for the introduction, warning James before he took him to the Prince's house, that he would find his host an interminable talker.[67]

At an early stage in their acquaintance the Prince asked James to produce for him a part of the Gospel in Scottish, written both in phonetic symbols and also in ordinary spelling 'in which' as the Prince expressed it 'Scotchmen like to see Scotch written'. After some months of effort James wrote to the Prince to say he found the task impossible. His letter giving his reasons was characteristic:

> I know no rule, no standard whatever for the modern Scottish forms of speech. The spelling of Burns for example is *simply English*, partly disguised by the fact that he uses a considerable percentage of *words not English*: these words unfortunately are such as can scarcely ever be pressed into service in the Gospel of Matthew, and the result is that when I try to write in Burns's orthography, my version looks scarcely different from the English certainly not worth publishing as Scotch, inasmuch as it conveys almost no idea as to the *actual living thing* a Scotch dialect, and its utter difference from English sounds . . . at present I feel that the work I have been trying to do is not worth the doing, and I would rather put it in the fire, than see anything of which I so fully disapprove issued under my name.[68]

This determination never to publish anything which fell short of the standards he set himself was to be shown again and again as James fought in later years to maintain the ideal of perfection he aimed at for the Dictionary.

The Prince had a great reputation as a linguist and as publisher of the parable of the sower in seventy-two different European languages and dialects, but James soon formed the opinion that he was very superficial and became bored by his incessant talk.[69] He agreed with Ellis that the Prince's one day tour of Buckinghamshire, testing various clergymen's use of 'I be' and 'I are', was insufficient evidence on which to base a theory. 'Another & equally good [principle] would be to classify dialects according to the colour of the eyes of the speakers;' James scoffed. 'I think I shall start it as a counter hypothesis to take the wind out of I is, I be, I are! We must classify on a broad view of everything in the dialects — not of some accidental "mite" of a word.'[70] James was no respecter of rank, especially where scholarship was concerned.

He had the right to speak with authority after the publication of his book, *The Dialect of the Southern Counties of Scotland*. It was almost finished when he met Ellis, who recognised at once that this was sound, original and very important work. In June 1868 he had proposed James as a member of the Philological Society,[71] the centre at which all the scholars interested in linguistic studies propounded their theories and argued about them, concerning themselves not only with Latin and Greek but also with the form, dialects and etymology of the English language and of non-European tongues. When the programme was drawn up for the winter session of lectures, James was offered three evenings[72] and his papers were delivered on 4 and 18 December 1868 and on 7 May, followed by a postscript on 17 December 1869.

There was no doubt about the impact of this research: Ellis wrote, 'Your paper on Scotch will make an era in the study of that language which has been hitherto thrown overboard, for no one has thought of strictly separating dialects before.'[73] Nevertheless James' attempts at finding a publisher were not at first successful. In April he had a disappointing reply from Robert Chambers of the Edinburgh firm of W. and R. Chambers, who wrote

> I have given a morning to the inspection of your manuscript, and now return it. It is a very learned work; but its very learning makes it dry, and unlikely to meet a good sale. It would not in the least suit W. & R.C. to publish it, and I much fear, in whatever way published, it would be a cause of pecuniary loss, whatever might be the amount of honour it would reflect upon the author.[74]

After the success at the Philological Society, however, Ellis supported its publication as Part II of the Society's *Transactions*, although the Secretary, Mr Furnivall, who had been bored by the paper, wanted much of the historical introduction omitted.[75] Finally a compromise was reached, the book was printed in its entirety but the cost of 200 extra copies was met by sale to subscribers organised by James himself. He was to spend a good deal of time in 1873 collecting orders and payments. The edition soon sold out and although in 1877 the Dialect Society suggested a reprint, by that time James was too busy with other work to have time to attend to it.

Between delivering the papers and publication, following suggestions from members of the Society, he issued a questionnaire to clergymen living along what he knew to be the linguistic frontier, asking them to say in what parishes Gaelic was still wholly or partially used in religious services. This enabled him to add a map and an appendix defining the Gaelic speaking areas.

The completed book of 250 pages drew together the fruits of his research in Hawick. The introduction, which is certainly not dull, incorporated his earlier studies of place names and of the legend of St Cuthbert's Chapel in the valley of the Slitrig. The whole book is the proof of the discovery he made as a little boy that the boundary between England and Scotland is artificial, and he established that the border lands which were historically a province of England belonged linguistically to the branch of Anglo-Saxon once spoken from the Humber to the Forth. His aim, he said, was 'to photograph the leading features of one of the least-altered' local dialects before it was lost, 'trampled under foot by the encroaching language of literature and education . . . corrupted and arrested by its all-pervading influence'.[76] It was the language which he himself had spoken before his speech had been 'corrupted'. Word lists of dialects had often been collected, but until this book the 'bad grammar' of the 'talk' was disparaged. 'I think,' he wrote in 1912

> that my own *Grammar of the Southern Scotch* . . . was actually the *first* attempt at recording minutely and lovingly the accidence and syntax of an English dialect; and it was at first looked upon with amused contempt by many. Even Burns thought that Scotch was defiled by 'bad grammar' and tried to conform his Scotch to *English* Grammar! transforming e.g. the Scotch '*Scots 'at hae*' into *Scots wha hae* which no sober Scotchman in his senses ever naturally said.[77]

The book was very well reviewed. In the *Athenaeum* for 26 July 1873[78] the writer, possibly Richard Morris, said it is 'all we could wish, and has our unqualified praise for the masterly way in which he has treated the Dialect . . . Mr Murray is a phoneticist as well as a philologist'. Henry Sweet, who reviewed it for the *Academy*[79] praised Murray's accurate phonetic notation and delicate sound distinctions, observing that he recognised nine, not three, degrees of tongue elevation in the case of some vowel sounds and praising the grammar as 'a unique combination of historical research and keen appreciation of . . . the living language'. The *Revue Celtique* reprinted his map and summarised his findings in an article on the 'Present Limits of the Celtic Language in Scotland' which made his work known on the Continent.[80]

The publication of the *Dialect* greatly impressed another distinguished English philologist, Walter Skeat. Skeat was also an amateur, whose career illustrates the old saying that if a man devotes all his leisure to a subject he is likely to find himself an acknowledged expert. Educated in the classics, he only knew English literature at school through examples used for translation into Greek and Latin.

7. Professor and Mrs Skeat.

He read poetry for recreation and his interest in Early English was roused by extracts from Chaucer and Piers Plowman in Mrs Markham's *History of England*. At Cambridge he read Mathematics and Theology, and when after ordination he had to give up his ministry through ill health, he returned to his old college, Christ's, as a lecturer in Mathematics. Finding that no one in Cambridge had any very accurate knowledge of Anglo-Saxon he decided to take it up, with the result that when the Bosworth Chair of Anglo-Saxon was founded in 1878 he found himself the first holder of it. He too owed much to Richard Morris, Ellis and Sweet, and recognised the revolution in the science of etymology brought about through their insistence that language is a living thing. He too believed in listening to the way people speak, finding obsolete forms of forgotten words often revealed by the chance words of a stranger.[81] This was exactly what James Murray had discovered himself and demonstrated in his book.

In 1875 Skeat had just undertaken the secretaryship of the newly founded English Dialect Society, with the objective of collecting lists of dialect words from published books and from field work—material which was eventually used for Wright's *English Dialect Dictionary*. Skeat at once recognised James Murray as an authority and asked him

84

to join the Society, looking to him for help in drawing up a bibliography of Scottish books and pamphlets in which dialect words would be found. 'You will say I am asking many things', he wrote, 'but I know what a keen interest you are sure to take in this. And if you are busy, by all means wait. Only a very *few* hints from *you* may go a very long way further than much talk from others who know less about it.'[82] A problem with which Skeat was faced was whether to adhere strictly to the criteria now established by Ellis and Murray for this work and to accept only material written in phonetic systems, which would mean rejecting lists made by collectors who had not, or could not, use them. Controversy over this had hindered the launching of the Society and now Skeat argued for a compromise, knowing that James was likely to be opposed to this.

> I am *for* phonetics, [Skeat said] where we can get 'em: but can't refuse collections because they have been made without. *Please to trust me at the helm* till you are well over the bar & well out to sea: for I assure you it requires very wary steering. Those who, like yourself, know what they are about, we shall be glad to leave pretty nearly to their own devices . . . If there is any part of the work you can take nearly off my hands, I shall be glad indeed. *Just* at present, I do all, and the task of letter-writing is incessant.[83]

This letter is typical of Skeat. He was a gentle, generous, optimistic man, very different from the cantankerous Sweet, but also often differing from James, who would not accept a compromise where he felt standards were concerned and whose views of recording dialects without the use of phonetics were the result of wide experience. James, only two years junior to Skeat, but without his academic training, soon realised Skeat's weakness—that of jumping at an idea and adopting it without considering it carefully enough. 'He never sees the weak points of his theories, till they are pressed on his attention', James said. 'To *me*, the weak points of mine are always more prominent & clamorous than the strong ones.'[84] He was able to demonstrate this failing in Skeat in 1875 in a review in the *Athenaeum* of Skeat's edition of the Anglo-Saxon and Northumbrian Gospels. Skeat, in his introduction, comparing two manuscript versions of glosses on the Gospels, said that one had derived directly from the other. James found that he had not looked far enough: what he said was not true of the Gospel of St Matthew and a few verses of St John. These, James was able to show, were in West Saxon, written by a

Midland man, whereas the remainder was in a Northumbrian dialect. He explained that he had noticed what had escaped Skeat and other scholars because of his very detailed knowledge of both glosses 'having (in the days . . . when I was a poor & lonely student . . . eagerly trying to find my way into the mysterious land of our early literature,) made a complete transcript of both versions from a copy of the Surtees edition.'[85] This had been one of the books lent to him by Canon Greenwell.

Although James was often very outspoken in his criticism of Walter Skeat's work, their friendship was never shaken. Skeat was extraordinarily humble. He early recognised the superiority of James' linguistic insight, and was always grateful for help and correction and apologetic about his mistakes. His sympathetic and practical support of James Murray through all the troubles that beset him in editing the Dictionary proved of the first importance in preventing him from abandoning the project.

The 'poor and lonely student' was now an image of the past. In less than fourteen years after coming to London as an unknown bank clerk, James Murray, now forty, had established his reputation as a scholar. In 1878 Henry Sweet in his Presidential Address to the Philological Society summed up the results of the past decade by referring to the extraordinary advances in English dialectology owing mainly to the colossal exertions of Mr Ellis and his school of disciples, among whom Mr Murray unquestionably took the first place.[86]

CHAPTER V

Furnivall's Henchman

JAMES Murray's research into dialects might be supposed sufficient leisure time occupation for a man in full employment, but this was only one of his preoccupations between 1868 and 1878. Just as when he was in Hawick, it is difficult to tell which of his many activities interested him most: he enjoyed them all.

On his introduction to the Philological Society in 1868, amid the sober, frock-coated members one was different and unforgettable. Bearded like most of the others, but unconventionally attired in corduroy trousers, with a tie of pink ribbon, having the most strikingly twinkling blue eyes, this man positively exuded enthusiasm and energy every time he opened his mouth. After the meeting, with jovial good humour he busied himself in handing round the coffee and while helping himself liberally, like a schoolboy, to the sweetest and most sugary cakes, he pressed them also on James and the other members. This was James' first encounter with Frederick Furnivall, a member of the Society from 1847, one of its two honorary secretaries from 1853 till 1862 and now its sole Secretary and leader. He was to hold office and be the heart and soul of the Society until his death in 1910. For those forty-two years he was a leading figure also in the life of James Murray, stimulating and persuasive, often meddlesome and exasperating, always a dynamic and powerful influence, eclipsing even James in his gusto for life.[1]

Frederick James Furnivall was born in 1825, the eldest son of an Egham doctor whose claim to fame was that he attended Mary Shelley in her confinement in 1817. Frederick showed an all-round brilliance in languages, science and theology, and after studying at University College London and reading mathematics at Trinity Hall Cambridge, he became a barrister. Although he practised for some years he

8. Frederick J. Furnivall with members of the Hammersmith Sculling Club for Girls, founded by him in 1896. About 1901. From a postcard from Furnivall to James Murray, 30 February 1907, complimenting him on progress with the letter '*P*'.

was never really interested in Law and his energies were directed into other channels. As a young man his life was one of ceaseless activity, chairing public meetings and speaking at street corners in support of causes such as that of the Thames ballast heavers against the tyranny of Thameside publicans, of wood-cutters on strike (in aid of whom he sold his books) or poor children for whom he organised parties. He was a leader in the move for popular education and taught grammar at the Working Men's College founded in 1854, where, in advance of his time, he supported student membership of the College Council and the admission of women and came into conflict with the founder and principal, F. D. Maurice over Sunday observance. He devoted his Sundays to sixteen-mile tramps and merry tea parties with the students. He invented a new type of rowing boat, formed a women's sculling club and used to row up the Thames to Richmond every week till he was 75. On Sundays in summer he took lively parties of men and women, students and professors, the girls who served him in a Lyons tea shop and anyone else available, for picnics up the river. Hurrying back in the evening he was well known for his unorthodox methods of getting his boat first out of a crowded lock which he had been the last to enter, disarming protests at his prodding boat hook by his merry laugh.

Besides his devotion to the Philological Society, Furnivall was an inveterate founder of organisations to promote the study of English literature through joint effort, inspired by the principles of the Cooperative movement of which he was a strong supporter. The Early English Text Society, to publish manuscripts and reprints of rare, inaccessible texts, was the first (1864), followed in 1868 by the Chaucer Society (the publications of which were mainly his own work), and the Ballad Society (1869), the New Shakespere Society (1873), the Wyclif Society (1881), the Browning Society (1881) and the Shelley Society (1886). In all of these projects he was motivated by a fervent patriotism and a zeal for popular education.

At first James Murray found in Frederick Furnivall a kindred spirit. His enthusiasm, his disinterested pursuit of knowledge, his democratic views and support of freedom, his love of walking and the open air, his geological and botanical expeditions with students, his teetotalism (he was also a non-smoker and a vegetarian), even the flowery language in which he couched his eloquent speeches and writings—all seemed to echo James' own interests and tastes. But James soon discovered other facets of his character which were less acceptable to him. From having in his undergraduate days been a keen Christian and founder of a branch of the Church Missionary Society, Furnivall had become an agnostic, a member of the anti-sabbatarian Sunday League and was now openly hostile to religion. His language and some of his tastes were crude and offensive to Victorian Society. He was defiant of convention and had shocked people by marrying a lady's maid, sister of one of his students, and he later shocked society even more by leaving her (this was considered such a scandal that James carefully stuck stamp-paper over the signature of the writer who gave him the news).[2] Even one of Furnivall's best friends and admirers said of him

> He never understood, or attempted to understand the quality of tact. It was a species of dishonesty. What he held to be true, was to be enounced in the face of all opposition, with unfaltering directness and clarity; what he held to be false was to be denounced with Athanasian intensity and resolution.[3]

Unfortunately, as James was to discover, he was often prejudiced and misguided in judgements formed too hastily. He also revelled in controversy and was a great mischief-maker and stirrer-up of trouble, partly owing to his inability to keep any news to himself. 'Furnivall is a regular sieve', Ellis warned James in 1873.[4] A friend admitted 'Reserve there was none: all his loves and his hatreds, his sports, his friends, and his labours—these he made other men's, as he freely made other men's his own. He held back nothing, not even his own shortcomings.'[5] This led to a habit of passing on letters intended to be confidential—'. . . his unfortunate annoyance-causing habit . . . strikes at the root of epistolary correspondence & has often caused much unpleasantness'.[6] He could also be rude: Professor Freeman said to James, 'Put Furnivall in an asylum and I will join E. E. Text Society at once!'[7] And on another occasion, 'I was not going to be bullied into joining it by the outrageous abuse which the Society's madman . . . thought good—I know not wherefore—to hurl at me in some of his prefaces. Why do not some of the sane members of the Society chain him up . . . or gag him.'[8]

He was involved in a notorious controversy with the poet Swinburne, who had been sarcastic about the methods of the New Shakespere Society.[9] Yet in spite of his faults, his disarming acknowledgment of his mistakes led his acquaintances to forgive him, judging his good points, and especially his warm-heartedness, to outweigh his bad. James Murray in his long contact with him found him always very difficult, and his contribution on Furnivall to the memorial volume, *A Personal Record*, was coldly factual and markedly lacking in the enthusiasm of other contributors.

At first, however, James, like nearly everyone else, fell under the spell of this extraordinary character and he allowed himself to be pressed into membership of the team of scholars working to produce volumes for the Early English Text Society, while at the same time continuing to work with Ellis on dialects. The work was put to James as a kind of mission. Furnivall spoke of it as 'a sort of debt to the past generations'. He thought of the unpublished manuscripts 'almost as if they were souls in prison' who ought to be released for the common benefit,[10] and if the public were unresponsive they should have the texts rammed down their throats. He argued for instance that subscribers must accept the issue of all the early lives of the Saints 'even though some are dull. The Sinners would doubtless be much more interesting.'[11] It was to him a scandal that so few of the 'inheritors of the speech of Cynewulf, Chaucer and Shakespere' were prepared to subscribe to publish their writings — far fewer indeed than the supporters of the Hellenic Society.[12]

The output of the Early English Text Society was prodigious. For the first ten years an average of five volumes a year appeared — in the vintage year of 1866 eleven volumes — and from 1867 an additional three volumes a year in an Extra Series. Furnivall's own contribution was twelve volumes in the first seven years. On speed of production James was very soon to find himself differing from Furnivall. Although in principle Furnivall aimed at accuracy and completeness, like Skeat he was anxious to see results and there was a hastiness about some of his own work and even more the work he commissioned which fell short of James' standards.

It was very difficult to find editors at a time when England was backward in textual criticism owing to the lack of English studies in the older Universities. Furnivall had perforce to resort to amateurs, many of whom had only very vague ideas on how to edit a text preserved in several manuscripts or to organise a glossary and were non-plussed when dealing with deviations from modern English usage because they even lacked a thorough grasp of Anglo-Saxon or Middle English. For the superficiality of some of the editing Furnivall's impatience was also to blame. He had a remarkable knowledge of the material and where it was to be found, and his practice was to get hold of the most accessible copy of the text and employ someone — often a clerk with no great expertise — to make a transcript. This was rushed into print and the proofs handed out to other scholars or clerks as available, to check with the various copies of the work. The official editor then cleared off the whole business of editing in the process of correcting the proofs, added a few notes and sometimes a glossary.[13] When Furnivall fell on James Murray as a potential editor he found a scholar who was prepared to resist this pressure for speed. As was the case in his research on dialects, James at once produced work of an unexceptionable quality in spite of his lack of training.

The first text that he undertook was *The Complaynt of Scotlande*, of which Furnivall sent him a copy in 1869.[14] This was a tract written in 1549 which survived in three early texts, two in the British Museum and one in the Advocates' Library in Edinburgh. Furnivall had never seen these but the work was known to James because it had been reprinted by John Leyden and he had a particular interest in it as an example of Border dialect, so that, as he said

I have everywhere found the language of the *Complaynt* familiar as the tones of childhood, and ever and anon have been surprised at the sanction which it gives to forms or idioms which I had thought to be modern 'vulgarisms' of the local patois, but which are thus shown to have a pedigree of three and a half centuries to plead.[15]

The first part of the edition was not published till 1872 and then appeared with an introduction of 123 pages, for the length of which James apologised. He referred to the 'very great labour which the work has cost me . . . under a heavy pressure of other work', and it bears evidence of his thoroughness. For instance, when he went to Edinburgh in August 1870 in order to collate the copy with that in the Advocates' Library, he took the opportunity to examine all the specimens they had there of early Scottish typography, from which he decided that it had been printed in France, a conclusion which he was pleased to find agreed with an independent investigation by the experts at the British Museum.[16] So engrossed was he in his work in Edinburgh that on one occasion he was locked by mistake into the library at closing time.

While in Edinburgh he noted with surprise and amusement how residence in London had already modified his speech. Writing to Ada he said

> How thoroughly Scotch even literary men speak here. I could hardly believe it. I never noticed it as much before. I find per contra that I am taken for out-and-out English by every one. How funny, since all Londoners could tell me to be Scotch at once—and even hear you as Scotch from your contact with me—and yet here nobody suspects me to be anything but English who does not know![17]

An anonymous review of the *Complaynt* in the *Athenaeum* in 1873 gave high praise to Murray for his editorial work and for discoveries of points which professional bibliographers had missed, while Skeat in the *Academy* in October found the introduction and glossary left nothing to be desired.[18] For the glossary James was indebted to Ada's 'painstaking labour': it listed all the words which differed in spelling or usage from modern English.[19] His work was only what would be expected from an editor today, but contrasted with Furnivall's frequent practice. A review in the *Athenaeum* in 1867, criticising the preface to Furnivall's edition of *Education in Early England* underlines the difference. Furnivall defended himself by saying 'these books cannot well go naked into the world . . . a preface is the natural coat and trousers with which to cover them . . . it is a "bore" to write it; a gift horse after all . . . a gift horse must not be looked in the mouth.' But the reviewer complained that the horse went from pillar to post and sometimes in a circle.[20]

Nevertheless Furnivall appreciated the standard of James' work, which brought credit to the Society, although he might chafe at his slowness. His plan had been that the *Complaynt* should go to the printer in the autumn of 1869—about four months after it had been commissioned—and would be published at the end of January 1870. Long before this he expected James to have begun work on another volume and in the same letter in which he accepted James' offer to edit the *Complaynt* he threw out a number of suggestions. He wanted him to undertake to edit a collection of miscellaneous Scotch poems from manuscripts in the British Museum, many of which he believed were unprinted, and also asked if James had an edition of Blind Hary's *Wallace* which he could do for the Extra Series.[21] It is interesting to note that James was now competent to read a manuscript, presumably he had taught himself.

Letters from Furnivall flowed in at the rate of several a week, sometimes two a day, all expecting James to respond with an energy equal to his own. They read breathlessly, as though Furnivall were catching a train rather than engaged on literary research, and they must often have been harassing when James had already more than enough to do. Furnivall drove his collaborators forward relentlessly and made them feel a little guilty if they pleaded lack of time, for he himself, however busy he might appear to be, seemed always ready to undertake to collate two manuscripts or correct a proof.

When James went to Edinburgh to check his text in the Advocates' Library Furnivall was ready at once with suggestions of other work to be done. He offered to pay James' expenses if he would devote ten days of his holiday to correcting a printed text of the Arthurian *Romances* by a manuscript there. He suggested that he should also see the Lindsay manuscript and if he could do any more in the time, he could check the *Sir Tristram* and *Bevis of Hampton*. Furnivall ended one letter of instructions with a plea 'If you could copy on bigger paper, & write bigger, the printer would like it much better. Write as fast as you like, only *big*, so that it doesn't strain the men's eyes. Childs says I've nearly blinded one man.'[22] Anyone who has read much of

James Murray's neat but microscopic handwriting would sympathise with Mr Childs, the printer.

In 1870 James experienced for the first time Furnivall in one of his less attractive lights. The *Complaynt* was set up in proof when Furnivall wrote indignantly objecting to 'a misbegotten monster' in the middle of words, a 'beastly big ȝ' (the Middle English letter *yogh*), which he accused James of having had specially cut. 'Hereafter,' he admonished him, 'before ordering unusual things, pray ask me about them, as much cost & trouble may be saved.' Not content with this, before James had time to reply, Furnivall involved Henry Wheatley, Secretary of the Early English Text Society. On Furnivall's instructions he too wrote complaining of the specially cut letter

> I am very surprised at this, [he concluded] because no editor before has ever given an order of this sort, and you will see that if editors were to do so without consultation . . . the Society could not be satisfactorily carried on . . . the loss of £5 in a useless expenditure . . . is a very serious matter . . .

It was now James' turn to be indignant, and he replied by return, not waiting till evening but writing from the bank where he was still employed, pointing out that he had given no order and was as surprised as anyone when he saw the offending sign, for which the printer was solely responsible. The idea of getting type specially cut had never entered his head. He had consulted Mr Furnivall on every point of doubt, and he ended, 'The idea that I should, after this, have ordered new types, or incurred expense in any way I could help, is really too bad.' He offered to meet the cost if he could be proved to blame. His letter crossed an apology from Wheatley, saying that he had written under an entire misapprehension and had now learned that it was the printer's fault.[23] The petty affair then died down, but it left a bad taste in James' mouth. He once said that it always gave him 'an uncomfortable feeling as to what a man is himself capable of, when we see him imputing mean conduct to another before experience compels him to do so.'[24] To Furnivall a tiff of this kind was just part of the spice of life—forgiven and forgotten as soon as it was over.

As Furnivall's programme did not allow for his editors doing only one text at a time, on 19 September 1870 he gave James an outline of his plans for him. 'Please tell me how many sheets of your Scotch paper for Phil. Soc. are done, & how many are yet to do. We want this finisht first, say next month, if possible: then *Complaynt* & Lyndesay by January, if convenient, if not, when you can.' On 8 November his further thoughts on the subject were 'Some day we must print the rest of that vol. in the Edinb. Coll. of Physicians from which Small printed his *Metrical Homilies*. I should think they'd lend it us, & if so, Mrs M[urray] might copy it next year, & you might bring it out in 1872 if you like, or later.'[25] James did not respond to the last suggestion, but he was already working on Lyndsay and had four sheets in proof early in September.[26]

Sir David Lyndsay (1490–1555) was a Scottish poet and Lyon King of Arms. The Early English Text Society had already started publishing his works and two other editors had been employed. Four volumes had appeared and James was to edit the Minor Poems as the fifth and final volume. He planned an introduction on the scale of that which he produced for the *Complaynt*, with chapters on the history and bibliography of Lyndsay's work, setting out the 'pedigree and peculiarities of the various editions and recensions which appeared before the close of the 16th century, and the characteristics of the language in which the poet wrote, as well as the Notes and Glossarial Index to the whole.' But he was setting himself an impossible task to produce two volumes for the Society simultaneously in addition to all his other work. The text alone was published in 1871 before the completion of the *Complaynt*, with a note that 'Owing to the Editor's removal from London [see Chapter VI, below], and the heavy and unforeseen demands made upon his time, during the past year . . . he has not had time to prepare for the press the large mass of materials which he has collected.'[27] He had been working on it until then under Furnivall's constant instructions. One text was copied and in proof in September 1869 and James was told that the Society would pay for a clerk to collate the proofs with a version in the British Museum. There was a 'money no object' attitude about this which contrasted with the fuss over the £5 spent on type for the *Complaynt*, but Furnivall was never very consistent. He busied himself making arrangements for James to see one of the Lyndsay manuscripts in the Library at Lambeth Palace, suggesting that James might go there one Saturday by boat![28] His approach was evidently tactless and provoked the Librarian to write,

Will you please not make remarks on the shortness the Library is open, to persons like Archdeacon Hale & others! . . . We give an

hour more each day than the order in Council sanctioned. For all
ordinary purposes except the E.E. Text Society it is sufficient!
  The stoves give good heat, so do not bring a great rug when you
come.

Nevertheless he agreed to lend the manuscript and Furnivall made
arrangements to put it in the hands of a copier at once.[29]
  Although Furnivall expressed the hope that James would go on
with the introduction to Lyndsay at leisure,[30] one reason why all the
material collected for it was never published, was that Furnivall had
lost interest. His aim was always to get the text—any text—into print
and made available as soon as possible. In an introduction to his own
edition of *Political, Religious and Love Poems* (published for the
Society in 1866), he owned that better texts of most of the poems
probably existed, but he was content to leave others with more leisure
to print them later. Most men, he stated, wanted '*some* text & that at
once'.[31] Lyndsay was therefore 'finished' so far as the Society was
concerned, and the editorial matter was of only secondary
importance.
  Instead, Furnivall now wanted James to get to work on other texts.
One was an edition of *The Pastel of Susan*,[32] another was the *Romance*
and *Prophecies* of Thomas of Erceldoune.[33] The *Pastel* was another
piece of work which James never found time to complete, but Thomas
of Erceldoune, a thirteenth-century writer, was of particular interest
to him. He produced in 1875 an edition printed from five manuscripts
with illustrations from the prophetic literature of the fifteenth and
sixteenth centuries and a full introduction. Thomas belonged to the
Border country, was associated with the village of Ercheldun (modern
Earlston) and the scene of his prophecies was the neighbourhood of
the Eildon Hills which James knew so well from his youth. Work on
the text led to enjoyable renewed contacts with antiquarian friends in
Roxburghshire. James' aim was to summarise 'all that History,
Legend and Tradition have to tell of Thomas', including Sir Walter
Scott's contribution in his *Minstrelsy of the Scottish Border*. In his
introduction, while acknowledging his indebtedness to all those of
whose writing he had made free use, James said that no statement had
been taken at second hand which was capable of verification. All
documentary evidence had been examined afresh and quotations
from manuscripts verified, leading to correction of some important
errors which had passed current from writer to writer for seventy

years. With the help of local friends James was able to identify the spot on which Thomas was supposed to have met the Queen of Faerie and to show that Sir Walter Scott, by changing the name of a ravine called Dick's Cleuch to Rhymer's Glen, had tried to prove that the meeting took place on the Abbotsford Estate.[34]

In 1876 James Murray was described by Furnivall as 'our learned E.E.T. Soc. Editor, the great authority on the Northern dialect etc.',[35] having for some years been looked to by him to act in a general advisory capacity with regard to the whole series. In 1869 Skeat had hoped that James would provide the glossary to his text of Barbour's *Bruce*,[36] —another piece of work which he never found time to undertake—and in 1870 Furnivall asked him to pass Skeat's proofs for a revised edition of his *Lancelot of the Laik*. James was evidently very outspoken and Skeat protested, 'I really think, however that you are in almost too great a hurry to fasten on me the name of "ignorant" . . . I think . . . that I *may* claim to know *something* . . . of the *older* Lowland & Northumberland language . . .' But he owned that his remarks on dialect in the original edition were 'as weak as anything I ever wrote', and said that he had made most of the corrections James suggested.[37]

Furnivall himself was gratefully seeking and accepting advice about his edition of Lauder's *Minor Poems*. In January 1870 he thanked James for help with the proofs, excusing some mistakes because he had done the work in a hurry, without his Scottish dictionary, and he asked what books he should read for the Introduction.[38] James was also in correspondence with the Rev. J. E. Lumby, editor of a poorly reviewed *Ratis Raving* (1870)[39] and Furnivall suggested he should keep a copy of his comments in case Lumby did not use them, for a later appendix of notes on all the Scottish texts published.[40] Everyone was suggesting what James should undertake. Skeat, for example said 'If you *want work*, I would beg to suggest a Glossary to *Gawin Douglas's Virgil* . . . Can you not enquire into this? Only consider the *importance* of it!'[41] Professor Zupitza, who was rightly critical of much of the work published by the Society, wrote to Furnivall in 1874 that he would be very glad if the invaluable help of Murray could be secured for the Guy of Warwick *Romances*. They planned to cooperate and James collated the text with an earlier printed edition of 1840 and with a manuscript in the Advocates' Library. In Part II Zupitza used these collations and stated that the side notes to its first section were nearly all Murray's.[42]

One of the astonishing aspects of all this work was the casualness with which valuable manuscripts were lent and borrowed. Private owners and librarians alike were quite willing in those honest days to let a scholar have possession of a manuscript on the security of a bond for its safe return. One of James Murray's many services to the Society was in collecting, standing surety and returning these priceless volumes. In August 1874, for instance, James insisted on the necessity of going himself to Cambridge and Lincoln to collate the Erceldoune manuscripts there, rather than trust the University Librarian, Henry Bradshaw, to do it for him. Furnivall reluctantly agreed, asking him to go on to Blickling in Norfolk to return two manuscripts to the Marquis of Lothian.[43] James set out carrying with him the Blickling Homilies (AD 971), which had been edited by Richard Morris, and an early psalter. It was a fruitful journey for him, as he met for the first time Henry Bradshaw, who later was most helpful in lending him books, which he took out of the University Library in his own name. When James failed to return them by the correct date Bradshaw incurred the fines.[44] It was Bradshaw who eventually made the awkward journey from Cambridge to Blickling and recovered the bonds which Furnivall had given for the safe return of the manuscripts.[45] This left James free to go to Lincoln, where he stayed with the Chancellor, Edward Benson, future Archbishop of Canterbury, and examined an Erceldoune manuscript in the Chapter Library.

Another very important loan was that of the Durham Ritual, a ninth-century manuscript which James borrowed in 1878 through his old friend Canon Greenwell, assuring the Chapter that he was well used to borrowing manuscripts and could arrange for its absolute safety while in his care. He wanted to transcribe it for a new edition he was planning and to get its various hands examined by experts in the British Museum.[46]

The most remarkable loan, however, was that which James negotiated in 1879 with the French government on behalf of the Philological Society. He borrowed from the College of Epinal the ninth-century glossary which Henry Sweet, who reproduced it in facsimile for the Early English Text Society, described as 'the finest one I have ever seen. It is probably the oldest English one in existence'.* Not surprisingly the French got anxious about its return,

---

* The MS was wrongly dated by Furnivall and Sweet to the seventh century.

for which they held James' bond. They wrote about it in the summer of 1880, sending the letter to the Society, care of University College, London. Arriving in the vacation, the letter was not forwarded and by the time it was received there was almost a diplomatic incident.[47]

James Murray's share in the work of the Early English Text Society in the ten years 1868 to 1878 were of crucial importance both for the study of English language and literature and for his own career. Edward Arber, later Professor of English at Birmingham, then busily engaged on his series of reprints, said that it seemed to him that the revival of English had been brought about by the voluntary and self-denying work of Frederick Furnivall, James Murray, himself and a few others.[48] This was true, and James' special contribution was in raising the standard of the editorial work. For himself he had gained an unrivalled knowledge of the sources for the study of Anglo-Saxon and Middle English. He now knew at first hand several of the key manuscripts, if and where they had been printed and how reliable the editions were.

By 1878 he had to his credit his important study of the dialect of the Border counties supported by a number of papers given to the Philological Society and the three texts, two fully edited, for the Early English Text Society. His reputation was established and when Thomas Baynes, editor of the ninth edition of the *Encyclopaedia Britannica*, failed to get Thomas Arnold to write a short history of the English language for it, James Murray was a natural choice. He asked him for four or five pages at four weeks' notice. 'A mere summary from you,' he wrote, 'would be of more value than a longer article from a writer of less authority.'[49] James took two months to produce an article of twelve pages and a chronological table. He described this as 'the most succinct account yet presented to Englishmen of the changes through which their language has passed, the causes of these changes, and the temporary phases of the long continuous whole, "which stands before us century after century like an evergreen tree".'[50] He planned to expand it into a fuller, more popular pamphlet and Baynes hoped that he would write a similar article on the Scottish language.[51] Neither materialised.

The reason for these unfulfilled hopes and his unfinished work for the Early English Text Society was that after 1879 James became wholly occupied in editing the Dictionary, a work for which, he felt later, all this busy research and writing had been an unconscious preparation and training. Gradually the random interests of his early years were being channelled in one direction. Even so, he might not have become a lexicographer had it not been for his membership of the Philological Society, the body which some twenty years earlier had first conceived the idea of a new English dictionary. It was through the Society that he left the bank in 1870 to return to teaching and it was through the Society that he was chosen to edit the Dictionary. The next chapters will show how, during the years when he was helping both Ellis and Furnivall, James had become once more a successful schoolmaster, while meantime Furnivall, like a busy spider, was spinning the web in which to entrap him in the toils of the Dictionary.

CHAPTER VI

Mill Hill: The Arcadian Years

JAMES Murray very quickly became a prominent member of the Philological Society, finding in it the stimulus and congenial fellowship which he had missed when he was cut off from the Hawick archaeologists by his removal to London. It was a fairly small group out of a total membership of under 200 who assembled on Friday evenings at University College and James soon got to know them all well. He rarely missed a meeting as long as he remained in London or the neighbourhood.

He was fortunate that when he joined the Society his work on the Scottish dialects was almost complete, as this at once established his reputation. In May 1869, a year after joining, he was elected to the Council, a position he held until his death. Over the next few years, besides contributing to the discussion on most of the papers read, he addressed the Society from time to time on his current research. In February 1871 he spoke on the dialectal varieties in the prose writings attributed to Rolle, and a year later on Shakespearian grammar, with illustrations from usages found in modern dialects, from which he deduced that the provincial terms used by Shakespeare were of northern origin.[1]

The members were often involved in controversial discussions into which James was drawn, usually in support of Alexander Ellis. In 1869 Ellis brought him into a committee considering recommendations for spelling reform, in order to get James' backing for his scheme against one pushed by another member. Ellis described the rival system as 'bad from every conceivable point of view . . . a disgrace to the Committee'[2] and 'all bosh to me'.[3] As the members of the Committee could not agree, a resolution was passed in November 1870 'That the Philological Society abstains from recommending the adoption of any spelling reform'.[4] Ten years later, as President of the Society, James confessed that he no longer believed in Ellis' scheme of introducing Glossic into schools for concurrent use with the present 'effete system'. Instead he initiated a scheme for a partial reform, approved also by the American Philological Association, to remove the most glaring anomalies in current usage by preparing a list of recommended amended spellings.[5] These were used for a time by the Society in its published transactions, and some were permanently adopted by enthusiasts like Furnivall. Fortunately, James did not use them in the Dictionary, but this introduction to the problem of orthography was yet another experience destined to be of value to him in his future work. He remained very sympathetic to the cause of spelling reform, although not convinced of the merits of any of the many schemes proposed to achieve it; and in 1905, following the examples of the other lexicographers, Walter Skeat, Henry Bradley, and Joseph Wright, he joined the American Simplified Spelling Board.[6]

His friendship with Ellis involved him in another of the arguments current among members of the Society—that on the pronunciation of Early English. In this Ellis' chief antagonist was Dr Richard Francis Weymouth, a senior member of the Society who had joined in 1851.[7] As a classicist his special interest was New Testament Greek, but he had taken his degree at University College London and there became acquainted with the new studies in philology and dialects. He had some knowledge of Anglo-Saxon and Icelandic and had very recently (1868) won the distinction of being awarded the first Litt.D. of the University of London. Furnivall, watching from the side lines in 1873, still hoped to see Weymouth overthrow the theories of Ellis on pronunciation[8] and already, on 17 June 1870, James had joined eagerly in the debate. He made some intelligent criticisms of a paper given by Dr Weymouth on this occasion, and this chance was to change the course of his life. Weymouth inquired who this young man was and how he came by his knowledge, and was told that he was at present a bank clerk, but had been a teacher in Scotland and might like to get back to school mastering again.[9]

Weymouth, formerly Head of Plymouth Grammar School, had just been appointed Head of Mill Hill, a school established in 1807 as the 'Protestant dissenters' Grammar School'. Although not exclusively non-conformist, it was founded to give sons of dissenters the public school education which at the beginning of the nineteenth century was still only open to Anglicans. The school had had a somewhat chequered history and Weymouth's appointment marked a new foundation which, it was hoped, would achieve the status of a public school.[10] Weymouth was now recruiting staff, and he followed up the hint given him by seeking out James Murray at the bank in Threadneedle Street one June evening. James later described their conversation in the courtyard. Weymouth began abruptly, 'I understand that you were a schoolmaster and might like to be so again?' To this James replied cautiously, 'Yes and no. I should like it on conditions.' Weymouth continued bluntly, 'Why are all you philologists Unitarians?' This was a rash deduction from the connection of the Society with University College which had been closely associated with Unitarianism and Utilitarianism from its foundation. When James explained that he was in fact a Congregationalist, Weymouth at once offered him an appointment on his staff, suggesting that he should come down to Mill Hill to see the place, holding out as a bait the chance of a philological chat.[11]

All through his life James found it difficult to make up his mind when faced by an important decision of this kind. He had hesitated almost till the last moment before deciding to leave Hawick and he was to have even more difficulty in committing himself to the Dictionary. Now he was doubtful, giving as his reason that the salary would entail financial sacrifices which would be unfair to his family, and it was a month before he came to a decision.[12]

In spite of his success at Hawick, James did not regard teaching children as his vocation. If he left the bank it would be for work which would secure him the time and money to enable him to continue his research and perhaps gain a qualification which might eventually lead to a university post. Any way to escape from the bank was tempting, because as he became more engrossed in his studies the commercial world seemed increasingly alien. It was also becoming increasingly demanding. In July 1870 James wrote to Prince Louis Bonaparte apologising for having failed to complete some work he had undertaken, and explaining 'My hours in the city have for many weeks and months been so long and my work so exhausting that I have on getting home, felt quite unable for any literary work almost.'[13]

On the other hand, as he well knew, a schoolmaster in term time has much longer hours than a bank clerk: it was a choice between having say four hours to himself after work on every day, or being tied for ten hours in term for the sake of ten weeks' holiday in the year, and on the whole James preferred the latter.[14] Moreover if he did decide to return to teaching, Mill Hill would suit him. Although Weymouth himself was a Baptist the school had strong links with the Congregational Church. It had also a broader; more progressive curriculum than the traditional public school. Because it was planned as a school for the sons of business men, there was less emphasis on the Classics: science and modern languages were taught and many boys took German as an alternative to Greek. The connection of Dr Weymouth with University College ensured that English studies would not be neglected and that he would be sympathetic towards James' research. In fact he was prepared to agree that James should only have a fourth share of out-of-school duties and promised that there would be no necessity for him to be in school till 9 *a.m.* (although if in fine summer weather he came over by 7.15 he would have a free breakfast), and he would never be required to remain after 8.30 *p.m.* even when on duty.[15] Mill Hill was near enough to London for James not to be cut off from the British Museum and he could continue to attend the Philological Society meetings. Finally the Murrays liked the idea of bringing up their family in the country and foresaw that association with the school would be an advantage when their sons reached school age.

Altogether there was enough to induce James and Ada to go down to Mill Hill one Saturday afternoon to have a look round. The founders of the School had deliberately chosen a site near, but just off, the main road and not too accessible to London in order to protect the pupils from the physical and moral dangers of the city[16] and in the 1870s it was still quite an adventure to get to Mill Hill. The newly built Midland station was some distance from the village, down a very steep lane, up which the Murrays went in a wagonette on this first visit.

The village is still surprisingly rural, in spite of the spread of London out to and beyond it, and the ridgeway along which the straggling village lies is still grass-verged and tree-lined. The Murrays were charmed by its country character—the ponds, the boarded cottages and the old inns were a complete contrast to the built up area of Camberwell where they were living. Above all there were views: here the country was quite different from the flat fields which had seemed so uninviting to James after the Borders. On each side of the ridge the land drops away and the school occupies a magnificent site with a terrace on the edge of the hill facing south. The grounds of the original house were laid out in 1747 as a Botanical garden and James was excited when Weymouth pointed out to him amongst the fine and rare trees, two huge cedars, said to have been planted by the botanist Linnaeus himself.

But the Murrays still hesitated. They had probably made inquiries about the school and found there was some anxiety as to its future. There had been frequent changes of staff and three headmasters between 1860 and 1868, when it was temporarily closed owing to financial difficulties. Before the closure the school had a bad reputation for indiscipline, academic standards were low, the health record was poor, and numbers had dropped to only 34 boys. It was not certain that Dr Weymouth could maintain a recent improvement, although James was favourably impressed by him. He was an imposing man, courteous and dignified — 'a superb figurehead'. Later he proved to have serious shortcomings as a Headmaster, but it was too early for this to be known.[17]

Whatever his doubts about the school, James kept them to himself and still based his reluctance entirely on the financial prospects. Weymouth, determined that James was the man he must have, continued trying to remove the obstacles. He promised, going beyond the terms at first approved by the Governors, a guaranteed salary of £150 based on £2 per annum for each boy in the school and 'a douceur of £5' on each boy James introduced. Weymouth was sure that James would soon equal and surpass his present salary. 'It would only be reculer pour mieux sauter', Weymouth said, and he would get £300 long before he would at the bank. If James obtained a degree he thought the Governors might even reconsider the salary.[18] But James wrote again on 11 July refusing to come unless the salary were increased. His remuneration at the bank was already £200 *p.a.*, the prospects there were permanent, and he had spare time in which to supplement his income by literary work. He added that he knew too well 'the cramping effects of an insuff. income upon a man's energies and powers of concentration'.[19] Ironically, it was exactly this situation in which he was to find himself as a result of undertaking the Dictionary, while in contrast, the years of full time teaching proved to be the most prosperous he ever knew and he was able to save a little. To his fourth son, Oswyn, as a small boy, the family at Mill Hill seemed 'rich, great and powerful' and it was a shock when one day he heard his father say that he could not afford a summer holiday.[20]

Dr Weymouth was very tenacious. Refusing to take no for an

9. Sunnyside, Hammer's Lane, Mill Hill. The Murray home, 1870–85. James Murray is sitting on the lawn on the left with his top hat beside him.

answer, he eventually overcame James' resistance by persuading the Governors to add to the salary a rent-free house and free medical attention which gave him the equivalent of a minimum salary of £200. On his part James agreed to work for an external B.A. degree of London University. On 25 July he gave notice to the bank to take effect from 27 August and went happily off to Edinburgh to use up the holiday still owing to him in research for the Early English Text Society, returning by sea from Newcastle.[21] From September 1870 therefore the work on dialects and on manuscripts recorded in the last chapters was accomplished in his spare time as a schoolmaster, and he was still teaching when he became involved in the plans for a new dictionary, and combined the editorship with his post at Mill Hill for six years.

The house the school rented for them finally won the Murrays over. Sunnyside, as it was called, is a most attractive house with Georgian features and parts which are much older. It was only five minutes from the school, standing at the top of Hammer's Lane, opposite the Three Hammers Inn and almost next door to the old butcher's shop. The white house stands at right angles to the lane, with a small garden on the north and a larger one of about a quarter of an acre on the south. Besides the lawn and some fine trees there was space in which James created a garden. He took great pride in the lawn, and games, such as cricket, which might damage it were taboo: fortunately for the children he never took much interest in vegetables, and they played *Lorna Doone* using the gaps between the asparagus and bean rows as the Doone valley.[22] Beyond the garden there was still open country through which the footpath to Hendon went across hay and corn fields and in summer the sound of the rattles used by boys hired to 'fray' the birds from the crops was familiar.[23] The chief delight was the view from house and garden. James' third son, Wilfrid, born at Mill Hill in 1871, described this view as a perpetual joy and refreshment to his father.

> Over finely wooded country, through which the thin trails of smoke from the trains on the Midland and the London and North-Western main lines could be followed for mile after mile, the eye travelled westward up to where the tall church spire of Harrow-on-the-Hill stood out boldly on the far skyline. From the spire the ground fell away sharply on either hand, and there was one spot where in the faint blue distance beyond it was possible with the help of a field-glass to distinguish the Round Tower of Windsor Castle and the Royal Standard floating above it.[24]

The house was a roomy one, a real family home. The front door opened into a 'room-like Hall' with a French window into the garden and at one end a door to a large drawing room. At the other end were two small rooms, used for nursery and study, or later school room. On the first floor there were three or four bedrooms and until their own family increased in number, the Murrays took two or three boys and a master from the school as boarders. There was plenty of room in a spacious semi-basement kitchen and attic bedrooms for servants, who were cheap and plentiful.[25] It was then exceptional for a professional man to have to perform any domestic tasks and James once reminded a son that it is 'easy to black your own boots; I did it all the 3 years I was Assistant Master at the Hawick Academy, & have done it hundreds of times since.' But at Mill Hill this was only in times of special crisis 'when the children were young, & Mother had too few or too weak servants'.[26]

To this delightful home the Murrays moved when James returned from his holiday, the carriage of their furniture from Hendon costing £3. It was the beginning of what he always spoke of as his 'Arcadian time', the happiest period of his life.[27]

Term started on 23 September and James was allocated to Form Three and gave his first lesson, which was in Geography. He flung himself into the work with customary determination, conscious that without a degree he had to prove his competence by results, and enjoying the challenge. Looking back at those early years he compared the atmosphere to that of the reign of Elizabeth I: Weymouth and himself shared in boundless faith in the school and hope for its future as they worked together to rebuild its reputation and numbers. Masters and boys alike were quickly impressed by James' phenomenal energy and ability to fill every moment and yet always to have apparent leisure to give help where it was needed.[28]

Unfortunately James soon discovered that although he himself got along well enough with Dr Weymouth, the Headmaster was a very difficult man to work with and there were constant changes amongst the assistants. Of the seven masters on the staff in 1870, only four were still there in 1874 and two of them left that year. An old boy, quoted in the history of the school, wrote of his former Headmaster as tactfully as he could,

> Dr Weymouth was a man with an unmistakable genius for teaching and ruling boys, and if only he had been of a more sympathetic disposition and had possessed a keener insight into human nature, and more consideration for human nature's little weaknesses and imperfections, he would have been nearer to the ideal Headmaster . . .[29]

This account gives the clue to Murray's role in the school. He was in sympathy with Weymouth's basic principles, with his strong moral and religious fervour, his insistence on accuracy, his scholarship and his expectation of hard work from his pupils. Like Weymouth, James believed in convincing boys that work 'is the great necessity of existence' and thoroughly approved the dictum which he first heard from Weymouth 'Know something about everything and everything about something'.[30] Like Weymouth he was intensely loyal to the school, identified himself with its fortunes and rejoiced to see the numbers build up, recognising the contribution made to this by Weymouth's gift of impressing the outside public. Where the two men differed was that whereas Weymouth was feared and unpopular, a narrow and rather unjust disciplinarian, without any real understanding of the needs of boys or sympathy with the more progressive ideas of his staff, James Murray, an equally firm disciplinarian, was known to be just and able to forgive and forget. It was he, not the Headmaster, to whom the boys went with their interests and their difficulties.[31] 'Dr Murray', a small boy once said 'knows everything', and he never turned a boy away who wanted information.[32] 'Knowing the willingness with which you always conversed with us . . . when we were boys', wrote an old boy in 1885, then a solicitor and wanting to know James' opinion about dancing . . . 'I have not the slightest doubt that you will be able to give me a minute or two.' 'They look to you for almost everything', a parent reported, asking him to continue her son's extra coaching.[33]

James' respect for Weymouth, in spite of not sharing his views on some very important matters, enabled him to maintain a position as mediator between the Headmaster, the staff, and the school monitors in clashes due to Weymouth's failures in personal relationships. Weymouth on his part recognised James' ability and appreciated his honesty of purpose and absence of partiality or self-interest. James was the one person who dared to speak frankly to the Head. Hence Weymouth came to rely increasingly on this assistant master, who soon carried so much responsibility and exercised so much influence in the school that it was later often mistakenly said that he had been Headmaster. Had he remained at the school he would certainly have succeeded Weymouth. Twice during his time at Mill Hill he was urged to apply for headships elsewhere, but he turned down both opportunities.[34] Prospects at Mill Hill seemed good, numbers were rising (they reached a peak of 183 in 1878) and with increased numbers his own salary rose too. He did not want to cut himself off from London and the literary work in which he was still engaged and preferred to stay where he was.

Always a strong personality with a distinguished appearance, James Murray was well remembered as he was at Mill Hill: very tall and thin, with a large head and a sandy beard and with a careful, 'somewhat affected' Scotch enunciation. He had a genial smile for everybody, and the boys soon found that beneath his austere manner he was very young in heart.[35]

One wonders what Dr Weymouth would have thought of some of the goings-on at Sunnyside, recorded by one of the boarders there from 1870–4.[36] In contrast to the bleak school Boarding House, Murray evidently determined that Sunnyside should provide a home atmosphere and be exempt from the rigid discipline of the school.

There he gave his sense of humour full play and was fond of unexpected pranks.

For example, at the beginning of one term the boarders returned on a dark evening. Taking their candles the boys went up to their room, which was at the end of a long passage running the length of the house, with a steep staircase to the attic half way along. They suddenly saw ahead of them in the flickering light the horrifying sight of a grimacing skeleton swaying about, some two feet from the ground. After a momentary panic, further investigation revealed it to be a realistic life-size drawing on black paper—the work of Murray himself.

Another story was of the master who lodged with them at first, Henry Tucker, appointed a year before James and responsible for introducing games and gymnastics. Tucker used to go over to the main school in the evenings to join the other masters in the senior common room, and he annoyed Murray by his habit of returning late at night. If the family had gone to bed, a chair used to be put against the door and the lights turned out as a hint that Tucker was late. Tucker did not mend his ways until one night, having negotiated the chair and groped his way to the table where the candle and matches were kept, he found himself suddenly seized by the knees—he supposed by a burglar, and a great struggle ensued, for Tucker was a good athlete. He and his adversary rolled together on the floor, until suddenly a quiet chuckle revealed that the supposed burglar was Murray himself! The boy who recalled this episode sixty years later remarked 'The joke caused some bitterness for a few days, but it came all right in the end, and the lesson was learnt.'

James understood boys and he was always prepared to support the Monitors' requests for changes if he felt them to be reasonable and especially if they would give the boys the freedom to acquire self discipline and opportunities for more self education. Although he often won the Masters' race on Sports day—a conspicuous figure with his flowing red beard and long raking stride—he was not interested in games and if he came out to watch a cricket match he usually brought proofs to correct.[37] He preferred to join the boys in exploring the countryside. His particular contribution to the extra-curricular activities was the foundation of a Natural History Society, modelled to some extent on the Hawick Archaeological Society. Members were encouraged to bring interesting specimens to the meetings and these became the nucleus of a school Museum. He was very anxious that the

Society should not lead to mere magpie collecting and told them

> I must . . . express my contempt for those boys whose whole idea
> . . . is that of getting a net, a killing bottle, a collecting box & some
> settling boards, before they have ever read or studied a book on the
> subject or know anything at all of the classification . . . Every boy
> who begins to collect eggs ought to begin by learning how birds are
> classed into orders and families . . . and he ought to arrange his eggs
> from the very first in groups . . . This alone is science; the
> formation of heterogeneous collections is only mischievous trifling.

He gave every year prizes to encourage serious collectors and
suggested special studies, capable of useful investigation, such as to
make a complete list of all the quadrupeds to be found locally, telling
them that he himself did not yet know which kinds of mice, voles,
weasels and bats were native to Mill Hill.[38] If he could not go out with
the boys himself, he was always glad if they dropped in at Sunnyside
to ask him about what they had found. 'Half the pleasure of an
afternoon's walk,' one boy said, 'was the prospect of a talk with Dr
Murray at the end of it.'[39]

A visit to Sunnyside was always interesting. He would invite the
whole of his class — the third form — to tea. They might begin with a
game of carpet bowls (an indoor version of the game, played with large
china balls), then James would begin to talk, perhaps on logic, or he
would tell them about his books, showing them for example a Bible
which had been thrown into the fire during the Marian persecution
and was half burned. The evening would end with one of his famous
recitations, or in summer they might adjourn to the honeysuckle and
clematis covered porch overlooking the garden. There as dusk fell, he
would tell them hair-raising Border tales of the occult or uncanny. A
favourite was that of a body snatcher, who went at midnight to rob a
vault in which a beautiful girl had been buried with a valuable ring
upon her finger. A passer-by saw the glimmer of his candle and ran to
spread the alarm. When a party reached the vault they found the
supposed corpse sitting upright and the thief lying unconscious on the
ground. Apparently the robber, unable to remove the ring, had
started to cut the finger off when — and here James uttered the most
blood curdling scream of pain — the girl, who was only in a swoon,
started up and saved her finger and her life![40]

Besides the Natural History Society, he identified himself closely
with the School Magazine, started in 1873 by T. A. Gurney, one of

the boarders at Sunnyside. Typically, James held that the magazine should be the boys' own responsibility, although he and other masters might contribute to it. He included in the Dictionary a quotation for the use of the word 'anamorphose' (to distort into a monstrous projection) used by himself in an article and said to be the only quotation in the Oxford Dictionary drawn from a school magazine.[41]

It was the deliberate policy of James and his colleagues to change the ethos of the school by introducing into its previously rather arid life something of the atmosphere which was at that time transforming the public schools. He had no first hand experience himself of other English schools, but because of his naturally friendly, unconventional approach to his pupils, he probably did more than any of the other masters to achieve this.[42] He had a strong ally in Robert Harley, who became Second master, chaplain and mathematics master in 1872. Harley was a man of means, and built at his own expense a new boarding house, but in his ideas on running it he came into conflict with Dr Weymouth.[43] Murray did his best to avert a crisis: he liked Harley, who became a life-long friend, but he also tried to be loyal to the Headmaster. This uncomfortable state of affairs was the one cloud in an otherwise very happy time at Mill Hill and was a source of great anxiety to James. When it was eventually decided that Harley must leave the School, the Governors relied upon James to prevent any demonstrations in his favour on the part of the rest of the staff and for the remainder of his time at the School it was James who held it together.[44] As soon as he left, the position rapidly deteriorated and in less than a year the Governors accepted Dr Weymouth's resignation.[45] When this happened James wrote to the Treasurer to the Governors, giving his frank opinion

> Dr Weymouth has been a failure: his personal failure was known to all of us years & years ago: but the school has been sustained in spite of him by the enthusiastic devotion of those who gave it their *disinterested* services, whose efforts were constantly directed to supplying and concealing his deficiencies . . . What has happened now would have happened 12 years ago, if Dr Weymouth had been left to himself.[46]

This then was the background to James' work as an assistant master, an additional burden which he carried. His actual teaching was very little trouble to him. The boys at Mill Hill, like the pupils at the Hawick Academy, appreciated his unconventional methods and his ability to share his enthusiasm and the excitement of discovery with them.

> His classes [wrote one of them] were always intensely interesting. You never knew where you might arrive before the lesson was done. A nominal geography class might easily develop into a lecture on Icelandic roots, and we often tried to bring him back to the days when the Finnish landed on the shores of the Baltic, on occasions when we had not given adequate time to the preparation of our set lesson. Then the tricks he could play with words. Such was his skill and knowledge that many of us firmly believed that by Grimm's law he could prove that BLACK really was the same word as WHITE; at least that was how it seemed to our poor intelligences.[47]

He would talk to the abler pupils about his most recent research and they remembered how once, when showing them a 1600 edition of Plutarch, he thrilled them by pointing out something which had been missed by other scholars and only noticed by himself just then for the first time.[48] His vivid way of teaching often enlivened what would otherwise have been dull. Describing how changes occur in the form of words he would warn the boys against speaking of words 'as if men carried them about in their hands & now & then let letters drop out: and sometimes when they are sleeping, stray letters, casuals, "creep in" for the sake of "euphony" or a night's lodging, or a bit of a lark.'[49] Teaching German to the Middle school he made the dry bones of accidence amusing by composing doggerel verses and stories to illustrate the declension of nouns. When he taught History to the upper school he made much use of original sources and led the boys to consider the motives of men and to trace events back to their causes and to recognise their after effects.[50]

James was not satisfied with the available text books and had plans to write his own as he had for English literature in Hawick. The first, and the only one to be published, was a *Synopsis of Paley's Horae Paulinae*, published in 1872. William Paley was an eighteenth-century exponent of theological utilitarianism and the *Horae* published in 1790 is considered his least successful work. Nevertheless it was chosen by the examiners for the Cambridge Locals as a set book. It is an elaborate logical argument to show that if history is true, then the Pauline epistles are true, and *vice versa*. James Murray thought it had some value in an age when Christians were challenged to give a reason for their beliefs, but he found schoolboys had difficulty in following arguments scattered over several pages. His *Synopsis* used different types and arranged the articles so that they would be 'eloquent to the eye', a single glance sufficing to show the correspondence between two documents and how their evidence supported each other.[51] The lasting importance of the book was that it led James to experiment with different printing types and this knowledge was used by him for the Dictionary. Twelve years later, his preface to its first part echoed his introduction to Paley as he described the steps taken to make the pages 'eloquent to the eye'.[52]

In 1874 James was working on the idea of a German Grammar, *A Declension of German Nouns arranged on Philological Principles for the Use of Schools and Private Students*. His aim was to make use of philological information about the history of nouns and the rules of change which had produced their modern forms, in order, he hoped, to simplify the learning of modern German. He consulted his friend Henry Nicol, who agreed that although these historical explanations were well known in Germany, nothing of the kind had been attempted in England. From his superior knowledge Nicol told him frankly that his work would need much revision to bring it up to date, as there had been big advances since Grimm's Grammar on which James had been relying. Nicol wrote that 'an insufficient knowledge of the older Aryan languages and their philology has led you into several confusions . . . and into several absolute errors', and a few days later he sent him seven and a half pages on the subject. Although the Grammar never advanced beyond the beginning of the first draft, the time spent on it was worthwhile for this informative criticism. It is doubtful in any case whether the Grammar would ever have been used, for, as Nicol wisely observed, 'I am not at all sure whether it is not often more confusing than otherwise to teach the science of a language, and the art of using it, together.' Such teaching was something which only a man of James' exceptional knowledge and enthusiasm could even attempt to do.[53]

The third text book he planned to write was a *Primer of English Grammar* in a series edited by John Richard Green for Macmillan. It was commissioned as a result of James' article in the *Encyclopaedia Britannica*. Green hoped it would 'help us break down that theory of education which was once put tersely enough by Bradley of Marlborough, "If once you interest boys in the work, you lose half its disciplinary profit."' Green thought the book would be particularly acceptable to girls' schools such as that of Miss Buss, because, he wrote, 'Girls' minds actually require the element of interest to enable them to gain knowledge from facts at all.'[54] The Grammar had been nearly completed by 1879 and was still hoped for in 1881 but then was dropped owing to the pressure of work on the Dictionary.[55]

Although Dr Weymouth had promised him a fairly light timetable, James' reliability and willingness soon led to involvement in additional responsibilities. Probably because of his banking experience he was asked to undertake the issue of the boys' pocket money and the sale of books, which gave his class-room a homely 'shoppy smell'.[56] One way and another he found he had to give a good deal of time to keeping accounts, and his approachability meant that parents increasingly wrote to him rather than to Dr Weymouth on money and other matters. In December 1873 A. J. Ellis wrote to him, 'I commiserate you with all my heart. The work of school accts. from morn to night must be simply dreadful. I was careful to say it was I knew *no fault of yours* . . . that you were . . . so late.' At times of the year when he was getting out the school bills James had to set aside other work and correspondence.[57]

Dr Weymouth, who seldom preached himself, also relied on James to help him in securing preachers for the School chapel and very often James delivered the address himself, rather than falling back on inexperienced theological students. A lasting impression was made on the boys by James' dramatic reading. 'It was a treat to hear him read the lessons, particularly the chapter in Kings about Elijah and the prophets of Baal. How he scorched them. Why, I am sure many boys of that period felt convinced that Elijah sure had a red beard and wore a scarlet hood.'[58]

The texts of many of James' sermons survive and show his sense of drama and his vivid imagination. Sometimes he would enlarge upon his own experience: one sermon likens the sinner's path to that chosen by a mountain traveller without map or guide, who, choosing what seems the easier route, finds it gradually change its character 'till the tourist finds himself on one of those dangerous screes where the loose, slippery slaty rock gives way beneath his weight, and he is hurled in a gathering avalanche of stones and dust over a sheer precipice into a dark tarn, or a rocky valley a thousand feet below.'[59]

The themes of his sermons naturally reflect the principles by which he lived himself. Two frequently recur—his doctrine of work and his belief in divine guidance. We tend to think of shoddy workmanship and lack of pride in craftsmanship as a product of our modern economy and it is interesting to find James saying in 1871 that it was a complaint of the times that honest work was almost impossible to find, men were only out for wages and did not bother about quality. In contrast he urged his audience to feel that all work is God's work, to be well done whether it is that of farmer, labourer, merchant, domestic servant or scholar.[60] His message for a new year was that 'God gave us no time to waste, no moment to pass unhonoured, unimproved', and that every man is given a life work to accomplish.[61] For himself he hated to be idle and he felt that all his life was a training for some work which he would be called upon to do. How do we know what our life work is to be? By divine guidance

> there will come occasions [he told the boys in 1871] . . . when the path of duty will *not* be *perfectly clear* . . . and you will be apt to exclaim, as I myself have done, Would that there were a Urim and Thummim or an Ephod now, as in the days of David, that I might enquire of the Lord in plain words 'Shall I go up or shall I not go up?' and 'Wilt thou deliver them into my hands?' and receive a distinct categoric 'Thou shalt go up', . . . to save you from the responsibility of a personal decision. And you will find . . . that tho' there *will* be occasions on which you will be shut up as it were to one course, when you will feel, 'I have no choice—circumstances compel me to do this or that', it will not be always so. Pray for help to decide, and then decide, on your own judgment, and with an eye to God's glory, and you will find that God's spirit has been *just as really present* . . . altho' you have not been able to distinguish his promptings & guidings from your own thoughts . . . reason and judgment. And looking back in after times, you will say, 'If ever I was divinely guided, surely it was *then*'.[62]

There is no doubt that he was describing his own problems in reaching decisions. Deep as was his trust in providence, this did not lead him to fatalism. He never felt a mere puppet in the hands of an almighty God, and although the issue was assured, decisions must be taken painfully and by the exercise of his own free will.

Within a few years of joining the staff of Mill Hill School James found that the work was more exacting than that of a bank clerk: not only were the hours longer, but because the work was more interesting he put more into it. In the years 1870 to 1875 it must be remembered that besides his school duties he was also working on dialects with Ellis and preparing his own book for publication in 1873.

He was helping Ellis, Nicol and Elworthy with their proofs: he was writing papers for the Philological Society: he was working on numerous texts for the Early English Text Society in addition to the three he actually published, namely the incomplete Lyndsay in 1871, the *Complaynt of Scotlande* in 1873 and Thomas of Erceldoune in 1875, and he was also reviewing books for the *Academy* and the *Athenaeum*. In addition to all this he was now studying for a London degree. For the first time in his life he was overworked and as a result succumbed to a severe attack of influenza in 1874. Furnivall, tiresome as he was, had a very kind heart, and wrote in real concern to James on 23 January:

> I'm glad to hear that you are about again, for, to tell you the truth, I feared the worst from your note describing your illness. . . . You must have a rare constitution to have pulled through. Make up your mind to work as little as possible . . . Give all your care to your health. Let your wife coddle you like a little one. If you go on thinking you *won't* be an invalid, you'll get finished off . . . P.S. Pray be *very* careful of yourself, Look on yourself as a hospital patient.[63]

But of course, the moment James was better Furnivall was as usual bombarding him with ideas about further literary work. 'The truth is,' wrote Henry Nicol to Alexander Ellis, 'you and Murray and I are all suffering from the old complaint—lots to do, and not enough time and strength to do it.'[64]

James found the work for a London B.A. degree for which he had begun to study on his appointment at Mill Hill, was the most burdensome of his many activities. This was sheer slogging, yet something he was very set upon, not so much from the point of view of salary, since he had a welcome addition to his income from the capitation allowance as the school numbers went up, but because he realised that the lack of a degree would stand in his way if he wished to get a university post, or even a headmastership, and he felt a sense of inferiority when his colleagues appeared in their academic gowns.

As soon as he accepted the post at Mill Hill he applied to the Secretary of the Scottish Educational Institute, hoping that its Council would take up the question of official robes.

> I have faith enough in the 'Clothes philosophy', [he wrote] to think that even in Scotland, it would be decidedly advantageous to teachers to wear them, for the Official status it would give . . . In

England, I need hardly say, any degree is practically valueless to a teacher, which is not accompanied by such a 'sensible sign', without which my own fellowship will, I find, be of no use to me.

The Secretary agreed that the question was an important one, and sent an extract of James' letter to the *Scottish Journal of Education*, apparently with no result.[65] Meanwhile James paid up his subscription of 15/- entitling him to use the degree, but the letters F.E.I.S. merely mystified people.[66]

He immediately entered for London Matriculation, which he took in January 1871. This he could do 'off the cuff' and he was placed fourth in the Honours List. The B.A. examination was in two parts. Again he passed with honours in June 1871. Part II, for which he offered Logic, Moral Philosophy and Physiology, was more demanding and he found it irritating to have to take time from his more interesting research to master the factual information for the examination. He should have completed it in the spring of 1873 but his father died on 8 March and he was unable to sit for the papers. This meant that he had not even the satisfaction of working for high honours and had to take a pass degree in October. He was disappointed and anxious about the result and relieved when he did better than he expected. Ellis commiserated with him: 'I hope you have thoroughly done with your exam? To "get up" anything you don't mean to pursue is abominable. I hope you have not hurt your health thereby into the bargain . . . I am sorry to have to ask you to do so much. But what should I do without you?'[67]

James had realised before this that a London B.A., particularly with only a pass in Part II, was not sufficient if he determined upon an academic career. Looking around him at the amateur philologists who gained important university positions it did not seem unrealistic to think that he might eventually obtain a professorship. He wanted a doctorate, but the thought of years of over-work to achieve this was depressing. By 1873 the encouragement he had received by the reception of his publications gave him the idea of trying to gain the support of friends in Scotland for the award of an Honorary degree at either St Andrews or Edinburgh.

He turned first to Sir Walter Elliot who had retired to his family home at Wolfelee near Denholm in 1860 after holding office as Provisional Governor of Madras at the time of the Indian Mutiny.[68] He was a keen botanist, antiquarian and student of local history and folklore and had taken a kindly interest in James Murray when he was active in these fields in Hawick. Elliot was grateful to James for supplying him with much of the material for a paper on the history of Denholm which he gave at a field meeting of the Berwickshire Naturalists' Club in May 1867, and he had always hoped that a career might be found for James in which his talents could be used. When James went to London they continued to correspond and to meet occasionally and Sir Walter lent him books from his library.

Sir Walter was very ready to help James to obtain a Scottish degree, and in August 1873 wrote that he had been in touch with Lord Neaves, Rector of St Andrews, who was sympathetic but cautious.[69] St Andrews had been criticised for awarding honorary degrees too easily in the past, and Neaves wrote to James in October 'I suspect they might think that you had not such a long standing or conspicuous position in literature as to justify them in preferring you to many others to whom they must refuse it.'[70]

At this James put the idea out of his mind as an immediate possibility, but Sir Walter kept up his pressure on Neaves and persuaded him to approach Sir Alexander Grant, the Principal of Edinburgh University, who having read Lord Neaves' letter to the Senate, reported that the matter had been viewed with favour.[71] The deciding factor was undoubtedly the very warm testimonials sent on James' behalf from members of the Philological Society. Furnivall, with his customary enthusiasm, wrote

> I consider him the first living authority on our Northern Dialects . . . he is our standard referee on this point . . . He takes also first rank among the phoneticists of the day, alongside of Mr Ellis, Mr Sweet etc . . . Whatever paper turns up at our Meetings, Sanscrit, Persian, Russian, Mr Murray has always knowledge of the subject, & something pertinent to say of it . . . if he lives, as I hope he will, long, he will by a series of editions & books of & on Scotch authors & linguistics do credit to the University that allies him to itself.[72]

Others who wrote were A. J. Ellis, Robert G. Latham, former Professor of English at University College, Prince Louis Bonaparte, and Dr Pauli of Göttingen. James said that he could if necessary have obtained letters also from French, German, Italian and American authorities—a measure of the reputation and contacts he had built up in the nine years since coming to London.[73]

The success of the efforts made in his behalf, however, remained in doubt until the last minute and on 25 March 1874 James wrote to Sir Walter 'I *do not* and *will not* build upon any hopes till they are realized.'[74] The application had been made after all the arrangements for the April degree giving were complete and there was talk of postponement till the autumn. The indefatigable Sir Walter kept urging speedy action to relieve James from any thought of further work for a degree, which would interrupt his commitments for the Early English Text Society. He was fortunate in happening to meet at dinner Professor Geikie, one of the Senators, who remembered James' help in solving geological problems in the Borders.[75] On 29 March Sir Alexander Grant told Sir Walter that the Senate had agreed to suspend standing orders in favour of Mr James A. H. Murray and to offer him the Honorary degree of LL.D., to be conferred on 22 April.[76]

Congratulations flowed in. James' brother Charles, who heard the news on 1 April, sent a card 'It could not be *all* Fools day when wise men do a wise deed.' Alexander Ellis wrote 'What an Easter egg! Hip Hip Hip Hurrah! And a happy Hatching.' Furnivall, more soberly, and with an eye to the additional work James would now be able to do on early texts said that the best part was the relief from the need to work for another degree.[77]

Unfortunately his mother had an attack of bronchitis and Ada her hands full with her young family, and neither was able to go to Edinburgh but James' brother Alexander, his former pupil Thomas Hunter and James Parlane, the Congregational Minister from Hawick, were present. James tried to use the opportunity to work in Edinburgh libraries, but was disappointed to find them shut for the Lent holidays.

As soon as he heard about the degree James wrote off to the gown makers. He chose, without hesitation, the full-dress gown of extra Saxony light scarlet cloth, faced with rich blue silk, price eight pounds, ten shillings, with a black silk velvet bonetta cap for fifteen shillings. These had recently been introduced in place of the 'undress robes' of black silk with college cap and were to be used not only for general purposes but also for 'state and ceremonial occasions'. He was disappointed that the robe makers were out of the Saxony cloth, but they offered him instead 'one of the thinnest cloths we have ever seen & we had it, expressly to make these gowns of, as it has a finer look & we think hangs better than the extra thin.'[78] Little did they know that they were writing to a tailor's son who knew all about good cloth. He was particularly delighted with the cap, which he always wore to work in for the rest of his life. He went on from Edinburgh to give a paper to the Hawick Archaeological Society on the *Complaynt of Scotlande* and appeared in his robes ('which admirably became him'). He explained that the robes were a revival of the old dress worn at the University before the Reformation and that the cap was of the pattern which would have been worn by his hero John Knox. The museum room in which he spoke was densely crowded, and in the middle of the vote of thanks one of the benches collapsed 'causing not a little merriment'.[79]

Four doctorates in Divinity and six in Law were conferred at Edinburgh. Professor Maclagan, deputising for the Dean of the Faculty of Law, reminded the audience in presenting the candidates that the LL.D. was the highest honorary distinction which it was within the power of the University to give. Of James A. H. Murray he said

> I point to Mr Murray as a marked example . . . of a man who in spite of the want of influential connections and early advantages, has by sheer force of work and will fought his way to the front ranks of literature, and gained for himself a scholarly reputation of the very highest character. As a Scotchman, I rejoice exceedingly, and I think all leal Scotchmen will join with me in rejoicing, to think that the foundation of Mr Murray's learning was laid in a Scottish parish school.[80]

For James perhaps the greatest immediate triumph was in writing a letter to the Registrar of London University in April 1874 in reply to a formal notice of the degree giving on Wednesday 13 May, which stated 'appropriate Academical Costume is expected', asking whether it would be in order if he appeared on Presentation day in the costume appropriate to the Higher Degree that he had obtained at Edinburgh.[81] He was not above a little understandable vanity.

The London B.A. led to his appointment as an Assistant Examiner in English for London University, yet another bit of work which he contrived to find time to do until 1878, which brought him until then a welcome addition to his income.[82] The Edinburgh honour added to his prestige in the Philological Society. If Furnivall had not arranged in 1872 to fix the rotation of the Presidency for years ahead, Murray, rather than Henry Sweet, would have been elected to the office in 1876,[83] but he had his turn in 1878 and used the opportunity to introduce some changes. The Society had been criticised because under Ellis, Morris and Sweet, too much emphasis was placed on dialects and questions of phonology and too little on comparative philology. 'We have still half the world to conquer', complained Robert Cust, a member of the Society and also founder and secretary of the Royal Asiatic Society, 'and I have really no leisure to listen to the way in which a Dorsetshire peasant addresses his cow.'[84]

James tried, unsuccesfully, to persuade Cust to provide offprints of the Royal Asiatic Society papers for publication in the Philological Society transactions, but did get him to collaborate in sharing a task he took upon himself of translating into English any papers delivered to the Philological Society by foreign philologists. This was for the benefit of members, as was another of James' innovations—to arrange for abstracts of unpublished papers read to the Society to be printed at his own expense for circulation to the many subscribers unable to get to the meetings. His own regular attendance every fortnight meant quite an expenditure of time and energy, entailing a late return to Mill Hill and an often somewhat adventurous walk up the hill from the station by the pitch dark Hammer's Lane.[85]

While much that James did at Mill Hill seemed a continuation or development of interests first shown at Hawick, in one respect there was a marked break with the past. He now took little part in local or national politics: the School and the Philological Society were his little worlds. There were a few exceptions. In 1880 he was a member of Herbert Gladstone's election committee when Gladstone unsuccessfully contested the Harrow division of Middlesex. In the same year James took up a local issue, that of the enclosure of part of the verge in Hammer's Lane. He was anxious to pull down the fence, but was restrained by the advice of the lawyer acting for the Commons Preservation Society, who told him that although he might be within his rights to do so, he did not recommend this course of action.[86]

Although there were times when James certainly felt overworked during the years 1870 to 1880, looking back later when under the strain of his labours on the Dictionary, these years seemed by contrast a time of freedom when he had leisure to enjoy his growing family.

The fourth son, Oswyn, was born in 1873, the first girl, Hilda Mary Emily Ada Ruthven, in 1875, followed by Ethelwyn born in 1878, Aelfric in 1880, Elsie in 1882 and Rosfrith in 1884. Reporting the birth of his eighth child, born on 1 May—'A little May-queen or May-princess', James wrote to his sister-in-law, '. . . Ada has gone through it bravely as is her wont, & successfully as is her due', but Ada herself was becoming troubled by the size of the family and the expenses to which they would be put to educate them all. She sought advice from the Mill Hill doctor as to how she might put an end to these frequent pregnancies. 'Madam', he is reported to have replied, 'I can only suggest that you should slide down the stairs head first on your stomach!' The stairs at Sunnyside were narrow, with a curve near the top and descended steeply into what would now be called the lounge, and the remedy was certainly never put to the test. It was only after moving to Oxford and after the birth of two more children that better medical advice was obtained.

The unusual first names chosen for the children were due to their father's interests and prejudices. For their second or other names they were called after relations on one side or the other, or given specially appropriate ones—Elsie was Mayflower and Rosfrith, the ninth child was called Nina. But for their first names James insisted on ones from Anglo-Saxon literature and history. Writing in the *Border Magazine* in August 1863 on 'Names' he had given examples of the 'fine old Saxon names [of the] hardy northern tribes from whence we boast our Anglo-Saxon lineage . . . like themselves, hardy, rough and bold', such as Harold 'the champion' and Ethelbert 'the nobly bright'. Rosfrith was the name of a god-fearing maiden who, according to legend, had worshipped at the lost chapel of St Cuthbert in the Slitrig valley at Hawick. He contrasted these names with the Georges, Anthonys, Denises and Michaels who 'flourished in the legendary saint-lore, with which wily priests fed the ignorant love of the marvellous, and deepened the gloom of the middle ages.'[87] In the introduction to his book on the *Dialect of the Southern Counties of Scotland* James noted that the children of Malcolm, who at the head of an Anglo-Saxon army slew Macbeth in the eleventh century, bore southern names instead of Celtic ones such as Duncan. This change of name marked the turning point, after which the Scottish royal family may be looked upon as an Anglo-Saxon line.[88] Later James complained that his eldest son, Harold, chose 'nasty Pictish names'— Donald and Kenneth—for his sons, but when he moved to Oxford and was no longer so immersed in his Anglo-Saxon studies, James gave up this tradition and his last two children's names were chosen differently.

James and Ada were singularly blessed in their eleven children, and they were an unusually close-knit family. James fostered this unity, believing from his own experience in the importance of a good home.

Rather surprisingly, in view of his studious turn of mind he loved to play with babies. He attributed his children's strong legs to having danced them on his knees to strengthen them, and he used to play cat and mouse with a couple of them clinging to his coat tails while he whirled them round.

His children were well brought up and well mannered. Harold wrote rather smugly when he and thirteen-year-old Ethelbert were staying with their Uncle Alexander at Newcastle that 'Auntie always praises our tidyness & gives us as examples to the girls & Tom especially. She has wished thrice in one day I was her son as I offered to help her.'

On this occasion Harold and Ethelbert travelled alone by sea from London to Newcastle. They were very excited by the voyage and Harold reported that although they went to bed at 10 *p.m.* they got up again at 12, went back to bed at 1 and rose again at 4 *a.m.* when it was very cold and they 'took camphor as ordered'. Harold, then fifteen, was anxious to assure his father that he was 'strictly adhering' to the scheme for their holiday prepared by him for them in advance.[89] Children in 1880 were much more subject to parental discipline of course, and therefore less mature than teenagers today, but although James was strict, and could be stern, his children were not repressed: they were lively and often in mischief, but they respected their father and accepted punishment without lasting resentment.

Apart from childish complaints, the whole family was remarkably strong and healthy. Ada is said never to have had a thermometer in the house. She was a great believer in homoeopathy—the system of treating diseases by very small doses of the drugs which would produce in a healthy person symptoms resembling those of the disease treated—but she also believed in cosseting James, when sick, with beef tea, jelly, milk and soda water, eggs and oysters.[90]

The children were also all very intelligent, some of them outstandingly brilliant, and as a teacher their father took part in their education and provided the stimulus for the full development of their abilities. One of Harold's early memories was of an afternoon when he was about five years old and his father amused him by dropping lumps of sugar into a tumbler of water to demonstrate that eventually no more would dissolve. When young the three elder boys shared a governess with neighbours, and James took a close interest in what they were taught and visited the class to advise the governess and to examine the children. Later the Murrays employed their own governess and the three eldest boys went on to Mill Hill School at greatly reduced rates, but before this they already went to the school once a week for 'a dreary course of freehand drawing'.

James' own experience as a schoolmaster at Hawick and Mill Hill led him to two conclusions. First, that boarding schools were a mistake, chiefly because day boys were more profitably occupied on Sundays, and second that regular schooling should not be begun too young, early 'forcing' being in his opinion the cause of many boys of promise proving disappointments when they reached their teens. In view of his own early precocity this view of education is curious, but perhaps he drew a distinction between self education and formal schooling. None of his children went away to school, although in the case of the youngest son this meant forgoing a Winchester scholarship; this very brilliant boy did not start lessons till six and only learnt to read at seven. Of course all the family benefited from their father's conversation about whatever he was working on at the time and especially from the walks he took with them at weekends and on holidays.

Like most large Victorian families, the Murrays were self sufficient and had their own amusements, which reflect the intellectual atmosphere created by their father. His belief in liberty saved him from being authoritarian, but he did try to protect them from influences and knowledge which he feared might be harmful, and, for instance, followed his own parents' example in doing what he could to discourage the reading of novels. His children inherited his vivid imagination and wrote their own stories and poems and they produced a series of magazines, each child, on getting to an age when writing was a pleasure, starting his or her production and carrying on with more or less persistence. Wilfrid introduced 'the family handwriting', a small cursive script of extreme neatness and legibility which all except Harold and Ethelbert used throughout their lives.[91] The topics discussed by James in the family circle are illustrated in the minute books of the Sunnyside Amateur Debating Society, founded by Harold, which ran for two years and to which the younger members of the family were admitted from the age of six upwards. The four founder members were Harold (15), Wilfrid (12), Oswyn (10) and Hilda (8). Ethelbert made them a stand for the mace but was for long banned for his unfitness and 'bullying propensities' and the strong suspicion that he had killed a cat. The Society debated 'That an education based on Latin and Greek language is necessary for any person claiming to be educated'; 'That Scotland should have as many privileges as Ireland' (Oswyn, who proposed, objected that Ireland had more members of Parliament); 'That this House approves of total abstinence'; 'Should Phonetic spelling be adopted in England?' (Hilda on this occasion declared that she had voted in the wrong lobby): 'That a house of Lords irresponsible to the people and based on primogeniture is a political injustice and should be abolished immediately': 'That irreligion and frivolity are extending their sway over the English young to a frightful extent' (this motion was lost): 'That this House do emphatically condemn the coercive policy of Lord Salisbury and all preceding Governments and do approve of the Government of Ireland Bill wholly and entirely' (this motion carried unanimously amid loud, long continued cheers for the Government). Oswyn on this occasion moved that the resolution be sent to Mr Gladstone and a long list of prominent M.P.s, but this was rejected because of the expense of postage.

When any of the family was away from home regular letter writing was expected. This became a family ritual and throughout their lives an interchange of weekly letters was the rule. Nor was a mere postcard or scribbled note acceptable: James himself always wrote in meticulous detail, even though it might be late at night and the pen had hardly been out of his hand all day.

The training began very early. Ethelbert, whose gifts lay in mechanical rather than literary directions, found it necessary as a small boy to excuse his omission by a plausible tale. 'I am sorry to tell you that I have lost 3 letters to you & 2 to Mamma. I left one at Whitchester, one here and lost one. I am sorry. I remain your affect son E. T. R. Murray.' Harold, on the other hand, with the responsibility of the eldest, set the perfect example, and his long daily letters when on holiday at Chepstow at the age of 12 are interesting because one hears in them James, the born teacher imparting to his son his own keen interest in the world. Harold wrote

My dear Parents, Brothers, Sisters etc ... After leaving Paddington I saw nothing of notice till Windsor. We did not go near the town but saw the Castle in the distance. We soon after crossed the Thames and came to Reading where we saw the Biscuit manufacture. The sun set between Uffington and Shrivenham. At Swyndon we stopped ten minutes. We stopped at Kemble junction for Cirencester. Shortly after we entered *the* tunnel from which we emerged into a valley through which a canal passes. This canal goes through a tunnel so low that men have to lie on their backs in the canal [boat] and push it along with their feet.

Subsequent letters described Roman roads, a Danish fort, a house 'which forms a parish in itself', geological formations and fossils, and wild flowers such as 'the red primrose and the cream growing on the same plant and also seperately'; he noted that the inhabitants never said 'Good afternoon, but always Good morning or Evening as the case may be'.[92] On another visit he wished very much that his parents were there, 'you would have enjoyed yourselves so much, & Papa could have pointed out the hills better than Robert or Mr Hobkirk'.[93]

The Mill Hill period was memorable for the first of a long series of family holidays. On these James would enjoy his family to the full and share with them his old hobbies, history and archaeology, botany and geology and in bad weather, philately.

In 1872, when the children were all very young, they went to Hastings, where James immediately began studying and collecting shells. The holiday was never forgotten on account of an incident which occurred there. James wanted to go at low tide to a rock reef where he was told a rare type of shell could be found. Leaving Ada sitting on the shingle beach with the babies, he set off, accompanied by a large black dog which seemed to be out without its owner, and attached itself to him. Having picked his way over a long stretch of rock he found that he was cut off from the further reef by a deep channel. Failing to find an easy crossing, he lay down flat and tried with rolled up sleeves and walking stick to plumb the depth of the water. While doing so he was suddenly seized with a panic stricken feeling of being in great danger. Getting to his feet he hurried, slithering on the wet, sea-weed covered rocks, back to Ada, without attempting to cross the channel. When he got near her, Ada called to him, 'It's all right, the man who was with you while you were out there spoke to me as he passed and told me that you could get across the channel.' 'My love', said James, 'there WASN'T ANY MAN WITH ME ON THAT ROCK!' And looking out over the wide deserted shore it was true, neither man nor dog was anywhere to be seen.

Second sight was a familiar phenomenon to James, whose mother, like his paternal grandmother Christina, claimed to possess it. As a boy he had heard his mother tell how, when returning home from visiting a sick neighbour, she was surprised to see the ill man coming towards her. The figure vanished and hastening back to his cottage she found that he had just died. Ada was equally convinced that both she and her mother had second sight. Stories were told of how she had premonitions of her children's examination successes and failures. In after years the story of the event at Hastings lost nothing in the telling.

In 1875 the Murrays let Sunnyside for the whole of August and took their holidays in the Lake District, partly at Kendal, Ada's father's home town, and partly at Ambleside. This holiday was such a success that it was repeated in 1877, 1879 and 1882, although in the other years they returned to Hastings, the Isle of Wight or Folkestone for the sake of the younger children. With six children under eleven Ada can hardly have found much relaxation in a holiday wherever it was taken. James never cared much for the sea-side, but developed a passionate love for the Westmorland mountains, getting to know most of them as an energetic fell walker, preferring this to rock climbing.

His feeling for the mountains is recorded in a sermon he preached at Keswick on the text 'I will lift up my eyes to the hills'.[94] In a passage which strikes a familiar note to us a hundred years later, he stressed the value of a mountain holiday in restoring a true perspective to the victims of modern society, which treats men like the wheels of a vast machine. His own keen enjoyment of nature was always closely linked to his philosophy and deep religious sense, and after speaking of the mountains as an image of eternal truth he concluded by recalling the geological history of the area and observed,

> How wonderful that these natural processes, earthquake, & Volcano, glacier & flood, destructive forces all should have worked harmoniously & constructively to produce such a scene of beauty . . . blind forces . . . [working] . . . out the plans of a creating God.

James never lazed about on holiday. He had no taste for sitting still but was always restless, wanting to be making some excursion and to see every place of interest within reach. Even when he gained a mountain top he would pull some proofs out of his pocket to work upon if the day was fine. In 1880 he offered to head a subscription list to build a shelter on Skiddaw, the absence of which he found discreditable to Keswick and ungrateful to their visitors. He explained he did not want a covered place which might become a nuisance, but just a substantial cairn in place of the existing 'despicable apology in the shape of a tumble of stones', with three radiating walls to provide a wind screen on ordinary good days.[95]

He always looked back to these holidays in the Lake District with nostalgia.

> Oh what would I give [he wrote to Harold in 1908] to recall the early visits to Keswick in the holidays of the seventies, when golden time fleeted by on the slopes of Grisedale Pike, or the recesses of the Coledale Valley. Those were the happiest days of my life, and the memory of them is sweet & precious. *You* can have them still, when you take a holiday with your two boys, and be their hero, as I was of mine.[96]

As soon as they were old enough he took his boys walking with him, although they had hard work to keep up with him: even in middle age he could still easily vault a six barred gate. Harold's diary of a holiday in 1877 when he was nine and his brother Ethelbert seven illustrates his father's energy.[97] The family left Mill Hill by wagonette to catch the 7 p.m. train. Occupying two compartments from Euston, parents, five children and the governess, they travelled all night to arrive at Oxenholme at 3.40 *a.m.* where they had to change trains. To fill in the waiting time till the connection left at 7.30 *a.m.*, James led the older children up Holm Knot to see the view of the mountains. Taking a horse coach from Windermere to Ambleside the whole party eventually reached their destination at 9.30 *a.m.* after a fourteen hour journey. After breakfast they were taken up Stock Gill Force and in the afternoon the two elder boys went with James by steamer to Bowness to row for an hour on the lake before meeting their grandmother who arrived from Hawick at 9 *p.m.* Every day there were excursions, culminating in a three day walk on which Harold was allowed to go with his father. His diary reads:

> THURSDAY. Dr Dove drove us to Chapel stile. We walked on by Dungeon Ghyll Hotel to Rossett Ghyll which we scaled with much toil. We passed Angle Tarn, got a peep down Borrowdale, & ascended Esk Hause. Here we sheltered behind the cairn from a heavy shower. We then ascended Scawfell Pikes, and though we encountered two hail storms, the summit was clear & the view magnificent: all Westmoreland & Cumberland, the Irish Sea, Isle of Man and Scottish mountains were visible. We descended a scree between the two pikes, & crossed to top of Lingmell, whence we found our way over a tremendous steep descent to Burnthwaite in Wastdale. Securing a bed & tea we went down to Wastwater & saw the Screes; & on returning, the tiny chapel. At night we watched

the Eclipse of the moon from a gate opposite Wastdale Head Inn. It could not be seen at Burnthwaite for the mountain.

In the three days they covered at least fifty miles as well as climbing two mountains of around 3000 feet. Clearly James was bringing up his son to be tough and expected of him an energy and endurance to match his own.

His reckless, keen enjoyment of a mountain adventure, his powers of vivid description, his detailed memory and his strong religious faith are all illustrated in an account of an evening walk in 1875 which he wrote in 1901 to occupy himself when confined to the house by an attack of influenza.[98]

It was on his first visit to Ambleside, from which he made many excursions and had managed, with the aid of a pony, to get Ada to the top of Helvellyn. The visit was drawing to an end, when on a sudden impulse one day at lunch, he determined to fit in Dungeon Ghyll and Pike O'Stickle that afternoon, relying on a harvest moon and his good knowledge of paths near Ambleside to get him back. He walked up Langdale at a rattling pace, covering the eleven miles to the foot of the Ghyll by 4.30 *p.m.* From there he had a very steep climb, made rougher going by taking the wrong bank, but he reached the summit (2323 feet) by 6 *p.m.* and sat for a while enjoying the view till sunset. The only map he had was the geological one made by Ada's grandfather, with very few place-names, but comparing it with his guide book he thought he could keep along the hill side to pick up a stream leading down by Coledale Tarn to Easdale Tarn, which he hoped to reach by dark. He had difficulty in finding the right stream and wasted more time, finally reaching the tarn after running most of the way, stumbling and falling and tearing off his big toe-nail on a stone hidden in the bracken. By now it was so dark he could not see his map and was in a quandary which way to turn, fearing that if he took the wrong side of the tarn he might find the mountain went sheer into it, making a passage on that side dangerous or impossible. He began to have visions of his anxious wife if he failed to get back before morning. In this predicament he fell on his knees in the heather, beseeching God to guide him. His account of what followed reads

> I rose from my knees and turning to the left ran at once in that direction, leaping from tuft to tuft of heath or firm grass. I ran thus fifty or a hundred paces, then, without . . . any deliberation or effort of will even, but as it were by a pure, irrational impulse, I

wheeled about as a runner wheels who turns a post, retraced my course, passed the heather tussock on which I had prayed, jumped across the stream which flowed into the lake, ran straight on without stopping across the level and up a slope, and all at once found my foot on a good firm path across which I came at rightangles.

Soon, following this path, he fell in with the Easdale guide, who gave him some coffee in his hut and then took him by moonlight down to Grasmere, and so 'running, limping, shuffling and hopping', back to Ambleside between ten and eleven o'clock at night, having walked at least 20 miles and climbed over 2000 feet since lunch. Thinking over this adventure and the incident at the head of the tarn he felt it to be 'one of the most mysterious' in his life, 'as wonderful to me at the moment, as it is now; only I was in too breathless a haste to speculate upon it'. For the left hand route he had, he said,

> a sort of dim prepossession that this was the likely side to get round the lake ... This, I say, may be explained as semi-conscious cerebration; but of the sudden and instantaneous wheel-about I have absolutely no explanation save that it was God's answer to my prayer: and such I have ever felt it. One does not proclaim these things on the housetops or write about them in the magazines: they are too sacred; but they are among the most profound convictions of one's soul: and, many a time since then, my faith in the invisible has been restored by remembering my experience at Easdale Tarn.

The incidents at Hastings and at Easdale Tarn were paralleled by another at about this date. He was caught in a thick mist on a mountain with the children, when once again a black dog appeared and they halted. When the mist lifted they found they were on the edge of a dangerous precipice and the dog had disappeared. All these happenings combined to give James a sense of a special providence protecting him. As the years went on he came to believe that it was for his work on the Dictionary that his life had been preserved.

In 1878 James was forty-one and it seemed as though he had really found his vocation. In spite of its problems, he loved the life at Mill Hill school and his contact with the boys. He was likely to become Headmaster there, if not elsewhere, before long. He had time for research and no lack of literary work to do: he had secured his doctorate and his recognition in his chosen field of study. It was at this stage that he took the most important decision of his life, and in agreeing to undertake to edit the *New English Dictionary*, he bound himself to an exacting servitude which was to last the rest of his life.

To explain why this came about it is necessary to describe how the materials for a new dictionary, which Furnivall had been collecting for the Philological Society for the past twenty years, were accepted for publication by the Clarendon Press at Oxford, on condition that James Murray was the editor.

CHAPTER VII

The Web is Spun:
Abortive Negotiations with Macmillan

ALTHOUGH, as will be seen, James Murray knew something of the project of the Philological Society to publish a new English Dictionary, he had not been directly involved and the first suggestion that he might turn his hand to lexicography came to him as a complete surprise. On 4 April 1876 he found in his post a letter from Alexander Macmillan, head of the publishing firm, saying that Richard Morris (at that time President of the Philological Society) had suggested his name in connection with a work they wanted done, could he come and have a talk?[1]

When the interview took place, James learned that Macmillan had been approached by the American publisher, Harper, to cooperate in producing a new standard English Dictionary and that they were looking for an editor. Since the publication of Samuel Johnson's famous Dictionary over a hundred years before, apart from fresh editions of his work, only three important dictionaries of English had been produced—that of Charles Richardson in England (1836–7) and those of Noah Webster (1828 and later) and Joseph Worcester (1846 and 1860) in America. Harper's idea was for something 'like Webster, in bulk, and as far superior in quality as possible'. This was a challenge, since Webster's original Dictionary, published in 1828, had been very much improved and enlarged, and the latest edition, the 'unabridged' of 1864, had acquired an international fame. It was held to be superior to every other dictionary and taken as the leading authority on the meaning of words, not only in America and England but also throughout the Far East.[2]

Although James had up to this time made no special study of lexicography, he was interested. He knew that existing dictionaries were out of date, not only because of the new words that had come into the language since they were compiled, but because in aim and method they had been superseded by advances in lexicography on the Continent.[3]

The most original feature of Johnson's Dictionary was the illustration of the use of words by literary quotations, but though his book was remarkable as the work of one man, he could not hope to cover the vast field of English literature and even his prodigious memory sometimes played him false. He also started with the idea that the purpose of a dictionary should be to establish a permanent standard of good literary English, by registering the sense of every word and phrase as used by writers of the Golden Age—'the wells of English undefiled'. Although he soon realised the fallacy of this ideal—language is a constantly changing, growing thing and cannot be standardised and preserved forever as it was at any particular point in time by excluding new words because they are considered decadent—none the less he restricted his field. He took his examples mainly from writers between Sir Philip Sidney and the Restoration.[4]

Charles Richardson, like Johnson, sought to guide his readers to the true meaning of each word and developed Johnson's idea of quotations to the extent of relying wholly on these to convey the meaning of words and dispensing with definitions. A serious weakness of his work was that he was a disciple of the school of English philologists represented by John Horne Tooke, to whose *Diversions of Purley* (1786) is attributed the backwater into which English philology was channelled in the early years of the nineteenth century. This school confused the scientific study of the established facts relating to language with philosophical speculation on the origins of thought and speech and sought to prove their theories by conjectural etymologies based on superficial similarities in the forms of words.[5]

From its foundation the Philological Society had avoided these speculations and its members were largely responsible for bringing English studies into the main stream of linguistic research as it had developed on the Continent. James Murray would have heard reference to this and no doubt discussed the matter with Alexander Ellis, who had spoken eloquently on the subject in his presidential address in 1873, at which Murray was present. Ellis argued that questions on the origin of language were outside the field of philology, maintaining 'We have to investigate what *is* . . . We shall do more by tracing the historical growth of one single work-a-day tongue, than by filling waste-paper baskets with reams of paper covered with speculations on the origin of all tongues.'[6] We have already seen how closely James applied this principle in his accurate research into dialects.

Although Webster's etymologies, which had also been guess-work, had been completely revised by a competent scholar in the later editions, James thought he could do better in what was a comparatively new science. He also saw in Macmillan's proposal the chance to compile a dictionary with a different emphasis, which, in line with new theories of lexicography, would attempt to trace the history of every word included. He knew that the Philological Society twenty years before had proposed to publish just such a dictionary and had started to get together materials for it.[7]

The project to collect words for a supplement to existing dictionaries, had been launched in 1857 by three members of the Society, Dr Richard Chenevix Trench, then Dean of Westminster, Herbert Coleridge, and Frederick Furnivall. To this end they had enlisted volunteers to read books. Less than a year later, Furnivall, having come to the conclusion that the Supplement was going to be bigger than the originals and that it was too laborious to have to check every dictionary to see whether a word was already registered or not, persuaded the others to change the scheme. The more ambitious idea of producing a complete *New English Dictionary* was launched with all the patriotism and enthusiasm of which Furnivall and his friends were capable and with the flowery eloquence with which James Murray was at that time addressing his Hawick audiences. They felt it to be a national disgrace that there was no adequate dictionary of English. Trench wrote 'the love of our own language, what is it . . . but the love of our country expressing itself in one particular direction?' and in another place 'language may be regarded as "a moral barometer", which indicates and permanently marks the rise or fall of a nation's life.'[8]

In planning the work Trench adopted the historical principle in lexicography, first stated by a German, Franz-Passow, in 1812, which had already been followed in England by H. G. Liddell and R. Scott in their *Greek-English Lexicon* (1843). The aim was to show the life history of every word, its origin and any changes of form and meaning. As an historian of the language, not a critic, the lexicographer's task was to collect *all* words, rather than to select *good* words, and whereas quotations were used by Johnson and his successors to define words, now their chief use would be to show historical changes of sense.[9]

The method of work was also borrowed from the Germans. Although Noah Webster had compiled the early editions of his Dictionary single handed, and in France Émile Littré at sixty-one was about to begin his thirteen year task of producing an historical dictionary of the French language, these were the last great dictionaries to be the work of one man. In Germany the brothers Jacob and Wilhelm Grimm were working on the *Deutsches Wörterbuch* with the aid of a team of helpers. Building on their experience Trench declared that

> this almost boundless field could only be made available for dictionary purposes through the combined action of many . . . this drawing as with a sweep-net over the whole extent of English literature, is that which we would fain see; which we would count it an honour to be the means of organizing and setting forward; being sure that it is only by such combined action, by such a joining of hand in hand on the part of as many as are willing to take their share in this toil, that we can hope the innumerable words . . . which are lurking unnoticed in every corner of our literature, will ever be brought within our net.[10]

Herbert Coleridge as editor had a set of fifty-four pigeon-holes made which would hold 100,000 slips and confidently announced in May 1860 that when these were full—probably in two years time—publication could begin, 'unless any unforeseen accident should occur to paralyse our efforts'.* Unhappily, just such an accident did occur. Coleridge died in 1861 at the early age of 31, from consumption brought on by a chill caused by sitting in damp clothes during a Philological Society lecture. When he was told that he would not recover he is reported to have exclaimed, 'I must begin Sanskrit tomorrow', and he died working on the Dictionary to the last, with quotation slips and word-lists spread on the quilt of his bed. In these tragic circumstances he persuaded Furnivall to take on the editorship and to promise to see this magnificent project through to a conclusion.[11]

---

* The pigeon-holes are preserved by the Oxford University Press. Some 2500 holes of this size would have been needed to hold the 5–6 million slips eventually collected.

In a report on progress in 1862 Furnivall issued one of his characteristic clarion calls for helpers:

> We have set ourselves to form a National Portrait Gallery, not only of the worthies, but of all the members, of the race of English words which is to form the dominant speech of the world. No winged messenger who bears to us the thoughts and aspirations, the weakness and the littleness, of our forefathers; who is to carry ours to our descendants: is to be absent, —
>   Fling our doors wide! all, all, not one, but all,
> must enter: for their service let them be honoured; and though the search for them may sometimes seem wearisome, and the labour of the ingathering more irksome still, yet the work is worthy and the aim unselfish. Let us, then, persevere.[12]

When Trench became Archbishop of Dublin and left London in 1863, the whole burden fell on Furnivall, who continued to persevere and was to be associated with the Dictionary until his death in 1910. As an editor Furnivall lacked the accuracy and the patience essential, but his sustained enthusiasm—however misdirected—was impressive. He felt himself bound by a solemn obligation to his dead friend and to his country to overcome all obstacles to the publication of the 'Society's Big Dictionary' launched with such fervour by the original committee.

It was the first work to which Furnivall applied the cooperative principle which he used in each of the many societies he later founded. The plan laid down by Coleridge was to appeal for voluntary help from members of the Society and from the public. Owing to Trench's books and lectures which had popularised language study, the response was, surprisingly, better from non-members. The helpers were asked to undertake to read books and to extract quotations illustrating the use of the words in them. These quotations were written on half sheets of notepaper with the head word in the left hand corner. For convenience, Coleridge divided English literature into three periods: 1250–1526 (Tyndale's *New Testament*), 1526–1674 (death of Milton) and 1674 onwards. The aim was to find at least one quotation for every word and sense for each of the three periods, including the earliest example for the period in which the word came into the language. To aid collectors in identifying unrecorded words, lists were provided as a 'basis for comparison'. Coleridge himself compiled a list for the first period, and the Concordances to the Bible and to Shakespeare were used for the middle period.

Frederick Furnivall as editor worked with more enthusiasm than order. A visitor in May 1862 found him in a dingy upstairs room 'the walls & floor and chairs strewn with books, papers, proofs, clothes, everything—in wondrous confusion; the table spread with a meal of chaotic and incongruous dishes.' After a vegetarian banquet of roast potatoes, asparagus and coffee, which lasted from seven till nine, Furnivall set his guests to work with him arranging and writing out words for the Dictionary. His future wife, the lady's maid he was educating, acted as secretary.[13]

From the experience thus gained two important modifications and one vital addition to the scheme were introduced. First, with a clearer idea of the time it was going to take to deal with the material, Furnivall induced the Society in 1862 to accept the need to prepare an interim publication which he called a concise Dictionary, the main purpose of which was to show the gaps still to be filled. At his own expense he made a contract with John Murray to publish this in three years: the full Dictionary would then, he considered, need 'only the sculptors' touches' and another three years would see it also finished.[14]

A second change was to introduce sub-editors, volunteers 'with any qualifications for the task', who should work on the slips sent in by the readers, each taking a letter or part of a letter of the alphabet, filling gaps, supplying definitions and if possible etymologies. At first Furnivall thought there should be no quotations in the concise version, then he changed his mind, and instructed sub-editors to give them where they seemed essential to prove the use and sense of the word, but only one 'and that the pattest'. Meanwhile the Big Dictionary was not to be lost sight of and he concluded his instructions with a typical piece of 'Furnivallese'

> Lastly, having finished the strict business of an Article, I exhort you, for the Full Dictionary, to indulge in a little chat with your Reader, noting for him the chief points of interest in the history you have set before him, moralizing shortly on them if you will, and giving any additional facts . . . in short, telling him all you wish him to hear. Being good sense and well put, as of course it will be, Editor and Publisher will be only too glad to find room for it.[15]

Furnivall's great contribution to the Dictionary was the recognition that as planned it could not be produced, or at any rate could not be complete, while the study of the early period of English literature remained in its rudimentary stage. The problem had been touched on in the original proposal for the Dictionary, and he now founded the Early English Text Society, the work of which has already been described,[16] as an aid to the Dictionary, to make accessible to the corps of voluntary readers the literature of the earliest period. First he persuaded the Philological Society to publish some texts as an appendage to its Transactions and when this led to financial problems, he set up the independent society.[17]

For the first few years Furnivall issued enthusiastic and encouraging reports: slips were pouring in every day from readers; the work of the sub-editors was going forward; lists of books to be read were circulated and the books taken up at once. The bad writing of some of the readers was a hindrance: an exasperated sub-editor wrote in 1865, 'Is there no punishment for illegible writing beyond the private maledictions of infuriated sub-editors?'[18]

To save time and make for clarity, Furnivall started buying books which were then offered to readers for marking or cutting up. He told James Murray later only to offer cheap or second-hand ones from Mudies Lending Library, explaining, 'I used to buy dear old ones, but men often bagd 'em & sent me no slips. One man had about £5 worth.'[19] Nevertheless a number of valuable old books did get cut up, and a lover of them would be horrified to see the earliest dictionary slips with bits of black letter editions of the sixteenth century pasted onto them.[20]

But as time went on there seemed no end in sight. For books read there were always as many still to be dealt with. Readers began to lose interest and fall off and so did sub-editors. Some grew too old or became sick. In May 1868 the *Athenaeum* reported that 'the general belief is, that the project will not be carried out'.[21] Furnivall himself had diverted his interest to his other manifold activities and without his drive the machine ground slowly to a halt. His reports to the Society became shorter and finally ceased altogether, but occasionally he was roused to fresh efforts by the impatience of some sub-editor inquiring what was being done with the fruit of his labour.

James Murray was a member of the Council of the Philological Society in April 1871 when, because of one of these prods, a sub-committee was set up to consider the present state of the Dictionary.[22] As a result in October Furnivall appealed for a new editor. He persuaded Henry Nicol to undertake the task, Sweet having already refused, but Nicol was a sick man with much work of his own on hand

and he did nothing. In 1875 the matter was again brought to the fore when the Rev. George Wheelwright of East Grinstead, sub-editor of F, complained that he had given ten years of his life to the work in the belief that the Philological Society knew what they were about and that they were not started on a 'Fools chace which should end only in a general fiasco'. He pressed Furnivall to make up his mind to do something to end what he described as 'the intolerable suspense under which we now groan'.[23]

Once again Furnivall took up the cudgels. He now realised that Henry Nicol's state of health made him a bad choice and he looked about for someone else. A chance remark of James Murray, who in discussing the matter with him had been rash enough to say he rather wished he could have a go at it himself—not intending this to be taken seriously—gave Furnivall an idea. Without telling James, he seems to have persuaded some prominent members of the Society that this man might turn out to be the editor they had all been hoping for.[24] At the same time he was exploring means of financing the project and in March 1876 James Murray was in the Chair at a meeting of the Philological Society Council at which Furnivall reported that Walter Skeat had been authorised to try to get £500 a year for at least two years from the Clarendon Press at Oxford to pay an editor's salary.[25]

When the Macmillans approached James Murray for their proposed Dictionary he at once got into touch with Skeat to find out what progress he had made at Oxford. He learned that Skeat had made no move, because his own experience as a sub-editor had convinced him that the 'Big Dictionary' was impracticable. As long ago as November 1865 he had warned Furnivall that it would be 'far more enormous than one would suppose could possibly *sell*—far too large to be printed at anything but a frightful expenditure of money.'[26]

Skeat liked the idea of the shorter work Macmillan had in mind and saw no reason why James should not be allowed to use the Society's materials for it, indeed he said it would be 'a great thing for England' if they could really get something done at last. He advised James that sooner or later Furnivall would have to be consulted, since he alone knew who the sub-editors were and where much of the results of their work could be found, but he warned him, in view of a request for confidentiality made by Harper that,

if it can be managed without Mr Furnivall till all is fairly in order, it will certainly be best. Without doubt, he will publish all he knows about it at the earliest opportunity. I have told him plainly, often, that this is often annoying: but, though he is at heart one of the best of men, he will not take *that* hint.[27]

Good advice—but almost certainly Furnivall was already informed about the project: he knew Macmillan well, having been a member of the 'weekly tobacco Parliament' which the publisher held for literary men in the early 1860s,[28] and he later claimed that Morris had acted on his suggestion in recommending James Murray.[29] Certainly Furnivall was soon happily scheming away with his usual good intentions but lack of tact.

The Dictionary, James now found, was not to be Macmillan's Dictionary, or Murray's Dictionary, but the Philological Society's Dictionary, and Furnivall in a number of letters made this quite clear.

> On the whole, I look on it, that Mcm. takes up the Phil. Soc. Dicty . . . & accepts our Editor, you. We don't use our material for his notion . . .[30]

> Of course we mustn't give Mcm. too much for too little. It must be *the Society's Dicty.* We must have the appointment of the Edr. from time to time, or a voice in it; & the material must be preserved & belong to us.[31]

Discounting the great capital outlay involved, Furnivall still believed any publisher should welcome the chance to print the Dictionary. He had learnt little from his dealings with John Murray. In 1858 John Murray had categorically refused to bind his firm to publish a work which he had not seen, over the contents of which he would have no control and the probable extent of which was 'undefined and unlimited'.[32] Furnivall was confident that the agreement with Macmillan would go through, and thought he could drive a hard bargain with them by threatening them with going to other firms if their terms did not seem good enough.

At first the negotiations went well. James and the Macmillans, father and son, took to each other and Furnivall began by urging James not to ask too much, telling him, 'There'll be pay hanging to future abridgments & the big book & a share in the royalty.'[33] The present scheme itself was thought of only as an abridgment—a selection from all the quotations collected which it was still hoped would be published eventually in the Big Dictionary. It was to be the Concise work which Furnivall had proposed but slightly better in giving some quotations as well as references.[34]

Furnivall was now jubilant at the prospect that at last the publication seemed in sight, welcoming this as a great chance on no account to be missed. He produced the quotations for C, which had been brought to a fair state of completion by the sub-editor concerned, and addressing James already as 'Mr Editor' sent the slips to him as 'The first lot of some thousands that'll come in to you I trust.' Acting as if everything were already settled he instructed him, 'You might as well begin at once to mark all the papers & books you read, & hand them over to your boy [surely not Harold, now aged eight!] to cut out the extracts & put references.'[35] He estimated that the publication would take ten years and should start three years after the agreement with the publishers was signed,[36] and in November he urged James to get

> a sorter and preparer of work *at once*, & use the 5 weeks before Xmas, so as to be ready to work early in the year. There's much to be done in sorting slips up for yourself & sub-editors, arranging what books are to be read, ordering printed slips for 'em etc. etc. When we appeal for fresh help, we want the material ready to put into volunteers' hands as soon as its askt for. It doesn't do to keep a man waiting 6 weeks: he cools. You'll want every day of your time.[37]

And five days later: 'Send me my illegible slips. When you've a Mus[eu]m Clerk, I rely on you not to set aside a slip because you're not certain of it. Let the Clerk refer & make it certain.' Once again he reminded James to write larger, 'Give *3 times* the space to each word that you generally do. My own sins enable me to advise you.'[38]

Meanwhile the main bar to the completion of the negotiations was that of size. Harper had thought of 2000 pages and would not go beyond 4000 as a maximum.[39] James was sure that this was too cramping and hoped to push them to 5000. The Society thought 6000 would be necessary, but Furnivall urged James not to worry. The book could no doubt be enlarged, and he asserted 'if Mcm sees the thing goes well, he'll extend it, I expect . . . 4000 pages'll let you do a good deal. Afterwards we can turn it into 12,000 or 20,000 if the Gods are propitious.'[40]

The Macmillans were in fact extremely anxious to reach a compromise and arranged with James that he should experiment with them in setting up a specimen in type.[41] Between mid October and mid November he worked away with proof after proof—nine in all—

trying to save space without using inconveniently small type. On 3 November he reported to the Philological Society Council that he thought he could get what he wanted into 4800 pages, and on the 17th that the Macmillans seemed disposed to agree.[42]

But all the time Furnivall was playing a double game. From the first he was anxious not to lose sight of the Big Dictionary, and in October once again he sought, unsuccessfully, to get Skeat to approach the Clarendon Press. He had in mind to try to get some publisher—if not Oxford then another—to make an offer so that he could threaten Macmillan with going elsewhere if he would not accept his conditions.[43] The first hint that all was not above board was conveyed to Macmillan at a meeting on 16 October. Furnivall created a bad impression by asking for the refund to himself of £610 which he had advanced to John Murray in 1858 for the publication of the concise Dictionary which had never appeared. The Macmillans were disappointed that it seemed as though the Society was going to give only 'grudging and difficult' cooperation instead of the enthusiastic help which Furnivall had at first promised. They were also disturbed to learn that there had been talk of seeking another publisher before the results of their experiment in type-setting were known. James did his best to allay their fears and like the Macmillans still hoped to reach agreement, and they continued to work on the specimen pages.[44] It was December when Furnivall finally showed his hand, setting out the conditions under which the Society's materials might be used in a tactless letter, charging the Macmillans with having from the first considered too much their own interests and stating that unless the firm would agree to give the Society half profits the Society would wait till they could get a fairer deal elsewhere.[45]

The Macmillans were furious. The letter went completely against the terms which they thought had been accepted the previous October and which had not been questioned since, and they considered that Furnivall had wasted their time and that there was now no prospect of any practical arrangements being made. Alexander Macmillan wrote to James: 'It is a pity that his pretty playful ways should ever be intruded into serious business',[46] while Dr Jack, who had conducted the negotiations on behalf of the firm, commented sarcastically on Furnivall's letter:

A more ingenious perversion of the spirit in which we supposed our famous interview [16 October] to have taken place, it is difficult to

imagine . . . The 'incredulous smile' which he was compelled by
considerations of higher policy to restrain, and the gentle but
unobtrusive efforts by which he proposed to lift us to a higher
platform then, reserving the completion of our education till he
should be ready to resume it a few months later, are to me
charming.[47]

Up to this point the Macmillans had been hopeful of getting Harper's
agreement on size, and they regarded Furnivall as entirely to blame in
breaking off the negotiations.

It was infuriating at the time, but in the long run the breakdown
was fortunate. It is unlikely that the Macmillans could have sustained
the great cost of publishing the *New English Dictionary* on the scale in
which it finally appeared, and the firm had no regrets later that they
had not gone ahead.[48] Had they produced the short Dictionary they
were considering, it is doubtful whether a more ambitious project
would ever have materialised.

At the time James Murray seemed less disappointed than the
Macmillans were. Having found out something of what would be
involved, he had become very doubtful if he really wanted to take on
the editorship. It was true there were things about it which tempted
him. He found the Macmillans people he could work with, and they
remained his close friends. Again, there was a fascination in the work,
and having handled some of the Dictionary slips he knew that the
material was valuable and ought to be used, while although the many
scholars to whom he showed his specimen sheets seemed to delight in
tearing them to pieces and finding endless matters of principle or
detail with which to disagree, some whose opinion he respected were
enthusiastic. Dr Jack, recognising the contribution that the
Dictionary could be to English scholarship, told James that the
Dictionary would make him famous; Russell Martineau, an
orientalist who was Assistant Keeper in the British Museum Library,
thought the general appearance and literary work 'simply perfect',
adding, 'Nothing must prevent your doing the work now'; while John
B. Mayor, Professor of Latin at Cambridge, who had been very
critical of the sample prepared by the sub-editor George Wheelwright
a few years earlier, thought it looked very promising.[49]

On the other hand, James now knew that the task of a lexicographer
was a very burdensome one. He had slaved over the specimen sheets
in the only time which he could spare from his teaching and other

work, which was at night. '*Do* sleep! *Please* take this advice' Ellis urged him[50] as for two months he tried out his solutions to the problems and sought to meet the suggestions of others, which he found 'a timewasting and wearying task.'[51] His keen conscience and desire for perfection would not let him rest until the work was as good as he could make it, and criticism worried him. Friends who were bluntly outspoken were sometimes upset to find how seriously he took ideas meant just for consideration. He was very different from the tough-skinned Skeat, who described himself as rarely depressed and 'buoyant as a cork'. Skeat advised him to follow his example, use what criticism he could, disregard the rest and do exactly as he pleased, telling everyone 'This is how *I* mean to do it: & when *you* rewrite the book, then & not till then you can do it *your* way.'[52] He said that he himself would ask for no reason if James rejected his suggestions. Furnivall also told him, 'Don't be disgusted by criticism. If you'd only had as much abuse as I, you wouldn't mind it, except as giving you a chance of telling critics what geese they are.'[53]

This was sound advice, echoed by Alexander Ellis and Henry Nicol, but advice which James found it hard to act upon. He remained always extremely sensitive to the opinions of others and was to spend much time he could ill afford writing long letters justifying his point of view, or showing where adverse critics were at fault.

So now he was torn between reluctance to throw into the waste-paper basket all the work that he had done, and relief to be quit of it. Fundamentally he was not ambitious: if the work was worth doing and he found it enjoyable, that was enough, and though convinced that the Dictionary ought to be published he was hopeful that another editor might be found. He persuaded himself that he was glad now to be free to continue his teaching and retain the hope of a headship. At about this time he was considering an invitation to apply for the Principalship of Huddersfield College. He had been shocked at Furnivall's suggestion that he could easily combine this with doing the Dictionary, by letting his name appear on the title page 'for fame & ultimate profits' sake', while someone else should do the actual work and take any pay, he himself just giving a couple of hours a day to the final revision. The suggestion illustrates the difference between the two men.[54] For Furnivall the end would always justify the means, for James hoodwinking the public was unthinkable.

In imagining that he could get out of the Dictionary so easily James misjudged the persistence of Furnivall and the effect of the work he

had already done on his fellow philologists. In spite of their criticisms
they realised that he had gone further in investigating the practical
details of the work than either Furnivall or anyone else had yet done.
Furnivall, for instance, dismissed the important questions of
principle which James raised as a result of his experiments for
Macmillan, as not needing a minute's hesitation to answer, saying
'We folk of the old Dict. settled 'em all, 18 years ago, and I've never
seen cause to doubt the judgement since.' He declared that every boy
of ten knew the answers to James' 'quibbles'.[55] Reacting to Furnivall's
superficial ruling that the criterion for the admission or omission of a
word was whether a quotation had been found for it or not, James
poured out his indignation to Alexander Ellis saying:

> Very good! but the world learns a little in 18 years, & even school-
> boys of 11 become men of 30 in that time & a little less certain about
> things they received as gospel at 11. And I can only say, that, if the
> Committee of 18 years ago, decided in cold blood that 'carriageless'
> and 'carriagewards' should go in because a quotation for them has
> been found, & e.g. 'wheelbarrowless' and 'wheelbarrowwards' to
> stay out because quotations have not been found, I think they were
> wise men of Gotham and I'm glad I was not one of them. In short if
> the Society holds to this principle now, the Dictionary shall not be
> edited by *me*; that is certain. I have *some* method in my madness,
> and I dont for words of that kind believe in the quotation test at all
> . . . because you know that not one millionth of current literature is
> read, & that it is the veriest chance or succession of chances which
> has caught *carriageless* and 'carriagewards' & missed a thousand
> others as good . . . I certainly will not agree to the dicta pronounced
> in Mr Furnivall's letter—nor will any possible editor but himself,
> & the thing may go to rest for another 18 years, till all who left
> Egypt have fallen without a sight of the promised land.[56]

In long discussions in the Council of the Philological Society, other
members came to recognise that James was right: there were indeed
very great problems to be settled, and Ellis replied to his letter

> The great advantage of our last week's discussion was to shew the
> crudeness of all our thoughts, arising from not having worked out
> the matter by actual trial. Furnivall wd say that's not true, he has.
> But I don't think he has at all, so as to come face to face with these
> difficulties.[57]

The result was that the leaders of the Society were prepared to back James against Furnivall, and to agree that whoever became editor must be free to go his own way and could not be bound by the *Canones Lexicographici* issued by the 'old men' in 1860. Moreover James had demonstrated what an amount of exact, tedious work would have to be done by the editor and they all knew now that they did not want the task and that James Murray alone was the man with the qualifications and the character to make the ideal cherished for so long by the Society into a reality. James might think that he was still free to say no. In fact it was already too late to escape.

CHAPTER VIII

The Fly is Caught:
Negotiations with the Delegates of the
Oxford University Press

FREDERICK Furnivall took the breakdown of the negotiations with Macmillan merely as a challenge to show that he could do better. He could not afford to accept defeat: his unfulfilled promise to the dying Coleridge and the complaints of the voluntary readers and sub-editors whose time he had wasted, weighed upon him. Paradoxically the history of the prolonged attempts to reach agreement with a publisher shows that while no one worked harder than Furnivall to get publication started, no one did more to cause difficulties. His impetuosity, tactlessness and frequent downright rudeness, time and again imperilled the whole project, and yet it was his persistence which saved it.

Two days after wrecking the Macmillan proposal, Furnivall asked James when he would like a committee to meet to discuss the next step and instructed him to prepare specimens to tempt publishers. He had already asked Walter Skeat to make a start by approaching the Syndics of the Cambridge University Press.[1] Skeat however soon found that his mission was foredoomed to failure, because Cambridge would have nothing to do with any scheme with which Furnivall was associated.

> Somehow, he isn't believed in at the Universities [Skeat told Murray later] . . . It has arisen from his odd prefaces, etc., & modes of expression—And your present chance, a good one, will all come to grief unless you listen to all he says, & then *systematically & effectively disregard* it all in practice.[2]

> None the less, Skeat was willing, if Furnivall agreed, to try Oxford next, but with a modified scheme, 'a big reference book of dated quotations, in fact, something like Richardson, multiplied by 6 or 10', with only very brief definitions and no etymologies or pronunciations.[3]

Neither Furnivall nor Murray was interested in such a limited project; Skeat's offer was not taken up and he and other influential members of the Society seem to have been kept in the dark as to the next moves of the Dictionary Committee, which consisted of Furnivall, Ellis, Morris, and Sweet, who as President of the Society took the initiative.[4]

The first matter was to settle the editorship. Furnivall had led Skeat to suppose that as James had decided not to apply for the post at Huddersfield he was now quite prepared to undertake the Dictionary. But James told Skeat that this was not the case. The abortive negotiations with Macmillan had, as we have seen, left him discouraged and much inclined to wash his hands of a project which from his experience of the past year, seemed a very doubtful starter. Henry Nicol's name was again suggested and he was willing to be editor, but not until he had completed other work.[5] Any delay was unacceptable to Furnivall and by April 1877 James Murray had been named again. Furnivall later claimed that it was at James' request that he nominated him, but James' version was, 'This is absolutely untrue, I never requested, never intended to be Editor'. He remained resistant to the schemes of Furnivall and the persuasions of Alexander Macmillan, who continued to interest himself in the Dictionary and who now helped to pave the way for an approach to Oxford.[6]

It was Henry Sweet who wrote on 20 April 1877 to Dr Bartholomew Price, Secretary to the Delegates of the University Press, suggesting terms (which were substantially identical with those agreed by Macmillan), under which the Society's materials would be made available, and mentioning James Murray as Editor, apparently without having obtained his consent.* Sweet's father was a solicitor and advised on the legal aspects, while Furnivall provided the data. The letter was a piece of clever salesmanship and presented the project in a most attractive light. The material offered was the fruit of nineteen years' labour, for the quality of which the reputation of the Society was a guarantee. Half of it was said to be already sub-edited and ready for publication, the remainder was sorted and would be prepared by James Murray under the general supervision of the Society. 'We are not', Sweet wrote, 'asking [the Delegates] to subsidize an unremunerative undertaking, but are rather offering them a share in what promises to be a very safe and remunerative one',

---

* See Appendix I, p. 342.

in return for providing the editor's salary and expenses and making the business arrangements. An historical dictionary of this kind would be without rival and would have an assured sale in Great Britain, its colonies and dependencies, the United States and the civilised world generally. Sweet reminded the Delegates of the success of Littré's French Dictionary, published in four large quarto volumes of 1000 pages each, at £4 the set, of which upwards of 40,000 copies had been sold.[7] Unfortunately, for both publishers and editor, Sweet's account was misleadingly optimistic: it deceived James into thinking that his task would be much less formidable than it proved, and still more disastrously for him, it gave the Delegates an expectation of handsome profits within a comparatively short time.

The letter came before the Delegates on 1 May, and was deferred for further consideration, but Sweet and Furnivall, in touch with influential Oxford friends, thought the auguries were good and reported that some of the Delegates were very taken with the idea.[8] Dr Price himself had some doubts about Murray because he associated him with a book of specimens of Scottish texts, for which James had entered into an agreement in 1873, for completion by September 1874, and for which the Press was still waiting. Naturally Price wondered if this man could be relied upon to edit a great work like a dictionary if he could not produce a small text book.[9] He also had some doubts about the viability of the work financially, but he was directed by the Delegates to ask for specimens of the material, of the work of the sub-editors and of the text as finally revised by the editor.[10] This gave Furnivall an opening, and he wrote persuasively to Price telling him 'with what is done, & what can be added during the editing of the book, we can produce a Dictionary which, with its abridgements, can beat everything in the market.'[11] 'As to the *paying* . . . Do ask yourself whether such a keen set as Macmillans firm would have proposed to take it up if they didn't see their way clear to a certain success.'[12]

At once he sent Price lists of readers and books read and directed sub-editors to send samples of their work direct to the Press. Soon Price had to write begging Furnivall to stay the flood of Dictionary slips which threatened to overwhelm him.[13] The Macmillans consented to the specimens which had been prepared for them being shown,[14] although James explained that these had been for a work limited to four to five thousand pages and that he could do better if Sweet's suggestion of six and a half thousand were accepted. Sweet warned him to expect some criticism, and to show the Delegates every deference in considering their comments. 'When we have once got over their chief objections they will leave the Editor entirely to himself', he commented, adding cynically that the Delegates 'naturally like to make as many criticisms as possible in order to show their sharpness and wideawakeness'.[15]

The Delegate principally concerned was Friedrich Max Müller, trained in philology in Leipzig, who had come to Oxford in 1848 and was now the first Professor of Comparative Philology, with a reputation as an orientalist and Sanskrit scholar. He recognised that the Philological Society's materials constituted a nucleus which could well form the basis of a work of national importance, in the same class as Littré in France and the Grimm brothers' German Dictionary, but that this would depend on how thoroughly the preliminary work had been done. He saw clearly that only the editorial work would reveal whether the instructions given to the voluntary readers had been adequate, and that there was a danger that they might have concentrated on the exceptional words used in exceptional senses and overlooked the common words. He noted that while there were scholars of repute amongst the contributors, others were unknown men, and that the list of books read—in some respects in his opinion too long—included some unimportant works and omitted some classics.[16] However, no doubt on Max Müller's recommendation the Delegates asked James to prepare further specimens.[17] This he agreed to do, choosing, after some experiment, four words, *arrow*, *carouse*, *castle* and *persuade*, for which sub-edited material was available. These were to be written up during the long vacation for submission to the Delegates in the autumn.

James thought his task would be easier this time, because he had already settled some of the technical problems, so he did not allow it to interrupt the family holiday in the Lake District. Back at Mill Hill, however, it proved gruelling work on top of the school demands, and it took till the end of November to get the proofs into the form which he and Price agreed were good enough to show to the Delegates.[18] But first, on Price's advice, he asked Max Müller for his comments. Unfortunately this led to difficulties about which James unburdened himself to Alexander Ellis. He found Max Müller's criticism of his etymologies impossible to meet. Having said that the derivations were 'as far as he knows, quite right', Müller had then proceeded to differ about one.

Now this [wrote James] drives me to my wits' end. Here is a third hypothetic derivation, which one cannot say is either better or worse than the other two. But Max Müller prefers it: he is a delegate, & one might offend him to omit it. But to give all 3 . . . traverses his expressed opinion that it is hardly the province of the work to enter on conjectural etymologies. What shall I do? I am sorely tempted to confess ignorance & say 'Der[ivation] quite uncert[ain] . . . Yet as Etymologies *have* been offered, it seems as if one did not know, to omit them entirely . . . If I add M.M's to the other 2, it makes 3 lines more & I don't know where to save them.[19]

It was in a dispirited, exhausted mood that James awaited the verdict of the Delegates. On 4 December 1877 Dr Price conveyed their views on the specimens to him. It was as bad, or worse, than he had anticipated. First they asked for more evidence that the search for words had been thorough and efficient. Price said that they only asked this because they were sure that the information would be easily obtained, but in fact this was just the question that the system of voluntary readers made it impossible for anyone at this stage to answer. Apart from this the Delegates concentrated on two features vital to the whole plan of the Dictionary.[20] They rejected James' scheme for indicating pronunciation, and what was more serious, suggested that the etymological part, which they did not much like, should be very much modified, or entirely omitted. In this view they were influenced by the fact that at the very same meeting at which James' specimens were considered, they had accepted for publication an etymological dictionary by Walter Skeat.[21] Well-meaning Walter, concluding from the lack of news since March that the idea of getting the Society's Dictionary published had again been dropped, had on his own account approached the Delegates with a dictionary on which he had been working for some years. He told James about it when the Press had set up some trial pages, explaining that he wanted to keep it secret from Furnivall until the agreement was signed. The last thing he had intended was to enter into competition, but he had acted on his own idea that the Society's Dictionary, if ever produced, would not go fully into etymologies but would concentrate on definitions and usages supported by quotations. He still hoped that his work would save the time of James or any other editor and that they could help each other by exchanging proofs. James sent him his specimens and Skeat was enthusiastic about them. 'What a splendid bit of work it is, & how delightfully legible!' he wrote, but he also suggested space and time-saving expedients.

> *Arrowsmith* [he commented] I don't think it is *modern*. I shouldn't bother to find out. You will have enough to do to arrange what you have in hand: & I don't think you ought to do more than supply *quite obvious* gaps. The fault should be thrown, in the preface, on the occasional lack of materials. You may be sure that, in most cases where materials fail, it is because the quotations are very hard to find, & to find 'em would shamefully waste your time. You can but take *reasonable* trouble![22]

James' ideas of what was reasonable were very different. Much as he liked Walter Skeat as a person, he considered his standards far too low. Walter did not aim to produce an authoritative work, but, like Furnivall, to publish something quickly. His method was to use the materials nearest at hand and spend not more than three hours on any word, making the best he could of it within that time and then letting it go.[23] This was all very well if the dictionary was to be just a rough draft for a later fuller work: the fear was that it would be accepted as a substitute.

James was full of foreboding. Skeat's own dictionary was a threat to the scope of the Society's Dictionary, which James planned to be fully comprehensive in all aspects, because it seemed to be extremely doubtful whether the Press would publish two dictionaries which must to some extent duplicate each other.[24] Although the Delegates were apparently still interested, it seemed to James that there was no prospect of agreement on a form which would satisfy him and justify his labour and the sacrifice of his other prospects. Once again he pushed the papers aside and resolved to have nothing more to do with it. But once again he had reckoned without Frederick Furnivall.

Furnivall had been kept more or less successfully in the background, but in this crisis he again took the lead, regretting that he had not been to see some of the Delegates sooner. Early in March 1878 he went to Cambridge to call on Skeat, discussed his etymological dictionary with him, tried to persuade him then and there to write to Oxford to ask the Delegates to reconsider their decision on omitting etymologies, and came away convinced that a compromise was possible. Skeat still doubted whether James Murray would consent to be editor and delayed taking any action for fear of damaging the prospects for his own dictionary.[25] Meanwhile

Furnivall went off to take up the negotiations with Oxford at the point at which they had been left in December. He saw Henry Liddell, Dean of Christ Church and co-editor of Liddell and Scott's *Greek-English Lexicon*, who was a prominent member of the Delegacy and known to be in favour of publishing the Society's materials: he also did his best to answer the doubts expressed by Max Müller on the quality of the work already done. He now produced a list of 393 readers, admitting that there were gaps, but guaranteeing that the Society would get more volunteers to read and would see that known authors were sub-stituted for quotations which had been criticised because they were taken from the daily press. Then he wrote to James, persuading him to write a conciliatory letter, because 'we must humour the Dons as much as we can'.[26]

James was still demurring. He did not want to get caught again. He had wasted the best part of two years on this futile word chase and he was badly behind with his other literary work. But when he tried to back out he was told that then it would be 'all over with the Dictionary', the Delegates had understood all through that he was willing to be editor and had only considered the project on that assumption. If he 'drew back' and another man was looked for and found, the whole proceeding must begin anew 'off at the ground'.

In March James spent an anxious fortnight, trying to make up his mind. Looking back more than twenty years later, it seemed to him that although he had allowed his name to be mentioned, he had never until this point really considered if he should commit himself. In the hours he had spent preparing specimens, the fascination was in solving a problem and seeing what could be made of the material and he said, 'My interest in it was purely unselfish. I wanted to see an ideal Dictionary & to show what I meant by one.'[27] Now he realised that he could not go on letting everyone believe that his mind was made up and yet retain private reservations: this was neither honest to the Society nor fair to the Press. Nor could he any longer deceive himself that this was a work which could be done at his leisure. It would take all the time hitherto devoted to the Early English Text Society, to his work with Ellis on dialects, his reviews, his school text books, his University examining and even something over and above that. He would have to ask to be relieved from the extra-curricular duties at Mill Hill School, perhaps even from some hours of teaching. This meant that for the ten years which it was thought would be needed in order to complete the Dictionary he would have to put out of his mind any prospect of promotion to a headmastership or to a university appointment. On the other hand, if the Dictionary were a success it would gain him a reputation which might eventually lead to a higher position in the academic world. Useful as it was to edit early texts, the Dictionary would fall into a different class, it would be a work of national, even international importance: the loss if it were not done would be great and he could be held to blame since there seemed no one else to take his place. He listed the pros and cons over and over again, weighing one against the other with Ada. He said, 'It was the most anxious fortnight my wife and I ever passed or ever may'—one of those times of choice to which James referred in his sermon to the boys at Mill Hill, when in spite of prayer there seemed no answer, when he longed for an oracle or prophet who would give him a clear Yes or No. Eventually he made his decision—or rather Ada made it for him—saying that he should choose the Dictionary and do one big thing well, rather than dissipate his energies on a number of minor works. He felt at the time that it was a great sacrifice: it seemed a greater one as the full realisation of all the implications of the task he had set his hand to were borne in on him. It was many years before he came to say 'Yet I think it was God's will.' It is of interest that Émile Littré, the French lexicographer, went through a similar crisis before deciding to undertake his Dictionary. In Littré's case he was already sixty-one, and he saw that the work would take him till old age. Given twenty-four hours in which to make his decision, he did not sleep all night. It was a time, he said, of anguish, and it was only at dawn that his courage triumphed.[28]

Furnivall was now constantly at James' back—writing on 24 March to thank him for his 'capital diplomatic letter' to the Delegates—sympathising with his misgivings, and counselling 'seeing that Oxford is our only hope, & that a little humouring & teaching them will bring 'em round to let you do just what you like, I am sure that it is best to put up with a little undeserved fault-finding at first.'[29] At his suggestion James prepared a statement of his plan for the Dictionary in a form suitable, Furnivall said, for Delegates who 'haven't evidently got up the facts & don't know much of the Hist. of English'.[30] Furnivall had won again, and in April Dr Jack of Macmillans', whose firm always took, as he said, 'a kind of avuncular interest', was glad to hear that 'the Great Dictionary . . . is again on the lines & thinking of moving'.[31] James for his part began to consider the branches of knowledge in which he might find himself most limited and took up the study of chemistry again by way of preparation.

Now for the first time James Murray was invited to Oxford to meet the Delegates. This meant breaking off a holiday that he and Ada were spending visiting Fred Elworthy, the Somerset dialect amateur, at his home at Wellington, but Price advised that it would be impolitic to ask for a change of date, and the meeting was fixed for 2.30 *p.m.* on 26 April.[32] William Morfill, a Slavonic scholar with whom James was acquainted through the Philological Society, invited him to spend the night at his home in Park Town, apologising for the fact that it was a little way out of the city — a reminder that the spread of North Oxford had then hardly begun.[33]

The meeting was in a lecture room at Christ Church, to suit Dean Liddell, and the assembled Delegates must have been rather awe-inspiring.[34] They included, besides Liddell and Max Müller, who were the most competent to judge a dictionary, William Stubbs, the future Bishop of Oxford, Regius Professor of History and already noted for his publication of medieval historical texts; George Bradley, Master of University College, whose reactionary views on education have been quoted above,[35] and the Rev. Edwin Palmer, a classical scholar who was a Canon of Christ Church. Among the older men were some who had been much involved in the religious controversies which had divided Oxford some thirty years before, the Vice Chancellor, James Sewell, Warden of New College, a conservative high churchman who had defeated Mark Pattison in the elections to the Hebdomadal Council in 1855; the forcible and humorous William Bright, Regius Professor of Ecclesiastical History, also a Canon of Christ Church and a high churchman; and the elderly John Griffiths, keeper of the archives and Warden of Wadham, who was one of the four tutors who had protested against Newman's famous tract XC in 1841.

The meeting was a success. The Delegates took to James Murray just as the Macmillans had done. No doubt they recognised his evident knowledge and enthusiasm, and his disinterested, scholarly attitude and they found him straightforward and courteous. James, a little shy and diffident was on the whole agreeably surprised. He wrote to Ada the same evening:

Seen the great men — a very long and withal pleasant interview, increasing I think our mutual respect and confidence — but I don't

> think it decided anything or that we are much nearer a decision. Max Müller played first fiddle and talked as everybody's friend. It struck me that we were playing Congress with myself as Russia, the Dons as England, Max Müller as Bismark, and the result—nothing yet. *Absit Omen!* But they are decent fellows and shook me v. warmly by the hand at leaving as a man and a brother![36]

In fact things went much better than he expected, and the Delegates decided to proceed. Max Müller, who had committed himself to the statement that he had no misgivings on the commercial aspect of the undertaking, was left to complete the arrangements and wrote in a very friendly tone to seek Murray's personal views and wishes on the points on which there was still some difference of opinion. Max Müller confessed that the undertaking to publish Skeat's dictionary had certainly put them in a very awkward position. They wanted to avoid duplication, but on the other hand he was not alone among the Delegates in seeing that it would be unworthy of a work to which James proposed to devote ten years of his life, to restrict him unduly.[37] Finally a compromise was reached. On 3 May Max Müller met the Council of the Philological Society, not as an emissary of the Delegates, but as a member, and persuaded them to agree that etymologies should not be traced beyond the immediate feeders of the English language. 'We want for Saxon words their antecedents in Norman-French and Latin', he reported to the Delegates, 'everything else belongs to an Etymological, not to an Historical Dictionary'. If James had a new etymology to suggest, he should be free to give it, and where he used accepted etymologies he should supply full references.[38]

James was left to settle the other outstanding disagreement, on whether or not pronunciations should be given. Dr Price explained to him 'They think that the principles and rules of Phonetics are not as yet sufficiently established and recognised: and as there may be considerable change in the matter, it is not expedient to commit a Dictionary of a permanent form and value to what may be a shifting theory.'[39] James' reaction to this was forthright

> I am at a loss to understand what the Delegates mean by the principles and rules of phonetics to which they fear to see the Dictionary committed ... I really cannot see what *that* has to do with the simple point of stating the present pronunciation or pronunciations of a word, in some simple and intelligible form.

The statement that 'one' is now 'wun' is no 'shifting theory' but a solid fact which everybody admits—and a fact of great importance in the history of the word. Whether we are to represent this by (wun), or (wŭn) or (won) or in any other way is also not theory, but a practical expedient, permanently intelligible, by the key which will be given. I do think that some of the Delegates must be conjuring up a ghost and then trembling at it.[40]

With this he seems to have had the last word and his own way. On 17 May the Society's sub-committee was given instructions to negotiate an agreement with the Press and James took office as President in anticipation of his Editorship.[41]

The drafting of the necessary documents was by no means a simple matter: there were in fact three separate items of legal business to be dealt with before work on the Dictionary could begin.

First there was the agreement between the Delegates and James Murray as Editor, settling his remuneration, his expenses, the size of the Dictionary and the speed at which it was to be produced. Then there was an agreement between the Delegates and the Society for the use of their materials and for their share of royalties. Before this could be finalised the Society had to be registered under the Companies Act in order to enter into a contract. Each of these documents depended to some extent on the others and in each there were problems to be surmounted. James found it impossible to estimate time, speed and expense: the Society had to handle Furnivall's idiosyncracies and in particular his demand on behalf of their work for a large share in the profits. Another ten months of protracted, troublesome negotiation lay ahead and James had soon cause to wonder whether he had made the right decision when he accepted the Editorship.

James, like his father, was no business man. He was a scholar, who would have liked to undertake the work for the love of it. He was almost naïve in the terms he suggested. His one anxiety was to place no obstacles in the way of the production of the Dictionary and he was prepared to limit his salary to the bare minimum, saying,

> My views and intentions with regard to my own remuneration have been that in order to keep down the working expenses I should ask only such remuneration as would actually leave me not a loser by taking my time from other work which I have, or may have, and devoting it to the Dictionary. And as at present I do a considerable amount of unpaid work in the interest of English Literature, and

for its own sake, I have considered, that I ought to reckon upon giving a portion of time without remuneration ... as my own contribution to English Literature.

Probably as a result of the intervention of his much more practical wife, he did add that he felt he must ask for a fair share in the profits of the work to balance the fact that he was surrendering all prospect of promotion for so long as he was tied to the Dictionary.[42] This request did not please Furnivall, and the Council of the Philological Society recorded (with Murray in the Chair) that they thought the amount of the Editor's share should be a matter for negotiation with the Society rather than with the Delegates.[43] It was agreed that three years preparatory work would be needed before copy could begin to flow into the Press for publication and that the Dictionary should come out in parts. Although James said that he could not wait for payment till printing started, he was willing to accept a very nominal salary during these preliminary years. He had no evidence to show that the assumed rate of production would be possible and said that if after six months he gave up the work because he could not keep to the timetable he would willingly forgo all payment for what he had done; 'I had better lose £100 than bind myself to what was impracticable.'[44]

The Delegates were also scholars rather than business men: it did not occur to them to make sure that James was being fair to himself and probably they did not realise the degree of self-sacrifice to which he was prepared to go.

The basis for negotiating an agreement was the document prepared for Macmillan in 1877 by George Sweet, Henry's father.[45] This suggested that the total remuneration, to cover the editor's salary, payments to any assistants engaged by him, the cost of a room to work in, postage, stationery and reference books, should be a fixed sum of £6500. Of this, £162 *p.a.* was to be paid during the first three years in quarterly instalments: thereafter the Editor would be paid by results at a rate of £1 for every page completed for press. There was a dismissal clause to be invoked if the Editor should not proceed with the work as fast as the Delegates considered reasonable. Since it was really impossible to estimate expenses in advance, there was considerable discussion before a figure acceptable to all parties was arrived at.

Furnivall, wavering between desire to screw the last penny out of the Press and anxiety lest negotiations should break down, gave conflicting advice. Having argued that for the first three years an additional skilled assistant at say £100 a year would be needed and that to cover everything the Editor's salary should be at least £1000 a year, he then changed his tune and began to suggest ways to economise.[46] James made his estimate by taking his actual earnings in 1878 and fixing his loss of income at £400 *p.a.*; he did not allow anything for possible increments, nor consider the expenses of his steadily growing family. He added £270 for the salaries of one sub-editor and two clerks, probably women, one to work with him as a sorter and one to check references in the British Museum. He included only £45 *p.a.* for the first three years for all the incidental expenses, having no idea what these would amount to.[47] He told Furnivall,

> I . . . expect the Society's Library to be put at my disposal for the use of all works of reference which may be useful . . . I shall have, as it appears, heavy immediate expenses for *matériel*, and all that can be done to save this will help me. I have been advised, as you know, not to ask the Delegates for any initial aid . . . Probably I shall have to expend £250 at once on starting, which is of course somewhat different from the original idea of being willing to give one's work merely.[48]

James did not complain unduly; he had this strong feeling that he should give some service to Literature, and by December 1879 he had accepted the situation that at present his own work for the Dictionary was gratuitous and would be so for the first three years, because the outlay on assistance, books, printing and postage was so great.[49]

Price, finding Murray so easy to deal with, had in June 1878 reached the stage of arranging with the lawyers to draft the necessary documents and hoped that everything would be settled in time for the work to begin in the Long Vacation.[50]

At this stage trouble began. First Henry Sweet, on seeing the terms, objected to the dismissal clause, since there was no provision for arbitration in case of dispute between the Press and the Society. He distrusted Price, and his sour nature came out when he warned James of the policy of the Delegates, saying,

> At present it is their interest to make things as pleasant as possible, till they have effected their main object, viz., of depriving the Soc[iet]y of all control of the material & the way in which it is worked up. You must be prepared for a good deal of vexatious

interference & dictation hereafter, liable to be enforced any moment by summary dismissal. You will then see your materials & the assistants trained by you utilized by some Oxford swell, who will draw a good salary for doing nothing. I know something of Oxford, & of its low state of morality as regards jobbery & personal interest.[51]

Fortunately, to Sweet's annoyance, Furnivall was set on getting the contract signed and refused to rise: instead, he saw Dean Liddell and afterwards reported that James might dismiss the idea completely that there was any scheme to put an Oxford man in his place or to deal harshly with him. Max Müller assured them that the offensive clause was a 'mere legal fiction' and it was accepted.[52] James, however, unduly sensitive about the fact that he had not had a full University training, may have remembered Sweet's words when untoward events later led to a loss of confidence between himself and the Delegates.

By now there was no hope of getting the contract signed before the Long Vacation[53] and further complications were introduced by quibblings of the lawyers. They asked whether the sub-editors had really handed their work over to the Society absolutely and whether it was certain that they would not claim their share of the profits? They wanted Furnivall to produce proof that their work was a gift to the Society, and were still fussing over this detail in August. At this point Dr Weymouth, trying to be helpful to James, gave some substance to their fears by asserting that the small amount of reading he had contributed himself was not for the Society but for the Dictionary, and he claimed a share of the Royalties, which he proposed to hand over to the Editor.[54] Furnivall must eventually have satisfied the lawyers and no more was heard of this red herring. Feeling that agreement was in sight, James now fixed the terms on which he could become a part-time member of staff at Mill Hill. On this there was no difficulty: he hoped that it would be sufficient if he gave up looking after pocket-money and stationery and dropped his private pupils. It was settled that if necessary he could also be relieved of up to half of his teaching with a *pro rata* reduction in salary.[55]

A third, and most serious objection was now raised. It stemmed from the misleading information given to James by Sweet and Furnivall as to the readiness of the material and the very exaggerated idea Furnivall had of its potential value in terms of profits. In the desire to see the Dictionary started Furnivall had dropped his original demand for half a share and in June he and Price reached a compromise agreeing that the Society's share should be 40 per cent, of which the Editor should have half.[56] Then, at the eleventh hour, when the articles of Association and the agreements with the Society and with James were all ready for signing, there was a bomb shell. Price wrote on 2 December to Furnivall saying that James' estimates for editorial expenses had been increased from £6500 to £9000 because he had found that the material provided by the Society would need more preparation than he had supposed. To meet this increase the Press now asked for 65 per cent of the profits: Price suggested that James' share should remain at 20 per cent but that the Society should have only 15 per cent.[57] Price did not yet realise the fanaticism with which he had to deal in Furnivall and he innocently and optimistically hoped that the Society would accept the change so that all could be settled without further delay and James might begin work on 1 January. But Furnivall was enraged. 'It's that mean old skunk Bart. Price, damn him!' he wrote, hoping to see James in an interval as he dashed between work in the British Museum and a performance of *Cymbeline* at Drury Lane. 'Tell Price at once that all this means putting off work. I told him I couldn't conceive that the Council would accept the proposed reduction.' Once again the future of the Dictionary trembled in the balance.[58]

On 20 December Furnivall gave the Council of the Society a vivid account, covering five pages in the Minute Book, of an interview which he and James had had with the Delegates—'some dozen of them'—on Friday 13 December.[59] It must have been a painful experience for James. Furnivall had accused the Delegates of unfairness, if anyone was to have less of the profits it should be Dr Murray, because he was getting more payment now, or else the Delegates should bear his increased expenses themselves. At the least all parties should be treated equally, but they had thrown the whole charge on the Society, on the principle, it seemed, of 'it has least, let it have less'. He had spoken sarcastically of Dr Price's 'liberality of disposition' and slightingly of Dr Murray 'who came to us an unknown student' and now was forced to take his additional allowance as Editor out of their pockets. He had ended with an impassioned appeal:

Why do you deal thus with us? We are (in the main) University men, as you are: we are a learned body working for the science we are devoted to, content to be poor that it may be advanced. Why, because you have the capital or the command of it, why screw us? I won't insult the understanding of any one among you by supposing that you think the result of the Dictionary will not be a certain success . . . you know, as we do . . . that the Dicty. *must* pay, and that right well.

He told the Philological Society Council that he could not have spoken more strongly or straightly than he had done. There is little doubt that this exhibition confirmed the Delegates in their opinion that Furnivall was a very tiresome customer to deal with; on the other hand their refusal to alter their decision was his justification for the conviction that the Delegates were mean and grasping.

Unfortunately the meeting left other lasting scars. When Furnivall had finished his tirade, James had taken the opportunity to make a plea to the Delegates for assistance in his initial outlay for books and materials. 'If they had wished to offer it, after having heard from me . . . what expenses must be incurred in starting, they could have done so, but did not', he recorded bitterly.[60] All that was promised was that he should have copies of any books published by the Clarendon Press that would be of use for reference, and that the Press would print the slips for readers if James paid for the paper and the cost of postage in their distribution.[61] It seemed grudging and unhelpful, especially in the light of a letter James had received from Price in March 1878, offering to pay all the expenses of his visit to Oxford, which ended 'you will not, I am sure, feel any hesitation in letting our University Chest carry this burden. It is a kind of *bottomless* pit.'[62]

The state of anger in which Furnivall had left the Delegates by his attack on them is sufficient to explain their attitude on this occasion, but James took the decision as final, never asked again for books, and nursed a lasting grievance. It is certain that the Delegates, who later provided a library for his co-editors,[63] would have responded if they had been aware of the situation. 'I cannot understand why you should feel precluded from telling the Delegates . . . in plain terms that the work cannot be adequately done with the existing means. [Frederick Pollock told James in 1892] To start a national undertaking of this kind and then starve it seems altogether absurd.'[64] As late as 1912 William Osler, Regius Professor of Medicine, was astonished to find that the Press did not supply all dictionaries as they came out, and willingly lent a medical one in his own possession.[65] James suffered also a rebuff from the Government. The Treasury, approached on two occasions with a request for copies of all Record Office publications, refused, although sets were being donated to libraries up and down the country. 'This', James commented ruefully, 'is the end of the nineteenth century, and what some of us had fondly believed to be liberal and enlightened England!'[66] At first he was probably too proud to ask the Delegates again, later he enjoyed a certain sense of martyrdom and did not want to destroy this image of himself. Some organisations and friends did help. In contrast to the English Government, the United States, unsolicited, sent copies of publications which it was thought should be read for the Dictionary; Professor Arber supplied copies of all his series of reprints; the Royal Society lent copies of their publications; Skeat was most practical and generous in lending books, some of which from 1881 onwards he bought specially for the purpose, and later he made a small annual money payment to this end. But it would have saved the Editor a considerable sum, and the time of himself and his staff going down to the Bodleian to look up references, had a proper library been provided for him from the outset. The failure to communicate between the Editor and the Delegates was often to have unhappy consequences of which this was but one example.[67]

In 1879 everyone would have thought it unwise had James pressed the point that books should be provided: the aim was to get the Dictionary launched at all costs and to leave details to be worked out later. Macmillan had given Furnivall strong advice to raise no further difficulties of any kind saying, '. . . there've been enough, let the thing go thro' now'.[68] Max Müller too, wanted to see the thing settled and could not understand what all the fuss was about. After all, when it came to profits, they were talking of only a few thousand pounds that no one now a member of the Society was likely to be alive to enjoy.[69] In point of fact there was never any suggestion that members of the Society would benefit personally, the intention was to devote any profit to the furtherance of philological and literary studies. Max Müller proved right, they were arguing an academic point and within a few years the question was not of entitlement to royalties, but whether the Press could afford to go on publishing the Dictionary at a heavy annual loss.

The later history of the Society's contract with the Press is interesting. In 1900 it was cancelled because Furnivall hit upon the idea that the Society should solve a financial crisis by surrendering its rights in the Dictionary, in return for an undertaking by the Delegates to contribute £50 a year for ten years towards the publication of its Transactions.[70] Today, although the work of the Society in collecting material is still acknowledged on the title page, the only legal relic of the Society's early connection with the Dictionary is the fact that its official address is University College, London, at which it was registered as a Company for the purposes of the agreement of 1879. At that date it met regularly at the College, but it has not done so for nearly fifty years. The agreement with James Murray was never cancelled, but neither he nor his heirs ever received any profits from a work which cost some £300,000 to produce.

The crisis of 1878 took six months to resolve because Furnivall was now fighting, with enjoyment of course, for a principle. James, who had been taken by surprise when the Delegates asked for the reduction in royalties, told Furnivall that it was very improbable they would alter their resolution, and if the Society stood out for a higher share the Press was likely to break off the negotiations. In order to avoid this and to remove the charge of 'invidiousness' which Furnivall had made on several occasions, James now offered to share profits equally with the Society, taking $17\frac{1}{2}$ per cent each.[71] This upset Price, who strongly objected, saying 'the work you are undertaking deserves every farthing of the money you are to receive, and you or your heirs ought to have it. "Thou shalt not muzzle the ox that treadeth out the corn." And I hope the Society will be generous enough to decline your offer.'[72]

The seven members of the Council who, with James Murray in the Chair, were present on 20 December, were divided.[73] Sweet wanted to break off negotiations, and when this was not accepted, refused to take any further part in the debate. Furnivall moved a motion to accept James' offer, the generosity of which did not prevent Furnivall from later accusing James of acting rather 'as President of the Delegates than of the Society'.[74] He further moved that the Council should agree to the Delegates' terms under protest while 'vigorously denouncing' their conduct as a breach of honour and good faith. Both motions were lost by three votes to four. At this Furnivall remarked sarcastically that, 'as the majority had taken the kicking of the Delegates so quietly, they might like to lick the Delegates' boots by sending them the humble letter.' This referred to a compromise proposed by Price, who acted throughout in a most helpful manner and certainly did not deserve the strictures of Furnivall. Price's advice, eventually accepted, was that the Society should request the Delegates to pass and minute a resolution recording the confident expectation that should the profits prove larger than they now anticipated, their successors would entertain favourably any application made to them by the Society for an increase in their share of the profits. Price's view was that although it was too much to hope that this would remove all antagonism, it would show friends the true feeling of the Delegates towards them and their enterprise.[75]

Meanwhile Furnivall and Sweet remained obdurate. The Philological Society was registered as a Company on 2 January 1879, but they argued that the terms now proposed by the Delegates had led to so strong a difference of opinion that the Council was morally bound to submit the ratification of the decision of 20 December to a special general meeting of the whole Society. This meeting was fixed for 7 February, which happened to be James' forty-second birthday.[76]

The atmosphere was still very tense and James, as President of the Society, was in a most difficult position and under very great stress. It was probably at this time that he had the conversation with Price, recalled in a letter to Lord Bryce in 1903, when Price told him that if the decision went against the agreement 'it will never get as far as this again in our time'.[77] Fortunately some of the Council felt that there was no point in 'throwing more hard words at the Delegates', since Furnivall had already given them a fair dose.[78] At a stormy Council meeting on 24 January, which lasted so long that there was no time for the ordinary Society meeting which should have followed, they supported James in insisting that the draft of a statement giving the history of the dispute in great detail, which had been prepared by Henry Sweet for circulation to all members, should be drastically cut.[79]

At the special meeting of the Society on the fateful Friday, 7 February 1879, Ellis took the Chair and urged the acceptance of the agreement to secure publication of the Society's long contemplated Dictionary. He was supported by James, who said that he believed 7000 pages would enable the work to be well done, and that in his view the Delegates had been liberal, taking into account the very heavy cost of publication. Once again he repeated his offer to give the Society part of his share in the profits and he appealed for the voluntary help of the members because the funds would allow for only one paid assistant and two clerks. Quite unshaken, Furnivall created an opportunity to go over all the old ground once again, by moving an amendment that the Society was fully entitled to its 20 per cent—'the poor little 20%'—of which it was to be robbed while the Delegates' 'big 60%' was left untouched. But even he could not afford to wreck the agreement now, and he said that if his protest was recorded he would sign. Sweet, on the other hand, still wanted to break off the negotiations. Good sense prevailed, the amendment was lost, and the motion for acceptance carried by a large majority.[80] At once Furnivall wrote to James to say that now the matter was settled he was willing that bygones should be bygones and they should get the joint work forward.[81]

On 1 March 1879 Dr Price sent James Murray two copies of his agreement duly executed and a cheque for £175 as the first instalment of his salary.'Let us all congratulate each other [he wrote] on having arrived at this resting place in our enterprise. Believe me to be with the best wishes for you in the large undertaking.'[82]

It was the starting point of what was to prove for James a marathon lasting for the rest of his life and for the Press of a commitment for fifty-four years to a publication, not of the 7000 pages originally contemplated, but of over 16,000 pages.[83] The agreement just signed proved far from solving the problems of Editor and Publishers, for it had a completely unsound basis, owing to general ignorance of what would be involved in a project of this magnitude. George Sweet's draft of 1877 used information supplied by Furnivall which was far too optimistic. On this model the Delegates and James Murray made a detailed and precise agreement as to the size of the Dictionary and the time, and therefore cost, of completing it—matters which neither was in a position to assess accurately.

The agreement which James was allowed to sign tied him closely to a programme which he knew was too tight. He had told the Delegates that he would do his best to send at least 800 pages to the press every year,[84] and at the meeting on 7 February he told the Society that this would mean turning out 3 quarto pages and correcting and revising at least 3 other pages in proof every day.[85] If he did not keep up this speed an extension of up to five years was allowed, but without any increase in his total payment, now fixed at £9000.[86] It has been said that the experience of all lexicographers, including Johnson, is that 'to be certain of a date by which his dictionary will be fairly begun or ended has been "the lie in the soul".'[87] In this case, it was particularly risky to accept a binding agreement because they were dealing with the work of volunteers which had been unsupervised and was of unknown quality. Both parties relied on the statement that half of the material was sub-edited and ready for publication and the rest on sorted slips needing only editing. True, it was known that there were gaps which would have to be filled, but it was assumed that the quality of the work already done was satisfactory. Moreover Furnivall had assured the Delegates that the task of collecting more material would not fall on the Editor, and James accepted this. He wrote to Furnivall on 14 December 1878

> In view of the unknown vastness of the work on which I embark, the Society will of course in its corporate capacity, & by influencing its members and others, do all that it can to aid the completion of the work, of the mere physical difficulty of which—even supposing all material in my hands to start with,—few men of our Council seem to have formed any real conception.[88]

Furnivall alone knew something of the true position and one suspects that he was deliberately misleading in his anxiety to secure the agreement of both Editor and Press to the undertaking: his optimistic nature made it easy for him to deceive himself as to the state of affairs.

From the very beginning all the problems of employing voluntary labour had presented themselves. This might have been foreseen, since the Grimm brothers, on whose system the scheme was modelled, had found that out of eighty-three helpers only six were satisfactory and only one of them ideal. Coleridge reported that fifteen of his early volunteers were inferior and another fifteen no use. He complained of those who forgot their promises or found the task more irksome than they anticipated and threw it aside, remaining dead to all requests to hand in their results, and of others who promised anything and everything and produced nothing.[89] Furnivall in 1864 spoke of the 'almost incredible' gaps in the material, for instance there was not one quotation for *imaginable*—a word used by Chaucer, Sir Thomas More and Milton.[90] It took some time to detect what James later described as 'a most pernicious and deceptive practice' in some readers, who had read their books for particular letters only.[91] This was discovered when it was noted that there were no quotations from an author when later letters in the alphabet came to be dealt with. Furnivall's defence was,

> . . . we of old were not, & you now w[oul]d not be silly enough to refuse slips for any 1 letter sent from a book. We took 'em, & said

please send the other letters in due course. And if folk didn't do so, we were powerless . . . Beggars can't be choosers, & no one beggar has a right to blame another for the poor case he's in.[92]

Much more had been done on the middle period than on any other, but even there important books had been omitted: work on the early period was held up because amateurs found difficulty with the language and because texts were not easily available: the bulk of the Early English Text Society publications had post-dated the peak of reading activity for the Dictionary. The eighteenth century had been left to American volunteers and the organisation had broken down. Comparatively little had been done on modern writers.[93]

It is ironical that after all the argument over the terms under which this supposedly valuable collection of quotations might be used, James later found that with a few notable exceptions the original material was so bad and so rarely to be trusted that he often wished he had made a bonfire of it and started afresh, so ridding himself of what he described as 'an incubus of rubbish & error'. In the end less than a sixth—probably only a tenth—of the quotations used came from the old material, and the statement on the title page of the Dictionary, on which Furnivall had insisted, that it was 'founded mainly on the materials collected by the Philological Society' was grossly misleading.[94]

The work of the sub-editors was equally uneven. Furnivall in submitting examples to the Press said that they had been selected at random,[95] but the section he handed to James Murray in *C* was the work of Henry Hucks Gibbs, one of the best. Furnivall's reports to the Society always included lists of letters of the alphabet lacking sub-editors, either because they had never been taken up, or had been abandoned. He also knew that what could be expected of some of the volunteers was very limited. He instructed them in 1862,

> If you find that tracing the etymologies beyond the first parents of the words requires too much time and research, leave it alone, I can get it done afterwards . . . Do what your time allows. If it allows of nothing [in the way of filling in gaps in the quotations] well and good: if it allows of little or much that will be better or best.[96]

Walter Skeat also had some inkling of the truth. When he wrote to James about the Macmillan negotiations he said, 'Dr Morris knows, as I do, that the papers of the Phil. Soc. are, *some of them*, but not all, in a sad jumble.'[97] He had perhaps forgotten a long letter he wrote to Furnivall in November 1865, when he was sub-editing *R*, complaining of lack of precise directions and suggesting that Furnivall should call in samples of the work of all sub-editors so that mistakes 'which *pervade* their *whole* work' could be pointed out, and the work standardised. He said, 'My idea is—you would thus have one or two unpleasant surprises—but better *now* than hereafter.'[98]

It was James Murray, not Frederick Furnivall, who was to have the unpleasant surprises.

CHAPTER IX

'Sundry Shocks and Serious Jars': The Raw Materials for the Dictionary

MONTHS before the agreement with the Press was finally signed on 1 March 1879, James Murray was being urged by Frederick Furnivall to start work and had optimistically made plans to do so.

His first concern was to organise a work room.[1] He had seen in Furnivall's house glimpses of the mass of material in the form of slips of quotations which had been returned as sub-editors completed or abandoned their work. It was impossible for any visitor not to be aware of the packages cluttering Furnivall's entrance hall and his rooms, crammed onto every available shelf, balanced on the tops of furniture, dumped anywhere where they could be temporarily disposed of. The accumulation had been last added to in 1877 when Furnivall wrote to various sub-editors asking them to send specimens of their work to be shown to the Delegates of the University Press, and some of this material had already been passed on to James at Mill Hill when he was preparing his sample articles.

Sunnyside, which had seemed such a palatial residence when the Murrays moved there from their little house in Camberwell, was now barely large enough for the family of six children, some of them in nursery and some at school room stage. There was no space for a study for James and his assistants and Ada was certainly not prepared to see her house permanently cumbered with all these dusty packages. Were they to give the Dictionary a home, or were they to inhabit a decreasing corner of the Dictionary's home, gradually ousted by a mountain of paper? Some solution must be found quickly. The first idea was to rent an adjoining cottage, but it was an old, thatched place, and James felt that the danger of fire would be too great. It could more safely be used to house one of the assistants. It was Ada, thinking about a fireproof room, who suggested that they should build a special place—a Scriptorium James jokingly called it—of corrugated iron, portable buildings made of which had recently appeared on the market. On the side of the house nearest to the village there was the small front garden, large enough to take a building thirty by fifteen feet: it would partly block some windows on the ground floor of the house but would be conveniently close to the door, so that it would be almost an attached annex.

The idea was mentioned to Furnivall at the beginning of December 1878. 'The iron building is a good notion', he commented. 'But can you keep one dry, & properly heated & ventilated?'[2] He never shared James' enthusiasm for his workshop, referring to it as the 'den' and blaming it for later bouts of staff ill-health, but he would accept any arrangements which ensured the start of the work. 'When are you going to have the Dicty. slips in?' he asked on 2 February, when the signing of the Contract was still in doubt owing to the difficulties he was himself making: 'Isn't your room ready for Herrtage to start work? If not, shouldn't he be copying Caxton words at Mus^m? Every day lost now'll be felt hereafter.'[3]

S. J. Herrtage was a protégé of Furnivall's whom he wanted to help. He had used him as an editor for the Early English Text Society and to index the Transactions of the Philological Society, and now recommended him to James as Chief Assistant. James found for himself a second assistant, his brother-in-law Herbert Ruthven, to be in charge of the clerical work. This was a source of disagreement with Furnivall, who argued that Ruthven could be better used, accusing James of employing him only for personal reasons, and grumbling

> I confess to wanting to see part of the equivalent of our lost 5 p.c. turned into extracts from old black letters. And I have a firm belief that it might be done forthwith . . . If you could look at Mr. R. not as a brother-in-law, but as the embodiment of a salary to be most efficiently employed for Dicty. work, I cannot doubt that you would put him in the Mus., or cut him in two, & do it.[4]

By the beginning of February James felt it safe to complete his plans. Approval for the 'shed' was obtained from the owners of the property and the School Governors, and the tentative arrangements with Dr Weymouth for release from part of his school work were formalised. James did not anticipate having to ask for more time than seven hours a week, which it was agreed should be on Wednesdays,

Saturdays and the last period on Fridays (to enable him to attend the Philological Society meetings).[5]

The ugly little iron room with its skylights, painted grey with a brown roof, looked rather like a chapel. It was up in about three weeks, then was lined with deal and finally fitted by Herbert Ruthven with over a thousand pigeon holes for the quotation slips. It was described by a visitor as strictly utilitarian

> plain deal pigeon hole . . . It is pigeon-hole higher than the arm can reach; going down so low there is need to stoop. It is pigeon-hole, all up and down, and anglewise, of this plain deal screen that shuts off the door, that keeps the inner side—where all is pigeon-hole again—snug and weather-tight for settled sitting. For the remainder, it is only just that much different from plain deal pigeon-hole that it is plain deal shelf . . . shelf erected above shelf; and upright divisions of shelf; and sloping shelf, with beaded stop-edge running all along, that books and papers can lie there open, escaping the danger of sliding off to the floor.[6]

The pigeon-holes were made on the model of those designed by Herbert Coleridge but later they were found awkward because the bundles so often had to be shifted to make room for new accessions and they were changed to shelves. Perhaps in memory of descriptions of Dr Johnson at work at his Dictionary, seated at the end of a table supervising his assistants, James constructed a foot-high dais for his own table and placed another at a lower level for the sorters.

By Lady Day the Scriptorium was ready to receive the 'copying and burrowing' of the host of readers who had been directed by Furnivall for the past twenty years. Dr Murray was prepared for two and a half million slips—about two tons of paper. Furnivall thankfully emptied the contents of his cupboards and shelves into his hall ready for collection. On 27 March he sent an S.O.S. that the van had failed to come for them.

> . . . the things must be got away from here on Friday, as my wife is coming home from the seaside. I hope you'll . . . send your carrier for the things . . . But if you can't send, I must find a man near here . . . & you can pay him. You have probably telegraphed in reply to my telegram. If not, pray do so *at once*.[7]

He sent everything just as it was, quotations, letters, newspaper cuttings, printed appeals, books of reference, books for distribution to readers to cut up, tied up with string or thrown together in boxes. As soon as he was relieved of the loads he began, on 28 March, sending his instructions to the new Editor:

> If you want the Shakesp. collations, you'll have to borrow, or buy for £9, the Cambridge Shakespere. Meantime you should subscribe for our* set of Qtos . . . You'll want a Secretary & Sorter at first, besides H. in preparing the A work for you. You shd have all the A slips pickt out first they're in packets, except such as are in the 2 or 3 G. Eliot packets whose slips want written catch words . . . I hope you have, or *very soon* will have your whole room shelved. Its the only plan of keeping the slips easily accessible & moveable . . . You've never acknowledged the receipt of any of the little Dicty packets I've posted to you. Pray don't treat stranger contributors so, or they'll put it down to indifference or rudeness. Have some receipt Post Cards or forms printed, & let H. acknowledge the rect. of everything . . . Some of the outer slips have got torn, &'ll need mending. You've probably laid in a supply of gum.[8]

Until the material was handed over, Furnivall gave James no hint of its condition. The load delivered to Murray at Mill Hill in the spring of 1879 and which stood on the floor of the Scriptorium waiting to be unpacked, was a shock to the newly appointed Editor. Many of the sub-editors had clearly found difficulty in packing up hundred-weights of slips. Some were sent in sacks in which they had long been stored, and when opened a dead rat was found in one and a live mouse and her family in another: one sub-editor's work was delivered in a baby's bassinet: there was a 'hamper of *I*'s' with the bottom broken, which had been left behind in an empty vicarage at Harrow.[9] Many of the bundles had stood for so many years in unsuitable places that the slips were crumbling with damp and the writing had faded; others had been so illegibly scribbled in the first place that Dr Murray exclaimed in exasperation that Chinese would have been more useful, since for that he could have found a translator. In spite of instructions, the slips were not all of a standard size: Furnivall himself nearly always wrote on scraps of paper or backs of envelopes.

The first task was to check if the whole alphabet was there, many letters having been split amongst several sub-editors and widely scattered. James set to work with the help of Herrtage, Ruthven and

---

* The New Shakespere Society's.

two young ladies from the village, Miss Skipper and Miss Scott, comparing what they found in the packages with the reports formerly given each year to the Philological Society by Furnivall. James later gave a lively account of the experience. He soon found that fewer than half a dozen of the original sub-editors had brought their work to a conclusion with their quotations and letters in order. More serious, by no means all had returned their work

> . . . in the case of some who had died years before, the materials in their hands had become a white elephant to their successors, who were fain to relegate them to cellars or stables, until they should be asked for: some persons even, in removing to a distance, saved the expense and trouble of taking some hundred-weights of written papers, and left them behind them in the vacant houses to the tender mercies of indignant tenants or grasping landlords, from whom they were recovered with trouble and expense.

James himself made journeys to various parsonages and country houses to ferret out these papers and arrange for their packing and transport to Mill Hill.[10] His difficulties were increased because a small note book in wrinkled purple brown leather, with a white paper label stuck on the side with sealing wax, in which Furnivall had kept a list of the addresses of those to whom he had entrusted slips, was mislaid. Furnivall was sure it had been sent to Price and passed on to James: James was sure he had never seen it and the result was that Furnivall had to rely on his memory.[11] At the same time James was trying to check the work of the original readers and to discover what books they had in fact read. Furnivall sent out 250 circular letters to them, but most came back marked 'dead', 'gone away', 'not known'.[12]

By 10 May the preliminary sorting was completed and James reported that they could find no clue to *H*, entrusted to Horace Moule, Thomas Hardy's teacher and friend, in 1862 and marked in 1871 'no return':[13] *Pa*, marked in 1871 'part done' was also missing, and *Q*, stated in Furnivall's report of 1862 to be taken by the Rev. T. H. Sheppard, appeared not to have been heard of since.

> Why [James asked Furnivall], do you tacitly drop it in every report, not even saying 'No Report'? . . . I think we have all the rest or know where it is; but it is not very easy to tell without a more detailed examination than we can yet give. Some of the letters being in utter confusion, and requiring a month or more to sort, we may

find sections wanting. There are some cruel jokes in your reports G 'done', 'nearly done', 'will be done in 1872' — a mass of utter confusion, which will take many weeks to put even in alphabetical order. It was nearly burnt you remember as rubbish by Mrs. Wilkes after her husband's death: fortunately she bethought her of informing you first . . . I am sorely troubled about H. Q, & Pa.[14]

To this Furnivall replied cheerfully and unrepentant. He scoffed at James for complaining about illegible writing, 'Why, it's almost as plain as print!'

. . . H is, perhaps, (I think, certainly) with the Hon. G. P. Marsh, U.S. Legation, Rome . . . Q & Pa I forget altogether. But doubtless W. Middleton at the old address'll tell you where Q is. Write at once to him . . . Also write to Mr Bailey about Pa. I thought you *had* written a month ago. The last entries about sub-editors were, I think in the lost book. As to the cruel jokes, I of course only gave the Sub-editors' own Reports. *S* & *T* all the slips were professedly sent back: the stock of S is immense. X? wasn't this returned done.

In another letter on the same day he wrote to say he had found *X* in his own manuscript cupboard, and reverted to the missing *Pa*, 'did Mr Palmer have it? I can't recollect anything about it. Don't remember *Pa* being separated from *P–Py*. W. I forget; but if the main part of the slips is in all is, as the letter's not likely to have been cut in two.'[15]

H was in fact in Florence: George P. Marsh wrote on 4 May from Rome: he had stopped work many years ago owing to failing eyesight. He had read recently that a lexicographer was going to tackle the Dictionary and he wrote to ask where he should send his slips when he could recover them from his summer villa at Florence.[16] *Q* also miraculously survived and came back from near Loughborough. The sub-editor, J. G. Middleton, who had undertaken the task twenty years before, had for long thought that the project had been abandoned or that at all events his part would not be wanted. At the time he had been living in Cumberland, later his family moved to Leicestershire. He explained

Had I been present I think it very probable I should have destroyed the papers. Being absent, persons who were wiser, or *less wise* than I, preserved them in whole or in part . . . You will find them, I expect, in some disorder as may be reasonably expected after being in idleness for so many years.[17]

Pa eluded discovery for years. After following various clues in vain, in November 1880 Furnivall suddenly discovered the missing book of addresses which he was so sure James had taken: it was somewhere on his first floor, not on the ground floor where he had looked for it. He now found the address of the brother of the sub-editor, and owned, 'I must have told Mr. G. Smith to return all the *Pa* papers, and then forgotten to see that he did it.' Smith's brother who had sub-edited *Pa* was an Irish clergyman who died in 1869 having left his living on the disestablishment of the Irish Church. His brother had collected the slips and handed them to someone for safe keeping: eventually they were traced to a stable in County Cavan, where only a few survived, the rest having been used for lighting fires. A great number of books had to be re-read to make good the loss.[18]

In May 1879 James gave the first of many reports which he was to make to the Philological Society on progress and said that the Scriptorium was in 'full orderly work', and the Editor was prepared to receive interested visitors. At the same time he told Members that even the somewhat cursory examination that he had been able to make showed that the readers' work was very much less complete than he and the Delegates had been led by Furnivall to suppose. Not only had many books been taken to be read and never returned, but the number of important books which had never been allocated for reading at all was far greater than he had expected. Furnivall had always admitted that some further reading would be needed, but Murray now realised that nothing short of a new appeal on the scale of the original one could remedy the situation. He had spent some time trying to compile a list of books for which volunteer readers were required. This proved a long and arduous task, some titles on it were later found to have been read while many were omitted which should have been included and further supplementary lists were needed.[19] Later he said 'Few have any conception of the many days' work involved in preparation of one of these, while the reading is going on and slips continually coming in, so that our series of quotations is growing and changing under our very hands, while we are trying to define its limits.'[20]

In April 1879 he had issued, through the Society, 2000 copies of *An Appeal to the English-speaking and English-reading Public* in Great Britain, America, and the British Colonies, asking for a thousand readers for the next three years, and saying, 'Anyone can help, especially with modern books; thus, from these, Dr Murray's own pupils have supplied him with 5000 good quotations during the past month.'[21] At the same time he issued lists of *desiderata* — words for which quotations were still needed, especially those illustrating the earliest or latest use. The first of these lists was issued in December 1879 and for the next fifteen years at least one appeared every year. It was discouraging that after all the labour of preparation the response to these lists was usually very small, but as a result of the Appeal some eight hundred readers in Great Britain and four or five hundred in the United States offered help and between them they added a million slips to those already in the Scriptorium.[22]

Instructions differed from those given to the original readers, who had been asked to pick out quotations only for words not included in the Concordances to the Bible and Shakespeare and the works of Burke.* This direction was now recognised as a major cause of the very meagre presentation of common words. James reported that 'the editor or his assistants have to search for precious hours for examples of common words, which readers passed by . . . Thus of *Abusion*, we found in the slips about 50 instances: of *Abuse* not five.'[23] Readers were now instructed 'Make a quotation for *every* word that strikes you as rare, obsolete, old-fashioned, new, peculiar, or used in a peculiar way', and also 'Make *as many* quotations *as you can* for ordinary words, especially when they are used significantly, and tend by the context to explain or suggest their own meaning.'[24] Although the main reading was concentrated into the first three years, the flow of slips never wholly ceased. As each letter of the alphabet came to be dealt with, gaps were found needing to be filled, while all the time new books were published and new words coined. Eventually there were five million slips in the Scriptorium and it was years before sorting and incorporating the new slips into the original series was up to date.

Dictionary slips and their sorting became a major element in the lives of the Murray family. In the earliest photograph of the Mill Hill 'iron room', Harold is visible,[25] but normally the Scriptorium was 'out of bounds' and the family work went on in their own quarters. Every afternoon the children went to the Scriptorium to collect some packets of recently arrived slips. As each child reached an age when he or she could read, they were pressed into service. Rosfrith, the ninth, remembered her father catching her by the pinny one day as he passed her in the hall, and exclaiming, 'It is time that this young woman started to earn her keep.' The little girl, left handed and rather delicate, was more backward than the others had been and had hardly

* See Appendix II, p. 346.

ne'er-do-well

1887 *Beatrice Potter*. [*Mrs Sidney Webb*] *M.B. Nineteenth Century* *since 1892* Oct, 1887, p. 483, *The Dock Life of East London*,

For the popular imagination represents the dock labourer either as an irrecoverable ne'er-do-well, or as a down-fallen angel.

10. A typical Dictionary slip.

as yet mastered her letters. She was soon in tears and the nurse had to come to her rescue. When there were complaints that Emma was neglecting her normal work, it was decided that Miss Nina was too young, and she was let off for a time. In April 1885 Wilfrid brought in a bill before the Sunnyside Debating Society, titled 'The Appropriation Act: That the members of this House do steadily henceforth keep to the work of half an hour's slips per day for the gain of 6d a week.' Jowett, the youngest son, described slip-sorting in the 1890s

we received no pocket money as a matter of course, but had to earn it by sorting slips. Hours & hours of our childhood were spent in this useful occupation. The motive actuating us was purely mercenary: we wanted money for Christmas or birthday presents, or to spend on our summer holidays, & the only way to get it was to sort slips. We were paid according to age, not according to skill or speed. The standard rate was one penny an hour, but this rose to two-pence, three pence or even sixpence as you mounted up in your teens.[26]

The dictionary slips were the size of a half sheet of notepaper, written on lengthways. In the left hand top corner was a catchword (which was all that concerned us) . . . The slips were all written by hand . . . except for cuttings from newspapers, which were sent in great numbers by Dr Furnivall with the catchword somewhat illegibly written so that we often had to read the printed paragraph to find out what the word might be. These slips were tied up in bundles of several hundred and had to be arranged in full alphabetical order . . . The sorting into first letters was easiest: that into second letters was a little harder, because you often had to read the whole catch word. The final sorting and combining two or perhaps three bundles were hardest of all; but we became skillful with practice &, I believe, quite as quick as the junior assistants in the Scriptorium . . . Financially considered, I am sure the Oxford University Press did very well by our labour.

The work was not uninteresting if done for only an hour or two at a time. But when we wanted to earn half a crown or even five shillings in the space of a week, we had to work long hours. We enlivened the task by reading out tit-bits from Dr Furnivall's newspaper cuttings, & bundles of slips from Dr Furnivall were in demand, in spite of the bad handwriting.[27]

Rosfrith recalled one of Furnivall's cuttings for the word 'toe-rag' and 'you dirty toe-rag' became a family term of abuse. Sometimes the slips were on coloured paper and there would be a competition to see who could get the highest score in these. When they worked long periods it was an established rule that after each hour they would take a run round the garden. It is not surprising that all the children gained unusually wide vocabularies and that some of them shone at doing cross-words in later life. In 1899 James acknowledged in his report to the Philological Society that the alphabetical arrangement of quotations had been done mainly by his younger children, but in the many accounts of the making of the Dictionary, the child labour goes unrecognised.

Several members of the family gave help in other ways when older. Harold, who is recorded in the preface to Volume I as having supplied 27,000 quotations, worked in the Scriptorium between leaving school and entering university: Hilda, while reading Modern Languages as an Oxford Home Student, regularly undertook to provide statistics for the Introductions to the published parts, by counting on the final proofs the numbers of main and subsidiary words, combinations, current, obsolete and alien words and the total of quotations. Elsie and Rosfrith on leaving school were employed as full time paid assistants in the Scriptorium and Bodleian checking references, and they continued their work after their father's death. Elsie was employed from 1899 until 1920 and Rosfrith from 1902 till 1929.

In the early years, when readers were working in large numbers, James found that the task of organising and instructing them took almost all his time. He had to dispatch books and slips and acknowledge their return, chase the tardy, answer queries about their work, and deal courteously with irritatingly stupid questions from volunteers upon whose goodwill he depended.

He wrote on an average thirty or forty letters a day—he had no secretary and of course no typewriter—if he wanted to keep a copy he wrote the letter out all over again (occasionally Ada did this for him). Often his letters ran to several pages in his minute handwriting. In the early years every letter he received was numbered and pasted into quarto volumes, thirteen of which had accumulated by 1882 containing some 5000 letters.[28] In spite of suggestions from friends, and directives from Furnivall, that he should hand over all this correspondence to an assistant,[29] and a later offer of the Press to lend him the services of a part-time shorthand clerk,[30] James preferred the personal touch. The fact that in writing to consult specialists he so seldom met with a refusal was undoubtedly because he wrote himself, and so warmly. He took great pains to make his helpers realise how much he appreciated their trouble and he was meticulous in recording their names in the prefaces to each part of the work. On the other hand he did waste an enormous amount of time in writing needless, and especially needlessly long, letters. Again and again someone who asked what the writer thought would be a simple question was embarrassed to receive four or five pages giving a whole history of a word. 'It is too bad of you', one expostulated, 'to write me a couple of pages when half a dozen lines would be ample.'[31]

He could not resist teaching: rather than throw a stupid letter in the waste-paper basket, he must show the writer why it was foolish. In 1880 a Mrs Pott sent him lengthy lists of words which she imagined were peculiar to the works of Francis Bacon, asking which other authors first used them. James wrote out a draft and then a fair copy of his reply, running to five octavo pages. He explained that it would take him three weeks to look for her words among the still only partly sorted dictionary slips, 'and with 15 years' work before me, 3 hours is more than I *ought* to spend on it. I have nevertheless spent three times three in testing your work at various points.' One hears the school master as he went on to expose her ignorance

> I wish to say, with all kindness, that I seem to see on every page evidence of a want of that preliminary study of the language which was surely necessary to enable any one to grapple with a delicate linguistic problem. Suppose one undertook to correct current opinion on the Gunpowder Plot, and included among the possible

persons implicated therein, Hengist & Horsa, Simon de Montfort, and Jane Shore; what would you say? . . . Probably suggest that he might with advantage peruse Little Henry's History, or Mrs Markham, and learn when these persons lived. Now, I find in your pages, words as old as Hengist and Horsa, words introduced before Simon de Montfort was born, words that Caxton was printing while Jane Shore was in honour. Surely it would have been worth your while to acquire the preliminary knowledge before dealing with a subject that required it![32]

Pen in hand, the words flowed easily, and one cannot doubt that he really enjoyed letter writing. One suspects that he must often have used attention to the pile of letters as an excuse for not beginning the grind of proof correcting and that it gave him satisfaction to feel he had achieved something positive. At least he had posted a dozen letters and had not to record at the end of the day that he had done absolutely nothing but wrestle unsuccessfully with an elusive definition. He remained therefore as meticulous in his correspondence as in his editing and nothing anyone could say would persuade him to change his methods.

Like Coleridge and Furnivall before him, James soon found that the voluntary helpers fell into different categories—the good, the bad, the indifferent and the dishonourable who returned nothing—not even the books they had borrowed. James had a long struggle to recover the slips for the first part of the letter *O*, entrusted for subediting to a Mr W. J. E. Crane of Brixton. He visited the man himself and obtained a promise that he would send the materials within a month: he sent Herbert Ruthven to collect them and he came away empty handed because in the absence of Mr Crane himself no one else had authority to surrender the slips. Finally a lawyer was consulted, who advised that because of the danger that Mr Crane might destroy the material, James should 'perseveringly pursue the course' he had adopted 'and apply again & again to Mr Crane, without letting him rest, and so obtain the material by great importunity.' This he eventually did, with Furnivall's help, but it was a time-consuming process.[33]

The class of readers who predominated were those who showed more enthusiam than ability and failed to grasp the object of the exercise. One laboured to produce 1000 quotations from Lane's *Modern Egyptians* only two of which were any use, the rest being

Arabic terms never used in English: another found a botanical book unsuitable for reading for the Dictionary because the bulk of it was just 'descriptions of flowers'. Inevitably there were also the cranks who predicted failure unless their own peculiar ideas on etymology or spelling were adopted.[34]

James had never expected to be involved with recruiting readers and supervising their work, for Furnivall had assured both him and the Delegates that this part of the task would be undertaken by the Society, but only seven members responded to the Appeal.[35] James asked in vain for a score to undertake to read the daily and weekly papers, magazines and scientific periodicals, but no one except Furnivall sent him a word: in 1880, asking members to read technical books and to lend him rare ones, he said that he had never had the help in this respect which had been promised.[36] Not the least of James Murray's contributions to the success of the Dictionary was that by his Appeal he tapped a new source of helpers, and that he never neglected the important work of retaining their enthusiasm. He knew how eagerly they turned the pages of each Part as it was published, counting the number of their contributions which had been used. He often wrote to console those who reproached him because not one of the thousand quotations sent from a book which he had urgently asked to be read had been selected.[37]

The contrast between the zeal of the new recruits and the apathy of the Philological Society made Furnivall's concern for the Society's interest in the profits the more absurd, and added to the bitterness which in moments of depression James felt about the task in which he had been enmeshed. In view of the state of English studies at the time, he should have been prepared for a similar apathy on the part of the universities. He told the Society in 1880, 'only one or two Professors of English in this country have thought the matter of sufficient importance to talk to their students about it and advise them to help me.'[38] Oxford University, in spite of special involvement in the project, seemed to share in the general indifference. James' report to the Delegates in 1880 on the first year's work was received by them without comment,[39] and to his surprise and disappointment none of them found it necessary to come to Mill Hill to inspect the work. Dr Price informed him 'having full confidence that you and your assistants are taking all possible care of the undertaking, and are doing all that can be done for the perfecting of the Work, I was not instructed to make any further enquiry.'[40] This bald letter suggested that the Delegates were not greatly interested. It was the same in 1881, when the excuse was made on their behalf by Price, 'I can assure you that nothing short of almost incessant work has prevented these visits being paid.' But evidently realising that James felt dissatisfied Price did make the effort to call at Mill Hill himself.[41]

The more James worked on the materials the more convinced he became of the great potential importance of the Dictionary, but he also became increasingly aware of the sacrifices demanded of himself, and he badly needed the encouragement that recognition of the nature of the work could give him. It was fortunate that the American scholars responded enthusiastically. Professor Francis A. March of Lafayette College, Pennsylvania undertook to organise readers in the United States and met with great success. All over the States men and women began collecting words. Coleridge's idea had been to allocate the eighteenth-century books to American helpers, but the work had not been well directed and had not produced results.[42] Now, like the English volunteers, the Americans read generally literary and scientific works.[43] Reporting in 1880 James spoke gratefully of this help, saying 'I cannot sufficiently express my appreciation of the kindness of our friends in the United States, where the interest taken in our scheme, springing from a genuine love of our common language, its history, and a warm desire to make the Dictionary worthy of that language, has impressed me very deeply.' He particularly named the Rev. J. Pierson of Michigan, Professor G. M. Philips of the University of Lewisburg and Dr Henry Phillips, secretary to the Numismatic and Antiquarian Society of Philadelphia, who among them had already sent in nearly 17,000 slips.[44]

Another consolation for the editor lay in the friendships he formed with men and women on both sides of the Atlantic who continued to give help year after year. None of these readers and sub-editors received any pay whatsoever. Some of them could only find time for the work with difficulty. Typical of their zeal was John Randall who provided over 2000 slips. Writing in January 1884 Randall said

> I have made time to send quotations by taking a few minutes from dinner time or tea time; sometimes I have given an hour or two on Saturday afternoon, sometimes I have sat up till twelve on Saturday evening, and sometimes I have got up earlier than usual on Monday morning, that I might before going to work, copy those sentences in which I had noticed strange words . . . I have thus tried to contribute my mite.[45]

Another early volunteer, Canon J. T. Fowler, introduced through James' old friend Canon Greenwell of Durham, gave regularly eight hours a day to 'Murray slips' and looked back, after twenty years, to the Dictionary work as one of the joys of his life, saying he preferred collecting words for it to 'any sort of games, muscular or cerebral'.[46] Amongst the readers were some continental enthusiasts, such as the Dutchman, A. Caland, who for years read all the proofs and declared that the Dictionary work was the one thing which kept him alive — though his wife described it as 'that wretched Dictionary'.[47] He had a special link with James Murray in that both were keen philatelists, and they always added to their letters a sentence or two about the latest issue of stamps, or found room in the envelope for a new or unusual specimen.

The response from women was particularly warm: higher education being still exceptional for them, there were many very intelligent ladies, lonely widows or spinsters living at home looking after parents or housekeeping for brothers or sisters, who found some fulfilment in contributing to the work. Miss Edith Thompson of Liverpool, for instance, who sent her first contribution on 16 April 1880 and with her sister supplied over 15,000 quotations, quickly revealed a wide knowledge of Old English and of historical terms and local dialects. Correspondence with a strange gentleman who was a scholar and lexicographer, was quite a dashing enterprise for her, and when she ventured some expression of personal opinion she wondered if she had committed a breach of privilege. 'If it is', she begged James, 'treat it as confidential.'[48] Another contributor, Miss J. E. A. Brown, who lived at first with a delicate sister at Malvern, found her desire to reply to a letter in which James unburdened to her some of his worries, too strong to be resisted. She urged him not to over-work and revealed that she had for long been accustomed to remember him in her prayers, hoping that she had not overstepped the limits of what is permissible to a stranger. Later James and Ada visited her when she moved her home to Cirencester. She continued to work for the Dictionary and to send solicitous and encouraging letters and when she died in the spring of 1907 she left James a very welcome legacy of £1000.[49]

Largely through the interest of this band of readers the Dictionary attracted increasing attention: the Scriptorium became a place of pilgrimage, and accounts of the work there appeared in several periodicals. Gladstone, who met Dr Murray when presenting prizes at Mill Hill, often stayed with the Earl of Aberdeen in the village and made a habit of dropping in, bringing other guests with him, to see how the work was progressing — expressing the 'sorrowful conviction' that he would never see the completion of the work.[50] The Earl of Aberdeen himself first visited the Scriptorium through calling at Sunnyside in mistake for the Vicarage. The door was opened by Ethelbert, the second boy, who was sharpening a clasp knife on an oil stone in the hall. He redirected Lord Aberdeen and went into the sitting room to report what had happened. His father, in joke, said, 'You should have invited him to come in and see the Scriptorium.' Childlike, Ethelbert took this seriously, and rushing out of the house and down the lane, waving the knife in one hand and the oil stone in the other, he overtook the astonished Lord, who promised to call on another day, which he did.[51]

German professors and Americans were among the most frequent visitors, the latter especially after Professor Child of Harvard advised his friends that the three things to see in England were Westminster Abbey, the Tower of London and the Scriptorium at Mill Hill where the Big Dictionary was being made.[52] Murray welcomed these visitors because he enjoyed talking about the work and used the opportunity to enlighten people on the importance of what was being attempted and the need for help.

Several descriptions exist of the Doctor at work. In the words of one visitor[53] 'The master looks up from the semi-circle of open reference-books amidst which he is sitting; he pushes away his chair, and comes smilingly down to give his hand. Wearing his academic cap, he is wearing, even more conspicuously, his academic breadth of courtesy and gentle learning.'

He then patiently explained how the work was organised, putting it in a different way if he saw that his audience had failed to understand any point. The visitors were shown how the slips, pouring in at the rate of 1000 a day, were passed through the various processes of sorting and classification in the course of which every slip was handled by five people. When a packet was received it was first looked through to see if there were any obvious errors, such as the omission of a full reference or a doubtful spelling which could be settled by a question to the reader. One of the two young women sorters (or the children) next put them into alphabetical order, for a more skilled assistant to sort words spelt in the same way into different parts of speech and senses, and next arrange the quotations for each group chronologically. By then the slips were ready for a sub-editor experienced enough to do further subdivision to show the various changes and shades of meaning through which the word had passed and to pin to each sub-division a slip attempting a definition. Finally, the sub-editor arranged his bundles in order of their historical development so far as he could determine it. The Editor's part was to check the work of the assistants, sub-divide still more if necessary, add the etymology and pronunciation and select the best quotations. When the copy was ready for the Press the slips were not transcribed, as this would introduce the possibility of clerical errors and necessitate re-checking, but those in each bundle were numbered 1 to 1000, so that if a compositor at the Press were to drop the bundle of loose papers accidentally, he could restore them to correct order.[54]

As he showed the guests round, Dr Murray would give examples of the unique feature of the Dictionary, the application of the historical method. His task was to trace the life history both of every English word now in use and of all those known to have been in use at any time during the last seven hundred years.[55] His starting point was 1150, and the early history, variations of sense and form of every word current at that date, was to be given in the same detail as the changes which took place in succeeding centuries. In this he was applying the historical principle much more completely than had been attempted in any country. Littré's French Dictionary, completed in 1872, took the classical French Language as used in the seventeenth century as his starting point, while the brothers Grimm, whose work was completed only in 1960, long after both were dead, started from the New High German of the mid-fifteenth century, and neither work paid attention to words obsolete earlier. For the words treated, Littré applied the historical method only for the centuries from the ninth to the sixteenth inclusive, and although the policy followed in Grimm was somewhat modified in the course of publication, Jacob Grimm himself was a purist who inclined to exclude words in current usage such as those Germanised by the addition of the termination —*iren*.[56]

Although James knew that there would be additions and changes in English vocabulary in future ages, he would stress that, 'Every fact faithfully recorded, and every inference correctly drawn from the facts, becomes a permanent accession to human knowledge . . . part of eternal truth, which will never cease to be true.'[57] Finally he would appeal for help saying

If literary men and students of English in any department, had the faintest conception of the amazing and enormous light which the Dictionary is going to throw upon the history of words and idioms, they would work with enthusiasm to hasten its appearance[58] . . . If you desire no credit and feel no interest in helping my work I can do without you, weep not for me, weep for yourselves and your children.[59]

He was not always so serious. He liked to tell the story of a dream he claimed to have had of Dr Johnson. Johnson was speaking of his Dictionary and Boswell, in an impish mood, asked 'What would you say, Sir, if you were told that in a hundred years' time a bigger and better dictionary than yours would be compiled by a Whig?' Johnson grunted. 'A Dissenter.' Johnson stirred in his chair. 'A Scotsman.' Johnson began, 'Sir . . .' but Boswell persisted—'and that the University of Oxford would publish it.' 'Sir', thundered Johnson, 'in order to be facetious it is not necessary to be indecent.'[60]

It was as well that James retained his sense of humour and his power to respond to a challenge, for the organisation of the mountain of slips and the host of readers was perhaps the least of his problems.

CHAPTER X

Hoc Unum Facio:
Solving the Technical Problems

ALL THE time that James Murray was organising the readers and trying to find time himself to do the necessary research to complete the slips on words in *A*, he was also working on the technical details, on which decisions were needed before type-setting could begin.

He spent nearly three years on the problem of pronunciation, putting to himself first the question, 'What is current usage?' Was he to take the pronunciation of northerners or southerners, of Cockneys or Oxford Dons, of singers or orators? How many varying pronunciations of a word should he give?[1] The one thing of which he was certain was that it was not the function of the Dictionary to establish a standard of 'right' or 'wrong'. It was to record facts, and the fact was that usage differs for reasons to be found in the history of the language. When appealed to for a decision he always answered that pronunciation is a matter of taste: he told one correspondent,

> Language is mobile and liable to change, and . . . a very large number of words have two or more pronunciations current . . . and giving life and variety to language . . . it is a free country, and a man may call a *vase* a *vawse*, a *vahse*, a *vaze*, or a *vase*, as he pleases. And why should he not? We do not all think alike, walk alike, dress alike, write alike, or dine alike; why should not we use our liberty in speech also, so long as the purpose of speech, to be intelligible, and its grace, are not interfered with?[2]

He decided to give all possible pronunciations where several were current, he referred doubtful cases to his friends for their opinion, and where he had no guidance he followed analogies as far as possible. He found particular difficulty in dealing with scientific words and related in his preface to Volume I that he once heard *gaseous* pronounced in six different ways by as many eminent physicists in the course of a discussion. Such a notable scientist as Thomas Huxley, he found, had often never thought how the scientific words he invented should be pronounced, because he coined them for use in books rather than in conversation.[3]

Henry Sweet thought that James was at a disadvantage because of his Scottish origin, to which he retorted that, on the contrary, he had the advantage of having been a school master in the Borders and of having had to learn a standard pronunciation in order to teach English, and he well understood the danger of giving a pronunciation because it was his, without investigating authority.[4]

James walked into a veritable hornet's nest when he sought advice on how to indicate pronunciation. Everyone he consulted had his own system: a Mr W. R. Evans offered the use of his Compendious Script; Isaac Pitman proposed his alphabet of phonetic script and others favoured Henry Sweet's Narrow Romic Glossic.[5] In 1881 James appealed to the members of the Philological Society asking, 'Who will save me the time of thinking this matter out, by giving a broad and practical consideration to the question?'[6] A year later he complained that again the help and advice he expected from the Society had not been forthcoming and that he had had to work out a system for himself, the result of three years' incessant trial and practical experience.[7] By then Henry Sweet had come to the same conclusion which the Delegates had earlier argued—that as so little was yet known on the subject no attempt should be made to show pronunciation at all. Like Skeat he advised James, 'If I were you, I should seize every opportunity of lightening your present work, whose magnitude you cannot measure till you have corrected the last proof of the first part.'[8] When Sweet flatly refused to undertake this part of the editing himself, James sighed, 'I really don't know what I shall do: I am sadly in want of plain common sense men. I suspect it would be "Clear out of the whole business".'[9] Sweet's objections, he saw, could be applied equally well to every one of the different sections of the Dictionary:

> All that you urge against phonetic statements, can be urged with far greater force against sematological ones: for these I am absolutely a pioneer; nobody exc[ept] my predecessors in specimens of the Dicty has yet *tried* to trace out historically the sense-development of English words . . . I shall have to do the best I can at defining

probably 80,000 words that I never *knew* or *used* or *saw* before; why cannot you or I try to make out, & give our conclusions as to the pronunciation of these words, as well as to their meanings? I at least was not *born* with a knowledge of either: of both, my conceptions are alike acquired, artificial, personally-warped & garbled: I have no 'natural' pronunciation & no intuitive knowledge.[10]

At this point Furnivall stepped in as, he said, a practical man, telling him

And my strong advice is, that you should, on this 1 point, as on all others, give your own results. Hear what all the other phonetists have to say, & don't go against them in any details for whim's sake, or merely to show independence, but, having once made up your own mind, set down your result, & don't care a hang what anybody else says . . . I wouldn't care a brass farthing for all the theoretical objections of the special phonetists.[11]

In the same letter he gave encouragement to James,

I know your feeling well. 'Chuck it all up' has come to me a fair number of times. But I think this depends very much on bodily health. If you could get a good gallop or other refreshing rest or change, the old strong *will* 'ud revive.

You are playing for a heavy stake in reputation, position, & money, ultimately, & if you hang on to the work, I've no doubt that you must win . . . the cause is well worth sacrifice . . . Cheer up. All'll go well yet.

James took his advice. He disappointed the spelling reformers, because although he was known to be in favour of certain changes to remove anomalies, he decided that none of their systems were delicate enough to serve as a scientific guide. They had hoped that he would use one of the schemes of reformed spelling to indicate pronunciation with the idea that this would encourage its adoption as an alternative orthography.[12] The method of showing pronunciation which he finally evolved met with little criticism, and Henry Bradley, reviewing Part I of the Dictionary, said that it seemed to balance the conflicting claims of precision and intelligibility better than any other known to him.[13]

Unfortunately Furnivall was not so reasonable when the issue was one which interested him personally. Another of the technical problems was how to treat combinations, compounds and derivatives—for example, to decide how many of the 500 words in *anti-* or the 1500 words in *be-* deserved separate treatment—a problem which had troubled James when preparing his specimens for Macmillan. The Delegates, when worried about the length of the Dictionary, as they were periodically, always picked on these words and complained they were being treated in too great detail, but Furnivall took the contrary view. James told Dr Price in June 1882

> Mr F. J. Furnivall (who has an itching for annoying people) has been worrying me for some time, because in words like *Abider*, *Abiding* etc., I do not sub-divide & classify them as minutely as the v[er]bs to which they belong . . . As there is no saying what he may do in one of his mad fits—print a letter abusing me perhaps . . . I write simply to inform you. I do not choose to accept Mr Furnivall's dictation as to any point of the Dictionary, because I do not believe in the soundness of his judgement or the sufficiency of his scholarship; and therefore he tries to get me into trouble. He speaks of himself as a former 'Editor'; he never 'edited' one word— only superintended the Reading.[14]

Furnivall did write to the Delegates calling attention to alleged defects in the treatment of these words, but the new Editor had successfully established his authority, and after a few months Furnivall withdrew his objections.[15]

James was still left with the problem of compounds, which he had put amusingly to Ellis in 1876:

> The other day I found myself *chairless*, in one of the rooms, and I am sometimes all but *bootless* and *shoeless*, before I can stir up the local shoemaker. We are not quite *tailorless* and so not obliged to go *trouserless*, like the *thoughtless* & *careless* if not quite *shameless* inhabitants of the *treeless, cultureless, gasless, Daily-paperless* & once *schoolless* regions of the north. The subject is endless & exhaustless, *boundless* & *bottomless* but the raising of it is not *purposeless* I assure you. Then must I not, if a place is *carpenterless*, at times wield the hammer *carpenter-wise* myself—or if my floor is *carpetless* spread it *carpet-wise* with something . . . A great deal of this applies equally to -ful, -ly, -ism, -ize etc. Think of this when *sleeplessly* tossing on your bed, or *carriagelessly* scuttling home in the rain. Yours truly, if *breathlessly*, JAHM.[16]

In 1879 he told the Philological Society that after many trials he thought he had found a satisfactory principle on which to divide compounds into those which should be treated as separate words and those not requiring definition, but in 1882 he was still worried about the compounds and proposed printing an example of the combinations of the words *all* and *alms* in order to 'elicit the judgment of critics as to where an end is to be forcibly put to them'.[17]

A basic question he had to consider in these preparatory years was 'What is the English Language?' People spoke of it as if it were a known and well accepted mass of words which could be counted. James was often asked, 'How many words are there in the language of Englishmen?' To this he would reply

> Of *some* Englishmen? or of *all* Englishmen? is it *all* that *all* Englishmen speak, or *some* of what *some* Englishmen speak? Does it include the English of Scotland and of Ireland, the speech of British Englishmen, and American Englishmen, of Australian Englishmen, South African Englishmen, and of the Englishmen in India?[18]

In his Introduction to the first volume of the Dictionary Dr Murray said that the vocabulary of a living language is not a fixed quantity with defined limits.

> That vast aggregate of words and phrases which constitutes the Vocabulary of English-speaking men presents, to the mind that endeavours to grasp it as a definite whole, the aspect of one of those nebulous masses familiar to the astronomer, in which a clear and unmistakable nucleus shades off on all sides, through zones of decreasing brightness, to a dim marginal film that seems to end nowhere, but to lose itself imperceptibly in the surrounding darkness.

He compared its constitution to a natural group in botany, where typical species are linked to other species in which the typical features become less and less distinct:

> So the English Vocabulary contains a nucleus or central mass of many thousand words whose 'Anglicity' is unquestioned; some of them only literary, some of them only colloquial, the great majority at once literary and colloquial, —they are the *Common Words* of the language. But they are linked on every side with other words which are less and less entitled to this appellation, and which pertain ever

more and more distinctly to the domain of local dialect, of the slang and cant of 'sets' and classes, of the peculiar technicalities of trades and processes, of the scientific terminology common to all civilized nations, of the actual languages of other lands and peoples. And there is absolutely no defining line in any direction: the circle of the English language has a well-defined centre but no discernible circumference.

This he illustrated by a diagram:

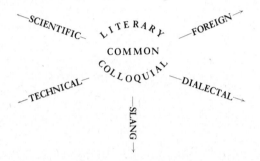

Foreign and scientific words enter the language mainly through the written word, slang through colloquial use: technical terms and dialect words are introduced both through speech and through literature: slang touches on the one side the technical terminology of trades and occupations (e.g. nautical slang) and on the other true dialect, while dialects similarly pass into foreign languages, and scientific terminology has links both with foreign languages and with technology. 'It is not possible to fix the point at which the "English Language" stops, along any of these diverging lines.'[19]

There was another undefined frontier, that of time. A living language is in a continuous state of change, of 'slow but incessant dissolution and renovation'. It is hard to fix the moment at which a word dies: our grandparents continue to use words which are already obsolete to us: new words are accepted by a few individuals before they become generally used, some may never become 'good English' or any other sort of English. Language begins with the spoken word and only gradually is recorded in writing and print: for the earliest periods when there were few books, of which few have survived, many words must have been unrecorded. Where then, does one fix the dates of entry and termination of a word's 'current usage'?[20]

The founders of the Philological Society's Dictionary had seen clearly that

> the mere merit of a word in an artistic or aesthetic point of view is a consideration, which the Lexicographer cannot for a moment entertain . . . the literary merit or demerit of any particular writer, like the comparative elegance or inelegance of any given word, is a subject upon which the Lexicographer is bound to be almost indifferent.[21]

James Murray accepted this as axiomatic, but it was not always easy to apply in practice. What, for example, was he to do about sexual words and colloquial coarse expressions, some of which have only in the 1970s become acceptable in print?[22] One of the voluntary readers, James Dixon, felt that the world *condum* was 'too utterly obscene' for inclusion and his letter discussing its etymology remains in its envelope marked 'Private'. On the other hand Dixon thought that it would be cowardly to shirk *pudendum*, but suggested it 'might be curtly dismissed—of course without a quotation,—a thing presque introuvable'.[23]

James did not exclude these words without careful consideration and advice, and left to himself he would have included some— especially those whose history showed them to have been originally reputable words later debased by vulgar usage—which contemporary opinion forced him to omit. He discussed the question with Dr J. S. Farmer, who was engaged in bringing out a dictionary of Slang and its Analogues. Farmer's policy was to include every word, but 'where the examples are coarse, to deal with them decently', wrapping up any explanations 'in language not "understanded" of the people'—i.e. Latin. In spite of his care Farmer was involved in a law suit with his publishers for breach of contract occasioned by their refusal to publish obscene words. Farmer asked Murray if he might quote one of his letters in support of his decision to include such terms. 'I am', he wrote, 'in a small way fighting your own battle in advance, and that may not be altogether without weight with you.'[24] James had really no choice but to leave them out of the Dictionary, but he was upset when a reviewer accused him of squeamishness and lack of courage.[25]

Another problem was to decide what words had really entered the language. The quotations were the evidence that a word had been used at a particular date in a particular way or sense, but was it sufficient if only one example had been found? What about words invented 'for the nonce', or as a joke, or mis-spellings by famous authors?[26] There was a special class of words, James found, which he termed 'dictionary or ghost words'—words which had never been used in speech or writing but had originated in some misreading or misprint, admitted to a dictionary and copied thereafter in all subsequent compilations.[27] Even the work of Johnson needed verification. James discovered that the confusion of the *coco nut* (fruit of the palm tree) and the *cocoa bean* originated in a printing or clerical error in Johnson by which the title word for *coco* was accidentally omitted and the word *cocoa* attached to the quotations for both nouns.[28] James made it a rule never to accept an unusual 'dictionary word' without finding a supporting quotation proving actual usage, and never to accept a word on the strength of a single quotation unless the form and derivation were otherwise perfectly clear. He was sometimes over-ruled by those he consulted. In 1893, for instance, he was advised to include the American words *cruster* and *crust-hunt* on the authority of the *Century Dictionary*. Furnivall and others adjudged them 'good words' but 'trivial', in as much as the derivations were easy and the words such as anyone might coin if this had not already been done. The advice was, 'We cannot act as if we had unlimited time to look for trivial words'. But it went against the grain and James did not often take such an easy solution.[29]

He relied much on the judgement of Henry Hucks Gibbs, the able sub-editor of *C*, in these matters, although he did not always agree with him. Gibbs would have taken a more rigid line, because his personal judgement was influenced by his literary prejudices

> It is well—very well—[he wrote] to fix the first entry of a word into the language; but you must be quite sure that it *has* entered . . . and is not a mere vagrant knocking at the door & who will be deservedly sent about his business. Don't allow slovenly or conceited writers to deposit their $\alpha\pi\alpha\xi\ \lambda\epsilon\gamma o\mu\epsilon\nu\alpha$ in your demesne—to shoot their rubbish over land that you are tilling so carefully! If you must honour such words as 'accommodated' (D[aily] T[elegraph]) 'accidented' 'accouche' and 'accoucheuse' by taking notice of them, in case they should ultimately creep into the language . . . you should have a separate limbo to which to relegate them—a hot one, I should suggest.[30]

Gibbs was also influenced by the need to set limits to the work from a practical point of view and echoed Skeat's advice

I would abandon to future investigators all such words as *alamite*, *alpeen*, and many others which now tire your brain and use up valuable time . . . Waste no time and thought in correspondence about them . . . reserve your time & brains for those words you do know and can easily get explained, and let most of the others slide.[31]

Never, at any time, did James Murray yield to the temptation of omitting a word because it was difficult or because it would save time: his own criterion for exclusion was that *inclusion* would not improve the Dictionary and might cumber it needlessly.

Although inevitably the Dictionary was not perfect, and the mere fact that it took fifty years to complete resulted in a few inconsistencies, one of the great achievements of its first Editor was to fix guiding lines which ensured the standardisation of treatment throughout and established a pattern which stood the test of time. There has been change in the policy of what should be included, but no important change in form was required when the four volume Supplement was planned in the 1970s. That James was so successful was largely due to the infinite pains he took in the first years to seek the advice of every expert known to him, although in the end he had to use his discretion and find his own answer to each point of difficulty.

Another technical matter to which James devoted much time and thought at the outset was that of typography. Here, helped by the Press, he drew on his experience gained from printing his *Horae Paulinae* and from preparing the nine different proofs of his specimens for Macmillan. Now he set up a large portion, including the word *all*, with its many combinations and derivatives, trying various samples of type and obtaining the opinion of the Delegates and other scholars on the pattern suggested.[32] He took as his model Littré, and arranged the work in three columns to a page, but by allowing wider margins and by using different sizes and strengths of type he greatly improved on the French dictionary, which was described by Henry Bradley as 'a chaos through which the reader must find his way as best he can'.[33] Littré has hardly any paragraphs and he printed the illustrative examples in the same type and continuously with the definitions, while James succeeded in directing the eye at once to the key information. The standard form of each word, printed in large Clarendon type, stands out boldly. The various historical forms are given in smaller Clarendon, and the definitions in Old Style. The quotations in smaller Old Style, each preceded by the date in Clarendon figures, come after each sense of the word and serve to separate the definitions from each other. The result is easy and pleasant to read and again has stood the test of time: the typography was clear enough to allow of the production of a two volume micrographic 'compact' edition in 1971 with a magnifying glass with which to read it.

When James started work on the Dictionary in 1879 he underestimated the time he would have to give to the work. He still kept up his 'leisure' activities: he read Mr Ellis' proofs for him and corrected his own proofs of the text of *Guy of Warwick*, before he gave it to Professor Zupitza for publication. As President of the Philological Society he was regularly in the Chair, indulged in a spirited attack on Henry Sweet's definition of dialects and helped to translate some of the foreign papers submitted. He was of course teaching for most of the week and deeply involved in troubles within the school. In the Scriptorium he found he was working against time and whenever he spent too long in establishing a point he fell behind his schedule. The gas light shining out of the Scriptorium skylights late at night became familiar to Mill Hillians.[34]

In the spring of 1880 for the first time in his life his health gave cause for anxiety, he suffered from headaches and was absent from school for a time in February. Dr Weymouth urged Ada to take him down to the sea for a week or a month of complete rest without a single book.[35] Furnivall also advised him to 'go for a walk, have a bath, or do nothing & rest . . . mind, keep well first, do the Dicty next'.[36]

Ada did not succeed in getting him away to the sea at once, but in April he joined Harold for a short holiday at Chepstow, staying with John Yeats, a former pupil and staunch supporter of the Dictionary. James had unusual resilience and after twenty-four hours he wrote to Ada,

> I . . . feel already much the better . . . The air today was keen & northern; the general aspect too of the many stone walls covered with ferns, the limestone cliffs, & distant blue hills of upper Gwent, are a delight to one's eyes. We were up & out by 7 this morning & did over 3 miles before breakfast besides the 8 or 9 miles since.

They visited that day Caerwent, Caldicot Castle, the Severn tunnel, then under construction, and Sudbury British Camp. James added 'There is a tremendous lot of local fudge about Romans, & Danes, and Vandals & no end of people — I list to it all with pleasure but of course

I smile at the enthusiasm of the local antiquaries—I once was one, and know the amiable weaknesses of the race.' The only thing lacking was Ada's presence, but she was expecting another baby.[37]

After this near breakdown, James had to begin cutting out some of his commitments and when he gave his Presidential address to the Philological Society in May he apologised for his failure to produce the customary review of the work of the Society for the past year, being, he said 'one engaged in a special department, to which every hour is consecrated and who is bound by every tie of duty to restrict his attention to the immediate work.' 'Hoc unum facio' was from henceforth to be his rule.[38]

The work went steadily on during 1880, but by January of the following year James was so overworked that he said letter writing had become 'a loathing' to him.[39] Furnivall attributed everything to the worry of the crisis at Mill Hill school. He urged him to tell Dr Price about the difficulties, feeling sure that if the true state of affairs were known at Oxford one of the new Professorships, or one of the Fellowships for persons engaged in literary or scientific work, the creation of which had been recommended by the University Commissioners, would be found for him.[40]

In May 1881 James explained to the Philological Society that their calculation that the Dictionary could be produced in ten years was 'utterly fallacious' because much of the sub-editing had either not been done at all or so badly done that it must be revised.[41] Seven of the old sub-editors renewed work and James recruited twenty-eight others, three of them women, all, like the readers, working in their own homes. Realising the disastrous results of Furnivall's practice of leaving the sub-editors with little guidance,[42] James gave up many hours to their supervision. He found it best to allocate to each volunteer only a small section at a time, both to minimise their discouragement at slow progress and also give himself opportunity for frequent checking of their work. He would explain in long careful letters where they had gone wrong, do part of their sections himself as a model, and suggest how their work could be improved. He hoped it would save time eventually, but at the moment it slowed up his own editorial work considerably and as the years went by he came to question the value of the sub-editors' work. By the time it came to be used much of it was out of date and the original workers had died. It never paid to set new men to complete and re-sub-edit the work. 'In 9 cases out of 10', he said, 'they merely make a confusion of it,

upsetting what has been done perhaps by better men than themselves.'

On the whole [he concluded in 1910] the volunteer sub-editing tho'
done with the greatest good-will, and immense diligence, has not
been a great help. Out of nearly 40 who have tried it, it would be
difficult to pick out 8 . . . whose help has been appreciably worth
the trouble . . . I have had to come to the conclusion that practically
the only valuable work that can be done by the average amateur, &
out of the Scriptorium, is that of reading books and extracting
quotations.[43]

James also tried to convey to the Society something of the
magnitude of the task he had undertaken. By 1881 he had sent out
817,625 slips to readers—fifteen hundredweight of paper. He
estimated that if each new slip returned with a quotation took only
half a minute to inspect this would occupy him for three working
years, but since the new represented only a third of the total number
of slips and many of the original ones were so badly written and so
incomplete in their references, even a cursory examination would take
much longer.[44] The space allowed for the inclusion of only about a
fifth of the quotations collected, and selection was bound to be a
lengthy process.[45]

In spite of the activity of the army of readers the gaps in the
material were still a constant source of anxiety and delay:

For more than five-sixths of the words we have to search out and
find additional quotations in order to complete their history [he
told the Society in 1884] . . . for *every* word we have to make a
general search to discover whether any earlier or later quotations,
or quotations in other senses, exist . . . Nearly the whole quotations
for *about, after, all, also, and . . . any, as . . .* have had to be found by
myself and my assistants.

The directions given to the readers still put too much emphasis on
unusual words, now he wished that he had asked them to take out
quotations for all words which did *not* strike them as rare because so
often the common words had been neglected. Sometimes, he said,
after he had spent hours of precious time trying to find suitable
quotations from modern sources, he had had to concoct his own
illustrations.[46] Sitting by Ada's bedside just after the birth of Elsie
Mayflower (1 May 1882), correcting the proofs of the first section of
the Dictionary, he added to the first column of page 2, as an example

of *a* following an adjective preceded by *as*, 'As fine a child as you will see'. The next section to be published included the word *arrival*, in the sense of 'one that arrives or has arrived', and the quotation, 'the new arrival is a little daughter', again commemorated a Murray daughter—Rosfrith (5 February 1884).[47]

Even when all the slips were at hand and sorted much remained to be done: sub-editors might attempt definitions and etymologies, but the final responsibility for them lay with the Editor, and at this stage he had to seek help from experts. Every week he had to write twenty or thirty letters asking for information and in a lecture James gave examples of what this involved

I write to the Director of the Royal Botanic Gardens at Kew about the first record of the name of an exotic plant; to a quay-side merchant at Newcastle about the *Keels* on the Tyne; to a Jesuit father on a point of Roman Catholic Divinity; to the Secretary of the Astronomical Society about the *primum-mobile* or the solar constant; to the Editor of the *Times* for the context of a quotation from the Times of 30 years ago; to the India Office about a letter of the year 1620 containing the first mention of *Punch* [the beverage]; to a Wesleyan minister about the *itineracy*; to Lord Tennyson to ask where he got the word *balm-cricket* and what he meant by it;[48] to the *Sporting News* about a term in horse-racing, or pugilism; or the inventor of the word *hooligan* in June 1898; to the Librarian of Cambridge University Library for the reading of the first edition of a rare book; to the Deputy Keeper of the Rolls for the exact reading of a historical M.S. which we have reason to suspect has been inaccurately quoted by Mr. Froude; to a cotton manufacturer for a definition of *Jaconet*, or a technical term of cotton printing; to George Meredith to ask what is the meaning of a line of one of his poems; to Thomas Hardy to ask what is the meaning of a word *terminatory* in one of his novels; to the Editor of the New York *Nation* for the history of an American political term; to the administrator of the Andaman Islands for the exact reference to an early quotation which he has sent for the word Jute, or the history of *Talapoin*; to the Mayor of Yarmouth about the word *bloater* in the herring fishery; to the chief Rabbi for the latest views upon the Hebrew *Jubilee*; to a celebrated collector of popular songs for the authorship of 'We don't want to fight, But by *Jingo* if we do', which gave his name to the political *Jingo*.[49]

Usually he solved the problem, but sometimes nobody knew and after writing twelve or even twenty letters about one word he had to give up because it was time to go to print.

As the Dictionary and its Editor got known the traffic of letters became two-way, almost as many inquiries coming to the Scriptorium as were sent out from it, and sometimes amusingly going in a circle. Early on, James wished to find the origin of the word *aphis*, first used by Linnaeus for *green fly*, and he wrote to the Zoological Secretary of the Linnaean Society for help. The Secretary replied 'I have sent your letter on to the one man who can answer it, Mr So & So, who has written the Monograph on the British Aphides, and I have no doubt he will send you a full answer.' This was encouraging, but in two days came another letter from a clerical friend in London, marked Immediate, which ran

> Dear Dr Murray
> Will you send me by return if possible, the etymology of the word Aphis? Dr B. a clergyman in Surrey, a friend of mine, a great Greek scholar, has been asked by a very distinguished naturalist, who lives near him, if he can tell him its derivation. Dr B. has looked up the Greek Lexicon and can get no light on it : but he is very anxious not to admit his failure; he knows that I know *you* and that *you* know everything, and he begs me to get the etymology from you to save his reputation as a Greek scholar.[50]

Even when the experts had provided the required information the actual writing of the definitions was not always straightforward. A case brought against the Clarendon Press as recently as July 1973 illustrates the possible pitfalls. A merchant claimed that the definitions of 'Jew' in the Oxford Dictionaries were 'scurrilous and defamatory'.[51] James Murray took infinite pains over the wording of his definitions of such words as *Altar* and *Catholic* where religious sensibilities might be offended.[52]

Most difficult and time consuming of all was the historical side of the work. While making full use of existing dictionaries and the etymological work of Walter Skeat and others, he found there were many corrections to make and that no one previously had traced the etymology of Middle English words, so that he and his assistants were like pioneers 'pushing our way experimentally through an untrodden forest where no white man's axe has been before us.' The great collection of quotations made it possible for the first time to illustrate

11. The Dictionary: a portion of James Murray's manuscript as sent to the printer.

the successive changes of form and sense which words had undergone. This was the most valuable feature of the new Dictionary and one of the most difficult to produce as James found:

Only those who have made the experiment [he wrote] know the bewilderment with which editor or sub-editor, after he has apportioned the quotations for such a word as *above* . . . among 20, 30 or 40 groups, and furnished each of these with a provisional definition, spreads them out on a table or on the floor [James often carried them to his drawing room floor or his dining table] where he can obtain a general survey of the whole, and spends hour after hour in shifting them about like the pieces on a chess-board, striving to find in the fragmentary evidence of an incomplete historical record, such a sequence of meanings as may form a logical chain of development. Sometimes the quest seems hopeless; recently, for example, the word *art* utterly baffled me for several days: something *had* to be done with it: something was done and put in type; but the renewed consideration of it in print, with the greater facility of reading and comparison which this afforded, led to the entire pulling to pieces and reconstruction of the edifice, extending to several columns of type . . . those who think that such work can be hurried, or that anything can accelerate it, except more brain power brought to bear on it, had better try.[53]

It was at the proof stage also that the quotations and surplus words in the definitions had to be pruned in order to keep within the limits of space and all this meant a new cause of delay when the proofs began to flow in. James' estimate of the work and the time needed was wildly out. In February 1882 he told Hucks Gibbs that it was '*very* hard work to finish 33 words a day. Often a single word, like *Approve* . . . takes $\frac{3}{4}$ of a day itself', and yet he needed to do more than this to complete the Dictionary even in sixteen years.[54] When proofs had to be corrected every day he found that he was taking at least six hours on this, leaving only three hours for preparing new words.[55] The task was beginning to look utterly hopeless.

CHAPTER XI

The Triple Nightmare:
Space, Time, and Money

WHILE the strain of over-long hours of work and the troubles of Mill Hill School were certainly contributory causes of ill-health and depression, the root of James' troubles lay deeper and was mentioned as early as Christmas 1879 in correspondence with Henry Nicol. 'I am sorry to hear the Dictionary is likely to take so much longer than was expected [Nicol wrote] and that you will suffer pecuniarily by it; I can only hope that, in the end, your share of the profits will more than compensate for the immediate sacrifice.'[1]

It had now become clear to James that he needed much more space, more time and more money, and that these needs were inter-related. Space, time and money were to be the problems which haunted him for the thirty-five years spent in editing the Dictionary—a triple nightmare which removed much of his enjoyment of the work.

The more he progressed in compiling the first section, the more certain he became that the calculations which he and others had made of the size of the Dictionary were wrong: a much bigger work was needed to do justice to the wealth of material. Any attempt to condense it to the agreed size would detract from the value of the Dictionary to such an extent that he would feel no pride in it, and the labour of abridgement would be so difficult that it would add much to the time needed for the editorial work. But more space would mean that the Dictionary would cost the Press a great deal in excess of the anticipated sum. Since size had been one of the reasons for the failure of the Macmillan/Harper negotiations, James faced the alarming prospect that it might lead to another breakdown. The need for more time had also financial implications: it would postpone the day when the Press might hope to recover its outlay in profit on sales, while for himself, under contract to edit the Dictionary for a fixed sum, it might mean ruin.

12. Henry Hucks Gibbs, Lord Aldenham. 1862.

At first he kept his worries to himself, sharing his anxiety only with Ada and one or two close friends, but at length he turned for help to Henry Hucks Gibbs.

Hucks Gibbs, later the first Baron Aldenham, was both scholar and businessman. As a scholar, he had not only, with his cousin Charlotte M. Yonge, the authoress, worked for the Dictionary from its early years, but had also edited editions for the Early English Text Society and the Roxburghe Club. He was a keen churchman, a restorer of buildings, including St Albans Abbey, and as a benefactor of Keble College he was influential in Oxford circles. As a businessman and head of the family firm of Bankers he became Director and Governor of the Bank of England and M.P. for the City of London.[2] Above all, he was a man of great common sense and insight into human nature. He could understand the different points of view of employers and employees and knew how words and actions could be misinterpreted. During the difficult years from 1882 to 1896 it was Hucks Gibbs whose statesmanship prevented Editor and Publishers of the Dictionary giving up the enterprise.

James greatly valued his judgment on technical matters connected with the Dictionary, finding that he always showed the capacity to look at questions from a broad, wise point of view. At first Hucks

Gibbs had not wanted to become involved again, feeling that he had brought his sub-editing of *C* to a conclusion, but when he realised how far from ready the material was as a whole, he became again an active helper and read every proof.[3] James enjoyed discussing philological details with him, and found in him unfailing kindness and integrity at a time when he felt he was surrounded by hostile critics and intriguers. If he had ever written the history of the Dictionary himself, it was James' intention to see that Gibbs' part was made known and that 'honour, and credit, and praise, are richly given where richly due', to one whom he termed 'my best of friends'.[4]

The first problem which James put to Gibbs was that of space, because Dean Liddell, Gibbs himself and others had complained that the quotations were being shortened too much and losing their literary interest.[5] In 1881, when settling typographical details with the Delegates, James had hinted at this problem and had explained to Mark Pattison, with whom he had walked up to the Bodleian library after the meeting, that with more space he could actually work more quickly, by saving this work of abridgement.[6] Pattison's reaction was encouraging, and when Hucks Gibbs agreed to act as intermediary in October of the same year, he found Dr Price, now quite convinced of the success of the Dictionary, in spite of his initial doubts, took 'a very reasonable view'. Max Müller also realised the impossibility of trying to fix a rigid limit, saying, 'the work would extend itself willy nilly'.[7] But by this time James had realised that even with 20,000 pages it would still not be possible to include quotations of the length of those enjoyed by readers of Richardson's Dictionary. 'I fear', he now reported to Gibbs, 'that we cannot dream of giving to the book this *literary* interest of being a readable collection of pithy sentences or elegant extracts, without abandoning altogether our distinctive character — that of actually showing . . . the history of each word.' The problem was not merely that of contracting quotations but of reducing the actual treatment of the words to fit the whole into the agreed limit of 7000 pages, which was four times the size of Webster's *Dictionary*. James found that in treating an interesting word like *Alms* he had exceeded Webster by ten times and that on an average it would be impossible to manage with less than 10,000 pages — representing six times the older Dictionary. 'If you can bring the Delegates up to that point', he told Gibbs, 'it will be a great boon, I may say rather a *necessity* of the Dictionary's practical usefulness.'[8]

The Delegates duly agreed, but only to an extension of 2000

pages—six volumes of 1400 pages each, instead of the four volumes of 1600 pages originally planned.[9] Once again Furnivall had intervened with unfortunate results. His ideas, as so often, were sensible and would have saved much future trouble. He wanted an open-ended agreement, with the 8400 pages as a minimum only, but there was little hope of the Delegates' accepting this, especially when it was pressed with Furnivall's usual lack of tact. He only hardened their attitude. Warning Price that Furnivall was showing his customary 'cantankerousness, and fondness of quarrelling', James exclaimed with exasperation that the man gave him more than trouble enough in other ways. He sent a strong letter of protest to him, saying 'As I hope to induce them to go to 10,000, and have found them not unreasonable on the matter, I regret your remarks, which are not those likely to be successful. I should have thought that you would by this time have seen enough of the impolicy of quarrelling with people who are better as friends than as enemies.'[10]

James was very disappointed with the new limit of 8400 pages, which barely gave him the space the specimens he had already prepared showed was likely to be needed, and allowed no elbow room.[11] Henry Hucks Gibbs also was not at all happy, and asked James whether he felt in honour bound to confine himself so strictly to the authorised total. It seemed to him very unwise to accept a rigid limit in advance, and that in any case it would be impossible for the Press to establish 'proof of damage' and to impose a penalty should the work turn out to exceed the agreed number of pages.[12] He got a firm and characteristic reply from James

> Yes; I consider myself in honour & duty bound to confine the work to whatever limits they prescribe, and by constantly seeing, say every 10 pages, that I am marching at even ratio with Webster to secure that the result is attained. I am not quite marching through an untrodden region—there are abundance of footsteps before me, and it means merely following one of these predecessors & taking 4, 5 or 6 steps to his one.

He explained that with Webster's *Dictionary* as his standard—an unfortunate legacy from the negotiations with Macmillan—the 10,000 pages he had hoped for would have been six times Webster, while the 8400 pages would be only $5\frac{1}{2}$ to 1. In either case he could never plead ignorance if he over-ran the limit.

James was obsessed by self-blame because his underestimate of the size of the work would involve the Delegates in additional cost for paper and printing. When the idea was that extra space would be used for longer quotations he calculated that this would save him time and that therefore he could offer to undertake the longer work without extra remuneration.[13] It was a very different matter when it was found that the extra pages would be needed for longer articles, since this would mean more editorial work. None the less he proposed that however much the new Dictionary exceeded the old, his payment should only be for the number of pages covered by the same words in Webster. In order to secure this, he accepted an agreement that he should receive only seventeen shillings a page produced, instead of the twenty shillings a page fixed by the original contract.[14]

For a Scotchman James was certainly extraordinarily lacking in hard-headedness and Gibbs not unnaturally could not see why it was unreasonable to ask for more money for more work.[15] James' attitude may be explained by his reaction to the mention of 'honour' and by the importance he attached to his contract and the employers to whom it bound him. His code of conduct had been given to him in childhood, typified by the story of his ancestor who found the pot of gold and at once handed it to his landlord. Any idea that he might 'take a chance' that the Delegates would not notice if he exceeded the limits they had set, or gamble that, if he did let the Dictionary run to too many pages, nothing would, or could, be done about it, was to him unthinkable. He also took his contract seriously—it was after all the only document which protected his position and included his eventual share in the royalties. Some at least of the Delegates might share his view of the document, holding that 'business is business' and a bargain must be held to, good or bad.[16] Gibbs regarded it as a contract which should never have been accepted in so far as it imposed limits of time and space; he was confident that the Delegates as reasonable men must come to recognise this, and he thought James should stand out till they did. James, on the other hand, conscious of his humble origin and lack of university background, felt he must defer to the 'great men' at Oxford, exaggerating their authority and attributing to them the arbitrariness of a remote hierachy—a view in which Furnivall had originally encouraged him.

With the problem of space temporarily settled, James Murray turned to Gibbs again, this time with his two other problems, those of the time he now estimated would be needed to complete the Dictionary and the effect of this upon his own financial position. He sent Gibbs a very long letter which he had delayed writing till February 1882 owing to pressure of work.[17] As the date of going to press approached and with many of the materials for Part I coming in at the last moment—or not at all—he said that he had had no moment since Christmas for anything but work, work, work! He began by telling Gibbs that it was now patent to him that the Dictionary could not be completed in anything approaching to the time named in the contract. He estimated that the very shortest time needed, including the three preliminary years, would be sixteen or seventeen years. He revealed his anxiety that he was not being straightforward because he had not told the Delegates:

> In the interests of the Dictionary I have desired not to raise the question of time, or any other, till we get the work fairly launched, believing that then, when its value is realized, and it is seen that I am doing as much as mortal man can do, the Delegates would be satisfied, and if anxious that the work should be expedited, would offer me more skilled assistance.

He went on to refer to his fear that the majority of the Delegates, '(who care nothing specially for English & do not realize *a priori* the grandeur of the work) might put up their backs & say, We won't stand this, we will rather stop it ... the thing worries me, and interferes with my mental peace, more perhaps than you can realize.'

He was haunted by the fear that the publication of the Dictionary would once more be abandoned, this time perhaps for ever, to the shame of the nation and irreparable loss to scholarship. He dreaded to face the reaction to such a debacle from his 800 enthusiastic voluntary helpers. Both Dr Price and Max Müller had told him that some of the Delegates were very luke-warm and grumbled at so large a part of the resources of the Press being diverted to an object outside the University. Their failure to come and see the Scriptorium seemed to confirm this, while the fact that he too was an 'outsider' would no doubt be another reason why a majority might be only too glad of an excuse to drop the Dictionary.[18]

He went on to tell Hucks Gibbs of his own desperate financial position.[19] Of the £9000 total remuneration which had been agreed, £2100 had already been paid to him, leaving only £6900 for the thirteen or fourteen years for which he now expected his life still to be mortgaged to the Dictionary. For a married man, less than £500 a year, almost all of which would be needed to pay the salaries of his assistants and other expenses, was a daunting prospect.[20] 'I am filled with perplexity [he told Hucks Gibbs], and at times my heart quite fails me. It has done so a good deal of late: and the state is not favourable to work.' He had been prepared to give his services for nothing for the first three years, but now he found that expenses had been so heavy he was actually £200 poorer than if he had never seen the Dictionary, and his letter continued:

> I have really, in my anxiety to press on & complete the preliminary work, spent far more than I ought upon it: partly also goaded to it by Mr Furnivall, who has continually said 'You must get this, & you must do that, & you must pay somebody to do the other thing,' and whose possessing idea seemed to be the fear that I should make money out of the work![21] I am not a capitalist, but a poor man, and have only saved a few hundred pounds in anticipation of the time when I should have to spend some on the further education & starting in life of my boys, by annual savings to which the Dictionary put a stop . . . I have had to say rather bitterly: 'I took up the Dictionary as a student, asking only to be repaid the income I sacrificed in its behalf, and to be furnished with the necessary assistance, and I find myself . . . with an incessant struggle to make ends meet, & failing in the struggle' . . . it is certain that we have all underestimated the cost to *somebody* . . . and that it is I on whom the consequences fall, & whom they threaten to crush.

In another letter, reverting to his Scotch dialect, he likened the Dictionary to a '*fifch* thing that never can be satisfied, a great abyss that will never cry "Enough"!'[22]

He did not blame the Delegates who, he felt, had acted generously in advancing so much money for the preparation of the work, and at first Hucks Gibbs was in favour of letting them know the facts at once. On second thoughts he advised James to wait till after the issue of Part I, when Oxford would surely think it an honour to be associated with a work certain to be acclaimed as a significant contribution to scholarship.[23] Gibbs was influenced by the discovery, when he examined the figures, that James was to some extent to blame for the errors in his estimates, and that Dean Liddell was rather annoyed that the Press should have been misled.[24] James had rounded off sums downwards rather than upwards—writing £900 for an actual £975 for example—and had reduced his figure for expenses to such an extent that it was obvious he would be out of pocket. He had done this partly from inexperience, partly because he wanted to make a personal contribution to the project and partly from fear that the Delegates would draw back if the cost seemed too great.

When James reviewed his expenses for the first year he found he had spent more than the £300, which should have covered everything, on salaries alone. The unexpected confusion of the slips had made it necessary to employ the two lady helpers for much longer than he had intended and although Furnivall continued to maintain that Herbert Ruthven was an extravagance and that Herrtage, the two girls, and a museum clerk at fifteen shillings a week should be all the help needed,[25] the advice was at variance with the facts, which were that the work was seriously behindhand. Moreover the inconsistent Furnivall would take it upon himself to employ additional readers for the Dictionary in the British Museum Library, and then expect James to pay them. James was particularly indignant about a personal friend of Furnivall's, Eleanor Marx, daughter of Karl Marx, who claimed to have spent 110 hours collecting 144 words. The work should not have taken more than twelve hours and was of no use as all the words were from modern dictionaries and glossaries and none were new.[26]

In addition to salaries, James had paid £150 for building the Scriptorium and over £100 for reference books. He complained in 1880 that he found 'the cost of books is enormous . . . and I seem about as far off having everything I want as ever'.[27] He had made insufficient allowance for stationery and postage. Under the arrangements with the Press he had to supply the paper (costing him £50) for the ready printed slips with which readers of long books were supplied, to save them the labour of entering particulars of the title and edition for each quotation. These slips had to be sent to the readers, often with a copy of the book to be read, and the carriage both ways mounted up to £75 in the first year.[28] He became an expert in finding cheap methods of transport by road to all parts of the kingdom and wrote in angry protest to the Postmaster General in July 1879 to complain of the 'serious ignorance of the regulations of the Department on the part of the Post Office Employés at Codford St. Mary', who had forced one of the readers to send two packets by letter post at over a shilling each instead of a few pence printed rate. 'As I shall have many thousands of such packages during the next 10 years . . . I cannot afford to lose money thus overcharged by incompetent persons in your employment.'[29] He subsequently established a good relationship with the Post Office: the district Inspector visited the

Scriptorium to see the work, with the result that if any packets broke open in transit, the slips strewn about in the post-bags were collected and delivered after a little delay. When he moved to Oxford, out of consideration for his convenience, the Post Office placed a pillar box outside his house, where it still stands. 'Dr Murray, Oxford' was a sufficient address. He was also successful in persuading the Postmaster General of the United States to allow manuscript Dictionary slips to count as printed matter, which he was at first doubtful could be allowed under the terms of the Postal Union. This extended to packets from European countries. He attributed the scarcity of contributors from the British Colonies to the niggardliness of the Government in refusing any such concessions. Even with all his care, postage ate into his private savings.

In 1882, when he acquainted Hucks Gibbs with the story, James had already received the whole payment due for the first three years' work, and could not expect any further money until the publication of Part I. Having advised against an approach to the Delegates at this stage, Hucks Gibbs began lending him money to meet the salaries of the assistants and other expenses.[30] It seems strange that it did not occur to Dr Price, who took charge of the financial arrangements for the Press, that the Editor might be short of money.

Unfortunately all James' friends were not so wise as Hucks Gibbs. Ever since the controversy over the Philological Society's share of the royalties, Furnivall had regarded the Delegacy as an enemy and constantly referred to the meanness shown. Now he would not wait to see what would happen when the facts were made known, but assumed that the Delegates must be shocked or shamed into action. In March 1882 he launched a scheme for a public appeal for money to meet editorial expenses for which it was fairly evident that the Press should be responsible.[31] Ellis was entrusted by Furnivall with a very naïve strategy. He was to ask the Delegates to print the appeal and sanction the use of a specimen page of the Dictionary with it, in the hope that they would put matters right themselves, rather than allow so damaging a document to be circulated to the public.[32] Not surprisingly the reaction was a chilly one; the Delegates would not be parties to any such appeal and strongly objected to its circulation.[33] They did, however, see James and authorised an advance of up to £300 on account for the money due to him on publication of Part I, with the assurance that the whole question of future arrangements for the Dictionary would be reviewed in the autumn.[34] Ellis took credit for this result, but it seems more likely to have been achieved through Hucks Gibbs, and Ellis probably did more harm than good.[35] The Delegates naturally did not like being driven to act by a pistol at their heads. James was also upset. He had been obliged to supply Ellis with the facts of his position, but felt a culprit, although Ellis told him that his only fault had been an error of judgment in entering upon a certain engagement for the Dictionary before he had all the facts.[36]

By 1882 it was abundantly clear to everyone concerned, Delegates, Editor and Philological Society, that things were not proceeding according to plan. Under the contract, publication should have begun in the spring of 1882 and then gone forward at a steady pace. It was another two years before Part I (*A* to *ANT*) was published (29 January 1884) and four years more before, with the end of *B*, the first complete volume appeared. It might perhaps have been foreseen. Furnivall knew that he had been deceptive as to the state of the material: James had outlined a programme which could have been seen to be over optimistic: the Delegates might have taken note of the very slow progress of Grimms' *Wörterbuch*. In that case publication had started in 1851 after thirteen years' preparation; the first volume took three years to complete and Jacob Grimm had died in 1863 in the middle of the letter *F*. Altogether the Germans took seventy-five years to cover only five sixths of the vocabulary. When the Oxford Dictionary was completed, seventy years after the inception of the work by the Philological Society and fifty years after James Murray became Editor, the speed of production was a matter for congratulation, but at the start the delays filled everyone with despondency.[37]

The next fifteen years in the history of the Dictionary were taken up by the attempts to grapple with a problem of production of which no one had any previous experience. It is a long and involved story, and one cannot follow it without feeling sympathy for the participants. In the chronicle of the years the letters of the alphabet stretch on and on ahead: the seeming hopelessness of the task is depressing: the Delegates at times were singularly clumsy in their demands. Yet, through it all, for most of the time, James Murray retained his enthusiasm and buoyancy. The tremendous vigour of his early years was chained now to one objective. Only a man of his singular character and stamina could have carried the strain for thirty years, years when most men would have passed their prime.

CHAPTER XII

Editor and Publisher:
Confrontation with Benjamin Jowett

DURING the preliminary years, following the signing of the agreements with the Philological Society and with James Murray, the Delegates showed little concern about the Dictionary: it was just one of their many projected publications and not regarded as in any way an exceptional undertaking. From 1883 the situation changed as it became increasingly clear that the initial outlay was going to be very much greater and the period during which there were no profits very much longer than had been estimated. Henceforth the worried, discouraged Editor was to be confronted by equally anxious, dissatisfied Publishers, trying to solve their economic difficulties by dictating to the Editor how he should do his work.

The Delegates directing the Clarendon Press for the University of Oxford, under a constitution of 1757, consisted at this time of the Vice-Chancellor and Proctors *ex-officio* and normally ten other distinguished members of the University, five of whom were Perpetual. The other five were appointed by the Vice-Chancellor and the Proctors for a term of years, and could be re-elected, while the whole body filled from their number any vacancies in the ranks of the Perpetual Delegates.[1] There was thus a large measure of continuity, but a considerable influence was exercised by the Vice-Chancellor of the day and the Secretary. James was to find that his fortunes and those of the Dictionary fluctuated according to the holders of these key positions.

The Press, historically, was divided into the 'learned side' and the 'Bible side' and although in the nineteenth century Oxford was already publishing classical texts and school books, the financing of scholarly, not necessarily remunerative, books depended on the profits of the 'Bible side'. The world at large believed that the Press had unlimited resources, but in fact, just at the period when the Dictionary was accepted for publication, the finances were causing some concern. The Delegates recognised that in principle they ought to encourage scholars to contribute to the increase of knowledge and the advancement of learning by publishing their works, but some at least of them also wanted to put the affairs of the Press on a more business-like basis. In 1878 there was no separate account for the 'learned purposes' side, there was considerable vagueness about which of the books accepted could be expected to pay and how much money would be needed to subsidise those which would not.[2] The Delegates were trying rather unsuccessfully to put their business in order and their failure to establish the finances of the Dictionary on a proper footing must be seen in the light of this general background. The official Order Book of the Delegates does not reveal divisions of opinion, but the decisions made can only be explained by the supposition that they were not always all of one mind.

The Dictionary was apparently one of those works about which there was uncertainty: was it a learned, unremunerative work, or could the assurances of the Philological Society be accepted that it should soon bring in handsome profits? Many of the Delegates did look upon it as a commercially viable undertaking and became alarmed at the sums of money being invested in it with diminishing hopes of a return. Others, such as Max Müller, saw that it had potential as a work of scholarship with which the University would be honoured to be associated. Those who thought it should be judged as a commercial undertaking were evidently not powerful enough to get the project abandoned, although this was considered from time to time: those who valued it as a learned work were not able to insist on a realistic subsidy to cover the cost of doing the work on the scale it deserved. The result was that they muddled along, at one moment attempting to impose stricter economies on the Editor and showing a cheese-paring disposition, and at the next reverting to a *laissez faire* attitude which seemed to contradict previous policy. The Editor was left with a feeling of constant insecurity and bewilderment as he tried to meet the seemingly arbitrary dictates of his masters. Only because James Murray was wholly dedicated to the task did he persist under these conditions. He was indeed often tempted to give up, and the effect on his personality was lasting.

He saw the pressure to accelerate production and to economise space, in order to save time and money, as a demand that he should sacrifice quality. Most of James' friends and the members of the Philological Society were sympathetic to the Delegates' desire to secure a more rapid publication and while they did not go so far as the Delegates, they did agree that James was too meticulous. Furnivall and Skeat both thought that he was setting a standard impossible of attainment, but he simply would not yield on this point.[3] Either he would be as thorough as he knew how, or he would have no interest in the work. Therefore he saved time only at his own expense, by sacrificing his holidays, his family life, his outside interests, his serenity and ultimately his health. Overwork made him at times very touchy and financial worry subjected him to continual strain.

It was unfortunate that neither Editor nor Delegates had much business experience or understanding. In spite of advice from Hucks Gibbs, James more than once accepted conditions which at best meant that he might break even and at worst would leave him out of pocket. His payment as Editor was based on the very minimum needed to cover estimated expenses and replace the salary he drew at Mill Hill School before he started work on the Dictionary. The hope of royalties was never realised and he gained nothing materially from the Editorship. The Delegates were probably not consciously seeking to strike a hard bargain: they had apparently not enough business expertise to recognise the unsound basis of the terms the Editor was willing to accept. They did not question the figures he gave them, and they did not protect him from the results of his idealism.

The first confrontation took place in 1883 when it was apparent that James was failing to meet the timetable for publication and various remedies were considered. Furnivall all along foresaw that the work would prove too much for one man and he now advocated the appointment of four additional editors.[4] James, although understandably reluctant to admit that he was defeated, nevertheless was not wholly averse to the appointment of a second editor, but the Press would not agree to the extra expense involved without a guarantee that production would thereby be greatly expedited. It took fourteen years before the principle of a team of editors was accepted.

Instead, in the summer of 1883 two alternatives were under consideration: either James Murray should resign his appointment at Mill Hill School and move to Oxford,[5] or he should remain at Mill Hill but with a larger staff for which the Delegacy would be prepared to find more money. If he moved to Oxford he might either be full time, or, to save the Delegacy the full replacement of his school salary,

13. Alfred Erlebach.

he might be found a light University appointment. Since either scheme was dependent from the Delegates' point of view on the Editor giving an undertaking to produce two parts a year, and from the Editor's point of view on getting adequate staff, James, backed by Gibbs, refused to commit himself.

He had already experienced staff difficulties. Herrtage, his chief assistant, was discovered in 1882 to be a kleptomaniac, who was stealing the reference books James had borrowed or bought out of his slender resources, and had to be dismissed.[6] In his place James was fortunate in securing Alfred Erlebach, an assistant master at the school, who proved first class. Besides being a most conscientious man, he was an accurate worker with an excellent memory for detail and an equable disposition—all indispensable qualities in the Scriptorium.[7] He and James worked very well together, but unfortunately unless his salary could be substantially increased there was no hope of retaining his services. James' brother-in-law, Herbert Ruthven, had left in 1882 owing to his wife's illness, and James had since met with difficulty in finding men of the necessary calibre. Often those who came to him were recommended because they had qualifications in, and enthusiasm for, English Literature, but the discipline of lexicography is more akin to science than to literature and the qualities needed were rarely found. New recruits were a source of trouble for the first four to six weeks: it was six months before they began to be useful and a year before they ceased to be learners and became of value. Over the fifty years of production the total of assistants who had worked in the Scriptorium was thirty-eight, and of these almost a third stayed less than two years. They left because the work was not what they had expected, or they gave up because their health would not stand the strain of continually working against time in the insalubrious Scriptorium. Dr Murray, it was noted 'did not scruple to tire less chalcenterous [brazen-gutted] workers'[8] and some went because they resented the schoolmasterly censures of the Editor and found the standards he set himself and expected of them were too exacting. Many of those who showed most promise left because the pay was low, not rising above the poor salary of an assistant teacher: the highest pay was £300, the less qualified received £50 to £100 a year only and the prospects for advancement in this specialised field were almost nil. Changes of staff always meant a set-back, and although the Editor did not yet know that staffing problems were going to remain 'the most disheartening and often paralysing feature' of his task[9] he was wise now to be adamant that until he saw his staff at work and had tested their abilities it was impossible to commit himself to a set rate of output a year. Because, while the staff had fixed wages, he himself was paid by results—which were dependent on his assistants' work—he had a double interest in their efficiency.[10] No one questioned the share he carried himself: in 1883 he was working twenty hours a week for the School and fifty-seven for the Dictionary—a seventy-seven hour week. He himself did wonder whether he could continue to work thirteen hours a day indefinitely, though he claimed that his health had not yet suffered.[11]

Temporarily things now reached a deadlock. The Delegates did not see their way to conclude either of the suggested new arrangements without a guaranteed increased output, and they departed for the Long Vacation.[12] Part I was still not out: James was in debt £400 to Hucks Gibbs and had borrowed another £100 at 4½ per cent from his former colleague, Mr Harley.[13] The amount he could expect for the work of the years ahead dwindled as payments for it were advanced by the Press. Ada took the younger children to the sea, and James went to stay with the Elworthys in Somerset. Fred Elworthy, sensible, cheerful and sympathetic, was always a good influence. James revived his antiquarian, botanical and horticultural interests in expeditions with him and found the atmosphere also conducive to writing, since Elworthy was at work too, producing books on dialect, local history and folklore. While at Wellington James was able to compile the prefatory matter for Part I which was expected to be published in October.

At this moment there was one of those sudden—and to James inexplicable—changes in the attitude of the Delegacy. At the very start, in February 1879, he had asked that a sub-committee be appointed to confer with him from time to time on literary problems arising from his task as Editor. A well qualified committee of Dean Liddell, Mark Pattison and Max Müller was appointed, but there is no evidence that it ever functioned except to consider typography and in practice any questions were resolved by Dr Price. The Delegates remained uninterested: they received the annual reports without comment and still none had troubled to visit the Scriptorium.[14] Now, at the eleventh hour, on the eve of publication, when James had made his many difficult decisions in the light of the best advice available, the 'great men' at Oxford suddenly presumed to suggest how he should have done his work.

The reason for this inopportune change lay in the person of the newly elected Vice-Chancellor—the redoubtable and famous Dr Benjamin Jowett, Master of Balliol College, who became *ex-officio* Chairman of the Delegacy from October 1882. Classical scholar and philosopher, he sought like Plato, whose works he translated, to use his knowledge for the good of society, and one of his aims was 'To arrange my life in the best possible way, that I may be able to arrange other people's.' Before entering upon his four-year period of office he drew up an agenda of seventeen items to be attended to in the University, and although the Clarendon Press was not included, he was soon interfering. He was interested in everything connected with books and their production and his restless energy and forceful initiative were directed to reforming the management, modernising the plant, adding to the business and encouraging the maintenance of the tradition of fine printing. He sometimes harassed the Secretary to the Press by urging impracticable ideas, but for the most part he swept opposition aside in an autocratic way, and won support by his evident good intentions. Highly intelligent and appreciative of sound scholarship, he at once seized upon the Dictionary, recognising in it a work of immense importance, but he saw also that unless steps were taken to change the arrangements for its production it would not be finished in his or the Editor's life time.[15]

Towards the end of July 1883, James received a personal letter from the Vice-Chancellor, inviting him to spend a night with him at the Master's Lodge in Balliol, in order to be present at a meeting of the Delegates the following morning. Dr Price wrote independently, urging acceptance of the invitation and telling James that the Vice-Chancellor 'takes a great deal of interest in the Dictionary, has many views about it and would like to become personally acquainted with the Author.'[16] James went to Oxford and apparently stayed the night at Balliol.[17] He recorded that the meeting with the Delegates on Tuesday, 31 July was hurried and unsatisfactory and the conversation with Dr Jowett, who said he needed to understand James' plan of action before he could help him, was limited to generalities. This might have been an opportunity to remove misunderstandings between them, but clearly it was not used.

At the meeting a document was handed to James which was certainly inspired, if not written, by Jowett himself. It presented the conclusions of the Delegates, formed after studying the final proofs for Part I, that steps must be taken to reduce the bulk of the Dictionary in order to cut the cost and speed the production. This printed sheet of *Suggestions for Guidance in Preparing Copy for the Press* was written in complete ignorance of the Editor's long labour in settling the pattern of the work, of the nature of his materials and the methods employed in the Scriptorium. He might well have exclaimed, 'You are teaching your Grandmother to suck eggs!'[18]

The *Suggestions*, for example, fastened upon the problem of what should or should not be included and ruled that slang terms and scientific words should both be limited to such as were found in literature. 'What', asked the exasperated Editor, 'is classed as literature?' He confessed to inability to give an answer

> I could at most omit those as to which I have a strong subjective feeling that they are not likely to be used at present in literature . . . running the risk that any day they may burst on the world as famous poisons, disinfectants, anaesthesiants, or cholera pro-phylacts, & so be in every body's mouths.[19]

This was exactly what happened over *appendicitis*. Dr Murray was advised in 1891,

> Surely you will not attempt to enter all the crack-jaw medical and

surgical words. What do you think of 'Dacryocystosyringoketok-leisis'?

Of these there is no end; and such jargon as they are! Only yesterday I met with 'appendicitis'—to mean an inflammation of the Appendix. You know doctors think the way to indicate any inflamm[atio]n is to tack on 'itis' to a word. Peritonitis is almost Anglicised, but Corneitis, and Gastritis, and Perichondritis, are euphonous in comparison with a thousand other abortions.[20]

James had consulted the Regius Professor of Medicine and on his advice omitted the word, only to find it universally used when Edward VII's coronation was postponed in 1902 because of the removal of his appendix.

Some of the *Suggestions* made were simply a matter of opinion, and James had already learned that there was room for plenty of this in Lexicography. On such points, he said 'no two men will ever spontaneously see alike . . . I do not expect that my treatment of words, especially difficult words, will strike other people as that which they would have adopted . . . the most that can be expected is "this is not an unreasonable way of exhibiting the facts".'[21]

Other suggestions made in the interests of economy seemed to threaten the very essence and quality of the work. It was proposed for example that quotations illustrating common words should be restricted to one or two early examples and the Editor should then say, 'this usage continues to the present day'. 'Absurd!' James noted.'No friend of the Dict[ionar]y would tolerate it. Why *show* usage at all? . . . Moreover it is suicidal: to an enormous number of men the "modern instances" are the favourite feature . . .'[22] On a suggestion that the treatment of derivatives should be abbreviated, he commented

If it must be so, I bow to a painful necessity. They will have to be done *some day* as I am doing them; and the feeling that my treatment of them is merely a stop-gap will greatly diminish my interest. I should like the Delegates to appoint a man to do the derivatives, on their plan, and I should initial my articles, (M.) & not look at the others.[23]

The Delegates' ignorance of the materials and of the work in the Scriptorium was obvious from their idea that the task of the Editor and his assistants was to find suitable quotations themselves. Jowett and his colleagues objected to the choice of quotations, for example they desired that passages showing the use of a word should always be quoted from the work in which it was first used in this construction or sense. James pointed out that if his staff were obliged to do this the Dictionary would *never* be finished. The example criticised in the *Suggestions* was *absence* in the phrase *conspicuous by absence*. James retorted

> I wrote *12* letters to journalists, critics and literary men . . . in the effort to find out the original use . . . and I had long passed the word '*Absence*' before I found the clue . . . a distinguished literary man wrote to me in reference to this very phrase; 'If you mean to do this with every word in the Dictionary, your great-grandson won't finish it'.[24]

Jowett wanted quotations taken as far as possible from great writers and James had to explain

> I use the quotations I have: if I must discard these, and search for others from better writers, the building will stand still, while the builders go searching for stones; and with what chances of success should I search for 'Famous quotations' which the reading of 25 years has missed?[25]

The Delegates, in common with many people at that time, including even Hucks Gibbs, still had the illusion that a Dictionary should set a standard of good literary usage and they could not grasp that this is not the province of an historical Dictionary. Opinion has changed completely and today the complaint has been made that the volunteer readers neglected the trivia and gave the impression that it was the giants of literature who formed our language.[26] In the 1880s the Delegates were not alone in objecting to quotations from newspapers and in the *Suggestions* it was stated that they should be avoided. James had to point out that often he could not illustrate the history of a word from any other source.

> Personally, [he told the Philological Society in 1884] I think this criticism by far the silliest that the Dictionary has elicited. I am certain that posterity will agree with me, and that the time will come when this criticism will be pointed out as a most remarkable instance of the inability of men to acknowledge contemporary facts and read the signs of the times.[27]

He was right. By the time the Dictionary was completed in 1928 the earlier policy of the Delegacy had been long forgotten and in describing the unique characteristics of the work, the Press boasted that quotations had always been up to date, citing *The Times* in praise of this feature: 'It is not the document so much as the use of it that counts; and to illustrate the general acceptance of a word ... any respectable and recognized publication—book or newspaper—may very likely be more apt for the lexicographer's purpose than a literary masterpiece.'[28]

To follow the *Suggestions* of the Delegates in the matter of quotations, as in some other of their directives, would have added to the Editor's work although the avowed intention of their intervention was to save time by such means as abridging the treatment of derivatives and limiting the number of quotations and subdivisions of senses. In many cases a more careful examination of the proofs would have shown that what was proposed was already the practice.

For the Editor the *Suggestions* were the last straw. He had expected at this stage to receive congratulations rather than criticism and was angry that if instructions were to be given they had not been drawn up long before, instead of waiting till the last moment. As a guide to economy of time he dismissed them completely, saying, 'the Dictionary can be made better in quality only by *more* care, *more* work, *more* time. It can be accelerated by less attention to details, and less attempt to make everything perfect.'[29]

He received strong backing from his friends and the members of the Philological Society who were more knowledgeable than Dr Jowett and his fellow Delegates on what was involved in editing the Dictionary. A hastily summoned special meeting of the Society resolved on 25 October 1883 that no general curtailment was possible without destroying the essential character of the work and that minor abridgements would not materially save either time or labour.[30] Hucks Gibbs, level-headed and diplomatic as usual, while agreeing, tried to put things in the best light and urged James not to speak of 'gratuitous impertinence'—it was only 'ignorant misapprehension' on the part of the Vice-Chancellor.[31]

Meanwhile Dr Jowett, accustomed to getting his own way, urbane and never seeking to start a quarrel, continued to take a lively interest in the Dictionary, seemingly oblivious to the annoyance he had caused. He was genuinely anxious to be helpful and he authorised further advances on Part I to prevent James from falling deeper into debt. He even found time on 17 October to pay a personal visit to the Scriptorium. He was accompanied by Henry Hucks Gibbs, who had probably suggested the visit, realising that the Vice-Chancellor's misconceptions could most easily be corrected by seeing the work in progress. Once James would greatly have appreciated this evidence of interest: now he was in no mood to entertain a man he regarded as interfering and presumptuous. His notes on the visit show his irritation. 'Prof. Jowett. A week past on Wed. Mr Gibbs showed him everything as well as his patience would allow, not very great — jumping at conclusions.'[32] James did not recognise that Benjamin Jowett had a very quick mind and took in more than he supposed: from his two meetings with him he had formed the opinion that the Vice-Chancellor was both impatient and superficial.

It was in fact quite a lengthy visit, and James wrote afterwards to Hucks Gibbs apologising for his having been inconvenienced by being unable to get away for another appointment. Hucks Gibbs found both men 'rather heated' and Jowett more ignorant than he should have been about the Dictionary, but not unreasonable and quite open to suggestions. Gibbs thought that he had managed to keep the peace very well. He was able to be more out-spoken than James himself would have found possible, and for this James was grateful, but even so the Vice-Chancellor's visit left him still very depressed. As it was a fine evening he had walked down the lane to the station with his guest, the burden of whose song to the last was 'ten years and condensation'. Jowett asked him for a scheme showing how the Dictionary could be completed in ten or at most twelve years and the cost per sheet, and he wanted an immediate reply.[33]

Jowett did not realise the highly nervous state to which the Editor had been reduced by overwork and worry, and a week later he committed a worse blunder than the last by an even more misguided attempt to show interest by teaching the Editor how to do his work. James had been expecting to receive from the Press the revised proof of his Introduction together with the Prospectus. To his astonishment the proof he took out of the envelope on 23 October was, when he started to read it, not his Introduction at all, but a redrafting of it. Even the title of the Dictionary had been changed from *A New English Dictionary on a Historical Basis* to *A New Dictionary Showing the History of the Language from the Earliest Times*, which James thought both 'weak and erroneous'. A Dictionary can only show a history of words, not language, and this one did not go back to 'earliest times' but only to 1150.[34]

No explanation of these changes was sent: James' own draft was not returned: he was not told whether the proof submitted represented merely suggestions for consideration or was a final form approved by the Delegates. There seems to have been a blunder. The Delegates on 19 October had appointed Dr Jowett, Dean Liddell, Mark Pattison and William Stubbs to examine James' proofs and suggest amendments and then confer with Dr Murray.[35] It must have been an error that the documents were sent to the Editor with no explanation. He was furious and in a private letter to Dr Price he said, 'I emphatically object to anybody altering it without consulting me . . . I will write my own Preface, or it shall remain unwritten,'[36] and he told Hucks Gibbs that if the Delegates sanctioned and insisted on Jowett's version 'we shall have a storm'.[37]

Henry Hucks Gibbs at once realised the danger when two strong-willed men start a tug-of-war, and that Jowett's suggestions, though 'superficially right' were 'fatuous in detail'. He went hurrying off to Oxford to act as *amicus curiae* and stop Jowett 'dipping his Vice-Chancellarian oar too freely' into the Dictionary waters. He determined to remind him that though he might choose to quarrel with Murray, this would not release the Delegates from their contract with the Philological Society, which bound them to continue publishing and to find another Editor. He would also call their attention to the specimen of the work approved earlier by them, which embodied all the points at which they now took exception.[38] He spent three days at Balliol and thought he had successfully smoothed everything down. He met Dean Liddell as well as Jowett and persuaded them to acknowledge that a mistake had been made.[39] Jowett now wrote to explain that the draft had only been put into print for convenience and was not intended to be final, nor did the Delegates wish to insist on the alterations.[40]

James was not easily mollified. He had a legitimate grievance and in his now overwrought condition he made the most of it, exaggerating the significance of some of the alterations made and taking them as a personal insult. Many of James' friends were equally indignant and encouraged him in thinking that the only course was to resign.

O o o o o o o o o—hhh. I don't know how to groan enough [wrote A. J. Ellis on 8 November]. What an awful conceit of himself the man must have!

But what business have the delegates as such to edit the Dictionary? This is what it amounts to. Edited by Jowett! No! The

Ph[ilological] S[ociet]y has the appointment of editor or the approval of editor, by contract. No delegate be he even Jupiter Pessimus Maximus, has any right to edit . . .

It is quite clear that unless Jowett engages not to interfere you can't work the dictionary . . .

But . . . to think of the misery of it, to think of the disappointment of all connected with the collection of materials! to think of the utter shipwreck which one selfsufficient man can accomplish!

It may be—I think it is—the best thing for your health & wellbeing to give up, & insist on the removal of your name from the title page . . . But—I can't tell you how grieved I am in every way . . .

At present I am mum. But I boil over.[41]

None the less James did listen to Hucks Gibbs and agreed to go to Oxford to meet the Delegates, accepting Gibbs' counsel to 'listen to their suggestions just as you have always listened to mine, defending your own words where they need defence, and not sticking too closely to anything that is of no moment one way or other.'[42]

James wrote a long letter to Gibbs on 8 November telling how the battle was fought at Oxford.

The Delegates whom I met during the two days that I was there, treated me with great cordiality, and I thought I could discern the good effects of your interposition . . . We had a sederunt of 4 hours on Tuesday afternoon, another of $4\frac{1}{2}$ hours (9 to 1.30) on Wednesday morning, and still another of more than an hour on Wednesday afternoon, till the V.C. had to rush off in a cab, and I to run for my train; and we had got only to page x and the rest is adjourned *sine die*! Indeed there is no particular reason why it should not last till a new V.C. comes in. Prof. Jowett said in his letter that their alterations were mere suggestions . . . but it soon became evident to me that they were suggestions which he was simply determined that I *should* swallow willing or unwilling. We simply had to fight every word, my *wishes* going for nothing; and only when I could absolutely convince him, that my words were better, would he yield anything. I expected that they would at certain parts, at least, have said, 'Dr Murray we think we can leave this mere detail to you; we have expressed our wishes or stated our difficulties and shall be glad if you will do as much as you can to meet them.' But there was not an iota of such a spirit shown; dead through every line we must go, and I must be forced to accept either what he had written, or something else which he proposed instead, or something else which he concocted in lieu of that, & so on. They must be his words & not mine. The whole was done, in such a whirl that one had hardly time to collect one's thoughts, & I often simply ceased protesting, from sheer vexation & weariness. I told Prof. Price and Mr Bywater who alone were left as I rushed off, that I was quite disgusted, and that they need not wonder if they received my resignation in a few days. Mr Bywater ran to the Station with me, to show me that he had no sympathy with what had been done, and to assure me that Jowett meant well & liked me etc.

James went on to tell Gibbs that having thought about the matter on the way home and talked it over with Ada, he had now decided to resign.

I cannot [he wrote] do what I have been doing without enthusiasm and whole-heartedness: the result of all this despicable squabbling over my English, as if it were a school-boy's essay, has been utterly to chill & freeze me, and make me loathe the whole matter: Then comes up all the feeling of the sacrifices, which one can make when the heart is warm, but which seem madness when one looks at them in cold blood, and I leap once more at the thought of being free from the eternal grind, of having romps with my boys, & walks with my wife, & excursions into the fields of literature, & hours in my garden, and time to enjoy existence, from each and all of which I have had to cut myself off to till this thorny, stony, & thankless ground. And I say: I will do it no more.

He had even thought of his future: he would immediately return to work he had left unfinished and then he would let his American friends know that he was now moveable. He said that he had twice already been asked if it would be worth approaching him with regard to a Professorship in an American College, and the idea attracted him, because he believed 'The future of English Scholarship lies in the United States, where the language is studied with an enthusiasm unknown here, and which will soon leave us far behind. I think I could help on that future.' This prospect seemed infinitely brighter than that of struggling on with the Dictionary, facing, he felt sure, 'as stubborn a fight, as over this abominable Preface' on every point of detail.[43] The attack made upon him by Jowett, insulting as it would have been to any editor of standing, was particularly hurtful to James Murray with his concealed, but deep feeling of inferiority, because he was self-taught. Moreover criticism which might have been applied to the flowery prose of his Hawick days was now quite unjustified.

Hucks Gibbs realised that only such influence as he could command in Oxford could now save the Dictionary. He warned Furnivall, 'The V.C., a most energetic man in all that he undertakes, has, I fear, upset the Coach. Murray wont stand their tutelage, and will resign if he hasn't done so.'[44] But he wrote to James begging him to keep the matter private for the moment and not to act precipitately.[45] At the same time he wrote urgently to Dean Liddell and Dr Jowett warning them of the seriousness of the situation and the likely loss of their Editor. He told Jowett frankly that he was 'drawing the cord too tightly' and must let Murray write his own preface and having told him what he did not like in it, leave him to modify it as best he could.[46] On 12 November he was able to send James letters from both the Dean and the Vice-Chancellor hoping that the threat of resignation would not be carried out.

> The V.C. has much πολυπραγμοσυνη[47] in his character [Gibbs told James], and that leads him to rush hastily into matters of which he necessarily lacks experience. He feels his power & great ability and that I think leads him to neglect Talleyrand's caution, et surtout, jeune homme, point de zèle! He must always see this when he is in the middle of that into which he has plunged, and must feel vexed with himself—you know how a man usually exhibits vexation with himself—by venting it on his neighbours. Therefore his letters are not usually as pleasant as the Dean's, but I don't think the present letter otherwise than sensible and agreeable.[48]

In contrast to Hucks Gibbs' diplomatic letters were those James received from his friends. Fitzedward Hall, one of his ablest volunteer helpers and proof readers, for example, referring to the vexations caused by 'impertinent officiousness' and assuring James of the support of the Philological Society in the battle, wrote

> The domineering Delegate who is interfering with you, and his colleagues, ought to know that the Dictionary, if it passed out of your hands, would be, if only from its patchwork character, very far inferior to what it promises to be ... And then where, among

English speaking men, could the Oxford Delegates hope to find your equal, or even approximate equal, for special competency, or for energy?[49]

Where indeed! The letters from Jowett and Dean Liddell to Gibbs showed that in spite of the impression given, they had a very high opinion of Dr Murray and that the last thing they wanted was that Part I should appear without his name on the title page.[50] None the less two very obstinate men were still facing each other. Jowett maintained that if serious injury were not to be done to the work, the Preface required re-writing, and he could not see that this was a matter for resignation.[51] James, on the other hand, argued that the changes in the Preface which Jowett was forcing on him could not affect the sales and reiterated his objection to petty criticisms and changes which, he said, vexed his soul and clothed his thoughts in a vesture which did not fit them, thus instead of making them clearer, bemuddling and spoiling them. He too had heard from Jowett and told Gibbs 'It is the old story, "we think a great deal of you, we are anxious to help you all we can, and to make the Dictionary perfect" which means "we are *determined* to help you, and *determined* that you *shall accept* the help, whether you want it or not".' After all their advice, he claimed, they must leave him to do the thing in his own way and characteristically he ended his letter to Gibbs 'What work has ever been done on any other plan? It is God's own way with his human instruments, and every attempt to set it aside has resulted only in discomfiture.'[52] Fortunately Hucks Gibbs was equally tenacious and he sent another of his tactful but outspoken letters to Jowett, spelling out yet more clearly what should be the limits of the Delegates' responsibilities and interference and concluding with a plea for sympathy for the Editor

... please to bear in mind that he has had a very heavy strain on him, both because the work has exhausted his money resources, and because this discussion carries with it much anxiety and much mortification to him; so that you must not wonder if he is irritable and inclined to doubt whether he can bear to continue the struggle.[53]

At length Gibbs' efforts were rewarded. Jowett had by now, as Gibbs suspected, reached the stage of realising that he had gone too far and wanted to extricate himself without losing face. This he did by informing James that the Delegates had resolved that he should be free to write his Preface in his own way. It scandalised James when he later learned that this was in fact not a decision of the Delegates at all, but a resolution taken by Jowett himself and conveyed to James on his own authority, without reference to any committee and without the knowledge of Dr Price as Secretary to the Delegates.

As soon as Jowett had capitulated, James set himself to alter the Preface back to his own words, retaining, however, as many as possible of the changes the Vice-Chancellor wanted. It was a patchwork job which took him a week, and once done and set up in type, he decided to take the corrected proof to Oxford himself, to avoid further delays. There was nearly another disaster. The Delegates happened to be meeting and hearing that James was coming to Oxford, Jowett proposed that he should join them again to discuss some points. Luckily James' friends on the Delegacy adroitly suggested that rather than this, Mr Doble, the assistant Secretary, should settle these minor details with him. James was nervous that he might have damaged his reputation in Oxford by having crossed swords with the Vice-Chancellor, but he found, on the contrary, that he was something of a hero. Price, indignant at the delay, expense and trouble that had been caused, hoped that Jowett had burned his fingers a little and would be more cautious in the future. Others, such as the Librarian of the Bodleian, who had themselves suffered from the Vice-Chancellor's interference, were amused and pleased at James' stand, and he learned that he had gained the reputation of being a very persistent man, with whom it was best not to meddle.[54] So James had won a notable victory and thanks to Henry Hucks Gibbs, the Dictionary was saved.

The quarrel had two immediate results. It meant that the publication of Part I, the price and binding of which had been fixed by November, was still further delayed and it appeared only at the end of January 1884.[55] It also decided the title of the work. James' suggestion *A New English Dictionary on Historical Principles* was now adopted, although the original proposal *on a historical basis* survived on the first page of the text. The amended title desired by Dr Jowett was abandoned.[56]

Defeated on the issue of the preface, Jowett was the more determined to have his way over the problem of production. The deadlock arrived at in the spring was still unresolved in November.

Although Jowett wanted him in Oxford as a full time Editor, until James produced a scheme showing how he proposed to accelerate the work, the Delegates were not prepared to suggest new terms for his employment to replace those now proved to be totally inadequate. No mention of the Editor's financial difficulties was made when James saw Dr Price and some of the Delegates in November 1883, and he was driven to raise the matter himself and to ask for at least a provisional arrangement to enable him to carry on until Easter. In reply Price asked once again for a statement for the Board.

> I have 'made statements' *ad nauseam* already [James complained to Gibbs], and I feel quite disgusted to have to do so again ... of course I really cannot go on with the pecuniary harassments of Part I to be repeated. But I think that it is quite certain that as long as I try to do so the Delegates will leave me to do it. So, disgusting or not disgusting, I shall be obliged to stir them up again. It would be a deal easier to slip out of the bother of it![57]

Henry Hucks Gibbs, Fred Elworthy and later Walter Skeat, all used their influence to urge the Delegacy to action. Elworthy, in Oxford in November, took the opportunity to impress on the Vice-Chancellor that worry was telling on James more than the actual work. He said that his visit did not inspire him with any great admiration for Jowett, but he did find that everyone was anxious to welcome Murray to Oxford. He also got the impression that Furnivall was a stumbling block and that the Delegates thought Murray would be easy to deal with without him. Elworthy did not contradict them, thinking that if this was their idea it should encourage them to bestir themselves to remove James to Oxford soon, away from such an evil influence![58] But still nothing was agreed because the Delegates did not accept that no profits could be looked for in the immediate future. Advances to James now totalled £500 which was £200 more than was due to him for Part I under the revised agreement of 1881. Yet the Delegates would not acknowledge that the financial arrangements had broken down and in sending him the last cheque Price warned James that they desired it to be distinctly understood that they reserved all their rights under the contract.[59]

On the other hand James' calculations of the work entailed in producing the 500 or even 600 pages a year which the Delegates thought should be the target, clearly showed that they were asking the impossible. It would mean that every day he and his assistants would have to work out the full history, etymology, definitions and logical order of senses for forty-five words, some of which might be easy, well prepared by sub-editors, but others would be of great complexity, or words for which the materials were in some respects deficient. In addition, six columns of first proofs must be corrected, often involving altering the order of senses or re-writing definitions; at the same time they had to check another six columns of revised proofs, carrying the notes of scholars such as Hucks Gibbs, Fitzedward Hall and others to whom the proofs were submitted for comment and additions. A further six columns of 'second revise' had to be scrutinised with exact care by the Editor and at least one assistant, to detect the smallest errors. This much was all daily work, but in addition every four days eight pages of final proofs must be passed for printing. At this stage James would try to put himself in the position of a user of the book and make his last improvements. 'Now, this', he observed to Gibbs with obvious truth, 'is an appalling amount of work: manifestly beyond the power of any one man to do in a day — and *every* day.' The question was what part of the work could he delegate and to whom: where could men be found of the quality needed and where was the money coming from to pay them?[60] James was as worried as anybody about the slow progress and told Price that he was willing to try anything short of changing the character of the Dictionary. If that were decided upon he would no longer feel justified in making it his life's work, although he would always be willing to give voluntary help.[61]

Gibbs, still working hard to achieve a settlement, was afraid that the Editor would again bind himself to conditions impossible of fulfilment. He knew that James was always embarrassed about bargaining on money matters and he had already urged him not to be 'mealy mouthed' when he met the Delegates. Now he advised him not to ask for the least possible sum to meet present expenditure, but an amount sufficient to enable the work to be done really efficiently. To save proof correction, he considered, drawing on his own experience, 'you want three Erlebachs instead of one'. He was particularly anxious that James should not make the mistake again of accepting a contract which tied him rigidly as regards time and expenses. The period now entered upon, when the material was to be processed for publication, was just as experimental as the earlier stage when the material was being collected, and only experience would enable the Editor to decide what money he would need for assistants and how much they could do in the time. Any arrangements for the first year should be subject to modification.[62]

With nothing settled for the future, Part I, consisting of 352 pages, at long last appeared on 29 January 1884. This was five years after the signing of the contract and two years after the first 'copy' had been sent to the printers. Price wrote to congratulate the Editor on sending out the first portion of a work which would carry his name all over the known world,[63] and many philologists on the Continent and in the United States gave it enthusiastic reviews. In England there were few scholars qualified to appreciate the work, but Henry Bradley, the future co-editor of the Dictionary, then little known, who had been a corresponding clerk with a Sheffield cutlery firm and had just come to London, wrote two articles in the *Academy*. These showed both an ability to criticise and a sincere well-informed appreciation. 'Happily for the credit of English scholarship' he wrote, '. . . it may be confidently asserted that if the level of excellence reached in this opening part be sustained throughout, the completed work will be an achievement without parallel in the lexicography of any living language.'[64] James at once got into touch with Bradley and began consulting him on etymological problems. In June Bradley asked whether there might be work for him on the Dictionary staff.[65] He could not come without financial security, but in the discussions with the Press about engaging a second editor James now had Bradley in mind as a possibility.

In spite of the general approval of Part I by those capable of judging it, its appearance was in a way something of an anticlimax. James had always hoped that with publication his troubles would be over, he was confident that the Delegates must then recognise the quality of the work and realise that it could not be hurried. But there was no letter expressing their appreciation, no change of attitude that he could detect. His disappointment, though he did not say much of it at the time, cut very deep and thereafter he carried a chip on his shoulder, feeling that his work was inadequately recognised and that he must be satisfied with his own knowledge that it was good.[66] Always sensitive to criticism, he was irritated by the reviewers who were insufficiently informed to comment on the finer points of lexicography and confined themselves to citing triumphantly quotations showing earlier usage of words than those given, or listed words they believed (usually mistakenly) to have been omitted. If only they had responded to his appeals for help earlier these comments could have been looked into, and if need be attended to, before it was too late. It was fortunate for James' morale that early in 1884 he was invited to the Tercentenary Celebrations of Edinburgh University as an honorary graduate and found himself something of a public figure there on account of the Dictionary.

A little shy at first, James was soon at ease with old and new friends among the assembled visitors. Max Müller was there and also Dr Jowett, who welcomed him, saying he did not know anybody who so much deserved a holiday. He met also Professor Zupitza of Berlin, with whom he had worked for the Early English Text Society and was delighted to find among the guests Signor Saffi, one of the three tribunes of the Roman Republic in 1849. He had helped to entertain him at Hawick as a friend of Italian freedom, and he surprised the old man by being able to quote to him a sentence from his speech of twenty-seven years before.[67]

He also found there James Russell Lowell, the American poet and diplomat, who was already known to him. Lowell's book of literary essays, *My Study Windows*, was one of those read for the Dictionary, and James had found amongst the slips of quotations from it a strange word—*alliterates*. So he wrote to Lowell to ask its meaning, at the same time expressing warm appreciation of his writing and enclosing a copy of the annual report on the progress of the Dictionary. Lowell replied, saying that the unknown word was certainly a misprint for *illiterates*. He was, he said, 'deeply interested in the Dictionary', and if he were at home in America he would have helped in the work, as he had for many years been in the habit of noting words in his own reading. He said he would like to pay a visit to the Scriptorium, and this he later did. Lowell was now delighted to report how well Part I had been received in the United States.[68]

Another literary figure at Edinburgh was Robert Browning. James had corresponded with him also, asking about the meaning of the word *apparitional* used by Elizabeth Barrett Browning in *Aurora Leigh*, but they had not met before. Browning told him that he found the Dictionary 'most delightful' and intended to read every word of it. Years later, when his son Oswyn mentioned that he much admired Browning's poetry, James' comment was, 'Browning constantly used words without regard to their proper meaning. He has added greatly to the difficulties of the Dictionary.'[69]

The publication of Part I had one immediate and important result—the award to James Murray in 1884 of a Civil List Pension of

£250 a year.[70] This was due to Furnivall's initiative. He had hoped that the government would make a contribution towards publishing a work of national importance, but was advised that the only form such help could take was a pension to the Editor. He was much gratified by the success of his move because the award of the pension seemed to set an official stamp on the work and he hoped that Oxford would now feel obliged to see its completion on the present scale.[71] Hucks Gibbs, on the other hand, though pleased for James' sake that he should have this recognition, was very much surprised that Gladstone as Premier would even consider a Government grant under the circumstances, and pointed out 'Dr Murray ought not to have to spend 5/- . . . He is employed by the University of Oxford. Surely they don't expect him to find capital for their speculation. The pension . . . would be that capital.'[72] It was certainly a curious award. In writing to express his thanks to Gladstone, James accepted the pension 'not for myself, but for the Dictionary', saying it would help him to increase his staff.[73] It was often said that except for a gift later from the Goldsmiths' Company of £5000, the whole cost of the Dictionary was borne by the Oxford University Press, but in fact the pension of £250 was used to relieve the Press of some of the burden of remunerating the Editor, and meant that the Government paid a third of his salary for nearly thirty years.[74]

The award immediately solved for the Delegates the problem of compensating James for the loss of his salary at Mill Hill School if he became full time Editor, and left them with only the necessity of providing the money for the salaries of his assistants and his incidental expenses.[75] It therefore saved them from having to look for another source of income for him, such as a University lectureship or fellowship. James never understood this. The prospect of some sort of University appointment had been held out to him and influenced his decision to leave Mill Hill and remove to Oxford, and although it is difficult to see how he could have carried a lectureship without interfering with his work on the Dictionary, a research fellowship would have been possible, and this he continued to hope for. The fact that none ever materialised was a source of lasting disappointment and resentment. Probably no one realised how much store he had set on the idea, nor how widespread amongst his friends had been the expectation that something of the kind would be the inevitable result of the move to Oxford, and it certainly had been in Jowett's mind. Hucks Gibbs reported in November 1883 that Dean Liddell was thinking of a University office for Dr Murray, with a few lectures, and Elworthy, after his talk with the Vice-Chancellor, told James, 'from what he said, I look forward to visiting Professor Murray here [at Oxford] before long'. A few days later Elworthy sent James a cutting of an advertisement of the Sherardian Professorship in Botany, saying 'Now it strikes me this would exactly suit you. Of course Botany is not your speciality, but you know more of it than most Professors (?) of their subject . . . it is very likely you could get it.' A few months later he suggested James could get one of the Readerships of £300 or £400 a year of which he had seen notices. James' friend Edward Arber assumed that when he was settled in Oxford he would get one of the first appointments vacant, while his former colleague, Robert Harley asked, when he heard he was leaving Mill Hill, whether the new post was a Professorship, Lectureship or Readership.[76]

When no move was made by the authorities, James later tried to secure a fellowship by his own initiative. Having been disappointed at Trinity and Merton,[77] in 1895 he applied for one at Exeter, for which he seemed well qualified. It was offered for seven years at £200 a year for some definite literary or scientific work and he hoped to use the money for the purchase of books and for increased salaries for his staff. His comment when he was unsuccessful was, 'Alas! I was born too soon! People will just begin to appreciate the Dictionary, when it is too late for *me*.'[78]

Even with everyone agreed that the move to Oxford was desirable and even with the pension, it took months more before the terms were finally settled. The Delegates, with Jowett still convinced of the rightness of his policy, continued to press James for a guaranteed annual rate of production and for a firm estimate of the money he would need for assistants. James still refused to commit himself and although he was urged to take immediate steps to recruit and train additional staff, he was still so cumbered with debt that he dared not even fill existing vacancies until he was certain of the means to pay his helpers. The deadlock therefore persisted in which the two parties, in growing misunderstanding, each waited for the other to move.

Once again it was Hucks Gibbs who brought them together and in June 1884 at a meeting at the Bank of England obtained the agreement of both Murray and Price to terms on which the transfer to Oxford might take place. These represented a compromise in which James' better judgment was over-ruled, even by Hucks Gibbs, who in his great desire to get the matter settled placed too much faith on the hope that after their experience of the first contract, the Delegates would regard the new agreement to a certain extent as experimental and flexible. Payment by result was now dropped, which was an improvement, and the Editor was guaranteed a salary of £500 a year, which the Civil List pension made up to £750. This sum was arrived at on the assumption that working full time with an increased staff, James could produce 700 pages a year, rewarded therefore at about the original rate of £1 a page which had been fixed in 1879. When one considers the calculations James had made of the amount of work to be done in a day if only 500 pages a year were produced, it is difficult to credit that anyone would not have realised that this new target would prove impossible of attainment. Great importance however was attached to a further concession that the Editor should now be paid £1175 a year for the wages of the eight assistants he asked for. In addition he would receive £75 a year for postage and stationery and £100 for the removal and possible enlargement of the Scriptorium and in future the heating and lighting of it would be the responsibility of the Delegates. Nor was the idea of a University appointment lost sight of, although its value to James would be merely honorary, since provision was made that if money became available from any other source the amount to which the Press was committed would be proportionately reduced.[79]

On Gibbs' advice on the vexed question of output James stated, 'I expect to be able to prepare 700 pages in each year, and I engage to do so unless prevented by unforeseen difficulties.' Hucks Gibbs also proposed that this undertaking should only take effect when the new staff had been trained and James stipulated that the Delegates should do all they could to help in what he still regarded as the greatest difficulty, the recruitment of satisfactory assistants.

Henry Hucks Gibbs thought another advance had been made in combating the influence of Dr Jowett and was optimistic that the compromise would be acceptable to the Delegates and end the long deadlock. James did not share his confidence and wrote that he felt his courage was failing and that he was undertaking indefinite new liabilities. He foresaw his time being frittered away supervising eight assistants, a prospect of harder work, a less satisfactory kind of work and a less satisfactory quality achieved.[80] He wrote a grudging acceptance of the terms to the Delegacy. Gibbs wished he had been with him to induce him to look upon the new phase more hopefully, telling him his letter had too much gloom in it.[81]

Unfortunately James' gloom was justified. Although Dr Price approved the suggested terms, the Delegates did not. Presumably, as Jowett was still their chairman, he was the cause of their obstinacy. They continued to demand 'the strongest assurance' and firm undertaking and introduced a new safeguard, that should output fall below the target, the agreement would only be binding for two years. This stand was a matter of principle, for they confided to Hucks Gibbs that money was not a difficulty, they were prepared to pay a sum greatly in excess of that suggested, provided the desired speed of production was secured.[82] Once again James reiterated his refusal to be bound in this way:

> I cannot ruin myself absolutely for the Dictionary; [he said] I will not undertake pecuniary risks after I have done my utmost, nor put myself in a position in which it may be said to me 'You came to Oxford under an absolute promise to prepare 500 pages* a year.' I cannot give such absolute promise, where not my own work, but that of many men is concerned, and where I cannot even dismiss an inefficient assistant, and employ another, without loss of time and diminution of results. If such is insisted upon, I must withdraw, and ask the Delegates and Philological Society to arrange for the future of the Dictionary.[83]

To Gibbs he said that he was now so weary of all this worrying that he would cheerfully resign and help as a volunteer, if someone could be found to give the guarantee they required.[84] Characteristically, Furnivall warned James that if he did resign, he should not surrender the Civil List pension, but hold onto it as long as possible, and use it to benefit the Dictionary,[85] while Hucks Gibbs, bemoaning the foolishness of the Delegates, gave them, through Dr Price, 'a good dressing'.[86]

By now it was too late for James to leave Mill Hill that year and the idea of moving to Oxford was temporarily abandoned. Instead, the Delegates began to look for a second editor, as Jowett was getting seriously worried that the Dictionary would outlive them all.[87]

This suggestion pleased Furnivall, who was convinced that doing the Dictionary single-handed could kill Murray. 'The Society won't get its Dict[ionar]y so well done as if you did it all', he told James, 'but it will see the Dict[ionar]y finisht in 10 or 12 years from now, & you

---

* *sic* an error for 700 pages.

left alive to work on.'[88] Unfortunately neither of the possible editors suggested by James, namely the Rev. A. L. Mayhew and Henry Bradley, were free at that time and in October 1884 both parties at length accepted an agreement, based on Hucks Gibbs' earlier proposals, but with the proviso that if the Editor failed to produce 700 pages a year, he would be prepared to accept the division of the work between himself and a co-editor. As an additional inducement it was agreed that should Murray become incapacitated, owing to illness, before the completion of the work, he should be entitled to a pension of £100 in addition to his share of the profits. At the same time money was paid to meet the current salaries of the staff and an additional £100 to clear the debt to Mr Harley.[89]

The only outstanding question now left was that of James' debt of £400 to Henry Hucks Gibbs. This had remained unsettled since Furnivall's attempt to shame the Delegates into paying the debts under threat of a public appeal. Furnivall was very restive and in November 1882 Dr Price suppressed an injudicious letter from him on the subject.[90] Skeat raised the matter again in 1884 after the publication of Part I, but yielded to the request of the Delegates that no action should be taken for the time being.[91] Furnivall was of course indignant at this further delay and in April Hucks Gibbs had to restrain him from a plan to expose the Delegates in the daily press, telling him 'It *is* a shame, as you say, but don't write to the papers about it. You'll do no good at all, and will more probably do harm. You do well to be savage, but you need not flaunt your war paint and feathers! I have no doubt they are brewing something at Oxford.'[92]

The matter came to a head again when Gibbs realised that James was having great difficulty in finding a house in Oxford at a price he could afford to pay, and that this was causing further delay to progress on Part II of the Dictionary. He urged James to make a direct appeal to the Delegates to free him from any outstanding debts.[93] James followed his advice, but once again injudicious letters from Furnivall hardened their attitude.[94] Nevertheless, they were sympathetic when James provided them with figures showing that in order to produce Part I, he had spent £1822 (including the loss of his Mill Hill salary and allowing for the Civil List pension), and had received only £1194 from the Press.[95] They might have paid the debt had not Walter Skeat challenged them to recognise that under the Contract they were liable to pay all costs. On the advice of their lawyers, the Delegates denied this, but withdrew their objection to the Society raising the money by

14. Sunnyside, Oxford, from the garden. The shed on the right is the Scriptorium. About 1887.

public subscription.[96] Furnivall reacted violently, declaring 'They are a Board, they've got no conscience and no feelings',[97] but in fact the Delegates all subscribed in their private capacity 'to show their personal feeling towards the work and Dr Murray'.[98] James was very unhappy over the whole thing, and but for the pressure of his friends he would have tried to prevent the appeal being made. As it was, he considerably changed the wording so that no offence would be caused to the Delegates—in the opinion of the Appeal Committee thereby very much lessening the impact on potential subscribers, although the *Murray Indemnity Fund* successfully raised the £400 to repay Hucks Gibbs and left a balance of £180 towards James' other out-of-pocket expenses.[99]

The *Fund* came too late to help with the house problem, but in May 1885 James found one, 78 Banbury Road, recently built on St John's College land in the developing North Oxford suburb.[100] Furnivall had suggested that he should try for a house three or four miles outside the city, advising that 'the exercise for you & the Press folk going to & fro w[oul]d do you all good'.[101] The house was not right in the country, but it was the last but one on the east side of the road with fields, now all built over, beyond.

A site for the Scriptorium was a problem. St John's College refused to allow its erection in the front garden and agreed to its being placed just behind the house only on condition that the next door neighbour, Professor Dicey, had no objection. The Diceys became very good friends, and Mrs Dicey later was sure they had made no difficulty but the fact is that in May 1885 Professor Dicey asserted that it would injure his outlook, and the Scriptorium had to be sunk about three feet into the ground before he would accept its position. As a result part of the garden was filled by a six foot high mound of the excavated soil, later planted with shrubs.[102] A less desirable outcome was that the Scriptorium was always somewhat damp. It was also ill ventilated. In summer it was stuffy, in winter dank and cold. Furnivall's fears as to the suitability of 'that horrid corrugated den' were confirmed by the bad health record of the assistants.[103] James himself dreaded the winter and seldom got through without chills which several times led to pneumonia. A minute of the Delegacy in 1889 refers to 'Proposals for improving the sanitary condition of the Scriptorium'. Plans and estimates were obtained for improved heating and ventilation and the Secretary wrote to James advising against his idea of drawing more air in from below the floor because 'It is known that in winter the ground is saturated to within a very few feet of the surface and air drawn from under your floor will be as damp & unwholesome as if you were all living in a cellar ... your feet will always be enveloped in chill unwarmed air.'[104] There was a stove to warm it in winter, but owing to fear of fire it was always extinguished at night and in cold weather James wore a thick overcoat and sometimes sat with his feet in a box to keep them from the draught. The spartan conditions shocked and surprised visitors to this crowded fifty by fifteen foot room looking, one said 'like a tool house, a washhouse or a stable'.[105]

The Scriptorium was a new building, slightly larger than the one at Mill Hill but built on the same pattern, though without a dais. The original workroom was presented to Mill Hill School and the cost of its removal to the school grounds was paid for by an appeal to Old Boys. Dr Murray wished it to be a place where all boys who wanted to read, study or pursue any quiet occupation, especially on Sundays, could do so without distraction. He expressed the hope that it would some day be viewed with interest as the original home of the Dictionary. Unfortunately it was accidentally burnt down in 1902, the 'fireproof room' being perhaps proof against external fire but not internal combustion, since its wood lining must have been highly inflammable. It was replaced, and there is still a Murray Scriptorium or Reading Room attached to the school library.[106]

The house at Oxford, which they named Sunnyside after the Mill Hill home, was ready for occupation in June and the Murrays moved on the 11th. James went ahead with the furniture, the older children and the pet doves, while Ada remained behind with the cat, to help the assistants pack the contents of the Scriptorium in some forty boxes. She complained that she slept very badly, 'the bed was *so* hard and *so* lonely'.[107]

There now only remained to make his farewells to the school and James and Ada returned for Foundation Day, a family occasion with Harold, the eldest boy carrying off most of the senior school prizes.

So ended another phase in James Murray's life and in the history of the Dictionary. With the removal to Oxford the confrontation with Benjamin Jowett ended. Surprisingly a close friendship grew up between the two men, each coming to have a great respect for the other. The Vice-Chancellor had had in his earlier years enough of the bitterness of controversy and he needed to make friends: by nature he was warm and kindly, and could exercise considerable charm.[108] His concern for the Dictionary was genuine, and as he got to know James better he recognised in him a man after his own heart. Both were deeply religious and both believed that every man should develop his abilities and do his chosen work to the limit of his powers as his response to his Maker. Jowett was unorthodox. He had been brought up in an evangelical tradition and had later become involved in controversy as a supporter of liberal views, condemned by both high and low churchmen as heretical. Although now a minister of the Church of England he could therefore appreciate James Murray's firm dissenting principles and James on his part became a regular worshipper in Balliol College Chapel when the Master was preaching. Jowett, like Murray, had had to help himself to advance in the world of scholarship. He had reached academic distinction by solitary study and in spite of a family background of unsuccessful businessmen. Hard work and self discipline were the qualities he most admired, and in James Murray he found them abundantly. It was Jowett who had fought to get the Editor of the Dictionary based in Oxford, and it was Jowett who welcomed the Murrays on their arrival. He made James a member of Balliol and frequently invited him to dine there. He also took to Ada and they both were often the Master's guests at the famous Balliol concerts. Dr Jowett would fill the Lodge at weekends with distinguished guests and on Sunday evenings take them all to the

College concert, trooping in with his galaxy of visitors while the audience rose to its feet as they walked the length of the Hall.[109] The Murrays were there on their very first Sunday in Oxford and in the interval the Master came down from the High Table to where they were sitting and said, 'Welcome to your own College', and led them up to sit with him.

When it came to choosing colleges for two of the Murray boys, Harold and the third son, Wilfrid, it was natural to turn to Balliol and another link was forged. Harold, who was an Exhibitioner, quickly distinguished himself; and one evening Jowett, walking across from the Hall after a concert, with Ada on his arm, told her, 'Your son Harold is, without exception, the very best undergraduate I have ever known.'[110] Harold obtained a First Class in Mathematics, but Jowett was probably referring as much to the family qualities of hard work and integrity as to his intellectual brilliance.

The friendship between the two scholars was sealed when a tenth child, a boy, was born to the Murrays in 1886, less than a year after their arrival in Oxford. The child was born on a Sunday and James, present at a Balliol concert that evening, decided to ask the Master's leave to name his son Benjamin after him. In reply Dr Jowett said that he had never cared for the name and would not willingly inflict it on the child, but he added that if he had had a son of his own he would have called him after his two close friends, Arthur Stanley and Arthur Hugh Clough.[111] He suggested that they should name the boy Arthur Hugh and that if they cared to add Jowett perhaps it would do the little fellow no harm. So Arthur Hugh Jowett he was. The Master was very fond of children and used to call on Ada to see the child, letting him play with his gold watch, and running round the room in a game of horses with his little namesake.

When the child was seven Benjamin Jowett died. Little Jowett was taken to see the dead man lying in state, which filled him with terror, and to the funeral, when he enjoyed a sense of importance in bearing the name of such a great man. He grew to be one of the most brilliant of the Murray children, obtaining a triple first in Classics and Law.

The friendship with Benjamin Jowett was one of the few happy results of the break with Mill Hill and the move to the new Sunnyside. In other respects Oxford marked for James the final end of his freedom. Henceforth he was Lexicographer and nothing more. He had to reconcile himself to the hard truth, that he was committed to the Dictionary for the rest of his working life, and must put out of his mind any other schemes and projects he might have entertained. It was now too late to draw back. He was well and truly caught, bound, as he said 'to never ending toil'.[112]

CHAPTER XIII

The Bête Noire of the Press

THE removal of Murray and his Scriptorium to Oxford was greeted with general relief and optimism. The Delegates marked the occasion by a public announcement in May that they 'confidently hope that it will be possible for the book to appear henceforth at the rate of two parts a year',[1] while Walter Skeat told James 'when you are *on the spot*, I think you may hope for far better things. [The Delegates] will begin to feel at last a real personal interest in the work & will warm up wonderfully . . . Take the cheerfulest view . . . for that is half the battle!'[2]

But James remained very depressed. He was sad to leave Mill Hill and to cut himself off from the society of school boys and the pleasure he found in teaching them. He felt deeply the loss of the wide views from his garden in which he found something of the peace of mind that always came to him when he could escape to the mountains. The Thames valley with its sluggish rivers and enervating atmosphere held no attractions. He was leaving behind many friends in the Philological Society and others whom he had known since he first came to London twenty-five years before or had met through the School. In Oxford, by contrast, he had few connections: he knew well only three philologists, W. R. Morfill, A. L. Mayhew, and a clergyman, C. B. Mount, who had been introduced to him by Professor Price in 1879 and had become one of his best voluntary workers, regularly checking references for him in the Bodleian Library.

Academically also, the reputation of Oxford in the field of philology was discouraging. In spite of changes resulting from the Royal Commission on the Universities of Oxford and Cambridge in 1850, Oxford, compared to the Universities of Scotland and of London, stood for the traditional Classical—and in James' view reactionary—system of education. Both in Hawick and at Mill Hill James was accustomed to a wide curriculum suited to boys who would enter professions or the business world, while Oxford still catered largely for the social elite, who could afford to go to the University as a cultural luxury rather than as a stepping stone to earning their living. Little progress had been made there in developing scientific and linguistic studies, and James had been warned that he must expect to find no interest in his work. 'They are hardly aware of the existence of Shakspeare & Chaucer yet', Henry Sweet told him in 1870.[3] The historian E. A. Freeman, also known to James Murray, expressed the same opinion even more strongly: 'I wish I could call Oxford the home of any language' he complained

> It, or at least a majority of it, will have nothing to do with English or any other Teutonic tongue . . . Their ignorance is not that negative darkness which consists in the mere absence of light. It is something positive, Egyptian darkness that may be felt. It is an aggressive contempt for all wise learning.[4]

Max Müller, in his inaugural address as Professor of Comparative Philology in 1868, speaking of his disappointment at the outcome of the reforms in the University, declared that 'knowledge for its own sake and a chivalrous devotion to studies which command no place in the fair of the world and lead to no place of emolument in Church or State, are looked down upon and ridiculed by almost everybody.' On another occasion he said that what he missed most after Germany was stimulating discourse in literary and scientific circles.[5] James' experience of the limited interest shown by Oxford dons in general in the Dictionary led him to conclude that there had been little change for the better in the last fifteen years. His own attitude to the University is revealed in a letter he wrote to Dr Price about the move to Oxford. Referring to the need to lower the foundations of the Scriptorium, he observed that he supposed it must be buried 'so that no trace of such a place of real work shall be seen by fastidious and otiose Oxford', going on to quote 'one of the most widely known men in Oxford' (possibly Max Müller) describing the University as a place 'where even men who work, do it in secret & pretend openly to be merely men of the world'.[6]

So far from looking forward to residence in a University city, therefore, James was only anxious lest he should be exposed more directly to interference by the Delegates.[7] None the less, encouraged by his friends, he still hoped for academic recognition and was disappointed to find that the University Statutes did not allow him to be given a doctorate *ad eundem* by virtue of his Edinburgh degree.[8] He accepted the Honorary M.A. arranged for him by Dr Jowett, but regarded the award simply as a necessary formality to enable him to use the Bodleian Library.[9] For someone not an Oxford man, and holding no college appointment, it was not easy to gain an entrée to University circles: the Colleges and their Common Rooms tended to be exclusive and it was possible for even a Professor or a scholar of European fame to live for years in the city without making the acquaintance of the leaders of the University.[10] Although Dr Jowett did his best to make the Murrays feel at home, James never lost the sense of being an outsider and as late as 1913, after nearly thirty years he said he still felt himself to be 'to a great extent only a sojourner' in Oxford because his work was there.[11] By then he was quite active in city, if not in University affairs, but the fact that he was a Congregationalist in a University where the leadership of the Colleges was still in the hands of ministers of the Church of England may have contributed to this impression.

Dr Murray's arrival in Oxford was heralded by an unfortunate intervention by an injudicious well-wisher. About a month before he took up residence in Banbury Road, an anonymous article appeared in the *Oxford Review*, headed 'How *not* to treat a man of letters'.[12] This was an outspoken criticism of the Delegates for their refusal to pay the debts for which the *Murray Indemnity Appeal* was made. Having outlined the situation leading up to the launching of the Appeal, the writer continued:

The spectacle of a University of ancient repute, when engaged in producing a work of more than national importance, driving a hard bargain with an eminent man of letters, taking advantage of legal technicalities to escape moral obligations, ... is not one that any friend of Oxford can observe without shame and disgust. We only hope that, despite the miserable parsimony and sharp practice of the Delegates ... Dr Murray will not abandon his great project in despair ... The Delegates should learn that cheese-paring is not the truest economy, that it is not wise to over-drive a willing horse ... They might also, if happily they were in a docile frame of mind, be taught that they are something more than tradesmen, that they are, in a sense, trustees of the credit of the University.

It is not difficult to recognise in this the hand of Frederick Furnivall, but it may well have made James some enemies and swayed the balance against him if there was still any question of offering him a University appointment.

Other more serious worries haunted James. The move cost more than expected and he would not have been able to buy the house at all had not Walter Skeat come generously to his help with a loan of £1500, for which he asked 4 per cent interest—the equivalent of an annual rent of £64. Twelve years later Skeat reduced the interest to 3½ per cent and asked James to pay the £8 thus saved into a fund for books and binding for the Scriptorium Library.[13] The mortgage remained a drain on the family resources, creating a crisis in 1912 when Skeat died and it had to be repaid. Initially James also had to find some three or four hundred pounds to complete the purchase and in addition an annual ground rent of twelve pounds ten shillings. Then, instead of the greatly reduced fees at Mill Hill, he had now to meet the cost of educating one son at the University and three boys and very shortly after, two girls at the Oxford High Schools. Education of the large family was a heavy burden for the next twelve years when there were always six or seven children at school or college. Thus, in spite of being now free from the debts incurred during the early period of the Dictionary, financial cares continued, and from 1887 until 1899 James supplemented his income by spending part of the short period he could take as a holiday from the Dictionary in acting as supervising examiner for the Oxford Local Examinations in various centres.

While his closest friends were aware of the difficulties, other people believed with Furnivall that the success of the *Indemnity Fund* had left James now comfortably off. Furnivall repeatedly hinted at this, contrasting James' position with his own, until in 1893 James told him in exasperation that he and Ada were obliged to draw on their small capital to the tune of £50 a year, adding, 'I don't know what the end will be. I shall be insolvent some day soon, and then the crash will come'.[14] The Delegates no doubt thought that James owned his house and had not the slightest idea that he had virtually no bank balance.[15] It did not occur to anyone, until at last James enlightened them, that twenty years was a long time to work with no increment or prospect of advancement. James' salary remained based on what he had earned as an assistant master in his early forties and no account was taken of the fact that had he remained in his profession he would certainly have become a headmaster long before. When the Delegates were made aware of the situation in 1905 they increased his salary by £100 to £650 *p.a.*, but by then, with savings exhausted, any exceptional expenditure, such as illness or university fees to be found for the youngest child, meant that James had to borrow from the older sons.[16]

In the 1880s however the immediate worry was that which James had communicated to Dr Price when the move to Oxford was first mooted, namely that he was gravely disquieted that the scheme rested on an expectation which might not be realised and that, as he said, 'this might cause the Delegates to conclude that they had made a mistake, while it would make me miserable'.[17] He had anticipated that the disappointment of the Delegates might be two-fold, first as to the success of the Dictionary commercially, and second in the possible acceleration of production, to which his full-time employment might not, he pointed out, make so much difference. Twenty hours a week was not such a very great addition, and the long days worked at Mill Hill were to some extent made possible only because the alternation between school and Scriptorium gave some relief through a change of occupation. His worst fears were to be confirmed: the Delegates were very disappointed on both counts, and he was very miserable.

It was unfortunate that the removal to Oxford coincided with important changes in the Delegacy. Jowett, now in a position to learn more about the work, would probably also have come to appreciate the Editor's difficulties, but he ceased to be Vice-Chancellor in 1886 and withdrew largely from University politics owing to the increasing ill health which led to his death in 1893. The other loss was that of Dr Price, whose resignation, as Secretary to the Delegates, announced in June 1884 took effect a year later. He had, with Murray, borne the strain of the difficult years of negotiation, had come to believe in the Dictionary and was always kind and helpful. He continued as a Perpetual Delegate to take a close interest in the work and was often able to intervene with effect, but his place as Secretary was taken by a younger man, without any first hand knowledge of the background to the establishment of the Editor of the Dictionary in Oxford.

Henry Lyttelton Gell, the new Secretary, was a Balliol graduate.

His appointment was said to have been engineered by Jowett, who called a meeting to confirm the arrangement in the Long Vacation when he knew most of the Delegates would be unable to attend. Lyttelton Gell had had some experience in commercial publishing with the firm of Cassell and Galpin, and Jowett hoped that he would be useful in carrying out his ideas to put the business of the Press on a better footing. He lacked the tact and courtesy of his predecessor, and the change was noticed at once. James' friend and reader for the Dictionary, Lucy Toulmin Smith, was in process of settling the terms for the publication of her edition of the *York Mystery Plays*. 'Who & what is Mr. P. Lytellton Gell in the Clar[endon] Press?' she asked James in a letter of July 1885. 'Between you & me his letter shows more zeal on behalf of his employers than on the side of the author.'[18]

Disastrously for James and the Dictionary, Lyttelton Gell fastened upon its production as an obvious example of the inefficiency he had been appointed to remedy. Even if, as Max Müller thought, it must be classed as one of the literary undertakings from which no commercial profit should be expected, that was no justification for vast sums of money being squandered because the Editor was not being held to his contract. Regardless of James' reiterated warnings of the doubtful possibility of producing two parts — 700 pages — a year, Gell persisted in treating the removal to Oxford, and the provision of money for the salaries of the Assistants, as dependent on an absolute undertaking on the part of the Editor — something to which James had refused to commit himself.

Looked at from a business angle the Dictionary was clearly a failure. When the original contract was signed in 1879 it was with the expectation that once production started, the interest on the capital investment would be met by the sale of the Parts, each of which, it was planned at first, should cover a letter. If the rate of progress had been at least two letters a year and the Philological Society had been correct in thinking 40,000 copies would be sold, a profit should have been realised within a reasonable time and then a very substantial profit from the sale of abridgements. The grounds for disappointment were obvious. The letter *A* alone took from 1882 to 1885. *B* was not completed till 1888, ending Volume I nine years after the work had commenced, and Volume II, containing *C*, was published only in 1895, three years after the whole work should have appeared under the original scheme.

The effect of the delay on sales was serious. When in 1886, 1890 and 1892 the subscribers, who had bought the first part with enthusiasm, received no parts at all, they became disgruntled, while potential subscribers refused to commit themselves to a work which seemed unlikely to be finished in their life-time, if ever.[19] Criticism of the slow rate of production was voiced in reviews of the Parts which did appear. The *Athenaeum* noticed the long wait for Part I and earnestly hoped that the whole time required for the completion had not been similarly underestimated, and in 1895, while sympathising with the desire for perfection, the reviewer wished those responsible were more impressed with the advisability of reaching *zyc* as rapidly as possible.[20]

Under the terms of the agreement, annual accounts were submitted by the Press to the Philological Society and these made increasingly gloomy reading. In 1885/6 there was already an opening debt of £7000 and expenses for the year amounted to another £3500.[21] The price of a Part (350 pages) had been fixed at twelve shillings and six pence which was thought very reasonable, 'the price of ... a small barrel of oysters or a hat',[22] but the sales in 1885/6 totalled only 400 copies of Part I (in addition to those sold when it was first published), and 3600 copies of the new Part—a figure very far short of the anticipated 40,000. By 1897 the debt was £51,452 and still rising by some £5000 a year.[23]

The situation bothered the Editor from the first. He had said in 1883 that amid all the financial difficulties which surrounded the enterprise, he had often been tempted to wish that someone could be found who would work more economically and faster than himself

> in favour of such a one [he added] I s[houl]d-not without a struggle & much pain, yet, if I felt that it w[oul]d better secure the end, with some sense of duty, resign my responsibility. The work is greater than I, or any worker, and while I will never desert it, I will never stand in the way of its better or more speedy achievement, if that seems attainable.[24]

In February 1886 he actually consulted the Philological Society on the possibility of finding a second editor at a salary of £300.[25] The financial aspect remained for him 'a load of vexation and solicitude' which worried him far more than the technicalities of the work.[26]

While Lyttelton Gell and James Murray were equally anxious to expedite production, they differed as to how this might be done and to what extent, because they viewed the problem from very different angles. Gell had a first class degree, but he had very little appreciation of scholarship or understanding of the difficulties of research. He saw it as his duty to the Press to run it as a profit-making concern and he was wholly lacking in imagination and the sensitivity to assess the impact of his brusque letters on their recipients. While Benjamin Jowett, of whom he was the literary executor and with whose ideas of the Dictionary he was certainly conversant, thought himself capable of telling Dr Murray how he ought to write it, Gell in his turn thought he could direct how the work should be organised. All his experience told him that if you put more money into a business you should get more return, and he was perplexed to account for the fact that in spite of the increased allowance for assistance, the work was proceeding more slowly than before. He could only conclude that the Editor was to blame, and if he was really working to full capacity, then his methods must be wrong. James, on the other hand, believed that if a task was worth doing at all it was worth doing well, and that those responsible should expect to make some sacrifices to ensure this. He could not understand how the elite of an ancient University could fail to recognise the fruits of real scholarship and could niggle at using what he believed to be their vast resources to promote a work of such universal value and importance. Thus while James was concerned to justify expenditure in terms of pure scholarship and high quality, Gell was determined to make returns balance the investment, even if this meant a less perfect production.

At first Gell thought it was just a matter of applying pressure to the Editor. When he found that this did not work, he concluded that the system was at fault, and he reverted to the earlier idea of a second editor with a second team of assistants. This was the right solution, but still not one which could achieve the target of 700 pages a year, as he would have realised had he not been so unappreciative of the quality of the work, and so fixed in his belief that it could be turned out like a machine product at a steady pace which could be calculated in advance.

Meanwhile James wanted to be given a fair chance to see what he could do under the new arrangement. He still believed that this would work if only he could find good enough assistants and had the money to retain them, but he underestimated the problems of delegation and the difficulty of finding men who matched his own standards of perfection. Unlike Gell, he had no illusions that the work could ever be produced at the pace the Delegates hoped, except by the sacrifice of those standards. The next ten years became a battle between the two men, with the Delegates and the Philological Society in the background, supporting now the one and now the other.

James had by 1885 lost his sense of humour and his serenity: he bothered over trifles and took offence easily, but Gell, knowing nothing of the overwork of the past years, did not recognise that the Editor, in spite of his fine stamina, was now on the verge of mental breakdown. If Gell knew of the reluctance with which James had accepted the target of two Parts a year, he ignored it, nor did he note Hucks Gibbs' stipulation that increased production could not start until the Scriptorium staff was complete and trained. Disregarding these warnings, like a worrying sheepdog he endeavoured to drive the Editor forward.

Within a month of work starting in Oxford, making no allowances for the upheaval that the move must necessarily have caused, Gell told Dr Murray that the Delegates were inquiring 'with great anxiety as to the weekly progress of the Dictionary', earnestly hoping that the arrangements would soon be completed so that the production of 700 pages could be secured.[27] James replied that he was not resting on his oars, but having 'intolerable trouble about assistants'. He kept trying them out, but after four or five days rejecting them as hopeless. His last, a strongly recommended Oxford B.A., had proved to be 'an utter numb-skull ... a most lack-a-daisical, graspless fellow, born to stare at existence.'[28]

In spite of these difficulties, Part II, *Anta to Battening*, appeared in November, but that was the result of work which had been done before leaving Mill Hill, and to Mr Gell's way of thinking, Part III should have been in the hands of the printer by the end of the year, and was due to be published in April 1886. He called the attention of the Delegates in January to the slow progress and the fact that it was already evident that the agreement to publish two Parts would not be kept. A special Committee was appointed to report and in March 1886 Mr Gell told them that only fifty-six pages out of the 352 for Part III had reached final proof stage.[29]

Full of impatience, less than a year after the move to Oxford, Gell decided that the new system was a failure, and he now got Henry Bradley appointed in May to assist in the work on *B*, with the intention that he should later become an independent Editor of complete letters.[30] Gell used the opportunity to remind James that this step was taken because he had not carried out the conditions attached to the increased grant for editorial expenses, and the 'copious financial assistance' the Delegates had contributed had 'resulted in a scarcely perceptible acceleration in the work'. He put the blame for this ungracious complaint on the Delegates and directed Mr Doble, the Assistant Secretary, to write a covering letter assuring the Editor that his whole intent was to make things easier in future. Mr Doble hoped that there would be 'no occasion for these harassing communications' hereafter.[31]

To Gell's irritation, Bradley's help made no appreciable difference, and he continued to complain. At the end of June he told James that the Delegates were viewing 'almost with consternation' his lack of progress: only fifteen pages of the new Part had been passed for press after more than six months work.[32] James challenged him to suggest how any of the longer Dictionary articles, such as 'the terrible word *Black* & its derivatives', could be done in half the time. This word had taken his best voluntary helper, Mr Mount, three months, a Scriptorium assistant another three weeks, and he himself a week more to master. 'I wish', he ended

> from the bottom of my heart that I could do without your money, and honestly give you what you would consider a commercial equivalent for it. It is an embittering consideration for me that while trying to do scholarly work in a way which scholars may be expected to appreciate, circumstances place me commercially in the position of the *bête noire* of the Clarendon Press, who involves them in ruinous expenditure.[33]

But Gell was not impressed and in August he begged James to think of some way of putting all his assistants onto finishing any material partly set up so that at least something might be published before the end of the year.[34] In September, looking for some reason to explain the apparent failure of the appointment of Bradley, Gell pounced again to complain that Bradley was now working on 'new' material which had not been prepared for him in advance by the assistants, saying, 'it is obvious that there could be no hope of his proceeding at the rate which you & the Delegates desire if he is to fritter away even a single hour upon work which a subordinate member of the staff could do as well.'[35] In October the Delegates, returning from the Long Vacation, recorded that progress was still unsatisfactory.[36]

Every month James came to expect some rebuke: in November he was informed that the Delegates were perplexed that there were no adequate results to show for the £1250 given for the assistants' salaries.[37] The New Year brought a more sinister communication. On 31 January Mr Gell begged James to remember that in spite of the need of maintaining a high standard 'the work is *wanted* by students *now*, and that it would be vain if in the end the pursuit of an unattainable standard in particular minutiae were to end in the non-completion of the Dictionary.' The present Delegates had pledged him all consideration and assistance, but they could not foretell the policy of their successors in years to come.[38]

In February 1887 Part III was at last published, but there were no congratulations from the Delegates. Instead it was resolved that the Secretary should call the attention of the Editor to the serious increase in the cost of corrections.[39] The March communication was the worst yet. The Delegates, James heard from Gell, 'will be appalled to learn that the whole completed result since Feb[ruary] 1st is two sheets', and he asked James to suggest any means whereby he could achieve a 'less vexatious discrepancy between expenditure & results'.[40] The final complaint before the Long Vacation was that only a single sheet had been passed between 5 May and 6 June. The current Part which should have been produced in six months seemed likely to take three to four years and James was warned that the Delegates would come to 'some serious & critical resolution', unless he would immediately pass Bradley's materials now believed to be ready but held up waiting his revisions.[41]

All these cracks of the whip were useless. The immediate delays were due to James' determination that nothing should be passed that was capable of improvement and insistence on checking all proofs himself. While he was reading Bradley's work the assistants complained that they were at a standstill waiting for him to attend to theirs.[42] James' only reaction was to work still harder, bringing himself nearer to a breakdown. In 1885 and 1886 he took no proper holiday and only two weeks in 1887. His friends begged him to rest, Walter Skeat urged him to spend even a couple of days at Cambridge: he had already arranged with several Oxford friends, Professor Rhys, a Celtic scholar and the philologists A. H. Mayhew and W. R. Morfill, to come and drag James out for an afternoon walk sometimes. Calmness, courage, and a cheerful state of bodily health, he advised, were essential to mental well being. He wondered whether James was getting enough oxygen and pressed the need for exercise.[43]

In July 1887 James was ill and even Mr Gell encouraged a short holiday, although on James' return his task-master made the depressing comment that he hoped the Dictionary would be the better and more vigorous as a result, saying ' "Without haste, without rest", will remain the only mottoe for its completion.'[44] James was missing the regular pattern of term and holidays he enjoyed at Mill Hill and he said in 1896 that this was only the second year in ten in which he had taken three weeks consecutive holiday. He had asked years before for the Scriptorium to be shut altogether for two weeks in August, but Mr Gell had said this was impossible, as it would mean the compositors working on the Dictionary would have to be put on some other work and would not be able to return to the Dictionary till that was finished, which would cause intolerable delays. The result was that James was always shorthanded during the holiday season but had somehow to complete the usual amount of work and in addition accumulate enough copy to keep the printers occupied if he went away himself. 'This I do at enormous personal cost', he said. At the end of the holiday 'the accumulation of proofs, revises, 2nd revises, finals ... to say nothing of the pile of letters etc. a yard deep is so appalling that I feel inclined to sit down and weep, and vow that I will never go away again!' The good effect of the break seemed gone in two or three days while the consequent arrears were not caught up for a month. 'Such has been my fate', James moaned, 'since I gave up my liberty to be the slave of the Dictionary! It never leaves me, it always weighs on me.'[45]

Meanwhile Gell had identified the reason for slow production: so long as all proofs must pass through Murray's hands he was a bottleneck and extra staff, even of the quality of Henry Bradley, did no good. The solution then must be to press on at once with the promotion of Bradley as an independent editor and to justify the expenses of this new appointment by reducing Dr Murray's staff by half, to the number he had employed at Mill Hill. Instead of one Editor producing two Parts a year, each Editor would produce one Part of 350 pages. With James' concurrence Bradley was now asked to prepare a specimen of his independent work[46] and on 4 November 1887 he became second Editor.[47] Gell showed no more tact than when Bradley had been introduced as a collaborator and in notifying James of the new arrangements he said that the Delegates were not prepared to accept failure to produce two Parts a year, which would mean that the Dictionary would not be finished in the lifetime of either James or its chief supporters.[48] He left James feeling that the decrease in his own staff was a punishment for his unsatisfactory progress. This impression was increased by a petty annoyance when, as soon as Bradley started to work independently, Gell took it upon himself to reduce the number of presentation copies hitherto allowed to Murray as Editor. Murray was accustomed to distribute some of these copies to the voluntary helpers and to use some for reference in the Scriptorium. Gell now informed him that he feared the Delegates would not feel his claim to Bradley's Parts was on the same footing as to those he produced himself, and said that he should receive only one copy of Bradley's. Although Gell was soon over-ruled on this by the Delegates and James was allowed nine copies, Parts missed at the time caused irritation for many years.[49]

James was not opposed to Henry Bradley as second Editor, but he was convinced that it was no solution to the problem of increasing production to the extent that Gell and the Delegacy hoped. He felt, with some justice, that a fair trial had never been given to the arrangement under which he had come to Oxford. He had always said that its success would depend upon recruiting competent assistants, and part of the understanding had been that the Press would help to find them. This was quite forgotten and in March 1886 Dr Price told him, 'I have no commission from the Delegates to enquire for assistants to you in the work of the Dictionary ... That is your business'.[50]

One reason for the slowing up of production was that the disaster James had anticipated had occurred: Erlebach, his best and most experienced helper, had left. Erlebach could easily have become a co-editor and would have been James' choice. He had shared the work from the beginning and had been involved in all the decisions on technical details: he did not need instruction or reminder—on the contrary, he could often help the Editor from his own memory of what had been settled. He left to fulfill a promise to join his brother in running a private school, but he was still deeply interested in the Dictionary. Until his death in 1899 he continued to help by reading proofs and would come from time to time to take over supervision of the Scriptorium to enable James to take a holiday. James always thought that if he had been able to offer him a better salary he would not have left: he wished that the £100 he was directed to contribute from his allowance for assistants towards Bradley's salary, could have been given to Erlebach and he never ceased to regret the Delegates' policy of introducing outsiders as co-editors rather than encouraging his better assistants by promotion.

There were other reasons why progress at Oxford was slower than at Mill Hill. The letter *B* proved much more difficult than *A*. While it was obvious that some letters would take longer than others because there were more words to be dealt with—*Q* would be quick and *S* would be slow, for example—it took some time to realise that some letters contain a higher proportion of words with difficult derivations and that this meant production was likely to go in spurts rather than at a steady pace. Everyone—Gell, Murray and the members of the Philological Society—made the mistake of taking *A* as typical. Even Skeat, with his experience of dictionary making, gave the wrong advice. In his opinion all words beginning with consonants were simpler than words beginning with vowels, because the initial letters are more stable. 'Moral', he told James confidently, 'when you get thro' *A*, you will have done one of the most troublesome of all letters, & may safely make an estimate of time by it, knowing that you will *not* exceed that estimate.'[51] This was totally misleading. The letter *A* contains more classical words and derivatives with Greek and Latin prefixes and most of these words are only used in one or two senses and had been fully treated by earlier lexicographers. It was therefore one of the easier letters, but when James reached *B* he found that he was having to trace the long history, hitherto unknown, of words which had changed their meanings and constructions in every century.[52]

A third factor of which no account had been taken was that all the while the Dictionary progressed, new material was coming in; there were more slips to be considered and more decisions to take in choosing which quotations to use, and no one could tell how much extra time would be needed for this. Bradley's view was that the reduction of four million quotations to the one million which could be used, was the most time-consuming task of all. He suggested that the sub-editors might make the preliminary selection so that fewer slips would need to be handled by the Scriptorium staff,[53] but James would not consent to this because in his experience there were few if any competent sub-editors; his instructions to them were that no slips might be removed.

If *B* had been as straightforward as *A*, if the material to be gone through had been no more than for *A* and if he had been able to fill all the vacancies on his staff with really competent men, James thought it

15. The Scriptorium, Oxford: at work on the Dictionary.

might just have been possible to produce the required 700 pages a year, but as things were he knew that it was impossible unless standards were lowered: 'the attempt to get on more quickly', he told Price in April 1886, 'will involve a sacrifice of much of the accuracy of the parts already published, as our standard must be not what is the best possible, but what is the most that can be done in the time. This is naturally a matter of profound regret and disappointment to myself.'[54] He claimed that the reduction of his staff to the size of the Mill Hill establishment would mean that they would have to deal with five words of average complexity every hour—40 a day: there would be no time for research in the Libraries, or to write, as was often necessary, to two or three specialists for information. The Editors would probably have to take some definitions from other dictionaries without verification, and they would certainly have to make do to a greater extent with the quotations they had, without looking for better. James probably exaggerated, but his words are indicative of his extreme anxiety at the time. 'Whether the result ... will be satisfactory or not', he said, 'a little experience will show ... and whether I find the necessary depreciation of quality so serious as to call for grave consideration.'[55] With the Press hinting at cessation of publication, and the Editor hinting at resignation, the fate of the Dictionary had again become precarious.

CHAPTER XIV

Shearing Samson's Locks:
The Pace of Production Must Be
Increased

IT WAS no surprise to James that Bradley's appointment did so little to improve production. He had done his best to convince Gell that this would be so and he may have felt a bitter satisfaction in being proved right. He knew that it was a mistake to bind Bradley like himself to a fixed output and to make his appointment conditional on this. He knew that he himself would be hard put to produce 350 pages a year and that Bradley was not strong and could not support long hours of work, added to which, although a first class philologist, he was a slow worker.[1] James warned Gell in June 1886 that his estimate of what it was possible to achieve was at fault and that the Delegates would soon be able to compare what Bradley could do and judge if his own slowness was due to any fault or unfitness on his part,[2] but it took some time for the truth of his opinion to be accepted. Meanwhile Bradley was also subjected to Mr Gell's pricking and goading. Without James' stamina he was brought to serious illness in 1890 and breakdown in 1892, when he was away for three months during which time James undertook to pass his proofs for press in order not to hold up the work.[3] By this time the Delegates were forced to acknowledge that so far from working as fast or faster than Murray, Henry Bradley would probably never exceed half of his pace, and it was decided to adjust his agreement and accept a rate of production of only half a part (176 pages) a year without any corresponding reduction in his staff.[4]

A second error in the terms of Bradley's appointment was that, owing to his wife's poor health and the advice of her doctor that the Oxford climate would not suit her, Bradley did not move to Oxford till 1896. In the interim he was living in Clapham, working in a room provided for him at the British Museum and paying frequent visits to Oxford. Mr Gell soon saw that this was absurd. 'Nothing' he wrote to

Furnivall, 'could be more unpractical or wasteful of a delicate man's powers than ... rattling his nerves to pieces in incessant railway journeys.'[5]

A third error was that Bradley's engagement was not even full time. Just before he was appointed the Press had entered into an agreement with him to make a new edition of Stratmann's *Middle English Dictionary*, and until this was completed he could give only four days a week to the *New English Dictionary*. Bradley hoped to have Stratmann off his hands in 1886, but it was not published till 1891 and meanwhile greatly hindered his new undertaking.[6]

In addition to these obvious miscalculations, James was troubled because he felt that Bradley had not yet enough experience to edit a volume on his own. Although the reviewers did not detect any falling off of standards in Bradley's first Part when it was published, James himself always felt that the two worst volumes of the Dictionary were *A* and *E*. Many years later he told Walter Skeat that of the two, *E* was much the worse

> because the Delegates were in such a hurry to get Mr Bradley on, to show that he could (as they thought) work twice as fast as I, that he neither had the practice, the knowledge of the weakness of the Philological Society slips, nor the resources of the Scriptorium to help him ... I have always said that the letter ought to be done again. *A* is not quite so unsatisfactory because I had been working provisionally for a year when I began to print it, and had learned how much had to be done to supplement the slips ... It *was* a pity to start Bradley so.[7]

As usual it was to Henry Hucks Gibbs that he voiced his anxieties. Bradley's knowledge of languages was extensive, but he was not yet practised in writing definitions, and during the time he supervised his work James found that he had frequently to do a good deal of correction and rewriting. He did not feel that the trial specimen Bradley prepared was a fair sample; the words were not typical from the point of view of difficulty, and the sub-editing had been done by an above-average assistant. 'What I fear', James told Gibbs,

> is that parts of his will be so bad, that I shall be ashamed of it, & have to say, I cannot go on with this: if you accept this I must resign my connection with it. I hope it may not be so; but, if some parts which he did prepare for press had been printed as he sent them, I should have had to speak very decidedly.[8]

No doubt his great regret at having to surrender the hope of editing the whole Dictionary himself, together with general depression, led James to take much too gloomy a view. Hucks Gibbs recognised this, and while agreeing that Bradley's specimen showed some weakness, thought there was nothing that greater experience would not remedy.[9]

Bradley himself was well aware of his limitations at this stage. Writing to Hucks Gibbs to ask if he would read his proofs for him he said 'I am very deeply sensible how far my qualifications for the work are below those of Dr Murray; but the task ... is to a material extent facilitated by the fact that I have so much of Dr Murray's work before me to serve as a model.'[10] Gell, anxious to separate the two Editors as completely as possible, suggested that Bradley should consult Murray only in cases of special difficulty, but Bradley begged James to look through his proofs if he had time to do so,[11] and he recorded later, 'I shall always remember with gratitude the abundant help which I received from him in the shape of criticism of my earlier efforts, and suggestion of the authorities to be consulted.'[12]

In the long run Bradley fully justified the Delegates' confidence, and James, who often consulted him on etymological problems, recognised his great ability. He particularly praised the arrangement of Bradley's article on the word *set* — the longest in the Dictionary — saying, 'I have seen no better treatment of a long word'.[13] Furnivall and some members of the Philological Society thought Bradley was the superior as Editor; Hucks Gibbs, who was probably in a better position than anyone to compare their work, because he saw it all in proof, did not agree.[14]

All in all, it was not surprising that Bradley's appointment did nothing to satisfy Mr Gell's longing for business efficiency and commercial success. The experience of Bradley merely repeated that of Murray himself: the system of payment by results meant that he had to ask for an advance in 1888.[15] He too discovered that the work of the voluntary sub-editors was often inadequate and complained that he could not proceed at the desired speed without further assistance.[16] In 1890 Mr Gell called the attention of the Delegates to the fact that Bradley had failed to adhere to the terms of his agreement,[17] and that although Murray had managed to produce his Parts in June 1888 and November 1889, Bradley had so far completed nothing, and in 1890 there was no Part from either Editor.

It was in the winter of 1889–90 that James was brought nearest to mental breakdown. He always dreaded the autumn term, when after the lull of the Long Vacation, the Delegates returned, 'keen for the fray, eager to discuss "what is to be done with the Dictionary?" ' The winter loomed ahead with the dark foggy November days when the Scriptorium felt so dank, and it was so desperately difficult to keep warm when chained to his desk.[18] Often as he rose before light to another day of toil he must have come near to yielding to the temptation to give up the long struggle and resign. Understandably he had begun to despair of completion. The task which he had undertaken for ten years now stretched on before him unendingly. The ten years were up and he had not finished even the third letter of the alphabet: Bradley's appointment as second Editor had been no help. Worse, he felt that his work was unappreciated. Sales were poor and although the reviewers of the Parts when they appeared continued enthusiastic, he was bitterly disappointed that the response from the Delegacy was so negative. With no word of encouragement he had begun to wonder if they really cared whether the Dictionary was produced or not. Furnivall totally misunderstood the reasons for his unhappiness and sent some of his bracing but unhelpful letters and postcards. 'As to work', he admonished James,

> the motive for it is not to get praise, or have one's vanity flattered, but to get knowledge increast & good work done which other folk may carry on. Only a girl wants continual praise. If a man knows himself that his work is honest, & a few friends know it too, that's enough, let the rest of the world call him a dd. fool if it likes.

When James retorted that he did not want praise for himself, but he was afraid he was sacrificing everything to a work which no one wanted, Furnivall had a quick answer: 'The Dict[ionar]y has to educate folk into wanting it, & ought to be produced tho' only 6 men cared for it.'[19]

James' other friends did their best to encourage him to go on and were deeply concerned by his talk of giving up. If he did resign it was very doubtful if the Dictionary would ever be completed. 'Would that some powerful friend would come forward to convince your Delegates of the injustice and cruelty, as well as the impolity, of hurrying you!'[20] wrote Fitzedward Hall, while the sympathetic sub-editor Miss Brown exclaimed,

> What I feel too is a cause for real regret is that a work which with your scholarly gifts and power *ought* to be such an intense

enjoyment should become a heavy burden ... I think your simile of the 'mountain and pick and shovel' very good, but you ought to have *time* to stop and realize the beauty of the crystals which day by day reveal themselves to your delving. A great national work should be slow to *be* perfect.[21]

Foreign scholars held the same opinion. 'I cannot understand', wrote Professor Sievers of Halle, 'why the Delegates should be so intent on ruining a work which will and can never be done again.'[22]

In this state of mind everything became out of proportion. James worked himself up into a state of agitation and indignation about the *Century Dictionary* which started publication in 1889 under the direction of Professor W. D. Whitney of Yale, who had already a world wide reputation in linguistic studies.[23] James worried that the work would be a commercial rival and dangerous competitor and claimed that the Editor was guilty of plagiarism. He thought the Delegacy should take legal action and took some of his valuable time to expose errors in Whitney's work in order to minimise its impact on the sale of his own work. All his friends were agreed that his fears were quite unfounded. They reminded him that the traditional practice of Dictionary makers was 'to copy shamelessly from one dictionary to another', and assured him that his reputation could not suffer. Furnivall told him

> Tho' I find your disgust natural at your own work being prigd, yet I hope it'll soon pass into satisfaction that your views are accepted by every one, & that right opinions prevail, tho' folk don't know whence they sprang ... You yourself get ... *all* the credit of our Dicty. The rest of us who've been at it — off & on — for 31 years are never thought of. What *does* it matter? The main thing is, the history of our language is made clear.[24]

In spite of the advice, James wrote such a scathing letter on Professor Whitney's derivation of the word *cockney*[25] that it called forth a protest and caution from his good friend Professor March, the organiser of the American volunteer readers. Murray's Dictionary, March told him,

> has been regarded here with affectionate pride as the greatest work of the linguistic scholarship of our time ... You can not write letters for the public belittling Prof. Whitney, Yale, and Americans and retain this affectionate regard ... It has been taken as a matter of

course that with all the materials entrusted to you . . . you will make many discoveries. It seems a sort of mis-user, a betrayal of trust, to make these discoveries a ground of sneers at your predecessors: your pride in them ought to be serene and gracious, ought not it?[26]

James convinced March that his criticism of Whitney's derivation was well founded and roused his sympathy by telling him of his anxiety about the financial position of the Dictionary and its future[27] and fortunately, at least temporarily, his serenity was restored.

A new friend, Robinson Ellis, the eccentric old Professor of Latin, had come forward with practical help. In the spring of 1890 he paid for James to join him in a first trip to the Continent. The holiday lasted a fortnight and they visited Brussels, Antwerp, Louvain, Waterloo, Cologne, Ghent and Bruges. James revived immediately. At the very outset, owing to the Professor insisting on a meal on arrival at Calais, the train went off with their luggage and without them, but James said he enjoyed the opportunity of exploring Calais. He found it delightful and felt like a schoolboy on a lark.[28]

Fred Elworthy, no doubt in league with Ada, also used his influence, and the European break was followed in September by a visit to Somerset. The party spent a day on Exmoor, lunching on the heather in broiling sunshine which dried a *papier mâché* squeeze the two antiquarians made of an inscribed stone, and left James' neck as 'tender as roast chicken'. He was triumphant in getting Ada to the top of Yes Tor and interested in discussing the derivation of the curious name.[29]

The effect of this much needed relaxation was good: in 1891 another Part of *C* appeared in the autumn, following Bradley's first Part of *E*. For the one and only time in the history of the Dictionary the dream of two Parts in a year was achieved.

It was an isolated triumph, and in November 1892 the storm which James had long dreaded burst upon the two Editors. Dr Price, writing with his customary courtesy, informed Dr Murray that the attention of the Delegates had lately been drawn (presumably by Mr Gell) to the delays in publishing the Dictionary, 'a progress indeed much slower than they have hoped for or expected'.[30] Lyttelton Gell wrote more bluntly to Dr Furnivall:

> I think there can be no objection to your knowing that the profound dissatisfaction of the Delegates at the steadily growing dispropor-
> tion between the money spent upon the '*Dictionary*' and the work

done has risen to such a pitch that the possibility of discontinuing it has been seriously urged upon the Board [by himself?], and the motion has only been suspended pending the receipt of a report from a Committee ...

The cost of 280 pages passed for publication (with material for another forty or so more) in the past year, representing the united efforts of the two Editors, was £2157. 'The Delegates', he continued, 'are impressed with the fact that the more they endow the Dictionary the slower proportionately it goes.' The Mill Hill rate of progress, he argued, ought to be regarded as 'the extreme *low* water mark, not the *high* water mark, of what is to be justly expected from the Editorial staff', and he reverted to his old charge against Dr Murray that he had broken the agreement under which the move to Oxford had been made. On the other hand, Mr Gell had to confess that although the Dictionary was costing £7 a page, expense was not really a problem and he thought that the Delegates would not draw back on that ground alone. What had moved them was the evidence of inefficiency—that they were now getting less for their money than they had in the Mill Hill days.[31]

Probably desperately anxious to demonstrate his business sense, Mr Gell was seeking for a solution, but could only fall back on the old scheme of two Editors with their separate staffs. He proposed that the present amateurish arrangements must end: Bradley should come to Oxford; both Editors should be established in separate but adjacent rooms at the Clarendon Press with easy inter-communication and a special telephone to the Bodleian Library, where an assistant and a boy should be available to look up everything referred to them. He had been outraged by a suggestion made in 1890 that the Press should publish 'A Visitor's Guide to the Scriptorium' which had been prepared by one of the assistants, Mr Sykes, and approved by Dr Murray. The Delegates had rejected the idea of encouraging the public to visit the Scriptorium during working hours, but now Gell went further and proposed that the opening of the Scriptorium as a show place should be forbidden as it was a constant source of interruption to Editor and staff.[32]

The threat of ceasing publication led to much discussion at the Philological Society and in Oxford among the two Editors, Frederick Furnivall, Henry Hucks Gibbs, Walter Skeat and others. All of them had had some experience of the actual work of making the Dictionary, and out of the discussion came a few practical suggestions to save time: Bradley's to reduce the number of quotations handled in the Scriptorium; Furnivall's to save the labour of correspondence by using printed inquiry cards wherever possible and that a shorthand clerk might be made available to the Editor for a few hours each day.[33] These sensible ideas were not acceptable to James, who, as we have seen, enjoyed writing letters even though he grumbled at the labour involved, and who was not prepared to learn to dictate and found printed forms too inflexible and impersonal for his needs. Another suggestion made by Bradley was that consultants should be engaged at a fee to do research on technical terms a long way ahead of the Editors. James had already raised this matter with C. E. Doble, the assistant secretary at the Press, pointing out that hunting down the senses of technical words took a great deal of time. He himself had generally been successful after writing many letters, but Bradley, having less interest in this department, had let it go by default.[34] Although funds were provided in 1896 the scheme never worked owing to difficulty in finding qualified people with time to give.[35]

What most upset James in this crisis was that, although his friends could appreciate the difficulties of the work in a way which Mr Gell could not, Furnivall and with him the Philological Society sided with Gell in his opinion that James was aiming at too much perfection and must lower his standards. Every great lexicographer must sooner or later face this problem. Samuel Johnson's decision is well known: 'To deliberate whenever I doubted, to enquire whenever I was ignorant, would have protracted the undertaking without end, and perhaps, without much improvement.'[36] Walter Skeat's advice to limit research to what was practical has already been quoted.[37] Émile Littré vividly described the temptation to flatter himself into believing that his dictionary, although not perfect, was good enough. He longed to abandon the high standards he had set himself in favour of a rapid completion, but after an inner struggle in which, as he said, he was both judge and defendant, ashamed of his weakness, he pursued his ideal with firmer resolution.[38] James Murray seems never to have even contemplated capitulation on this point. His tempters were external and his solution, if circumstances became impossible, was to abandon his task rather than depart from his standards. It was his obstinate resistance to all the pressures upon him to stop short of excellence which ensured the lasting quality of the Dictionary. In this he found a fundamental difference between himself and Frederick

Furnivall, who, in his desperate anxiety to see the Dictionary done and his life-long obligation to its founders discharged, was willing to make sacrifices.

Furnivall had always wanted the Dictionary to be produced on the cooperative principle he employed with some success in his other undertakings: he hoped that the appointment of Bradley was a prelude to the enlistment of a team of editors and he kept up his pressure on the Delegacy to accept this solution.[39] When James voiced his fears of possible loss in efficiency, Furnivall's reply was: 'well & good: I shall be content, & let my boy wait for the 2nd ed[itio]n & his son for the 3rd . . . No first try can produce a perfect work.'[40] Now, when James was fighting Gell and the Delegates for the survival of the ideal Dictionary he had conceived, Furnivall, whose hostility to the Press had made negotiations so difficult in 1878, suddenly changed his tack. Forgetting his old argument about the royalties and the stingy Delegates, he now told James, 'we *can't* expect the Press to go on for 20 years at the present rate . . . All life is a compromise . . . in this case between limited cash & efficient work.'[41]

In December 1892 Furnivall wrote to Gell to say that he and others of the Philological Society were convinced that it was vital for sales that the public should be shown that the work would be completed by 1900, adding, 'what I think it wants is the control of a business man, at the Press, not only that of research men at their homes.'[42] Gell recognised in Furnivall a man on his side. He at once confided to him his private plans for putting the organisation of the work on a business-like footing[43] and during this crisis in the history of the Dictionary, Furnivall, carrying the Society with him, was Gell's ally. For James this seemed treachery. He felt utterly deserted when he heard that the Society agreed that the Delegates were fully justified, in view of the financial situation, in insisting that all features causing delay should be modified or abandoned: that 'the research view must give way to the Business one & that the pace of production must be increast.'[44]

Help came from a most unexpected quarter. Unknown to James, Lyttelton Gell had his own difficulties with the Delegates. The role for which Dr Jowett had cast him—that of efficient business manager—was not generally accepted and he found himself hamstrung by Delegates who, in his opinion, kept far too much in their own hands.[45] When the report of the Dictionary Committee on the 1892-3 crisis appeared it was curiously inconclusive: the sting had been drawn—probably through the influence of Dr Price, and the result was a defeat for Gell. Although the report went over the old ground, asking for less attention to be paid to technical words or words of recent origin, and dealing with other minor details which, as Skeat said, only played around the fringe of things,[46] every comment in it was so wrapped about with qualifications as to be rendered meaningless. In effect the Editors were left with authority to use their discretion and do the best they could. The Report read:

> We are not prepared to say that these suggestions could, without detriment to the Dictionary, be followed as an absolute rule; but we believe that there are probably many cases in which Dr Murray and Mr Bradley may be in doubt, and we think it would be quite safe for them in such cases to bear in mind the opinions expressed ... as sanctioning some compromise between what is theoretically best and what is practically possible, in view of expediting the progress ... without laying themselves open to fair criticism or impairing the value of their labour. At the same time we should be sorry that any essential modification should be introduced into the work that would at all impair its character . . .[47]

Six suggestions on saving time were suggestions only: nothing was said about excluding strangers from the Scriptorium. A perceptive visitor once noted that some interruption and opportunity to talk about his work was good for Dr Murray,[48] and the Delegates might have judged that even if visitors did cause delay they also had very great advertisement value. Henry Bradley, still unwell, continued to work in London and the sensible proposal to concentrate the work in one building was postponed.

James did not realise that a victory had been won for him. He found the reactions of the Delegacy to the Dictionary always inexplicable and arbitrary: he never knew what stirred them to take too much interest or why they sometimes appeared completely apathetic. While thankful that the immediate crisis was over, he continued to worry about the cause of it, and to fear that something would trigger it all off again. So far as he was aware Lyttelton Gell was still very much in control and there was no way of getting round him. Still sure that half his trouble was lack of money to pay his assistants adequately, James hoped that some increase might be sanctioned. Mr Gell was obdurate: no increase without increased production. Once again Gell applied business techniques and in March 1893 he introduced an incentive bonus based on payment per page in excess of an agreed norm.[49] This proved yet another addition to James' problems and irritations and one which dogged him for years after Gell had ceased to be Secretary.

The application of the bonus scheme proved extremely difficult in practice. There was the initial problem of determining what was the normal basic rate of production: at first this was fixed at 200 pages a year and the expectation was that the bonus would encourage attainment of 300 pages — bringing the output of the two Editors close to the desired target of 700 pages.[50] In practice this meant that the chances of earning a substantial bonus were minimal and James said bitterly that it was only a way of saving the Delegates money.[51] Both Editors found that on the low basic salaries the bonus system did not give their assistants sufficient security and that there were too many factors which were beyond their control. Output, for instance, depended upon the availability of labour, when a man left and the vacancy was not filled immediately, or was filled by a beginner who had to be trained, or when the Editor or any member of staff was ill, the output was bound to drop and those who carried the extra work without additional pay lost their bonus also.[52] In these conditions it was naïve to suggest, as the Secretary did to James in 1908, that 'a bonus should be a bonus' to add a little excitement and stimulus to the efficiency of the team.[53]

The problem should have been brought to the attention of the Delegates at once, but instead James tried to meet the difficulties by giving each member of his staff a fixed salary which included the amount of bonus he hoped they would earn (he did not take any share himself — there was too little to divide). Thus at the end of every year he was working desperately to bring the output to the total needed to earn the bonus he had anticipated and nearly always he was out of pocket. In 1905 he estimated this loss over the past three years as £200.[54] Once or twice when his staff lost time owing to Bradley's illness, an adjustment was made, but generally he struggled on, dipping into his savings and, it must be confessed, getting some satisfaction from the sense of martyrdom. Even when the bonus was earned there was the difficulty of advancing the anticipated sum to the assistants throughout the year, aggravated by the fact that till 1898 the cheque from the Press for the basic salaries, totalling about £60 a month, was paid only at three monthly intervals in arrears. Meanwhile James had to keep sufficient floating capital to pay the assistants himself. The effect of the crisis of 1893 was to increase his fear that unless he practised the strictest economy the Press might suspend publication, therefore he himself always paid for any additional part-time help such as Erlebach gave in vacations, or for an extra clerk checking references in the British Museum.[55]

The bonus problem was eventually solved by a wiser secretary than Gell using increasing discretion in varying the amount paid for excess pages from year to year and adjusting this to the sum which James worked out as fair and necessary. In 1906 it was also arranged that part of the bonus should be paid in the form of a deferred sum calculated to give each member of staff the equivalent of a year and a half's salary if he were in employment on the completion of the Dictionary.[56] In 1893 however these solutions lay far ahead and in the meantime Mr Gell and his policy still cast a gloomy shadow on the Editor.

The threat of suspending publication and the support lent by the Philological Society to the plea for speed at the expense of quality, left James with a renewed sense of insecurity. He told Skeat that he felt 'all sort of enthusiasm and go crushed out of me'.[57] Skeat as usual did his best to cheer him up, reminding him that *C* is a letter of exceptional size, equivalent to as many as ten of the smaller letters. He begged James to take a few days in Cambridge over Easter, jokingly telling him that he need not lose sight of the words in *Cu* on which he was then working.

> I could find enough talk to *cumber* you. You could come by a *curvilinear* railway. Bring a *cudgel* to walk with ... We have *cutlets* in the *cupboard* & *currants* & *curry* & *custards* & (naturally) *cups* ... say you'll CUM![58]

James did not yield, but pressed on to finish *C* by the end of the year, when Skeat sent a congratulatory poem:

> Wherever the English speech has spread
>   And the Union Jack flies free,
> The news will be gratefully, proudly read
>   That you've conquered your ABC!
> But I fear it will come
>   As a shock to some
> That the sad result will be—
> That you're taking to *dabble* and *dawdle* and *dose*

To *dullness* and *dumps* and (worse than those)
To *danger* and *drink*
And—shocking to think—
To words that begin with d--------!

One more crisis was to threaten the Dictionary and its Editors, and this was brought about by James himself, with almost disastrous results. The trouble this time was the old one of the scale of the work and James' tender conscience about exceeding the proportion of five and a half pages to one of Webster. This limit James never succeeded in adhering to. He could not do anything about the extra words to be included—from *A* to *Age* he had almost twice the number of words in Webster—and in their treatment he could only save space by using rigid economy in writing his definitions, so that most of the saving had to be in the selection of the illustrative quotations. Although Liddell had criticised the quotations as being too short, he also objected that in the proofs of *A* there were superfluous quotations on every page.[59] Bearing this criticism in mind, with few difficult words, James managed to keep to six pages to one of Webster, but as soon as he reached *B* the scale crept up to seven and a half and in *C* eight pages to one. James continued to make strenuous efforts to save space on 'easy' letters in order to have more space for the difficult ones. He described this time-taking labour as a 'sorrowful necessity' and told the Philological Society in 1890 that it was 'like shearing Samson's locks', because the quotations were the essence of the work.[60] Describing the unremitting effort needed to keep the average of *D* to eight times Webster, he said that all his assistants and proof readers knew that he was ten times more grateful for a suggestion that resulted in cutting something out than for any additions, and that often when they wanted to add something he had to say, 'Yes, it would be an improvement, but we cannot afford the space'.[61]

James was always afraid that the Delegates would suddenly begin another of their periodic economy drives and that if one Editor exceeded the limit on easy letters they would both be faced with an impossible task of treating the difficult ones adequately on the most limited scale. As long as he supervised Bradley's work he went through his proofs marking quotations which he thought should be omitted. But Bradley, naturally, did not always agree, and on many occasions James felt it his duty to warn the Press that his colleague was exceeding the limit.[62] This he did, he explained, 'not in any spirit

of censoriousness but purely in the interests of the work, and in order
. . . to prevent future calamities'.[63]

Scale led to fresh difficulty when it came to planning the content of
future volumes, and on 27 January 1896 Murray wrote again to Gell,
this time to point out that it was no longer possible for Volume IV to
contain Bradley's *F* and *G* and his own *H* as planned, because *F* had
taken up much more space than expected.[64] Unhappily this communication gave Mr Gell, still unwilling to accept his defeat of 1893,
the opportunity to reopen the whole question of the future of the
Dictionary.

At James' request the Delegates now appointed a new sub-
committee, but this time it was without the sympathetic Dr Price.[65]
Of its two members, Ingram Bywater, Regius Professor of Greek, and
York Powell, Regius Professor of History, Bywater was the more
influential. He had joined the Delegacy under Professor Jowett's
chairmanship and his own conclusions on the Dictionary echoed
many of the views of Jowett expressed in the 'suggestions' of 1884.[66]
Bywater and York Powell had been members of the 1893 Dictionary
sub-committee and were known to be critical of the finances of the
Press.[67] Their terms of reference were to consider the divisions of the
remaining letters of the alphabet into volumes, but they at once
fastened upon the issue of scale. Negotiations were still going on
about moving Bradley to Oxford, but even before the Committee had
begun work he was told that if he could not keep within the correct
scale for the rest of *F*, his connection with the Dictionary must
cease.[68] Then on 12 February Bywater had an interview with Murray
which turned the attack from Bradley to James himself. Bywater had
made an important discovery. The issue of Bradley's scale, he
reported to the Delegacy, was of secondary importance: the real
question was whether the Delegates were prepared to sanction
Murray's disregard of his agreement, and to allow both the Editors to
proceed on a scale which, he calculated, would result in a work of
some 12,800 to 12,900 pages instead of the 8400 approved in 1882.
Such a work would run to eleven or twelve volumes and would be half
as large again as that authorised. Both Editors, he found, had
'systematically neglected' to observe the limits—Bradley to a greater
extent than Murray—but Murray on his own calculation was now
working at a scale of eight times Webster and Bywater thought it more
like eight and three quarter pages to one.[69]

None of the Delegates thought to question whether the Dictionary was better or worse for this expansion, neither had they learned that it was futile to tie the Editors to an agreement made at an early stage in the work, when it was impossible to give accurate estimates. A comparison of the English and American dictionaries should have shown that the size to which the *Oxford Dictionary* was growing was fully justified and should have been a matter for congratulation rather than complaint.

The merit of Webster's work lay in the definitions: the etymologies were very brief, the quotations illustrated use and not a complete history of the word. For many words there were no quotations at all, and where supplied they were undated: the references were to authors only, not to works, and the range of writers used was limited to well known names such as Chaucer, Shakespeare, Pope, and Walter Scott. Taking as an example the word *black*, which has a long history, Webster dismissed the etymology in five lines, where Murray took twenty-three, and the whole word and its derivatives filled nineteen columns to Webster's three and a half.

Do, another difficult word, occupied sixteen times the space given to Webster, while even a simple word like *doctor*, derived from the Old French and Latin and occupying less than a third of a column in Webster, required three columns when fully treated in the *Oxford English Dictionary*. These differences are obvious to anyone comparing the two works. The Delegates were not competent to judge of the subtler editorial problems, such as that some letters containing more difficult words required a fuller treatment than others.

Mr Gell was on sick leave when Professor Bywater's report was received, but Mr Doble, the assistant Secretary, informed both Editors that the Delegates had resolved to ask them for an undertaking that in future they would not exceed six times Webster, although in exceptional cases, if cause were shown before a section was begun, a scale of seven to one might be permitted.[70] A further resolution, not communicated to the Editors, but which soon leaked out, was that if the Editors refused to bind themselves, the Delegates would consider suspending publication. By calling attention to Bradley's failure to condense his section, James Murray had unintentionally brought a load of fresh trouble on both their heads and put the future of the Dictionary again in jeopardy.

Lord Aldenham (Henry Hucks Gibbs) was in bed with gout, but both Editors and the Philological Society reacted at once to this emergency, and this time presented a united front. All agreed that such a drastic reduction in size would change the whole character of the work, leaving the Dictionary hardly superior to its competitors and that this would result in disgusted subscribers cancelling their orders. The Philological Society suggested a public appeal should be made in Great Britain and the United States for funds to save the work from being spoilt and James agreed with Fitzedward Hall in feeling that rather than see the Dictionary deprived of its whole character it would be better to let it end at *F*, hoping that 'some future age, under happier conditions may be able to resume it.' James told Gell

> The only support which I personally have in labour which would otherwise crush me is the feeling of satisfaction that comes from the consciousness that the best possible has been done to realize, within the narrowest limits, the ideal of a Dictionary on historical principles; and if this is taken away, I shall have to bow to the inevitable and give up the struggle.

He added that all the financial and other difficulties were oppressing him by day and giving him long sleepless hours at night.[71]

James threatened resignation so often that the Delegates had probably ceased to take the possibility seriously. They were still groping their way to a solution of the problems and evidently divided as to future policy. Towards the end of March it was decided that a letter drafted by Professor Bywater, to be forwarded by the Vice-Chancellor to the Philological Society, should not go, as it did not in all respects represent the unanimous views of the Delegates. At the same time the revival of the pro-Dictionary party was reflected in a decision to proceed with arrangements for bringing Bradley to Oxford, to a house in the Press Quadrangle in Walton Street.[72]

The supporters of the Bywater Committee were still not defeated. Ignoring a strongly worded resolution of the Philological Society which asserted that to cut the Dictionary to six times Webster would ruin its special historic character, they sent a further report to both Editors. This reverted to the 1893 resolutions on measures to be taken to shorten the work. The qualifications which in 1893 left the Editors virtually free to do what they liked, were now omitted. The Delegates thought it necessary 'to lay down more definitely the principles on which the compilation . . . ought to proceed'. For example, the Editors must now 'rigorously adhere' to the principle that no quotations should be given for words of more recent origin than 1880, slang words must be omitted unless in general literary use: Americanisms were acceptable only if found in American and English writers of note, and so on—the whole to be taken as a guide to the preparation of materials from the earliest stages and not only in the final proof.[73]

At this point the whole agitation suddenly collapsed, once again revealing the divisions among the Delegates. The Editors had challenged them to take a page of recent proofs and to show how the required economies in space could be achieved. They estimated that to bring the work down to only six times Webster, each column in James' proof would have to be reduced by twenty-eight lines, and each of Bradley's by forty-four. Dr Monro, Provost of Oriel, a classical scholar, joined Professors Bywater and York Powell to do this, but they found the task impossible. So far from arriving at six times Webster, their deletions left the ratio at still rather more than eight to one. The Philological Society triumphantly concluded that this implied that the Press would be satisfied if the Editors pledged themselves not to exceed this higher limit.[74]

Meanwhile the papers carried the news of possible suspension of publication. The *Saturday Review* noted the astonishment and indignation with which the announcement would be received—it would be 'nothing less than a national calamity and an indelible disgrace to the University'. The anonymous writer, perhaps unfortunately for James Murray's popularity in Oxford, went on to express surprise that James' immense services to learning had received no official recognition there, saying that this was typical of English Universities' 'kindness in reserve', which (misquoting Samuel Johnson)

> Slowly wise and meanly just
> To buried merit rears the tardy bust.[75]

Letters began to pour in supporting the Dictionary, and the Delegates hastily changed their tack. On 9 May Gell informed Dr Murray that they had rescinded the order of 21 February and authorised the Editors to proceed as before. This he trusted would 'terminate the somewhat protracted crisis in the N.E.D.' and enable the Editor to go forward with new vigour.[76] At the same time Dr Price was instructed to see to the distribution of a notice correcting the damaging newspaper reports.[77]

Another crisis was over, again leaving its lasting mark on James Murray. He had been overworking to a dangerous extent since

August 1895, culminating in a spurt when he was doing eighty or ninety hours a week. He told Gell that he was fagged and weary already and the difficulties about the scale of the Dictionary coming upon everything else had taken the heart out of him. In April he was on the verge of collapse and complained his brain would not work. At last he yielded to the persuasion of friends and allowed Ada to carry him off to Malvern to try if a few days change, spending the whole time in the open air and walking on high ground, would brace him up.[78] He was only there the inside of a week — Monday to Saturday — but the effect was electric. His letter to his eldest daughter, Hilda, left in charge at home to water the flowers and lock up the Scriptorium at night, reads as if by a different man:

> Yesterday ... we had a splendid day on the heights. Mamma & I ... walked some $2\frac{1}{2}$ or 3 miles to the British Camp* — we went straight up the hill ... but by & by the f[oot] p[ath] vanished & we found ourselves on a slope of short grass a great deal steeper than the roof of a house and had a tremendous pull up to the top, Mamma lying prone on the slope and desperately clutching at the very short and dry herbage to pull herself up ... We reached the summit however, & recuperated our energies while we surveyed the stupendous entrenchment with which the summit is circumvallated. I also ran on alone to the end of the ridge about $\frac{3}{4}$ of a mile further ...[79]

It was a pity that the Delegates never saw this side of the petulant and despairing scholar they had to deal with, and it is sad that he continued to feel that he and the Dictionary were to the Press 'a kind of white elephant, an honour that they would gladly dispense with.'[80] Fortunately 1896 marked the end of this very difficult period in the history of the Dictionary, when both Delegates and Editors were making blunders as they felt their way forward on very unfamiliar ground. By 1910 James could look back at something he had said in 1895 as 'an echo of some earlier world ... the ashes of long gone troubles and bitterness, of which the world knows, and need know, nothing.'[81]

* Hereford Beacon.

CHAPTER XV

'Not the Least of the Glories of the University of Oxford'

AFTER 1896 there was a changed attitude on the part of both publishers and Editor towards the production of the Dictionary and while not all the problems were settled there was henceforth no serious risk of either party throwing up the project. There were various reasons for the change.

Most important was that at last, and by accident, an agreed pattern of production was established and although predictions as to the size of the work and date of its completion were still far from the truth, at least the speed of output became acceptable and predictable. Abandoning the hopeless demand of 700 pages a year, the Press adopted the policy of publishing sixty-four page quarterly sections at half a crown each. This was a target which the Editors were able to achieve, and every year from 1895 till 1915 they managed to issue at least one extra, or double, section a year, and sometimes a triple section. This arrangement resulted from the chance that owing to the unexpected bulk of *C* it was impossible to carry out the original idea of binding *C* and *D* together as Volume II. Instead, the volume was completed by a short section of *C*, numbering only 103 instead of the usual 352 pages published in November 1893, and then Volume III was started with a short section of *D*.[1] Splitting a Part in this way proved so popular with subscribers and the trade that it suggested the new arrangement which was adopted from the autumn of 1894. It ended the constant complaints and harassing of the Editors and although there were good and bad years and from time to time the Delegates commented that one or other Editor's pace was disappointing, the fluctuations could be explained by special circumstances such as illness or staffing difficulties. The new arrangement had an encouraging effect: instead of the disheartening experience of finding themselves falling more and more behind an impossible target there was the stimulus, if all went well, of being able to do better than was expected. Also, the splitting of the work into small sections made advance more noticeable and the magnitude of the task began to feel less formidable. It was such a simple solution it is surprising that it took ten years to find. Now it was possible to plan for a year ahead: each Editor worked steadily on at his own letter and the sections were published as they were ready in January, April, July and October. From 1891, when Bradley began publishing *E* while Murray was still on *C*, the Dictionary no longer appeared in literal order: by the time Bradley reached the end of *G* in 1900 Murray had completed *H* and *I* and from 1910 till 1916 *S* and *T* were appearing simultaneously.[2] The rate of production was also helped, though not to the degree that the Press had hoped, by the acceptance of Dr Furnivall's principle of team work. To Murray and Bradley were added in 1901 William Alexander Craigie (after an apprenticeship begun in 1897) and in 1914 Charles Talbut Onions, who had been an assistant since 1895.

The team was not formed without difficulty. Furnivall continued to press the need to divide the work and kept suggesting possible names. He irritated James by proposing salaries of up to £400 a year—far in excess of those earned by his most experienced assistants—for men who lacked suitable qualifications.[3]

At first James found it difficult to accept the idea of collaborators. It was hard to have to surrender the actual compilation to other men, when he had done all the preliminary work, and as has been seen, he felt it a confession of his failure to accomplish the task to which he had pledged himself. He continued to worry lest, because of the divided responsibility, the Dictionary would lack unity, or fall short of the standards of excellence which he had established.[4] Lyttelton Gell was not sufficiently sensitive to appreciate these undercurrents and the Delegates did not even realise the practical desirability of regularising the relationships between Dr Murray and those they appointed to share his task. It was only slowly that his position as Editor-in-chief was officially recognised.

Happily, Henry Bradley was a man of exceptional integrity and understanding. In the case of his appointment, Furnivall had rushed to insert a premature announcement in the papers, and Bradley at once wrote to James to explain that this was none of his doing, adding 'I have not been so insensible as I may have seemed of the difficulty of your position, and my sense of it has made me feel deeply grateful to you for the unvarying kindness which you have shown to me under circumstances which were so peculiarly trying.'[5] He later made it clear what in his view must be the relationship between the two Editors, and writing to Gell he said,

> I feel very strongly that it would be a serious injustice to Dr Murray if the new arrangement were put in the form of the appointment of a colleague on equal terms ... Few persons are as well able as I am to appreciate the extent to which the merits of the Dictionary are due to Dr Murray himself ... Supposing that half of what remains of the work is to be executed by another hand, the merits of that half will still be very largely due to Dr Murray, and I think this ought to be explicitly recognised.

His suggestion was that Dr Murray should remain the chief Editor, but it should be stated that it had been found necessary to depute certain portions of the editing.[6] The position, however, was not given any formal recognition and the appointment of William Craigie as third Editor was again badly mishandled and was sprung upon James Murray without consultation.

In 1897 James had set himself the target of completing half the letters of the alphabet by the turn of the century and to this end asked for extra staff in order to do five years work in four. The Delegates did not agree, believing that Murray was still a bottleneck and more staff would throw an intolerable burden on himself; but his request reminded them of the need to search for a third Editor, who might begin by working in the Scriptorium with full responsibility for the easier words, and Professor York Powell at once initiated inquiries.[7]

How far Lyttelton Gell knew what was happening is uncertain. He was overworked and unwell and losing what influence he had exercised upon the Delegates.[8] His letters by this date are more friendly, but James' resentment of earlier events prevented him from noting the change. Gell alleged that he had known nothing of the Delegates' plan until directed to write to offer a three months trial appointment as potential third editor to Mr W. A. Craigie, formerly of Oriel, now holding an appointment at St Andrews University. Craigie had accepted an engagement to work at first under Bradley, who had approved the appointment. Gell said he thought that it was his duty to inform James of Craigie's acceptance as a formality, assuming that he had already been consulted.[9]

It may have been a genuine misunderstanding, or it may be that

Murray was deliberately kept in the dark because some opposition from him was anticipated. In any event he was justifiably furious. 'I have not been consulted', he wrote,

> but merely 'informed of an engagement' made behind my back, and this, after all I have done, and all the labours and sacrifices which I have undergone for the sake of a work for which I have done and am still doing all the preliminary work, & to which I have practically devoted my life! It appears to me as the culmination of many minor acts recently pointing in the same direction, and if it represents the policy of the Delegates, it means that my connexion with the Dictionary must cease.[10]

He was deeply hurt by the lack of confidence suggested and also concerned at the effect of the appointment on members of his and Bradley's staff, some of whom might themselves qualify as independent editors (as in fact proved the case with C. T. Onions). These men would resent a man with no previous lexicographical experience being brought in over their heads, and if any were to resign, his own plans would be thwarted. The justice of the protest was obvious and the Delegates hastened to make amends. A sub-committee assured James that after a trial period he would be consulted before a permanent appointment was made. When the time came James had to point out that he had still not been given opportunity to assess Craigie's work himself,[11] and Furnivall as usual added his measure of irritation. First he invited Craigie instead of James to make the Dictionary Report to the Philological Society[12] and then, as he had done in Bradley's case, inserted a notice in the *Athenaeum* in 1899 anticipating Craigie's appointment as third Editor,[13] which did not in fact take place till 1901.[14]

Meanwhile the Delegates at last regularised the position by giving Murray an extra £50 a year in recognition of his status and special responsibilities as Editor-in-Chief.[15] At the same time the wording of the title page was agreed, and in Volume III, published in 1897, the first issued under a divided editorship, Murray's name stood as for his Volume I and II. Below, the responsibility for each letter was stated:

D	E
By Dr J. A. H. Murray, LL.D.	By Henry Bradley, M.A.

This was the pattern followed in volumes IV to VIII, although Furnivall continued to complain that it was unfair to Bradley.[16]

Once he had got over his initial disappointment, James was not opposed in principle to the employment of additional editors, nor was he worried about their linguistic ability. What did trouble him was to persuade them to conform to the agreed pattern of the work. Each brought his own special excellence to the Dictionary: Bradley and Craigie were outstanding as etymologists, and James had from time to time to remind them that it was the historical basis of the work which was to be its prime characteristic. His own special skill lay in his ability to trace the history of a word in its changing usage from century to century and to write, with the utmost economy of words, definitions which summarise the fruits of profound research.

James had reluctantly accepted the need to divide the editorship in the hope that this would expedite the work, but he considered the policy a failure because, even with three Editors, the original production target was never reached.[17] It was hardly to be expected that his collaborators would show his own single-minded devotion to the work: in spite of his remarkable stamina James drove himself almost to breaking point. A delicate man like Bradley was forced to go slowly in self-defence, and Craigie saw no reason to refuse first a University Readership and then a Professorship when these came his way. It was very rarely that James' annual output was less than that of Bradley and Craigie, and in the end nearly half of the whole work (7207 out of 15,487 pages) was produced by him.[18] He still held to the belief that the money would have been better spent in providing salaries which would attract and hold really competent assistants.

James' worries, apart from those of speed of production, continued to be mainly on the question of scale. In 1896 he and Bradley were both asked to estimate the number of pages needed for the remaining letters of the alphabet: both underestimated the space required, Murray more seriously than Bradley.[19] The task was little more possible of accuracy than guessing the number of peas in a bottle, but unfortunately the Dictionary had been advertised to Subscribers as a ten-volume work. It became increasingly difficult to fit the material into so few volumes.[20] Although the splitting of volumes IX and X each into two parts and the relegation of the Supplement and Bibliography, originally planned as part of Volume X, to an extra volume, eventually helped to overcome the problem, it was still essential to watch the scale anxiously.[21] James regarded this as his function as Editor-in-Chief, and he wrote frequently, both to his co-editors and to the Press, calling attention to the need to cut out superfluous quotations.[22] He hated to have to do this: 'No one knows so well as I do, how it grieves one to have to do this', he wrote to Craigie, 'but I have had to steel my heart & clench my teeth & do it, for years: and you will also find it, I doubt not, the most painful part of your work.'[23] Bradley and Craigie rightly protested that it meant more work with less result: Craigie found it took an extra day's work on each bundle of copy if he attempted to cut to anything below eight times Webster.[24] James waxed almost hysterical at their 'scandalous', 'unbearable' and 'heart-rending' waste of the space which he felt he had saved only for them to squander.[25] He himself became highly skilled in reducing his articles to a conciseness which did not sacrifice clarity, but it not only took time, but also meant that his bill for corrections exceeded that incurred by the other Editors.[26]

It says much for the dedication of all of them that serious quarrels did not occur. Henry Bradley was a most reasonable and placid man, an excellent foil to James' excitability and bouts of depression alternating with exhilaration. This was fortunate, for their good relations had to stand up to mischief-making by Furnivall. As long as he lived in London, Bradley regularly attended the meetings of the Philological Society and he was a close friend of Furnivall, sharing his Sunday river excursions and on several occasions joining him for summer holidays. Furnivall in return showed his customary warmth of heart in looking after his interests and helping to raise money to pay for convalescence abroad after his breakdown in health. Unfortunately Furnivall formed the erroneous opinion that James was jealous of Bradley and was not treating him fairly or giving him sufficient credit for his contribution.

Matters had come to a head in 1892, when Furnivall accused Murray of deliberately hampering Bradley by depriving him of the help of sub-editors. This was a misunderstanding of a half-heard statement made by Bradley in a report to the Society on the progress of the Dictionary and it was at once refuted by James as totally untrue.[27] Bradley, at that time President of the Society, with other friends, tried to persuade James not to take Furnivall seriously, since everyone knew that he was given to extravagant remarks and did not represent the views of the majority.[28] They were unable to prevent Furnivall from publishing his distortion of the facts in the *Athenaeum*, and this led to further acrimonious correspondence. 'I have not gone the length of some injudicious folk in praising your faults', Furnivall wrote to James, '. . . But personally there's plenty of room in the world for you & me apart . . . But if any act of yours seems to me selfish & unfair, I shall feel free to say so.'[29]

In the end James was induced to withdraw a letter resigning from the Society, after the Council had passed a resolution acquitting him from any unfairness. Furnivall said he hoped this was the end of what he described as 'a temporary difference',[30] but then kept it alive. He quoted a true, if unwise remark made by one of the Murray children, that Bradley's output was much less than his father's, as evidence that Murray ran down Bradley in Oxford,[31] and in 1897 refused an invitation to stay at Sunnyside so long as Bradley was not acknowledged as co-equal with Murray in the editorship.[32]

Bradley might well have felt it hard to be associated for forty years with a work for which the main credit was given to Murray, had he not been far too nice a person ever to question their roles. His behaviour was exemplary throughout and he never changed his original opinion that Murray must be given credit for having planned the whole work and organised and inspired the volunteer readers.[33] James was not jealous of Bradley as a scholar, although he was envious of the more generous terms under which his colleague was employed by the Press—especially in the provision of a rent free house in Oxford.[34] When he scoffed at Bradley's slow progress his remarks were not intended as a criticism of him but of the Delegates—a self-justification—proving how right he had been and how wrong the Delegates in thinking they could find a super-man who could better his own results in this meticulous work.

In his relationships with his co-editors, James observed a Victorian formality. It is difficult to tell how significant this was, since even with close friends like Walter Skeat or Fred Elworthy, Christian names were never used in correspondence. Certainly, although James would enjoy an occasional social evening with Henry Bradley or William Craigie,[35] spent mainly in discussion of difficult or interesting words, they did not form a closely knit team. He and Bradley shared the same problems in their dealings with the Press—shortage of money and pressure to go faster—but they never made a common front: each fought his battles independently and seemingly in ignorance of what the other was doing. This was mainly because the appointment of co-editors was treated as entirely a matter for the Delegates and the Philological Society, the terms of their appointment were not discussed with the Editor-in-Chief and James would feel that professional etiquette debarred him from seeking information from them about their private affairs.

Another factor reducing the possibility of close team work was that Murray worked apart from the others. The idea of one Scriptorium for the whole staff was dropped. James' reluctance to face the upheaval of another move and to leave his own workroom was respected and he decided against enlarging the Scriptorium to accommodate the others. It would have meant the sacrifice of more of his garden, the loss of valuable trees and of some of the privacy and convenience of his family and he was also worried about the wear and tear on the library he had built up at personal expense.[36]

When Henry Bradley came to Oxford he worked in a room provided for him at the Press, and when Craigie and later Onions joined him they were all accommodated in the Old Ashmolean, to which the remaining materials were transferred after Murray's death. The decision to keep two workrooms undoubtedly had some drawbacks. There was no telephone and James spent much time writing long letters when he wanted to consult his co-editors on any point: he advised Craigie if he wanted an answer urgently to send one of his assistants to Sunnyside on his bicycle, or in emergency by tram.[37] It isolated the chief Editor from the casual exchange and easy relationship naturally established in a common work room. On the other hand, there were certain advantages. Two centres of work, rather than one, encouraged a friendly rivalry and competitive spirit which helped to enliven the tedium of the work.[38] It also spared the co-editors and their staff from the interruptions which occurred in the Sunnyside Scriptorium which, in spite of Mr Gell, remained a show place, and the increasingly colourful and venerable Editor a show piece.

Perhaps it was as well that the Editors were kept apart: their methods were very different. C. T. Onions, who worked first under Murray and then under Bradley commented that 'To pass from the one to the other was a remarkable experience; it was to pass from the practical professional teacher to the philosophical exponent. Murray gave formal instruction; Bradley taught rather by hint, by interjectional phrase, or even a burst of laughter.'[39]

To some extent relationships were coloured by James' inability to throw off the schoolmaster; with pen in hand he could forget to whom he was writing. In 1902 in a ten-page letter to William Craigie he complained that Craigie had not observed the pattern of the

Dictionary in his treatment of derivatives. He stormed at the inclusion of *railway porter*, with a quotation 'it was a railway porter'

> Is there any purpose whatever served by ... this ridiculous quot[atio]n of 1894? ... Only because you have *named* it above, & think you are obliged, by hook or by crook, to furnish an ostensible quot[atio]n for it! The mistake is in the princip!e which invokes such miserable failure in its application ... It is very painful to me to have so to interfere, and I assure you that I do it with the most friendly feeling ... no part of my work is so onerous and unpleasant to me as that of looking through your copy ... I should be infinitely glad to have done with it ... And if you would earnestly set yourself to making my work unnecessary, it might soon be done.[40]

No doubt censures of this kind caused resentment in the Old Ashmolean and there is one proof corrected by Dr Murray on which Craigie has scribbled 'Please look at the enclosed ... but don't send it to the Scriptorium' and noted that he is ignoring most of the suggested deletions.[41]

Even the mild Henry Bradley hit back sometimes. In 1901 he complained that portions of his copy were 'constantly getting lost at the Scriptorium'. This allegation brought a pained reaction from the Editor-in-Chief:

> there are no holes in the Scriptm. floor through which such portions could slip, and as every table is cleared from time to time, and every stray slip found put into its place ... it is to us so inconceivable as to be utterly impossible, that even a single slip could be permanently lost. I believe that I have lost or mislaid only *two* slips since the Dictionary began ... one of these which I mourned for years and years, and spent hours in looking for, turned up a few weeks ago under *Ocean* to which it had been sent on from *charnel*, when not used there ... I mourned its loss for 13 years ... But it was *not lost* after all, and I do not believe that any slip was ever lost here. If a definite statement had been made at any time that certain 'portions of copy' were lost, there would have been a revolution here, and it ought not to be made *now*.

Bradley humbly apologised for unintentionally adding to the Editor's worries, but held to his point that disappearance of slips was in his experience not impossible.[42] One wonders at the Editor's confidence: odd slips still turn up amongst bundles of correspondence, and the risky practice was followed of sometimes loaning a whole packet of slips to an inquirer.[43] Even Murray had to own that the word *bondmaid* had been omitted from the Dictionary through having in some unaccountable way been lost either in the Scriptorium or at the Press.[44] In very many cases the fact that there were far more quotations than could be used made the loss of one slip of no great consequence; it was losses from the bundles prepared for printing which really mattered.

On the whole the work proceeded without serious disagreement. The co-editors respected the iron determination and capacity for unremitting work of the chief, and he was ready to help them when, through illness or other cause, they were falling behind in their schedule.[45] Even though their pace was slower than had been hoped, their contribution was substantial, and helped to allay the anxiety of the Delegates.

As publication progressed the Dictionary became widely known and approved. People began to believe in its eventual completion: references to it became more frequent and more respectful.[46] Allusions to it now occurred in Parliamentary and public speeches, it was cited by lawyers in evidence in the Courts and was the subject of frequent articles in the newspapers.[47] The recognition of the Dictionary as a national asset was sealed when James Murray suggested that the whole work should be dedicated to Queen Victoria. In August 1897 the Queen accepted, and the third Volume containing Murray's *D* and Bradley's *E* included a fly leaf with the dedication by the University of Oxford. For the first time the University itself was formally pledged to the production and any drawing back was now unthinkable.[48]

Another very important factor in the improvement in the position of the Dictionary was a change of personnel. The Vice-Chancellor in 1895 was Dr J. R. Magrath, Provost of Queen's College, and the new Secretary replacing Lyttelton Gell in 1898 was Charles Cannan, a classical scholar of Trinity. Both believed in the value of the Dictionary, were sympathetic to Murray and both remained associated with the Delegacy until after his death. The attempt by Gell to make the Dictionary pay was abandoned: it was accepted that it would be unremunerative for some time but would enhance the reputation of the University, and any doubts about it were forgotten. After 1897 letters to the Editor became increasingly friendly. In 1905 Dr Magrath assured James, 'We should be very sorry if anything which we could control had the effect of making you despondent as to finishing the great work to which you have given your life and your reputation.'[49] Cannan would remember to convey the congratulations of the Delegacy on exceptionally good output and their concern that James should take a holiday after illness, mentioning on one occasion the possibility of a grant of £10 towards his expenses.[50]

Dr Magrath first became involved with the Dictionary during the 1896 crisis, and his respect for the Editors had been increased when he had failed to cut their proofs to a scale of six times Webster. In his contact with James he became aware of his embittered attitude towards the University and the Delegacy and his need for encouragement. It was not want of heart, Skeat realised, but want of thought which had made the Delegates appear so unappreciative hitherto.[51] Now Magrath had the happy idea of arranging a dinner in the Hall of Queen's College on 12 October 1897 to which he invited representatives of all those involved in producing the Dictionary—Editors, Delegates, printers, the Philological Society and the voluntary sub-editors and readers. Writing to James about the details Magrath said 'I trust that the gathering will give you an indication that more people sympathise with you in your self denying labours than perhaps in moments of depression, disappointment or annoyance you have been fully able to realize.'[52] Characteristically, commenting on the occasion to Fitzedward Hall, James dwelt on the loss of working time the function caused him—three days in letter-writing and entertaining the guests, many of whom stayed a day or two—but he did acknowledge that it was a handsome act of the Vice-Chancellor and marked a decided advance on the part of Oxford.[53] Unhappily though, the wounds of the past had gone too deep and although this gesture was followed for James by the honour of being invited to give the Romanes Lecture in Oxford in 1900 on *The Evolution of English Lexicography*, the old grievance that the University had found no appointment for him and had not given him an honorary doctorate, continued to rankle.

None the less the dinner was a great occasion and secured new publicity for the Dictionary. There were fourteen lengthy speeches, Murray delivering an address which recounted something of the long history of Dictionary-making as well as the history of the *Oxford English Dictionary* and it is not surprising that the proceedings lasted till near midnight. Dr Furnivall gave a typically lively and direct reply to the toast to the Philological Society, taking the opportunity to attack the meanness of the Universities of Oxford and Cambridge in their attitude to the admission of women.[54] James must have smiled wryly at Sir William Markby's reply to the toast to the Clarendon Press, in which he asserted, 'We have never hesitated in the performance of what we consider to be a great duty which we owe to the University and to the nation, and we have never felt any doubt as to the ultimate completion of the work under the able editorship of Dr Murray and the co-operation of those associated with him in this great work.'[55] *The Times*, commenting on the occasion in a leading article, referred to the production of the Dictionary as 'the greatest effort probably which any University, it may be any printing press, has taken in hand since the invention of printing . . . It will not be the least of the glories of the University of Oxford to have completed this gigantic task.'[56]

On the subject of the completion James rashly committed himself in his speech to the hope that the end would be reached in 1910 or even 1908. He had some grounds for optimism. At last the immense piles of slips in the Scriptorium could be seen to be dwindling. In his report to the Philological Society in 1899 he told the members,

> although 'A' forms a perceptible part of the Dictionary, yet when we reached the end of A and had emptied all the A pigeon-holes, & packed up the A slips used and unused in strong boxes the additions to the later material were so great that we had more slips in the Scriptorium than when we began . . . the same thing happened again at the end of B; and even at the end of C when one fifth of the material was used up, the 4/5 that remained occupied more space than the original whole. Now however . . . it begins to be apparent that the material in the Scriptorium has undergone considerable diminution, and we shall now be able to use the vacant pigeon holes . . . for the materials for the letters after T which have hitherto . . . had to be stowed away in rather inaccessible positions.[57]

He took the opportunity of the Romanes Lecture to stress the fact that compared to the other great national dictionaries the English dictionary, now approaching the half way mark, was making exceedingly rapid progress.[58]

The Delegates ceased to complain of the cost, although in 1902 when five out of the proposed ten volumes were complete, the accumulated debt, not including interest, stood at £59,100.[59] In 1905, through the influence of Hucks Gibbs' son Alban, the Goldsmiths' Company gave £5000 towards the cost of Volume VI[60]. The leaf inserted in the volume to record this gift was printed in gold for the Company and a few privileged persons. In sending James one of these special copies Cannan told him that one voluntary helper had complained he had been given an ordinary copy by mistake, but Cannan had replied that the price of the gold leaf was to donate £5000 or else to edit a volume.[61]

James hoped that other wealthy bodies or individuals would follow the example of the Goldsmiths and he himself approached Andrew Carnegie, thinking he might pay for Volume VII if he knew that the Editor was 'a struggling Scotch student . . . whose life for a quarter of a century now has been one continuous sacrifice to the work.' Carnegie, who was a convinced supporter of spelling reform, replied that he was satisfied with the *Century Dictionary*, and having heard that the Oxford one was to continue the antiquated spelling at present in use, he did not see that its field of usefulness could be very great. He ended by saying, 'I have put your letter among my autographs. Whatever comes of the Dictionary, your own history is valuable.'[62]

James Murray's work received wide recognition. Through his old friend Canon Greenwell, Durham had made him an honorary doctor in 1886, and there followed degrees from Freiburg, Glasgow, Wales, the Cape of Good Hope, Dublin and Cambridge.[63] A story of the conferment of the Glasgow degree was told by Miss Constance Jones, Mistress of Girton College:

> I had the pleasure of being introduced to . . . Dr Murray . . . a very tall fine-looking old man, with a most charming manner—he had been wearing a great variety of hoods when capped, and explained that he owned seven degrees and corresponding hoods, and that his wife had packed for him a selection of four, all of which he had worn, by way of compliment to the University that was giving him yet another.[64]

In spite of his many Doctorates of Literature James always insisted that universities which chose this degree for a lexicographer mistook the facts. 'I am not a literary man', he would say, 'I do not write novels, nor essays, nor poems, nor history, I am not specially interested in Arthur & his knights, nor in the development of the modern newspaper, I am a man of science, and I am interested in that branch of Anthropology which deals with the history of human speech.'[65] At the Vice-Chancellor's Dictionary dinner Murray and Bradley were made honorary members of the Netherlands Society of Art, Science and Literature. Later James was given membership of the Academies of Vienna, Ghent, Prussia, Leyden, and Upsala, of the Royal Society of Edinburgh and the American Academy of Arts and Science. He was specially proud of being a foreign correspondent of the French Academy.[66] In England he was a founder member of the British Academy and a member of its Council, and in its early years he was influential in opposing those who wanted to narrow the original plan and make it a small and exclusive body.[67]

In Oxford he became well known. William Rothenstein included him in a volume of lithograph portraits of *Oxford Characters* published in 1896; he was made an honorary member of the Oxford Union, and from 1900 till 1911 a member of the Board of Studies of the newly established Honour School of English Language and Literature, for which he gave a series of lectures on Language and Words in 1911.[68] He was also from 1909 on the Committee for the degrees of Bachelor of Letters and Science. At last in June 1914 the Delegates proposed that the degrees of D. Litt. *Honoris Causa* be conferred on Murray and Bradley and an Honorary M.A. on Onions in recognition of their scientific distinction and their long and valuable service as Editors of the *Oxford English Dictionary*.[69] It is not known why the decision was taken at this point. Ada, who opened the letter conveying the news to James, exclaimed, 'At last!' 'Yes,' James said, 'I suppose they were afraid I might die first and make me a post-mortem doctor!'[70] This may well have been true: his health was already giving cause for anxiety and he was to die in July the following year. The Delegates may have thought that it was risky to wait till the award of the degree would coincide with the completion of the work.

State recognition had already come with a Knighthood. James received the offer of the award on 9 June 1908 from Herbert Asquith 'as a slight & too long delayed recognition of a great work greatly conceived & greatly executed'. James' reaction was revealing. He at once wrote long letters to his sons Harold, Ethelbert and Oswyn and to his daughter Hilda asking their advice as to whether to accept. His own instinct was to refuse, unless they felt that he should take it for the sake of Ada and the family. While he would have liked an Order of Merit as the equivalent of an academic recognition of scholarly work, a plain knight 'as if I were a brewer or a local mayor' did not please him: for a rich man or a country gentleman a 'sir' might be an asset, for a poor man it might prove a white elephant only encouraging tradesmen to put up their prices. He had observed that such honours tended 'to make people Tory and wean them from popular sympathies' and he did not wish to expose himself to such temptation. But the real reason for his hesitation was that to accept would destroy the image of martyrdom which he had built up for himself and which was in a curious way a help in sustaining him in his task. 'To tell the truth', he wrote to Oswyn, 'my work . . . was so long so little appreciated, that I learned . . . not to care a scrap for either blame or praise.' And to Harold he said 'I feel a great reluctance to come down from this position and accept the honour of this generation; I should prefer that my biographer should have to say, "Oxford never made him a Fellow or a D.C.L., and his country never recognised his work, but he worked on all the same, believing in his work and his duty."'[71] He had asked Asquith to give him time to consult his family, but he hesitated so long that on 18 June the Prime Minister wired to know his decision. James was resentful that consideration of the question had taken up working time and he yielded reluctantly to the persuasion of his family and friends,[72] but once the decision was taken he was excited by the flood of letters and congratulatory telegrams from all over Europe. He was glad for Ada's evident pleasure and had a hearty laugh with her at the nursery-maid's mother who wrote that she never thought a child of hers would ever 'live with quality'. He hired his court dress, which he described as a 'gew gaw', practised his bow[73] and thoroughly enjoyed a Gaudy dinner at Balliol for the Prime Minister and some thirty Balliol M.P.s, when he blushed to hear the Master unexpectedly referring to the knighthood as 'an honour to Oxford'. Asquith, to whom he was introduced, told him of his relief that he had accepted, as it was almost the only royal Birthday honour of which the newspapers had approved.[74] 'If I have not made money', James wrote to his son Aelfric in Capetown, 'I have had abundance of honour.'[75]

James valued all these honours not for himself but because they confirmed his belief that the Dictionary had maintained the standard he had hoped and striven for. The work was never easy, it never allowed of much relaxation if the end was kept in view, and it progressed only because he drove himself continuously towards his goal. Even the death of the King in 1910 was a set back: the holiday for the funeral came just after the Whitsun break and was 'a serious loss of time'. Yet although he spoke of being 'a galley slave chained to

16. Sir James Murray in court dress. 1908.

the oar' and his day was never less than twelve hours and for months at a time thirteen to fifteen hours, he never really minded hard work, and although he suffered periods of great depression these were probably outnumbered by his times of exhilaration. In a letter of 1900 to Edward Arber he had written, 'life is to me a tremendous struggle' but as he compared it to conquering a mountain one senses the excitement of achievement. 'Last year', he wrote, 'I worked harder, more desperately, more unremittingly than ever I have done in my life, and this year it must be the same, if I am to come near to completing half the Dictionary this century, so as to start next century on the mountain top, & advance each year down-hill-ward to the end.' He estimated that, on average, he and his team starting from nothing, had produced nearly twelve half columns in the finished state every hour. 'It is like the work of a machine & not of human beings struggling with some of the most difficult problems of human history—why, the history of the verbal suffix, -*ing*, alone took me nearly 3 weeks of research, and then two whole days to write it.'[76]

The spurt in which he felt the greatest pride was that to finish *D* in 1896. This year of crisis had started badly: the word *do*, begun at Christmas, proved so difficult that it was the end of June before it reached final proof stage. Eleven weeks had been lost through illness amongst his assistants and finally there was the alarm of the Delegacy's demand for curtailment to six times Webster which, James said, 'consumed a month of my time, and much more than a month of my energy and spirits, & reduced me almost to desperation'.[77] A friend, either Robinson Ellis or Walter Skeat, concerned for his health, provided money for three weeks' holiday in North Wales in the late summer. Ada dragged him away, with results which were, James said, 'simply marvellous'. He returned to Oxford on 5 September feeling fit for any amount of work. More than two thirds of the year were gone and barely a third of the section planned for it had passed through the Press. To catch up seemed impossible, but having carefully apportioned what was left, he

resolved if possible, & as long as I could hold out, to finish each day's work as allotted in its day, or where special difficulties made that impossible, at least *every week's work* in its own week, however many hours it might take. It really took 80 to 90 hours every week, and ... I was enabled to keep this up for 10 weeks without one failure; unfortunately, when within the one week of the end, I broke down with influenza ... with the result only that instead of finishing on Saturday night ... it was the following Tuesday evening* at 11 pm, that I was enabled to hand to my wife, who was sitting with me waiting for the end, the word Dziggetai,† and to say 'Here endeth the Letter D, τῷ θεῷ μόνῳ δόξα!' And indeed it seems to me almost miraculous; for ... it has surpassed in difficulties of all kinds any portion of the Dictionary heretofore.[78]

The faithful Walter Skeat was there as usual to cheer from the side-lines and with one of his poems to commemorate the end of *D* and the advance to *H* (*G* being left to Bradley).

To J.A.H.M. Jan. 1. 1897

I'm glad that you've done—so I hear you say—
With words that begin with D—
And have left H.B. to be Glad and Gay
With the Glory that waits on G:
And you laugh, Ha! Ha! defying fate,
As you tackle the terrible aspirate.

* * * * * *

We all rejoice, on this New Year's day
To hear you are fairly upon your way
To Honour and Happiness, Hope, and Health—
I would you were nearer to Worldly Wealth!

James was then approaching his sixtieth birthday, but he was to keep up his resilience and enthusiasm for another eighteen long years. In 1913 he wrote 'I shall complete 76 years tomorrow ... and yet ... I do not feel old or worn out, but—in feeling—as fresh & ready for work as ever. This is a mercy for I have to work as hard, or harder than ever I did.'[79] In November of that year he was described as coming to his desk every morning 'with the same, if indeed, not a greater enthusiasm: time does not bring weariness. Still he talks of words with eyes that light up with pleasure.'[80] Six months later he recounted to Ada a triumphantly successful hunt for information about the word *trillion* which had taken him from 10.30 till 1.15 in the Taylorian and Bodleian libraries, adding, 'Everything was lovely and fresh at 5 this morning, when I rose, I had a stiff morning's work before breakfast.'[81]

* Christmas Eve.
† A species of equine quadruped native to Central Asia.

In his later years he continued his life-long habit of rising early, and as an old man he wrote to his daughter-in-law, Katie, in a rather shaky hand, apologizing that his hands were numb, 'it is 6 o'clock & I have had my cold bath, & have not recovered heat yet'.[82] If it was summer he might spend a little time in the garden, or cycle round to the Press with 'copy', or work in the Scriptorium till breakfast at eight, but in winter he worked in the morning room till the stoves had been lit and the chill taken off the 'iron room'. One of his assistants, P. J. Philip, who worked in the Scriptorium for a short time in 1909, described coming into the work room at seven o'clock on an autumn morning. The tables, the chairs, the desks, even the floor were snowed under with the verb *to put*.

> With his fountain-pen in his mouth for safety—he lost it five times a day—Sir James ... was playing chess with the senses. He wore a grey tweed Norfolk suit, and with one hand he grasped his long white beard, as he always did when every cell of the alert brain below the black velvet skull-cap was busy with some great problem. For over an hour he worked in silence not heeding my presence. Then with a gesture as if he had conquered a province, he bundled the little slips into groups and smiled a 'Good morning'. 'Do you remember how Euclid defines a point as having position but no magnitude?' he asked in his curious Anglo-Scotch nasal accent, 'yet "point" occupied twenty one columns. I thought "put" was a little word, but it is going to take even more than that number.'*[83]

The Norfolk jacket was unusual, almost invariably he wore a black frock coat, and although there was a place for him at the tables where his assistants sat in one half of the room, he preferred to work standing for hours at a time at a high desk which divided the room into two halves and held the large Dictionaries of Johnson, Littré, Webster and the *Century* open for reference. From this position he could see what went on in the room, and his daughter Rosfrith, busy checking that references were standardised, remembered the wink he would exchange with her when one of the assistants, with a reputation for lateness would try to slip into his place without attracting notice.

The steady stream of visitors to the Scriptorium continued: those genuinely interested found Murray very accessible and ready to talk about his work with humour. That he could make the apparently dry

---

* It took 30 columns.

17. The Scriptorium, Oxford: Editor and staff.

subject of lexicography fascinating, even to the layman, was proved in
1887 when he lectured on '*The World of Words and its Explorers*' to
the Summer School for Extension Students. He invited those
interested to come and see the Dictionary in the making, expecting
perhaps a dozen, and was taken aback when tram load after tram load
came all afternoon. Nearly exhausted, he turned the last away, saying
they could come next day, and he got ready a small exhibition for
them in the garden: they came in even greater numbers, and some for
the second time, and this continued next day, until on the fourth day
James had to tell them that the show was over. Although exasperated
by the interruption, he was amused too, particularly by a prim,
decisive lady who he felt sure was the principal of a young ladies
seminary. When James showed her a copy of the Dictionary she
adjusted her gold pince-nez and then suddenly, with a startled cry as
if a bee had stung her, she ejaculated, 'There is a word I have never
seen before!' James explained that every day he had to write the
history of words new to him. But the little lady repeated with

irritation, 'I am sure I never saw that word before!' James again attempted to explain that the Dictionary contained, besides current words, obsolete ones and obscure technical terms, but the lady would not hear him out, but this time in towering indignation, repeated, 'No! I am positive that I *never* saw that word before', and shutting the book she turned away, having lost interest in a Dictionary that had the audacity to include *one* word that she, the distinguished head of a superior academy for young ladies, had never seen before. James' observation when telling this anecdote was, 'not even one educated lady's English is all English'.[84]

The casual visitor, who tended to turn up on a Sunday afternoon, was usually left to a somewhat reluctant Rosfrith or Elsie to be shown the regular exhibits such as interesting autograph letters, including one from George Eliot saying that she had used the word *adust* in *Romola* for *dusty* because it suited the rhythm of her prose, and one from Robert Louis Stevenson revealing that a mysterious word *brean* was a misprint for *ocean*.[85] James himself liked to welcome old Mill Hill pupils and distinguished scholars from the Continent, such as Dr Brandl of Berlin, who had a meal with the family and was reminded of Thomas More and his learned daughter and felt sure that as More's work for Greek bore fruit long afterwards, so would Murray's work for English.[86] Former readers and sub-editors would drop in if passing anywhere near Oxford: Heads of Houses and Professors of the University found it a convenient way of entertaining their guests, and every visitor from America still made a point of calling. Amongst them came Mark Twain in 1900, with the excuse that as a last resort he was thinking of making a dictionary, and wanted to see how it was done. James flattered him by saying he had had no such famous literary visitor since Gladstone.[87] Parties from schools or clubs sightseeing for a day in Oxford would try to include the Scriptorium in their itinerary and although the Editor would sometimes tell them it was not worth a visit, he seldom refused to receive them.[88]

Over the years James' own attitude to his work changed and although he was increasingly desirous to see the end, he lost something of his impatience and disappointment at being caught in the strangle-hold of the Dictionary. He had accepted that the time when he would pick up again the research he had laid down in 1878 would never come. At the end of 1896 he resigned from the Council of the Early English Text Society and any other of Furnivall's numerous societies with which he might have a connection saying, 'The

Dictionary is quite enough for me for the rest of my life, and to its service I must devote all my resources.' He retained his membership of the Philological Society and consented to hold office again as President in 1907, but accepted regretfully that he could seldom attend, saying, 'Alas! Oxford is so far away and it costs both time & money to come, and I have neither to spare.'[89] On his visits to London for any meetings he preferred not to stay overnight, since this meant the loss of the next morning's work which would have begun at 6 *a.m.* Instead he would catch a train at past midnight which got him to Oxford at 2.10 *a.m.*, to cycle, sometimes in evening dress, home through the empty streets.[90]

When he yielded to persuasion and undertook any work outside the Dictionary he always regretted it. A lecture to the Royal Institution in 1903 became a 'kind of hateful bugbear' and as the time for it drew near he moaned that he had made no preparation for it and it seemed that he had always far more demands upon him than he could possibly meet.[91] He had agreed in 1895 to revise his article on English Language for a new edition of the *Encyclopaedia*. His daughter Hilda helped him, but it dragged on till 1908 and he said he should never have agreed, 'I have no joy in it, but only trouble'.[92] In 1913 he told a reporter, 'I have given up everything extraneous and am happiest when I am writing away uninterruptedly.' He wished those who pestered him with unnecessary letters would remember the urgency of his work, requiring every ounce of his intellectual energy, and would leave him free to finish what he had begun.[93]

Besides being reconciled to his servitude to the Dictionary, James was also more relaxed because he had no longer to fight to preserve the quality of the work and even its continuance.[94] He had won his battle to persuade people that the plan was not too vast to be successfully carried out and that quality must not be sacrificed to speed, and now he became less dependent on the encouragement of the minority who could appreciate the scholarship required for the work. In his Christmas letter to Edward Arber in 1904 he wrote

I wonder sometimes whether anybody will ever realize the work that the Dictionary costs . . . but I do not seem to care: *I* know; and it pleases me, at any practicable amount of work, to get at the facts, and force them to yield their secret. When you receive the new issue, turn to the articles *pelican* and *penguin*, and try to realize what these articles cost. I could have written two books with less labour:

or read the note at the end of *Parish*, or try to estimate the brain work that is put into *Pass* which came near driving me mad, before I could see my way first *through* it; and second to exhibit it clearly & neatly after I saw it. No, the world will *never* know nor realize it, and it does not matter; once it *did* trouble me; now I know the work is too high & too intense for anybody to realize who only sees the result.[95]

On re-reading what he had written he felt it to be egotistic and self-centred and that this was only the experience of any earnest scholar, but it was a help in times of discouragement to remember, as he told the Philological Society in 1906, that he was working not for the present day but for the future. Good work once done and in print, he said, becomes an eternal inheritance which will remain of value for generations to come.[96]

CHAPTER XVI

The Sands Run Out

IT WAS as well that James had regained a more philosophical and balanced outlook, since one of the strains of the last years was that from 1900 onwards the passing months were marked by the breakdown and death of one after another of his team of voluntary helpers and personal friends who had given him moral as well as practical support. These losses naturally made him look with increasing anxiety at his own mounting record of years, measuring the tale against the letters of the Dictionary still to be completed. The sands, he said, ten years before his death, were running out.

Of his close friends, Fred Elworthy, with whom he had shared many interests and holidays, died in 1907, six weeks after the death of Henry Hucks Gibbs, without whose help the Dictionary would not have survived the early difficulties. Walter Skeat, ever optimistic, following every stage in the Dictionary's production with sympathy and understanding, died in the autumn of 1912. At about the same time Edward Arber was knocked down by a taxi-cab in Birmingham. Professor Robinson Ellis died in 1913. James told the Philological Society in 1908 'Thus one by one, they pass away, & one has ever the anxious question Who is to be the next? ... If good wishes & good counsel can prolong my days, they are not wanting.'[1]

The greatest shock was the death of Frederick Furnivall in 1910. He had seemed indestructible and even in his eighties he had lost none of his vitality. He still rowed on the Thames, he still sent his daily packet of clippings from newspapers, recording fresh words and usages for the Dictionary, with which he had been associated for fifty years. He wrote a characteristically courageous, forthright letter to James to tell him that he was suffering from an internal tumour. His letter began with an approving comment on James' article on *tallow*

18. Fitzedward Hall. 1862.

ketch and then continued 'Yes, our Dict. men go gradually, & I am to disappear in 6 months . . . It's a great disappointment, as I wanted to see the Dict. finishd before I die. But it is not to be. However the completion of the work is certain. So that's all right.'[2] Although James had often had occasion to wish himself rid of Furnivall, he was shaken by the news. 'The note from Dr F. quite upset me', he wrote to Hilda, 'and made me feel that my end might also come soon; esp. when he wrote that his great disappointment is that he is not to see the Dictionary finished; I asked myself "And shall I?" Alas! my friends seem to be dying daily, & younger men too.'[3] His reply to Furnivall was as characteristic as Furnivall's to him. Just as when a child James could think of no better gift for his baby brother than 'round O and crooked S', now he could think of no more appropriate token of sympathy for the dying old man than to ask 'Would it give you any satisfaction to see the gigantic TAKE in final? before it is too late?'[4]

Among others forced to abandon the Dictionary by death or illness were two whose daily contribution from the start had been indispensable, Dr Fitzedward Hall and Dr W. C. Minor. Both were Americans and both were sufferers from persecution mania.

Dr Hall went out to India as a young man and became Professor of Sanskrit at Government College Benares.[5] After 1862 he settled in

England and was Professor of Sanskrit at King's College London and Librarian at the India Office and he undertook some editions for the Early English Text Society. Then in 1869 things went wrong: he was accused of misconduct in a quarrel with Professor Goldstücker and suspended from membership of the Philological Society; he was alleged to be a foreign spy and a drunkard and forced to leave the India Office. When he retired to Suffolk he claimed that his marriage had been broken up by a neighbouring clergyman and he became practically a recluse, hardly going outside his gate except for an occasional visit to America. He asserted that his only offence was his nationality and that he was the victim of the 'fiendish hatred' which he believed Englishmen felt towards his countrymen.[6] There was some truth in his allegations: James received a scurrilous communication in 1906 from the former Rector of Dr Hall's parish, attempting to destroy both his moral and his academic reputation.[7] There is no question of the value of his help to the Dictionary. Persuaded by Skeat, from about 1881 until his death in 1901 he devoted four to six hours a day to going through the proofs and adding to them from notes on words and phrases marked when reading in his extensive library: 'there is scarcely a page', James recorded in the Preface to volume I, 'to which he has not added earlier instances of words or senses ... many rare words and rare senses have been added entirely from his stores.' And to Hall he spoke of it as 'the most generous literary assistance which the annals of literature can show'.[8] At his death James had to organise a band of 100 volunteers to go through the library and copy out Hall's marked quotations for the letters still to be done.[9] The two men never met, although they exchanged letters almost daily for twenty years; James was always too busy to make the long journey to Suffolk and although Fitzedward Hall came to London at least once he did not come on to Oxford and he refused the invitation to the Vice-Chancellor's Dictionary Dinner. Yet when Hall was ill James, for once abandoning the conventional 'yours truly' for 'yours very affectionately', told Hall that he looked upon him as a senior relative of his own.[10] Hall was his strongest supporter against pressure to sacrifice quality to speed and provided a sympathetic ear for James' complaints of Furnivall's misconceptions.[11]

The story of Dr W. C. Minor has often been told.[12] He was one of the early readers for the Dictionary and in the Preface to volume I he was named among those who had already contributed between 5000 and 8000 quotations. That was only a beginning, and until he gave up owing to ill health in 1902, Dr Minor's total was only exceeded by that of Furnivall. When James invited him to the Dictionary Dinner, urging him to spend a day or two at Sunnyside, Dr Minor said that, owing to physical reasons, he could not accept, but instead invited James to visit him at Crowthorne in Berkshire. James was impressed to find a liveried servant and a handsome brougham with two fine horses to meet him at the station. At the end of a two-mile drive through the country the horses turned into the courtyard of a large brick building of forbidding appearance. A little puzzled, James followed a servant up a gloomy staircase and along corridors to a well-furnished office in which an official looking man was seated at the desk. James advanced to greet Dr Minor, but the official hastened to say that he was not Dr Minor, but the Governor of Broadmoor Criminal Lunatic Asylum. Dr Minor, he explained, was an inmate. He was the son of a wealthy American and had joined the Army of the North as a surgeon-captain. He had been much upset by an order to brand a soldier who had deserted, and later, after an attack of sunstroke, he developed a mania under which he believed that Irishmen were pursuing him to take revenge. After a period in an asylum he was considered cured, and came to England on a visit in 1871. He brought with him introductions to various people, including one from a Professor of Yale to John Ruskin, but while staying in London a tragedy occurred. On the night of 17 February 1872 he was returning to his lodgings in Lambeth at 2 *a.m.* when he became aware that a man was walking behind him. Apparently his mania had been returning and he had already presented himself at a police station with confused complaints which the police did not recognise were symptomatic. Now he turned upon the man behind him, who was a night stoker from the Lion Brewery, and shot him dead. He realised immediately what he had done, and although there were no witnesses, gave himself up when the police arrived. On trial he was committed to Broadmoor for life, where he was allowed a private room and was able to buy and borrow books. One day he found in a book he had ordered, Dr Murray's leaflet appealing for readers for the Dictionary, and he started work, mainly supplying rare words from books in his possession. So great was his contribution over the years that in 1899 James said it would be easy to illustrate the last four centuries for these words from his quotations alone, which in that particular year had totalled 12,000. James found him always somewhat touchy. 'In his lonely & sad position', James told Craigie, 'he requires a great deal of nursing, encouraging and coaxing and I have had to go from time to time to see him ... it has been no light part of my unknown & unrecognised duties to keep him interested.'[13] In 1905 Dr Minor showed his gratitude by sending James a small gift of money towards unexpected expenses he might incur on a visit he was about to pay to the Cape of Good Hope.[14] James did not abandon his concern for this unfortunate man, and in 1910, through the interest of an American visitor to the Scriptorium, to whom he told the story, a movement was set on foot to obtain his release. Winston Churchill, then Home Secretary, approved his return to the States in charge of his brothers and James and Ada went to Broadmoor to say goodbye.[15] He was still kept in custody in Washington, where he died in 1921.

One other remarkable character amongst the voluntary helpers deserves special mention. The place of James Platt, junior, who died on 10 February 1910, was another which could never be filled.[16] Platt had been known to James Murray since 1882, when as a young man of twenty-one, he read a paper to the Philological Society in which was a trenchant criticism of Professor Toller's revision, for the Oxford University Press, of Joseph Bosworth's *Anglo-Saxon Dictionary*. James agreed with his criticisms since he had himself advised the Delegates to cancel publication. But other members of the Society took exception to the young man's brashness and moved a motion disapproving of Mr Platt's failure to observe the rules of literary decorum and etiquette, with the result that he dropped his work on Anglo-Saxon grammar and phonology.[17] In 1899 Platt contributed a criticism of the etymology of a word in the Dictionary to the *Athenaeum*, and this led to a renewal of his friendship with Murray,[18] and henceforth he directed his energies to equipping himself to help the Dictionary where help was most needed — in solving etymological queries related to obscure, little-known languages of America, Africa and Asia. 'I know no one, and cannot hope ever to find any one', James wrote on Platt's death, '... to whom I can send any strange alien word and say "What language can this belong to" with a very sure and well-founded expectation that in a day or two there will come an illuminating answer.'[19] Platt travelled on the Continent, spoke every European language and said that anyone who could learn twelve languages would have little difficulty in mastering a hundred, yet he was so quiet himself that he was described as a man who had learnt a hundred languages and forgotten his own! Like James Murray before him, he drew on the resources of London. He explored opium dens, and he looked out for foreigners in the streets and would offer them his services as guide or interpreter, often then inviting the stranger to his house for the evening in order to learn his language.

Platt worked in his father's woollen business in the City and philology was only a spare-time hobby: his visits to the British Museum Library were restricted to his lunch hour, when he was always tied for time and never stayed for more than about ten minutes, just long enough to order a book one day that he could look at the next. He kept alphabetical notebooks crammed with unusual words, but most of his knowledge was stored in his remarkable memory. James was astonished to learn after Platt's death how few books he owned, saying, 'He becomes more and more a marvel to me because I have no clue to the mystery how with only such books he was able to answer our queries.' James Platt's mysterious powers were just one of the many miracles that James Murray came more and more to find attended on the production of the Dictionary.

Even with his close knowledge of the working of the Scriptorium, James found it difficult to see how, in a good year like 1898, he managed to produce 272 pages, which he said

> means the production, completing, and printing, of every column of the work in less than $2\frac{1}{2}$ hours, a statement which when I consider all that the production of a column involves . . . seems even to myself incredible. Without any boastfulness . . . I may be allowed to question whether anything approaching it in the speed of thorough work has ever been witnessed in the world before.[20]

Increasingly his sense of a divine providence using him as an instrument grew, and the feeling that it was only by a miracle that he could accomplish his heavy task. He wrote more frankly on this to his son Aelfric, when trying to strengthen the young man's sense of vocation.

> I never could have stood the work that I have done at the Dictionary, and the special difficulties which threatened at times to overwhelm me without earnest prayer every morning for help to do my work . . . And many a time, unknown to anybody, . . . when absolutely at the end of my own resources in dealing with entangled & difficult words, when all alone at night in the Scriptorium, I have shut the door, and thrown myself on the floor absolutely on God's help, and asked him to use me as an instrument to do what He knew

to be right; and I believe I have never asked in vain. There are many articles in the Dictionary which could never have been done by me without this earnest and sometimes agonized appeal to higher wisdom to inspire me with fresh effort. To many a long article, but for affectation and the appearance of Pharisaism, I could gladly append *Deo soli sit gloria*.[21]

Eagerly looking forward to the end, James had again and again to confess that his predictions had been too optimistic and to move the date yet further off. In 1880 he was still hopeful that the whole work would be done before the end of the century: at the Dictionary Dinner in 1897 he had hoped to finish by 1908. In July 1912 he told Walter Skeat that he was now half way through *T*, which he had begun two and a half years before. In another two and a half years he planned to reach *U* and by then Bradley and Craigie should have completed *S* so that all three Editors could work on *U* to *Z*—the last half volume. *W* would be the only considerable letter of these and he hoped they could do this last section in two years. He estimated that the end of 1916 would see the Dictionary complete. 'If I live to then I shall be 80, and it will also be my Golden Wedding; let us hope that the Grand Conjunction of all these cycles will really take place.'[22]

He was then seventy-eight and although he still had surprising vigour of body and mind, he had lost something of his powers of resilience. He confessed to Aelfric in 1913 that he had begun to wish he were free of the burden of work, 'at least' he added, 'that feeling comes over me strongly at times, when I am not quite well'.[23] He found that he was more subject to colds and took longer to recover from them: the periods when he drove himself to sustained work for long hours to meet his self-imposed timetable took more out of him than hitherto. What finally undermined him was the collapse of Ada. Apart from a period when she was incapacitated by rheumatism in 1900–1, her constitution, despite all her child bearing, was almost as good as his own. She was 'the pivot on which the whole house revolved'; 'ever since I began the dictionary,' he told Furnivall, 'she has not done much *to* it, but ... everything *for* it; everything to save *me* to it ... and the loss of this help ... doubled my tear-and-wear, distracting me daily with incessant details of domestic and social duty.'[24] She was unpaid secretary as well as wife, and above all she never lost faith in his ability to accomplish his task. When he would have given up the effort to meet a dead-line for finishing a triple section, Ada 'with her usual optimism' would try to cheer him up and encourage him at least to do his best, and as James told Aelfric, 'her belief that all would turn out well, though it irritated me at the time, as believing against all grounds of belief, acted as a tonic & braced me up a bit.'[25]

Now for some years Ada had suffered from cataract in both eyes. In 1909 she had two operations and in 1914 a third, for all of which she went to a specialist at Bournemouth with her daughter Rosfrith, leaving James alone with his troubles. In 1914 everything went wrong. James' most senior and able assistant, Mr Balk, had resigned: unable to find a replacement James had had a desperate struggle to produce the double section planned for May. He managed it — another miracle achieved 'in a way I know not' — but the day after he had handed in the last proof his health broke down. Ada with Rosfrith was in the nursing home at Bournemouth and had suffered a set-back. Although eventually the operation was successful, for a time an infection of the eye delayed recovery and she was much longer convalescing than had been expected. James kept the knowledge of his own illness from her until she was better and he faced alone the anxiety about Ada, about his work, about his own health and about the heavy expense in which all this illness involved him.

The Regius Professor of Medicine, Sir William Osler, once laughingly remarked, 'The University pays me my salary to keep that old man alive till his 80th birthday in 1917 when the Dictionary will be finished.'[27] He was called in now as consultant and pronounced that what James had feared might be appendicitis was trouble caused by the prostate gland. The operation which today is common and normally successful was then unknown. Osler advised treatment by X-rays, then also still very experimental, and he warned James that internal burning might result and that the effect of the rays would not be known for six weeks.[28] At first he made little progress and remained very weak and subject to violent perspiration. For four months he was unfit for work, and it was seven before he felt he had recovered.

In April 1915 he complained of inability to work his customary long hours,[29] but he did not lose his hope. While finishing *T* he was already planning how to deal with words in *Un* — and able to treat his work with humour. 'It is not an easy job', he wrote to his son, 'but I have thought a good deal about it and think myself more capable of tackling it with less *un*-preparedness and *un*-wisdom than any one

19. The last day in the Scriptorium, 10 July 1915. Left to right, seated: Elsie M. R. Murray, James A. H. Murray, Rosfrith A. N. R. Murray; standing: A. T. Maling, F. J. Sweatman, F. A. Yockney.

else; but it will need skilful arrangement to keep the *un*-bounded prefix within bounds.'[30]

Early in July Henry Bradley called on him, and although he realised that James was a sick man, he said that he found 'not a little of the zest and mental lucidity' that he remembered of old. Bradley considered that the double section, *Trink* to *Turndown*, which James had just completed, was one containing an extraordinary number of difficult words, 'handled with ... characteristic sagacity and resource', a piece of work of which the Editor might be proud.[31] On Friday 10 July James was photographed in the Scriptorium with his staff, A. T. Maling, F. J. Sweatman, F. A. Yockney, Rosfrith and Elsie, but on the following Monday when he attempted work he felt too unwell, and when he returned to the house Ada found that he was suffering from pleurisy. He was ill only for a fortnight and died from heart failure on the afternoon of 26 July 1915.

He and Ada had already selected the spot where he wished to be buried in the Wolvercote cemetery, next to the graves of two friends, Dr Andrew Fairbairn, first principal of Mansfield College, and Dr James Legge, Professor of Chinese.

With his death some of the driving force was gone and the hope of an early completion faded once more. World War I would have thwarted James' hopes of the 'Grand Conjunction' in any case, for many of the staff and printers were withdrawn for military service. After the war further delays were caused by the death in May 1923 of Henry Bradley, who had become Chief Editor, and the fact that William Craigie and Charles Onions were not able to give their continuous and whole time work to the Dictionary. Thus it was not until the beginning of 1928, almost exactly seventy years from the date on which the Philological Society had resolved to prepare 'a new English Dictionary' that the last part appeared. Craigie and Onions then edited the materials which had already accumulated for a Supplement and this, with an Introduction and Bibliography to the whole work, was published in 1933.

Finally, in 1972, the first volume of a four volume Supplement edited by R. W. Burchfield appeared. This is planned to replace the 1933 Supplement and to bring the history of the language down to the present day. *The Times Literary Supplement*, in a leading article, took the opportunity of its publication to review the principal English Dictionaries then available. The writer, while admitting that the *Oxford English Dictionary* is not perfect, concluded that 'its overall reliability and fullness are astonishingly high ... As a broad survey of the history of English vocabulary up to the end of the nineteenth century, it does not seem likely that *OED* will be superseded for some generations to come, if ever.'[32] The announcement made by the Press in 1928 therefore still stands today. It reads

The superiority of the Dictionary to all other English Dictionaries, in accuracy and completeness, is everywhere admitted. The Oxford Dictionary is the supreme authority, and without a rival. It is perhaps less generally appreciated that what makes the Dictionary unique is its historical method; it is a Dictionary not of our English, but of all English: the English of Chaucer, of the Bible, and of Shakespeare is unfolded in it with the same wealth of illustration as is devoted to the most modern authors. When considered in this light, the fact that the first part of the Dictionary was published in 1884 is seen to be relatively unimportant; 44 years is a small period in the life of a language.[33]

The Dictionary has become the national achievement which James Murray fought to make it.

At their first meeting after the long Vacation, on 22 October 1915, the Delegates recorded their tribute to his thirty-five years' work for the Dictionary in these words:

> At the beginning Sir JAMES MURRAY laid the lines and drew the plan of the Dictionary, and when it is completed half the printed pages will be his; the Delegates acknowledge the debt which they, and with them the University and the world of scholarship, owe to the unremitting labour and the distinguished skill of the original editor of the Dictionary.[34]

One cannot however let his biography end there. The Delegates witnessed to the heroic achievement of a great lexicographer, but there was also another side to him, the side that he felt had been sacrificed to his life work: his family; his wide general interests; his wish to be involved in civic and religious affairs. These interests were never wholly ousted by the demands of the Dictionary, and to them we must now turn.

CHAPTER XVII

'The Dic and the Little Dics':
The Man and His Family

WHEN James Murray died in 1915 he was mourned not only as a great lexicographer who had tragically failed to see the completion of his life's work, but also as father and grandfather, friend, citizen and Christian.

The family was his constant care and concern. When he had contemplated resignation in 1883 he had put first in the list of pleasures to which he would escape, 'romps with my boys and walks with my wife'.[1] In a moment of nostalgic gloom in 1908 he wrote to his eldest son:

> The greatest sacrifice the Dictionary entailed upon me, by far, was the sacrifice of the constant companionship of my own children; and I doubt if it was worth the sacrifice. I have tried, as a husband & father, to do what should have been the work of a celibate and ascetic, a Dunstan or a Cuthbert: no wonder it has been a struggle. But has it been worth it?[2]

As so often, he was dramatising and exaggerating his plight for, in spite of the Dictionary, he did succeed in filling a patriarchal role too: he was the dominant influence in holding his large family together and moulding the characters of its members.[3]

The Murray home was one of the many villas which sprang up in North Oxford in the 1880s and '90s, roomy, brick-built and high gabled, standing back from the road with a space in front for a flower bed, two beech trees and a large old elm, while at the rear there was a walled garden on the site of an old orchard. To the children, looking back, it seemed that there was always apple pie and rice pudding for lunch throughout the year, and that besides what was picked and stored or given away, there was fallen ripe fruit to eat in abundance in

20. Sunnyside, 78 Banbury Road, Oxford. The Murray home from 1885.

the autumn. In summer James, sitting writing letters in the garden, would keep stopping to throw stones to scare the birds. He thought the Wild Bird Protection Act should be repealed because he believed that it had interfered with the balance of nature and had resulted in a ten-fold increase in the number of blackbirds.[4]

He kept up his interest in growing flowers: bulbs, primulas, forget-me-nots and wallflowers in spring, bedding-out plants and herbaceous borders in summer, none of which he liked to see picked. He also collected ferns, which did well at the side of the house where a draughty pathway between front and back gardens was known to the family as 'windy lene'. Although there was an elderly gardener, James liked to find time to attend to his plants himself—up early in the morning to put cotton to protect the primulas from the birds, or taking a couple of hours off from the Dictionary on a summer evening to carry sixty cans of water to save his flowers in a drought.[5] He was less particular about the lawn than in Mill Hill days, and the children played croquet and bowls. They were supposed to keep away from the vicinity of the Scriptorium—known as the 'scrippy'—during working hours, but when their father was safely out of the way they sometimes played 'German Bands', blowing down the watering can spouts as trumpets, with occasionally the desired result that one of the assistants would come out and give them a penny to go away. They remembered Charles Onions, the future fourth Editor of the Dictionary, also taking advantage of the absence of Dr Murray to slip

315

21. Family group. About 1892. Left to right, standing: Wilfrid, Hilda, Oswyn, Ethelwyn; seated: Elsie, Harold, James, Ada, Ethelbert, Aelfric; in front: Rosfrith, Gwyneth, Jowett.

out to turn the skipping rope for them. He was unimpressive as a young man and behind his back the children used to sing, 'Charlie is my darling'.

Indoors, Sunnyside, though lacking the charm of the old house at Mill Hill, had the advantage of providing more space for the family and the friends who always thronged it. It was three stories high with three living rooms on the ground floor: a small 'morning room' used mainly by the older members of the family, a large, crimson-plush furnished drawing room on the garden side and an equally large dining room facing Banbury Road. Here hung pictures of James' heroes, Gladstone and Bright, and his framed collection of British butterflies. The artistry of the family was represented in both rooms by the portraits painted by Ada's father and the etchings of James' brother Charles. The big dining table easily held not only the entire family when at home, but three or four visitors as well. On occasion it was also used for Dictionary purposes, and when working out the history of a difficult word, James would cover it with over 200 packets of slips.[6]

James was never happy unless the family filled the table. 'One looks back now as the ancients did to the Golden Age ... to that last Christmas of 1896 when all were here', he wrote to Aelfric in 1902, '... one did not half prize it, as one ought. I fear we shall have no one home this time, except Hilda ... and perhaps Oswyn & Mildred.'[7] He did not count the 'home family', Elsie, Rosfrith, Jowett and Gwyneth who were still permanently members of the household! When he thought of the 'happy, hopeful, bright days' when he had them all round him, he said he found it hard to keep his spirits up, but fortunately although three of his children migrated to South Africa between 1897 and 1902 and three of the sons in England were married by 1900, there were then daughters-in-law and grandchildren to join the circle.[8]

He retained his interest in even quite young children: he was delighted when a baby grandson wanted to be danced on his knee and tossed in the air.[9] He knew what would please children and honoured his eldest grandson, Leslie, at the age of six with a postcard addressed,

> To Leslie, Hydraulic Engineer.
>
> Now Leslie lad, you are a trump
> To make me such a portly pump
> . . . .
> With such a pump, with such a spout
> Our water never can run out!
>
> Oxford. 20 Jan. 1903.

Although the Oxford period, 1885 to 1915, fell only half into the reign of Queen Victoria, in framework and discipline the Murray household remained typical of that period. 'I use the old Queen's stamp', James wrote to Edward Arber in 1905, four years after the Queen's death, 'as you & I are of Victorian era, and History, if it remembers us, will so describe us.'[10] In early years the big family divided into three groups: 'the older ones' at the University, or already earning their living, 'the children' at school, and 'the little ones' in the nursery upstairs. Another important part of the household was the servants, cook, housemaid, nurse and nursemaid. In spite of the struggle to make ends meet, it would not have occurred to the Murrays or any other middle-class Victorians to economise on domestic help. It was, after all, cheap enough: in 1890 they paid a young girl one shilling and six pence a week, and an older one £8 a year,[11] and probably the total annual wage bill at Sunnyside was little more than £70. Following the practice of his own home, James did not expect his sons to help in house or garden: apart from the Dictionary slips, his rule for all, except the little ones, was systematic study for school or university.

The day would begin with the rattle of the window as James threw it up soon after 5 *a.m.* to let in the fresh air. The family rising bell was not until 7.30, followed by the prayer bell for all to assemble in the dining room at 8. This included the servants, but there was difficulty for the cook. James was fussy about his porridge, and would look critically at it, breaking into his Scotch dialect to exclaim: 'These porridge are waesh [liquid]', or 'These porridge are brose [thick]'. The cook maintained that she could not serve it as he liked if she was expected to attend prayers.

Lunch at 1.30 was the main meal of the day. Usually James arrived a few minutes late, carrying a handful of Dictionary slips, about which he would talk during the meal. If by any chance he arrived early and found no one else there, he would bang on the table with a knife handle till everyone flung down what he was doing and came running. Mischievous members of the family sometimes made this signal for the fun of seeing the pandemonium it caused. The children sat round the table and were served in order of age, and the youngest suffered pangs of hunger during the seemingly interminable wait. No fidgeting or chattering was allowed: older members of the family remembered being required to sit gripping the table edge with thumbs on top to keep their hands out of mischief, but later the rule was relaxed and it was possible to smuggle small toys in, to play with out of sight while waiting.

The pattern on Sundays was rather different. Religious observance followed the regular Victorian practice, and a considerable portion of the week was set aside for family and congregational worship. Apart from the daily family prayers there was an evening mid-week service at the church which Oswyn, even on the eve of his Finals, was rebuked for failing to attend.[12] On Sunday mornings a sight familiar to North Oxford residents was that of Dr Murray leading his large family down the Banbury Road to the Congregational Church in George Street. He walked very upright, grasping his umbrella by the middle, like a proud Drake with his ducklings behind him, and they were nicknamed 'the Dic. and the little Dics'. He was made a Deacon of the Church as soon as he came to Oxford and a life Deacon in 1912, and in early years he often preached and also conducted the service in the absence of the Minister.[13] The older children taught in Sunday school, and in the evening all but the nursery party again walked into Oxford for the service. There were no morning family prayers on that day, but instead, after supper, they all, with the servants and any visitors, gathered in the drawing room. After a hymn and a psalm there followed the lesson, each member reading a verse. They counted anxiously to see when their turns would come, but sometimes they were put out by James electing to read more than one verse himself, leaving a small child unprepared for a long word or unpronounceable name. Woe betide any who started to giggle: Rosfrith remembered rushing upstairs in an outburst of suppressed laughter on one occasion, and her father's stern voice booming after her, 'Who is disturbing the peace of the Sabbath?'

In his prayers James expressed his complete and simple faith. Those who heard him lead the Lord's Prayer at George Street said that in the very tone of his voice one could feel the reverence of a strong man conscious of his dependence on a higher power. Little Jowett never forgot the solemn start to every day and end to every Sunday: God, he thought, must be a very important person if his parents who ruled his home should kneel in reverence before Him. The prayers were extempore and very drawn out. Donald, the second grandson, was never quite forgiven for standing up in the middle and announcing, 'These prayers are much too long for a little boy like me.'

The upbringing of the family was austere, on principle as much as of necessity. James remained a strict teetotaller and the children were led to sign the pledge and join the Blue Ribbon Band.[14] No one dared to smoke in the house, and visitors would seek refuge behind bushes in the garden if they felt desperate for a pipe. James himself would never attend a theatre, although he would turn a blind eye if the younger members went for a celebration. But on the whole, anniversaries and feast days were kept very simply. The children had less pocket money than their friends, what they had was earned and they were expected to save it to meet their needs. For birthdays the rule

22. A Christmas morning walk.

was one present from the parents and one joint gift from the brothers and sisters. Parties and birthday cakes (cake was always a very rare treat) were for long unknown, until Hilda introduced candles after a visit to Germany.

Parental discipline was carried into adult life. Aelfric, often scolded for failure to write regularly from the Cape, remembered to send a cable on the occasion of James' honorary degree at Cambridge. This was not well received. He was told that he should have written a letter in time. Cables seemed to his father 'a very foolish piece of extravagance, & of very little use, and I hope that you will never think of such a thing again. It is a fad of the wealthy in a decadent age, which the poor think themselves obliged to ape.'[15]

Yet the lack of what James would have thought indulgence did not mean lack of uproarious fun. At Christmas the absence of real presents were made up for by 'haves'—gifts intended to take the recipient in, like April fool's day pranks. Large parcels with many wrappings concealed, when all the paper was removed, only a lump of sugar, or a more unpleasant relic, such as an old tooth-brush, offered 'with fondest love', and carefully cherished to be returned to the donor next Christmas. James joined in the fun and Gwyneth remembered her anguish as a little girl at finding nothing in her parcel but a Garibaldi ('squashed fly') biscuit, and then, as she began to cry, catching a twinkle in her father's eye and discovering the coin he had embedded in it.

True to James' Scottish upbringing, not much was made of Christmas as a religious festival but James would lead the family for a walk usually across Port Meadow to Godstow and back down the tow path through Binsey, and sometimes further afield to Boar's Hill, each to add a stone to the cairn on top. On New Year's day he went with them into the Banbury Road if fine, or into the drawing room to welcome the New Year by singing Auld Lang Syne, but the original fourth verse which runs, 'And we'll take a right guid willie-waught' was changed to, 'We'll gie a right guid hearty shake', in deference to temperance principles.

Easter was memorable mainly for the fact that the 'scrippy' was closed for three days, and while the assistants were away Ada with the help of some of the girls would spring clean it. Cyril Joad, the future philosopher and broadcaster, who as a small boy at Lynam's school used to spend Sundays at Sunnyside, described how he once climbed into the Scriptorium by a window and created havoc there. He claimed he did irreparable damage and delayed work on the Dictionary for at least six months by destroying slips, pasting the leaves of books together, and overturning ink pots. The family remembered the fat, spoilt small boy, but not this episode. It was probably what Joad would like to have done, moved by the resentment which he says he felt against the 'decorous regularity' of the Murray household.[16] It would have been unthinkable for any of the Murrays to have dreamed of doing any damage to the contents of the Scriptorium, nor would they have forgiven anyone who committed such an outrage on the centre of their world.

Hallowe'en was a memorable festival in which James joined, providing the model for turnip lanterns,[17] and hiding behind a bush in 'windy lene' to jump out on the children as they rode round the house on a broomstick. Guests would be taken up to the nursery to throw dragon's blood on the fire. When they had been suitably scared by the vision of a spectral figure which, manipulated by strings, rose up from behind the rocking-horse, James would finish the evening with his famous ghost stories and recitations.

Although he could be stern and was feared as well as revered by the family, James' strong sense of justice and his concern for every child made the Murrays' household a secure one in which to grow up, and they all looked back on days which seemed full of laughter.[18] A twinkle in the corner of his keen blue eyes often betrayed James' sense of fun just below the surface, and when amused his whole face beamed, every line of his normally rather rugged features reflecting his merriment. He enjoyed the sallies of wit and quick repartees of the children and he never lost his memory of his own high spirited youth, his appreciation of an innocent joke and his ability to join imaginatively in an adventure. He laughed when Wilfrid took them all in by posing as a visiting minister needing lodging for the night, and shared the excitement of exploring a sea-side cave in search, he said, of 'treasure, or kegs of gin, or bales of silk ... the White Lady who haunts it ... murderers' or murdered skeletons.'[19]

The high point of the year was the family holiday, continued on the pattern established in Mill Hill days.[20] Whatever other short breaks there might be during the year, nothing counted as a holiday unless the whole clan went right away for three weeks. Although James always took some Dictionary proofs with him, he renewed his youth, cast off his cares and turned every expedition into a joyous adventure. The years immediately following the move to Oxford in 1885 to 1889, when the Dictionary robbed him of this relaxation, were the black years. In these summers James made time for family picnics in two hired boats on the upper river, and they all waited to hear with delight the echo when he shouted 'Hoch!' as they passed under Godstow bridge: but it did not count as a family holiday, nor did James' sampling of the Welsh hills when he finished examining at Llanrwst Grammar school in 1887 and 1888.

Real family holidays were renewed in 1890 when the party at Torquay consisted of twelve children (including a friend's son), one a babe in arms and five under twelve, two adult servants, the little nursemaid and of course James and Ada. After a much delayed railway journey they reached their destination nearly eleven hours after leaving Oxford, with James still enjoying the adventure. He wrote next day:

when we arrived at length here all was dark, and we had the mysterious delight of striking a match at the door & entering a dark unknown house to explore its manifold dark passages & rooms. I

23. On the sands at Borth, North Wales.

24. James and Ada Murray at Killarney, Ireland. British Association meeting, 1908.

think we got to bed without exactly knowing where we were—
though I had the pleasure of determining by astronomical observation that our room looked west & south and that I should lie with
my head to the north.[21]

On sea-side holidays he would join in sand-building and there are
pictures of him astride a great sand-monster, big enough to hold all
the family.

In later years it was harder to gather the clan together, but there
was a red-letter year in 1895 when all were at Keswick, including
Harold and Ethelbert with their wives. The following summer and
until 1907, holidays in Wales at Criccieth, Penmaenmawr and (most
frequently) Borth, took the place of those in the Lake District. James
got to know all the Welsh mountains, but he preferred Westmorland
and was sorry that his younger children became so attached to Borth.
His belief in freedom was still too strong to allow him to insist that
they come with him, so in some years the family divided, with the
older members and their families at Keswick and the younger in
Wales. James himself on three occasions was tempted away by
Professor Robinson Ellis, who paid his expenses for the sake of his
companionship on trips to the Continent.[22] These, and a greatly
enjoyed visit to the Cape of Good Hope for the British Association
meeting there in 1905, for which the Delegates gave him £100
towards his and Ada's expenses,[23] were his only ventures across the
sea, except for a short holiday with Ada in Ireland, when he was given
his honorary degree at Dublin.

Robinson Ellis was James' closest friend in Oxford. On fine
afternoons he used to turn up in a hansom cab to take James out to the
open, high ground to the north of Oxford, known as the Plateau, now
covered with the suburban spread of Summertown and Wolvercote.
Here they would walk a little way, with the cab following behind to
pick them up when Ellis had had enough. They must have looked a
curious pair: James, tall and upright, light on his feet and still a quick
energetic walker; Ellis tall too, but moving in a shambling way, with
his head and short straggling beard thrust forward. He wore an ill-
fitting suit, shiny with age, and a top hat. He suffered from gout and
the toes of his very large boots turned up.[24] Apart from a common
interest in words, the two had very different tastes, and this was
evident when they travelled together abroad. Ellis was only interested
in classical manuscripts, he disliked night travel and early starts,

preferred towns, and found his relaxation in attending concerts. He did not mix easily with people, spoke Latin to scholars and seemed deliberate in his mis-pronunciation of French. James, on the other hand, was determined to see all there was to be seen, even if this meant uncomfortable journeys at inconvenient hours. He hankered for high hills and only tolerated music. He used every opportunity to practise his modern languages by talking to strangers and even hiring a boy to read the newspapers to him. He noticed that the women in Belgium spoke Flemish and French indiscriminately but that children in the park understood Flemish better.

Letters written to the family describing the 1904 holiday, which took them to Grenoble and Uriage-les-Bains, are typical of James in holiday mood. He rose every morning at four or five, climbed 3000 feet and came down again before breakfast. One night, when Ellis was attending a concert, he reluctantly agreed that James might be absent in order to climb the Pic de la Croix de Belledonne, a peak of 9500 feet in the French alps east of Grenoble. The ascent is usually fairly easy, taking about three hours from the mountain hut at La Pra, where James spent the night. Unfortunately freak weather for August occurred and he arrived at La Pra in snow, which was still falling at four next morning. Local people said snow would not last at that time of year, so he set off with a guide, in what proved to be the worst August storm in living memory. James was invigorated by the experience. 'It was glorious', he wrote, '... wading ankle-deep, sinking knee deep, thigh deep, waste [*sic*] deep in the loose dry powdery snow.' At the top there was no view and with a precipice on each side, he clung to the cross so as not to be blown over. Coming down, the snow was deeper, and when they reached the hut people would hardly believe they had been at the summit. 'But our appearance convinced them', James continued,

we were both completely encased with icicles like scale mail. I had a kind of woollen neckerchief with a fringe tied round my face to prevent my ears freezing, and every fringe of this had become an icicle surrounding my face like a crown of thorns. My hair behind under my cap was converted into a circle of icicles, which in the chalet began to melt & run down my neck. But my beard—oh! you should have seen my beard—you have seen Aber Falls frozen— that was nothing to my beard—frozen streams from my whiskers & moustaches flowed into the main beard & coalesced with it into one huge icicle of clear blue ice . . . They all burst into a great 'Vivat!' and ran for a looking glass . . . I did not know myself in the least . . . it was like a Frost-giant of the Edda . . . But my beard began to melt . . . and after various unsuccessful efforts to break it away, they brought a block of wood, held it under my chin, and then with a large carpenter's hammer, hammered away at my beard until they broke the clear blue ice into thousands of fragments.[25]

When he returned to Oxford Ada rushed at him crying, 'Jamie, Jamie, what have you done with your beard!' and it was never quite so long afterwards as it had been before.

Still a reddish gold when he left Mill Hill, his hair turned white before he was fifty and thinned to reveal a fine domed forehead, while the snowy beard reached halfway to his waist. Even after his adventure on Belledonne his beard was impressive and with his fine profile and tall figure, made him conspicuous in any assembly. 'Who is that old Abraham?' an undergraduate asked Oswyn when James was dining at the High Table at Exeter College. 'Abraham is my father', Oswyn replied proudly.[26]

For many scholars it is no hardship to sit indoors studying on a fine afternoon, but for James with his intense love of the open air, it required a stern discipline to hold himself to his task, seeing the spring or summer skies only through the panes of glass in the Scriptorium roof. He complained bitterly of the times when he hardly went outside the garden gate. Fortunately there were periods when the pressure was less.

When he first settled in Oxford, Furnivall advised him to spend part of the balance of the *Murray Idemnity Fund* on the purchase of a Humber tandem tricycle and a single tricycle, 'and then', he said, 'your boys could lark about with you'.[27] James followed the advice. The tricycle was kept under the stairs in the hall for use when he went round to the Press with copy, and the cumbersome tandem was in the garden shed for longer excursions. Neither was easy to ride. The tricycle became well known in the Banbury Road from its peculiar behaviour. Any sudden turn was apt to buckle one of the wheels and the machine collapsed. Undisturbed by this mishap, James would spring the wheel back into the true by hand, remount and ride on as if nothing untoward had occurred. The peculiarity of the tandem was the brake, which was worked by turning an upright handle round and round and released by turning it in the opposite direction, an

25. The Humber tandem tricycle. This was the type of machine bought by James Murray in 1885.

operation which it was difficult to perform quickly in an emergency. Very early on, before he was familiar with the countryside, James took Ada for a trial run. Unexpectedly they found themselves on the brow of the steep hill down from Elsfield. The heavy machine rapidly gathered momentum, and unable to get the brake on, they descended the hill at an alarming speed. James called 'Hold on tight love', and down they went to land, as James had done long before on his cousin's velocipede in Hawick, in a ditch by the roadside, muddy and wet but unhurt.

On another occasion James took a ride with Professor Skeat round by Eynsham. The two returned very hot and exhausted. Skeat confided to Ada that he thought James had left him to do all the work. A few minutes later James whispered to her that Walter had not put any force at all into his pedalling. Ada slipped out to the machine, suspecting what had happened, and found that the brake had been left screwed on throughout the trip.

The tricycles were fun, but the boys soon bought two-wheelers. Ethelbert, always the first to try out a mechanical invention, owned a 'kangaroo',* but no one else ventured on it. In 1896 James was attracted by Oswyn's safety cycle and with the help of his sons learnt to ride in quiet by-ways. Soon Oswyn reported that his father was becoming quite expert, could keep fairly straight and had raced three of the Girls' High School mistresses back from Summertown. James was so enthusiastic that he was getting up at sunrise to go out to Kidlington and back before breakfast. Eight or more cycles were now added to the mountain of luggage to be transported to Wales for the annual holiday, where James, riding with his beard blowing over his shoulder in the wind, was greeted by the local children with cries of 'Father Christmas!' When in Oxford James would often take a break from Dictionary work for an afternoon ride with one of the boys, Rosfrith or a grandson, and when Oswyn hired a trailer in 1903 which could be attached to a push cycle, James even pulled Ada round the country in it.

He never learnt to dismount, except by falling sideways, a manoeuvre apt to take by surprise any unwary cyclist following him too closely. Alone or with the family he always rode perilously, nearly run down on his new machine by an omnibus and a careering hansom cab in the centre of Birmingham: skidding on the tram lines returning at night from giving an address at the Cowley Congregational Chapel: scaring the milkman as he cannoned off his pony's side: arguing with the parent of a little girl with whom he collided in Holywell: falling when riding through Machynlleth carrying a parcel. Once there was a police court case, when meeting a trap driven by the local butcher in a narrow Welsh lane, James claimed he was thrown into the ditch. The butcher put himself in the wrong by striking at him with his whip, and was fined ten shillings and costs, but one wonders who was really to blame. James was delighted to be taken for a long drive by Ethelbert in an early motor car, but for himself he stuck to his cycle. A journalist described him in February 1913 on

> a day of bitter cold and splendid sunshine when Winter stood with naked sword in the streets of Oxford ... Age kept the hearth. Down the Banbury road came a picturesque exception, an almost prophetic figure, his long white beard shaking like snowflakes in the wind. His seventy-sixth winter, and he cycles still![28]

---

* The 'kangaroo' was a 'penny-farthing' type of high bicycle introduced in 1884. It had a 36 inch front wheel. See John Woodforde, *The Story of the Bicycle* (1970), p. 60 sq.

It was James' capacity to acquire and share new interests such as cycling with his children which helped to hold the family together. Over twenty years separated the oldest from the youngest child, and the seniors had left home for work and marriage before she was born: four went overseas and the eleven could easily have lost touch. That they did not was due to James. The training given to the older children at Mill Hill continued, especially the ritual of letter writing. Even if they did not correspond very often with one another, they all wrote home, and 'writing the mail-letters' was, like the twice-daily remembrance of them all in prayer, a duty which James and Ada never omitted. The replies they received were passed round the family circle, sometimes with unfortunate results if the writer had not considered that his news and views would become public property. Most followed their father's example and sent a detailed diary of all their doings: Aelfric, who was apt to leave letter writing to the last moment, was often reprimanded. His letter on arrival in South Africa was found to be 'rather jejune' and his father wrote that they were disappointed 'that it told us no more about life on ship-board, whom you got to know, what you tried at the Sports, etc . . . Kindly, tell us everything that is like to be of interest to us.' Later there was disapproval because when he mentioned wild flowers he did not give their names.[29]

It is remarkable that although Aelfric, as it seemed, could do nothing right, and was constantly reproved and exhorted to do better, yet he treasured these scolding letters from his father and brought them back from South Africa, undoubtedly retaining his affection for his stern parent. James had the gift of showing that although misdoing might call for punishment and censure, it did not influence his underlying love and concern. He could switch in a moment from rebuke to a lively account of things he had been doing and he knew what would specially interest whomever he was writing to. With Aelfric he shared an interest in botany and politics and he knew that the boy away in Africa would want news of the social life of Oxford and the titbits of local gossip. His letters to Jowett, on the other hand, added to the family news discussions of the derivations of words on which James was working at the time.

In any special crisis in their careers a son or daughter would be in James' mind all day. When Jowett went out to China as a missionary, James got out the atlas so that he could picture him at each stage and almost at each hour of his journey, while when Oswyn was worried about a promotion James wrote to him: 'The matter was never out of my head — it is not to advise but to express my deep sympathy and concern that I am writing.'[30]

The record of family successes — which was remarkable, especially in that, in contrast to so many large Victorian families, there was no weakling or ne'er-do-well amongst them — was a source of pride and rejoicing, not only for James and Ada, but by and for them all. A typical comment on an achievement was, 'All the family feel themselves taller by it.'[31] Two sons gained triple Firsts in Honour Moderations, Greats and Law: two other children First Class Honours, one in Mathematics and one in English. James took an active part in promoting their careers. Although he wished he had more money to start them in life, he spared no pains to do what he could, writing to people who might help to obtain scholarships for them, advising Harold on his applications for posts, collating manuscripts for Hilda and reading her proofs, writing frequent admonitions to Aelfric who he feared might not prosper in his profession unless he showed more diligence.

The older sons were expected to take their share of responsibility for the younger children and this duty could be burdensome. James, hard driven to complete the education of the youngest, kept pressing Aelfric as a bachelor in the Civil Service, to send regular contributions towards school or college fees. In writing a rather grudging letter of congratulation to this young man on his wedding (which James did not approve, as he felt his son's position was as yet too insecure), he remarked, 'It would have been a noble and generous thing if no brother had married, until they had seen their sisters married, or otherwise provided for! But alas! it has been otherwise.'[32]

He had firm ideas on matrimony. 'It is a very serious mistake', he told Aelfric when he was considering engagement, 'for a man to marry a woman older than himself ... a woman usually gets older so much sooner than a man that she ought if possible always to be younger than he to start with ... Mother is $8\frac{1}{2}$ years younger than I, and to all intents and purposes she is now as old, and might with advantage have been younger than she is.'[33] This remark was prompted by anxiety about Ada's health and not intended to suggest criticism. Ada was perfect, her ministrations 'angelic', 'really a queen of women, whom none of us can too highly love & reverence'.[34]

James' affection for Ada was very deep. As soon as he entered the house he would call out, 'Where's my lovey, where's my lovey?' and she would come running to attend to his wants. Without Ada with him he disliked the thought of going to give a lecture and found a social engagement only moderately enjoyable and a waste of time. Indeed, if she were not there to enter his engagements in a diary and to remind him of them, he was likely to forget them.[35] He was incurably absent-minded: once the bag of wages for the Scriptorium staff could not be found and there was a hue and cry, till Ada discovered it set down in the front garden, where James had left it when he noticed a flower needing attention on his return from the Bank.

Because he was so dependent upon her, Ada exercised a considerable influence, which on occasion strengthened James' own determination. One very hot day in July 1897, when he had been examining for the Locals in Birmingham, he collapsed in the street and was taken to hospital. 'They pulled off my coat & waistcoat', he wrote to Hilda,

> & in a trice had off my boots & socks, & were pulling at my trousers. But here I screamed 'No! No! you must not, you really must not. I must go home by the 4 o'clock train.' ... The doctor told me my temperature was over 100, nurses hung over me and implored me not to go, — but I was resolute & said I would go — not for my own sake, but for my wife's, who would be distracted if I did not arrive. They ... finally told me that I was a wilful man, and that my wife had spoiled me by letting me have my own way, and that if I went, I did it at my own risk ... So it was finally arranged that I should travel by the 7.45 train.[36]

He consulted Ada on every important decision and there are letters which have been altered and corrected by her. She had fixed ideas on certain matters. She did not, for instance, like reference to James' first wife, who was never mentioned in the family, and it was Ada who objected to Sir Herbert Warren publishing some autobiographical details which James had given to him. She disliked Maggie Scott figuring in the story and also thought the romance of James' humble birth and self education might injure their children, and that if the world knew of his limited education it might be thought that he could not be expected to do the Dictionary. 'Quite correctly', James commented, '—yet people sometimes do what they cannot be expected to do.'[37]

Although James gave Ada pride of place in his ideal picture of the family circle, in his children's eyes it was he, not their mother, who was its centre. She corresponded as regularly as James with the absent members, but it was his letters that they treasured, and few of hers survive. For the younger ones the nurse, Emma, was their mother-figure, who fed, dressed, bathed and put them to bed. They remembered Ada busy at her desk in the dining room, doing the house-keeping accounts and helping to answer James' voluminous correspondence, and when she had done with her writing, making smocks for the girls. A rare letter from her to Hilda in 1899 reveals the over-busy housewife. She described her full week. Professor and Mrs Skeat were staying in the house and she had invitations to go out with them: there were visitors to High Tea: Elsie was in the fever hospital with scarlatina and needed to be visited every day, which took two hours. Emma was utterly unfit for work, having taken to her bed on return from her holiday, and James had come back from examining at Birmingham upset by the food and the heat, while on top of all there were the preparations for the annual migration to Wales. 'I got so hopelessly behind hand', she concluded, '& heaps of things needing attention, that on Friday night I set to work after everyone had gone to bed & worked hard till 4 a.m. & then went to bed & had 3 hours sound sleep, with the satisfaction of having overtaken things again.'[38] She was quite content to take second place to James: he was her hero and had always the first claim to her affection and she was inordinately proud of him and of the family he fathered.

Although Ada and the family occupied so much of any time which James could spare from the Dictionary, his letters to his sons reveal that he also not only lived quite a full social life, but was able to keep up some of his old interests. They correct the gloomy picture of unremitting toil conveyed by the harassed letters to the Delegates and the Dictionary helpers.

Sunnyside was always full, sometimes over-full, with a constant tide of visitors. The married sons and their families were liable to arrive at holiday seasons or in a domestic crisis and James and Ada were too kind hearted to remain deaf to an appeal for help. 'Compassion ... and "As ye would that men etc.", left us with no alternative,' James explained on one occasion when they had taken in the nurse and two infants of old friends who were ill.[39] Fred Elworthy and Walter Skeat, sometimes with their wives, would come for long or short stays: foreign professors would lodge with the Murrays when they visited Oxford. The list of overseas visitors was extended when

26. The three Dictionary makers: Joseph Wright, James Murray and Walter Skeat in the garden at Sunnyside, Oxford. Before 1912.

Wilfrid obtained a post at the University of Cape Town, and Rhodes scholars from South Africa and later America and Canada became regular guests, many of them looking on Sunnyside as a second home.

In spite of not being attached to the University, James and Ada were invited to many functions and James often dined at College High Tables to meet distinguished guests.[40] Many people in Oxford knew him slightly and admired his work, and when he was seriously ill with pneumonia in 1892, Ada said they had forty or fifty callers every day inquiring after him.[41] At the same time, those who did not share his love of words found that his engrossment in his work made him somewhat of a bore, and on his part a natural shyness and a long habit of wasting no time, left him with little inclination to get to know casual acquaintances better. It was only those admitted to close friendship who discovered that his rugged appearance and sometimes biting tongue concealed a man described by Graham Bell as 'one of the kindest and gentlest men I ever met.'[42]

Apart from Professor Robinson Ellis, James' chief friend in Oxford was Joseph Wright, the editor of the *English Dialect Dictionary*. Between 1888 when he settled in Oxford and his marriage in 1896, Wright always spent Thursday evenings at Sunnyside and the two

333

scholars had a great regard for each other.[43] They had much in common: both came from humble homes and were largely self educated, and both made their reputation by books on dialect—in Wright's case the dialect of his native Yorkshire. In editing the *Dialect Dictionary*, which like the *Oxford English Dictionary* was based on collections made by voluntary readers, Wright drew on James' experience and learnt from his mistakes. He delegated more to his assistants, he never wrote a letter which he could avoid and he cut his social engagements to a minimum. He brought out the parts of his Dictionary so regularly that the subscribers said they could set their clocks by them, and he achieved what James had found impossible, the production of 700 pages a year.

In early years James spent considerable time and energy in travelling about Britain, as far afield as Blackpool, Newcastle, Glasgow, Birmingham, Leicester, Bristol and London delivering lectures on the Dictionary to help to advertise the work. He acquired a reputation as an amusing lecturer. Although he usually repeated the same lecture, with only slight changes, he found it impossible to throw off anything quickly, because he could not bear to put his name to a paper which fell short of the best he could offer. For important occasions such as the Romanes Lecture and the course for the Oxford English School he spent many hours in preparation. 'I could not *afford* to do it, even for £1000', he told his son Jowett, 'unless I could do something really good ... for I have a name to keep up, and that means work.'[44]

However busy he was, he never lost his curiosity or his keen interest in the unusual. In 1895 he wrote to the *Oxford Times* to give a minute description of a meteor-like object he had observed when walking up St Giles';[45] in 1908 he was excited by a magnificent display of the *Aurora Borealis* and took Ada up the road at twenty to eleven to see it, observing that they could read their watches by its light.[46] In 1913 when there were army manoeuvres in Blenheim Park, he walked three miles up Port Meadow with Ada to inspect an aeroplane which had landed, and next morning hurried out early to see an airship which had come down in the University Parks, which satisfied him that he now knew how flying machines worked.[47]

He also retained his early interest in politics, attended and occasionally spoke at public meetings, and was well known as a staunch Liberal. He held to the opinions he had adopted in Hawick days and now was outspoken in his condemnation of Joseph

Chamberlain and the Liberal Unionists, who he considered had put back the liberties of England more than two centuries, and were hand in hand with 'the brewer, the priest, the better and the devil'.[48] He was particularly indignant in the constitutional crisis of 1909 at the use of the House of Lords to obstruct the legislative programme of the Liberal majority in the Commons, culminating in the rejection of the Budget. After staying up till midnight at the Union to hear the results of the 1910 General Election, he began to hope for a revolution in which the aristocracy would share the fate of the French in 1790, having already said that if it came to a revolution he would not mind fighting.[49] He was of course only reflecting the very strong political divisions of his time. These were the days when the Tory Party was closely identified with the Established Church, and Non-Conformists were Liberals almost to a man. Party feeling, thus linked to religious conviction and prejudice, ran very high and 'Liberal' was as emotive a term as 'Communist' was to become later.[50]

Clearly it was James' religious views which determined his political allegiances. His son Wilfrid thought his father became more intolerant with years, Harold that he became less so: the truth was that his views changed very little, but that when he had pen in hand he was always apt to be carried away and so appeared more bigoted than he was in practice, when his naturally kindly nature kept his tongue under control.

One of his fixations was that the Established Church was inevitably tainted because of its partnership with worldly powers. He saw no place for a priestly hierarchy and abominated what he regarded as superstitious practices designed to deceive the believer. It was a blow to him when his eldest son married the daughter of a minister of the Church of England, with a Bishop officiating, but still more of a grief when the wayward Aelfric, on whose direction he had spent so much trouble, announced that he was not only joining the Church of England but taking Orders. 'I myself abhor the priest and all his claims', James wrote to Aelfric;

> in my reading of history, he has been the persistent enemy of humanity, the pretender who takes advantage of man's deepest spiritual emotions to trade upon them for his own advantage and exaltation. Far be it from me to say that every priest is of this character, but it has been historically & indeed naturally the character of priest craft in all ages and all systems.

335

Yet, strongly as he felt, even as he wrote, his natural affection for his son was leading him to find a way out. The Church in South Africa where Aelfric would serve had perhaps not the same political position as in England, and Aelfric might prove to be one of the exceptions who might serve without worldly ambition. Provided it did not lead to abuse, James was not opposed to the varying practice of the different denominations and in the same letter he said '... I have considered that if all these people were allowed voluntarily & without any state fear or favour to work their own systems, that we should probably then carry out most fully God's own plan.'[51] Where others might have allowed prejudice to split the family, James never lost his overriding need to remain the loving and just father-figure.

To some extent he was forced to modify his more extreme views by finding they did not fit the facts of his experience. Certainly as he advanced into the twentieth century he changed his philosophy from the unbounded optimism of his youth. The industrial revolution, the railway age and the great advances in knowledge now seemed to be leading less directly to an increasingly perfect world. By 1886 he was becoming troubled. The difficulties he experienced in that year in placing his son Ethelbert brought home to him that there were too many candidates for most sorts of work.

In earlier days when such congestion happened, wars, famines, & pestilence stepped in, & at the expense of those who fell made it more tolerable for the survivors [he wrote to Hucks Gibbs]. But all the efforts of Christianity have been devoted to the extinction of these 'scourges'—when the system of things is 'perfect' they will be entirely eliminated and what *will* become of unthinned humanity?[52]

In old age James was disillusioned and disappointed by events which showed a retrograde tendency. In 1911 the war in China and industrial unrest at home made him feel inclined to despair of the world, and the outbreak of the 1914–18 war seemed to him 'a lamentable outcome of centuries of Christ's teaching'. But he was not permanently depressed and remained confident that everything had its place in the divine plan. 'One can only hope', he wrote once when worried by events, 'that God has allowed it for good & strive to take it with faith & patience, looking to a "better country".'[53] Public and personal disasters were a challenge to show that the prayer 'Thy will be done' is really sincere.[54]

Belief in the efficacy of prayer was fundamental to him, and, as has been seen, he had throughout his life a sense of a divine force directing not only himself but the whole family. Writing to Hilda on her appointment to a lectureship at Girton College, he said 'We are all *exceedingly* glad; for we think we see the leading of Providence in it and the path of duty ... Circumstances have driven me, generally against my will or sentiment, and they will do the same with you.'[55] 'Few people', he told a son, 'can have had experience of so much guidance, so much actual pushing me forward and into positions of honour as I have had.'[56] They were all, he felt 'the favoured children of God' and this he attributed to the accumulated and continuous influence of the prayers of two generations of God-fearing Scottish ancestors.[57]

This belief was the basis of his philosophy. They could not, he was convinced, depend upon the continuance of this exceptional favour unless they responded by striving to perfect their natural gifts in order to use them in the service of God and man, and for the performance of the tasks to which they were called. The whole object of life was this dutiful response. His favourite text was a saying of Charles Kingsley, which hung in his bedroom, 'Have thy tools ready, God will find thee work.'[58]

Although James was human enough, as we have seen, to like his good work to be appreciated, he was lacking in ambition. He never sought friendship with influential people for the sake of possible personal advancement, he never undertook tasks because they would bring him into the public eye. His strong influence gave all his children this quality of dutifulness. His sons all did well in their chosen fields, but yet did not climb to the heights which would have been possible to them had they set themselves that aim. An obituary of Oswyn, who became Permanent Secretary to the Admiralty, could be a description of his father: 'He ... never spared himself ... His work was a striking example of the proverb that what is worth doing is worth doing well ... He was entirely unworldly, unassuming, and for himself unambitious.'[59]

James' unworldliness was linked to his attitude to money, which seems strange to the twentieth century but was not uncommon in men of his generation. Probably no professional man today would hesitate for a moment in claiming from his employer any expenses connected with his work, nor would he continue for long in a post with a salary below that which he found he could afford to live on, if he could remedy the situation. With James Murray it was different. He would have made a sharp distinction between the business man whose job it is to manipulate his trade so as to create and add to his fortune, and the professional man whose work is a vocation, something he offers in the service of his fellows and to the glory of God. Far from claiming all that was due, he wished to give generously and felt it an obligation to manage on his basic salary: it was extremely distasteful to him to have to confess to what he regarded almost as a failure in good housekeeping and to ask for more. He did not expect to become a rich man and only considered that a lifetime of conscientious work should have put him in a position to educate his children, start them in their careers and provide for their welfare without getting into debt. This attitude explains his failure to insist on a business-like contract with the Delegates of the Press and the sense of martyrdom that resulted.

Yet if the family suffered financially from his commitment to work which was poorly paid in comparison with other appointments he might have obtained, he was wrong in feeling that the Dictionary had prevented him from being as good a father as he would have wished. Just as his own character had been moulded by the influence of his parents, so he was a force in the lives of his children and they, and even their children, reflected his convictions and characteristics. It could even be argued that preoccupation with the Dictionary may have made James a better parent, since without it he might have dominated the family too much.

Again and again as one reviews James Murray's activities, opinions and reactions in his later years one is reminded of him at earlier stages in his career. His life was all of a piece, and varied as were his interests, they can all be traced back to his childhood and youth: in the boy at Denholm and the young man at Hawick one sees his character already formed. The seeds of all his future concerns were sown then. They developed from the toughness of his Scottish physique and his quite outstanding stamina producing his unbounded energy, which he retained till old age. He never lost his enthusiasm, and his resilience was hardly lessened with years—he could still renew his youthfulness overnight, as it were, in escaping from Mill Hill or Oxford to the Malvern Hills, to battle in the snow storm on Belledonne or to scale Cader in his seventies, still a boy at heart in his sense of fun and enjoyment of family pranks. These were all part of his joyous response to life, which gave him also his wide curiosity about all he saw and heard around him, his life-long interest in astronomy and the weather, in botany, geology, archaeology, and above all in words. Only this continual feeling of wonder, adventure and delight could have sustained him through the tedious advance, year after year, among the words of the English language, still finding a fresh excitement in tracing the long history of some little word like *put*.

His enchantment with the world around him also made him a born teacher: he could not avoid the compelling desire to communicate his discoveries and the pleasure of them to others. The toddler at once wanting to show his baby brother his letters, the schoolboy drawing maps on the house wall to teach his brothers geography, or troubling their tongues with strange-sounding words, the inspiring schoolmaster at Hawick and Mill Hill, the lexicographer who, busy as he might be, could not resist writing a long letter to enlighten some inquirer or to put some ignoramus straight, the editor who lectured his collaborator on how to do his work better—the teacher in him was never far below the surface. Less evident, but always there too, was the young journalist pushing his flowery articles through the letter-box of the *Hawick Advertiser*. His prose became polished and refined with the years, but his enjoyment in writing was always there in the long, fluent letters to his family and friends and strangers—letters which make such good reading because they are so vibrant with the energy of the man. The writer and reciter of *Macgregor* and the teller of ghost stories was also always present in his love of drama—not the drama of the theatre, but the drama of his own life. He enjoyed a crisis and he enjoyed even more writing it up as a good story. Difficult as the work for the Dictionary was and relentless as was the pressure it exerted on him, it certainly lost nothing in the telling, and between the lines which speak of despair and toil one senses the exhilaration of the fell walker, pitting his strength against the wind on a steep slope. Anyone driving himself forward with so much expenditure of energy must be subject to periods of exhaustion and consequent depression, but with James Murray their duration was seldom long and even his most lasting disappointments and anxieties—the failure of Oxford to give him academic recognition, the financial difficulties and the actions of the unsympathetic Mr Gell—were all made tolerable again by the story teller turning them into a tale of martyrdom.

James Murray's life is a reminder that equality of opportunity, which the twentieth century claims as its gift to the next generation, existed in a different form in the nineteenth century. The gifted lad, however much handicapped by the circumstances of his birth, could educate himself and rise high in the professional class. James Murray, Henry Bradley, and Joseph Wright are all examples of this. In an age when paper qualifications, however useful, were not yet the essential passport to advancement which they have now become, perhaps in some ways the opportunities were greater than today. James could have done well in any subject and at any task to which he applied himself: he could for example have become an outstanding minister, headmaster or professor. It was only by his accidental, or, as he would have said, providential involvement in the Dictionary, a work of national and international importance, that he achieved fame. But it was also only because of his unique qualities that the Dictionary was produced. No one else amongst his contemporaries could have edited it: Furnivall had already tried and failed; the work was at a standstill when James took it on and Furnivall had too many interests and was too volatile to show the persistence necessary to plan the framework and settle all the technical points. Henry Nicol died a few years after James began work. Henry Sweet would have quarrelled with his helpers and with the Press very quickly. Henry Bradley would not have had the physical strength. Walter Skeat would have produced a work of very inferior quality—a first attempt rather than a definitive dictionary.

Further, the Dictionary had to be produced at that point in time if at all. As Skeat once said, it could not have been compiled earlier because it was only after the publication of many of the earlier texts through Furnivall's Early English Text Society that the historical treatment of words became possible.[60] It would have been much more difficult to compile later, because of the enormous multiplication of printed matter and the invention of so many new words in the twentieth century. Nor was it mere chance that the project of a *New English Dictionary* was conceived in the reign of Queen Victoria. It is one of a number of monumental undertakings, chief among them the ninth edition of the *Encyclopaedia Britannica*, the *Dictionary of National Biography*, and the *Victoria County History*, which belong to this period of confidence in national greatness, of a belief in popular education and a disinterested love of learning.

James Murray, with his tough constitution, his hope for the world, his strong sense of duty and service, his wide general knowledge, was the right man at the right time. The successful undertaking of the Dictionary required someone who could say, as James said with all sincerity:

I think it was God's will. In times of faith, I am sure of it. I look back & see that every step of my life has been as it were imposed upon me—not a thing of choice; and that the whole training of my life with its multifarious & irregular incursions into nearly every science & many arts, seems to have had the express purpose of fitting me to do this Dictionary ... So I work on with a firm belief (at most times) that I am doing what God has fitted me for, & so made my duty; & a hope that He will strengthen me to see the end of it ... But I am only an instrument, only the means that He has provided, & there is no credit due to me, except that of trying to do my duty; Deo soli gloria.[61]

Appendix I

LETTER from Henry Sweet on behalf of the Philological Society, to Professor Price, Secretary to the Delegates of the Oxford University Press 20 April 1877. This document was the basis for the agreement made in March 1879 with the Society and with James A. H. Murray as Editor, for the publication of the Dictionary. It was the source of many of the misconceptions and consequent problems which subsequently occurred. (I quote from a copy made by Henry or George Sweet.)

[Dear Professor Price]

Hearing (through Mr Macmillan) that the Delegates were not undisposed to take up the English Dictionary of the Philological Society, I have been discussing the question with the members of the special committee (of which I am one) appointed by the Society to watch over its interests in any negotiations about publishing the dictionary, and they have commissioned me to open negociations with the Delegates on the basis of terms which our Committee consider reasonable. A rough sketch of these terms, together with some preliminary remarks on the nature of the dictionary and its prospects of success will be found on the annexed sheets. Will you kindly bring these details before the Delegates at their next meeting? I hope the Delegates may be induced to consider the whole question maturely before returning any decided answer. If once convinced of the feasibility of the undertaking, they will, I think, allow the reasonableness of the proposed terms, agreed on by us after hearing the best trade and legal advice.

The last clause in the terms was added against my wish in deference to the opinion of the other members of the committee, who did not like the Society to relinquish any future chance of getting the large dictionary done. I am certain that such a work will never be undertaken.

If the Delegates think fit, it will be easy to set up a specimen page of the proposed dictionary.

Hoping to hear from you soon
I remain dear Sir
Yours very truly
Henry Sweet

Preliminary Remarks

It must be borne in mind that in asking the Delegates of the Clarendon Press to undertake the publication of the English Dictionary of the Philological Society, we are not asking them to subsidize an unremunerative undertaking, but are rather offering them a share in what promises to be a very safe and remunerative one. We contribute the material—the result of 19 years' work—together with the reputation of our Society, and agree to provide an Editor and to exercise a general supervision of his work—in short to make ourselves responsible for the scientific and literary side of the undertaking. We ask the Delegates to advance the capital required for the Editor's salary and the other necessary expenses, & to undertake the business arrangements generally.

The state of the material is this. The workers for the Dictionary had different books assigned to them, from which they made extracts on separate slips of paper. These slips were all thrown together, and sorted under each separate word. 'Subeditors' were appointed, and to each was assigned a single letter, together with the task of working up all the words beginning with that letter into a shape for publication. About half the alphabet has been dealt with in this way, the other half consisting of sorted slips. The mass of material is very great. To utilize it fully a dictionary of about 18,000 quarto pages would be required, and, indeed, it is only on such a scale as this that a thoroughly full and satisfactory work on the plan contemplated by the Society could be produced. The dictionary of 6400 pp. which we now propose must be considered as an abridgment of the one originally contemplated.

Our reasons for believing that the undertaking will prove safe and remunerative are the following:

343

The great advance of Philology of late years has completely changed the conditions of a good dictionary. What is now required is fullness of citations and historical method, or, in other words, *a full number of citations from every period of the language arranged so as to exhibit the history of each word*. It is also requisite that every department, whether etymology or pronunciation etc., must be treated according to the latest results of linguistic science. But the essential groundwork is a full body of citations. Whatever may be the character of the editing, these will always retain their value, and their collection, it may safely be said, constitutes half of the whole undertaking.

Practical proof is afforded by the success of Littré's French dictionary,—due entirely to its fullness of citations and its historical and scientific character. Upwards of 40,000 copies have been sold of this work, published in 4 large quarto vols of about 1000 pp. each, at £4 the set.

No such dictionary exists of the English language. The most popular dictionary, that of Webster, has no historical or scientific value, and is almost entirely without quotations. Our proposed dictionary has, therefore, the field entirely to itself, and its fullness of material gives it many years' start of any possible rival. We feel confident that its intrinsic value, together with the prestige of our Society and of the University and the reputation of the proposed editor (Dr J. A. H. Murray) would at once make it generally adopted in Great Britain and its colonies and dependencies, and in the United States, and, indeed in the civilized world generally. Still more extensive sales would be commanded by the various abridgments.

We propose that the returns should be applied first in repaying the Delegates their advances with interest thereon, and then that the net profits should be divided equally between the Delegates and the Society (the Society paying part of their profits to the editor). We consider that the disadvantage of the Delegates having to advance capital is fully compensated by the value of the material for whose collection and partial casting into shape they incur no expense whatever, & the absence of risk and certainty of large returns in the future.

The whole work of collection and half of that of editing has been done without remuneration by the co-operation of a large number of members of the Society, & the only reward these workers look forward to is that of seeing the Society reap the fair reward of its labours in profits which will be applied solely to the advancement of philology & literature—in fact, to aims common to ourselves and to the University itself. We should also be quite willing to print at the University press any publications to which our dictionary profits may be applied.

Terms suggested as the basis of an Agreement

1. The materials in the possession of the Society and the copyright of all dictionaries, abridgments etc. to be founded on them will be made over to the Delegates.

2. The first dictionary will consist of 6400 quarto pages (like Webster's) in four volumes—to be published as the work proceeds in 5s. or 10s. parts. Ultimately, if the Delegates think fit a larger dictionary to be prepared.

3. The Delegates to pay all expenses in the first instance and get them back out of the gross receipts. The expenses will include a sum of £650 a year for 10 years to the Editor who will pay his own assistants. The Delegates to provide also remuneration to such experts as they may think fit to engage for revision of the proofs with reference to scientific and technical words—also a small payment to an American Editor (say Prof. Whitney) whose contributions in Americanisms and Etymology would justify the use of his name on the title page as one of the Editors and so (probably) protect the copyright in the United States.

4. £1950, part of the whole £6500, to be paid to the Editor in the course of three years by quarterly instalments of £162.10s. and the remaining £4550 by payments of 20s. for each page returned for press. Interest at 5 per cent on those advances to be reckoned as expenses.

5. Profits from whatever source to be equally divided between the Delegates and the Society. The latter will out of their share retain £3250 (one half of the sum paid to Editor—to be regarded as an advance of his share of profits) and then divide the remainder of their share with him in a proportion to be agreed upon.

6. Editor to be Dr Murray. Agreement with him to be terminable by Delegates, if he does not deliver ready for press the MS. down to E inclusive within 3 years, down to O inclusive within 6 years, and to the end within 9 years from date of contract.

7. Appointment of a new Editor to be agreed upon or settled by arbitration. New editor to have payment and share of profits in proportion to the work remaining to be done on the scale of the agreement with Dr Murray.

8. Provision for arbitration.

9. After 10 years from the publication of the 4 vols. dictionary the Society may use the materials for the preparation on their own account of a dictionary not less than twice the size, if the Delegates decline to undertake it.

Appendix II

On the following four pages is reproduced a facsimile of the instructions drawn up by Dr Murray in 1879 for the voluntary readers for the Dictionary.

DIRECTIONS TO READERS FOR THE DICTIONARY.

1. Write on a half-sheet of note-paper in accordance with the following models.

2. Give date of your book (if you can), author, title (short); give an *exact reference*, such as seems to you to be the best to enable any one to verify your quotation.

3. In *poetry*, as a rule, quote by *name* of piece, *Book, Canto*, and *Stanza*, or *line*; or in a play by *Act, Scene, line*. These references will serve for all editions.

4. In *prose* quote by *Vol., Book, Chap., Section*, and *page* (as far as the work is so divided—most books have *chapters*, and all have *pages*), and *name the edition* if not the first: thus

      1849. J. S. MILL, *Logic*, Bk. III. ch. xiv. § 35. p. 17 (ed. 1856).

*5. Make a quotation for *every* word that strikes you as rare, obsolete, old-fashioned, new, peculiar, or used in a peculiar way.

6. Take special note of passages which show or imply that a word is either new and tentative, or needing explanation as obsolete or archaic, and which thus help to fix the date of its introduction or disuse.

*7. Make *as many* quotations *as convenient to you* for ordinary words, when these are used significantly, and help by the context to explain their own meaning, or show their use.

8. Carefully preserve the spelling, capitals, etc., *underlining nothing but what is in italics* in the original.

9. It is not necessary to quote a full sentence; but the quotation must be sufficient to show the meaning, or use, and to make connected sense.

10. Put the *word* as a catchword at the left-hand upper corner, in its ordinary spelling and simplest grammatical form (as infinitive of the verb), adding the spelling in your quotation (if this differs much); also part of speech, and short definition, if convenient.

11. If convenient, sort your slips alphabetically before sending them in, and send with them the full title of your book, and your own name and address.

12. For books of any extent, Dr. Murray will be glad to supply slips having date, author, title, &c. ready filled in, on receiving a model slip giving all the particulars to be printed. (See the following specimens, and the example after No. 4, above.)

ADDITIONAL NOTES.

If Readers will send a note of their postages, Dr. Murray will be glad to repay them in stamps. In sending packets of slips by Book-post, care should be taken to comply with the Post Office regulations, which forbid the fastening of the cover to the contents by gum, or even by the projecting edge of the stamp. In consequence of the transgression of these rules, the Editor has had to pay double letter postage on many packets already paid by Book-post, making an unpleasant amount for fines weekly. *String* may be, and ought to be, used to secure the packets.

Direction 7 seems to have puzzled some Readers; one anxiously asked if *the*, for instance, was to be recorded *every time it occurred*; another disregarded this Direction altogether, and wrote to say that she had carefully gone through her book (750 pages) without finding a single word to extract; she would like therefore to return it and examine another in which there might be some rare words! If Readers will kindly remember that the Dictionary is to contain *all* English words ordinary and extraordinary, that it is to give, if possible, one quotation in each century for every sense or construction of every word, and that it is these quotations that we ask them to supply by their reading, they will at once see why we ask them to give us, not only all the *extraordinary* words or constructions in their books, but also as many *good, apt, pithy* quotations for ordinary words as their time and patience permit. The quotations for common words must come from *some* books; they ought to come from *all* books; and this can be realised only by each Reader sending some. The only difference is, that as quotations for *rare* words and rare uses of words are difficult to get, they ought to be seized at once, wherever they occur, and whether good or bad, for they may be the only ones; whereas quotations for common words in their common sense and construction need only be made when they are *good*, that is when the Reader can say, 'This is a capital quotation for, say, *heaven*, or *half*, or *hug*, or *handful*; it illustrates the meaning or use of the word; it is a suitable instance for the Dictionary.' Other things being equal, also, the shortest quotations, provided they are complete, are the best.

Rhinoceros, n. (*not yet naturalized*)

1616. PURCHAS, *Pilgrimage; Descr. India* (ed. 1864), 2.

In Bengala are found great numbers of Abadas or Rhinocerotes,
whose horne (growing up from his snowt)   *   *   is good
against poyson.

Diplomatist, n.

1860. J. L. MOTLEY, *United Netherlands* (ed. 1868), I. ii. 24.

If diplomatic adroitness consists mainly in the power to deceive, never were more adroit diplomatists than those of the sixteenth century.

Abbreviations Used in Notes

AAM	Ada Agnes Murray
AECRM	Aelfric C. R. Murray. Letters from JAHM in possession of his daughter, Mrs John Manning.
AHJM	A. H. Jowett Murray. Letters in his possession from JAHM.
AHJM Memoirs	Unpublished Recollections of Childhood, written in Internment Camp, Shanghai, 1943–5, completed in 1968–9. In his possession.
AJE	Alexander J. Ellis.
AMcm	Alexander Macmillan.
BJ	Professor Benjamin Jowett.
BP	Professor Bartholomew Price.
CC	Charles Cannan.
CED	C. E. Doble.
Clarendon Press Incoming Letters	OUP Unindexed files, Jordan Hill, Oxford.
COM	Charles O. Murray.
COM Reminiscences	MP Unpublished Early Reminiscences of Denholm (typescript copy).
CTO	Charles Talbot Onions.
DNB	*Dictionary of National Biography*
EA	Professor Edward Arber.
Edgar	James Edgar, *Hawick in the Early Sixties* (Hawick, 1913).

EETS	Early English Text Society.
FE	Frederick Elworthy.
FH	Dr Fitzedward Hall.
FJF	Dr Frederick J. Furnivall.
Furnivall Papers	Unindexed papers of Dr F. J. Furnivall. Manuscript Library, King's College, London.
G	Guildhall Library London, Henry Hucks Gibbs Correspondence. Letters were bound in volumes and annotated by Hucks Gibbs. They are usually numbered by leaves, but the references here are given always to the first page of each letter.
GFT	George F. Timpson, *Sir James A. H. Murray. A Self Portrait* (Gloucester, 1957). A transcript of an autobiographical letter to Lord Bryce, 15 Dec. 03. From the Bryce Papers, Bodleian Library, Oxford. There is also a draft in MP.
GMcm	George Macmillan.
HA	*Hawick Advertiser* (till 1 Sept. 1855 *The Hawick Monthly Advertiser*).
HAS	Hawick Archaeological Society.
HAST	*Hawick Archaeological Society Transactions*, 1863 onwards. From 1856–62 papers read at meetings were fully recorded in the Minute books of the Society (now in possession of the Secretary) and published or summarised in the *Hawick Advertiser*.
Hawick	*The History of Hawick from 1832* (Hawick, 1902).
HB	Dr Henry Bradley.
HG	Henry Hucks Gibbs, created Baron Aldenham, 1896.
HJRM	Harold J. R. Murray.
HJRM Biography	Life of James A. H. Murray by HJRM. Typescript in possession of K. M. E. Murray.
HMRM	Hilda M. R. Murray.
HN	Henry Nicol.

HS	Henry Sweet.
HW	Sir Herbert Warren.
HW Notes	MP Sir Herbert Warren's Notes on the Life of James A. H. Murray (typescript copy). The notes were taken down by Sir Herbert in interviews with JAHM and used by him for his obituary of JAHM. *The Times*, 27 July 15.
JAHM	James A. H. Murray.
JAHM Antiquarian Ramble	MP JAHM, 'An Antiquarian Ramble by Eildon Hills and the Rink', Paper read to HAS in 1859 (ms.).
JAHM Burgess Speech	MP JAHM notes for speech on conferment of the Freedom of Hawick, 18 Sept. 06.
JAHM *Dialect*	JAHM, *The Dialect of the Southern Counties of Scotland, its Pronunciation, Grammar and Historical Relations* (Published for the Philological Society, London and Berlin, 1873).
JAHM Peckham address	MP JAHM, a talk given in Peckham, about 1866 (ms.).
JAHM Sermons	JAHM Sermons, written mainly for Mill Hill School (ms.). In possession of Mrs Manning.
JAHM Up the Slitrig	MP JAHM, 'Up the Slitrig and Down the Liddell', Paper read to the HAS, 4 June 61 (cutting from the *Border Advertiser*, 14 June 61).
JAHM Visit to Ruberslaw	MP Annotated cutting from *HA*, 3 Feb. 51.
James	Norman G. Brett James, *The History of Mill Hill School 1807–1907* (London, n.d.).
JRM	J. R. Magrath.
Lady M	Lady (Oswyn) Murray, *The Making of a Civil Servant. Sir Oswyn Murray, G.C.B., Secretary of the Admiralty 1917–1936* (London, 1940).
LG	Philip Lyttelton Gell.
LLB	H.I.H. Prince Louis-Lucien Bonaparte.

MP	Murray Papers, in possession of K. M. E. Murray.
MP Doc.	Murray Papers. Correspondence and Minutes Privately Printed by Order of the Board for the Delegates of the Press, 24 Apr. 96.
MP Gurney Notes	T. Gurney, 'Dr. Murray and Sunnyside'. Unpublished Recollections given to HJRM.
MxM	Professor the Right Hon. Frederick Max Müller.
N & Q	*Notes & Queries.*
OARM	Oswyn A. R. Murray.
OD	Unpublished Order Books of the Delegates of the Clarendon Press. 1853–81, 1881–92, 1892–8, 1898–1904, 1904–13, 1913–24.
OED	*The Oxford English Dictionary.*
OUP	Archives of the Oxford University Press at the Oxford English Dictionary Annexe. Oxford.
Personal Record	*Frederick James Furnivall, A Volume of Personal Record* (Oxford, 1911).
PS	The Philological Society, London.
PSCM	The Philological Society Council Minute Book (In possession of the Society).
PSOM	The Philological Society Ordinary Meetings Minute Book (In possession of the Society).
PST	*Philological Society Transactions.*
RE	Professor Robinson Ellis.
RFW	Dr Richard F. Weymouth.
VG	Vicary Gibbs.
WAC	Professor William A. Craigie.
WE	Sir Walter Elliot.
WGRM	Wilfrid G. R. Murray, *Murray the Dictionary Maker. A Brief Account of Sir James A. H. Murray* (Privately Printed. Cape Town, 1943).
WJ	Dr William Jack.
WS	Professor Walter W. Skeat.

Notes

Notes to Prologue

1. GFT, p. 10.
2. MP JAHM to unnamed correspondent, 20 Apr. 86.
3. MP JAHM to HW, 19 Jan. 11 (draft). He here repeats his repugnance to a biography which would 'do away with the privacy of personal & domestic affairs'.

Notes to Chapter I

1. MP JAHM, Peckham address [1866].
2. MP JAHM, *Historical Sketch of Denholm*. Read at the Soirée and Presentation to James Douglas Esq. of Cavers, at Denholm, on the 21st December, privately printed (1863); Sir Walter Elliot, 'Denholm and its Vicinity', *Berwickshire Naturalists' Club* (1863–8), pp. 307–25.
3. For information about Thomas Murray and Mary Scott and their ancestry I am indebted to the genealogy traced by my father, HJRM. Details about Denholm and the Murray family's life there are from MP COM, Reminiscences, and HW, Notes.
4. J. W. Turnbull, 'Denholm and Its Memories', *HAST* (1938), p. 62 sq. and Elliot, *loc. cit.*
5. The plaque was placed there in 1971 by the Feuars' Association, the Hawick Archaeological Society and the Young Callants.
6. T. C. Smout, *A History of the Scottish People* (1969), p. 39.
7. *HA*, 15 May 58.
8. Smout, *op. cit.*, p. 63 sq. For the Douglas family see JAHM, 'Hist. and Antiquities of Cavers', *HAST* (1863), p. 14 sq. (Reprinted *HAST*, 1913, p. 30 sq.), and 'Notices of Upper Teviotdale during the Covenanting Times', *ibid.* (1864), p. 3 sq.

9. MP JAHM, Peckham address.
10. JAHM to AECRM, 14 Dec. 06.
11. Smout, *op. cit.*, pp. 73, 87 sq., 96–7.
12. MP JAHM to Sir Richard Tangye, 22/29 Sept. 95 (copy).
13. GFT, pp. 10–11.
14. MP *Hawick News Letter for August 1846*. Extracts from the *Border Watch*.
15. JAHM, 'The Roar of Guns', *N & Q*, 11th Ser., viii (18 Oct. 13), 310–11.
16. MP JAHM, Peckham address and 'Up the Slitrig'.
17. MP JAHM (under pseudonym of Chrysanthemum Leucanthenum), 'A glimpse of the wild flowers of the month'. (Cutting from *HA*, 7 July 55.)
18. JAHM, 'Hist. of Cavers', *loc. cit.*, and MP HW, Notes.
19. For Leyden's life see Dr John Leyden, *Poems and Ballads* with a memoir of the author by Sir Walter Scott Bart., and supplement by Robert White, Kelso (1858), also James Robson, *The Churches and Churchyards of Teviotdale*, Hawick (1895), p. 50 sq.
20. JAHM to AECRM, 2 Feb. 07.
21. MP COM, Reminiscences and A. D. Murray, 'The School and its Teacher', A sketch written for the *Bouquet* (typescript copy).
22. MP JAHM (under pseudonym of Surgere Tento), 'A visit to Ruberslaw'. (Cutting from *HA*, 3 Feb. 55 with ms. notes.)
23. MP COM, Reminiscences.
24. MP T. Oliver to JAHM, 16 June 80.
25. Elliot, *loc. cit.*, p. 16 sq. James Duncan was another link with Leyden: his father taught Leyden Latin.
26. *HAST* Nine papers (1863–7), also reprinted in *HA*.

27. Now in the British Museum of Natural History.
28. JAHM, *Dialect*, p. 161 n. 2.
29. J. M. Turnbull, 'Denholm and Its Memories', *loc. cit.*, p. 69; *Hawick*, p. 24 sq.
30. MP William Sanderson to JAHM, 13, 21 Aug. 07. Effie Dickinson to JAHM, 8 Jan. 07.
31. MP JAHM to Sir R. Tangye, 22/29 Sept. 95.
32. MP JAHM, 'A visit to Ruberslaw' and 'Notices of Upper Teviotdale', *loc. cit.*, p. 8.
33. JAHM, 'Hist. of Cavers', *loc. cit.*, pp. 15–16.
34. The Hazel Dog was born only in 1715 and could not have been the hero of the flight: his father was already settled in Rulewater in 1712 and the flight, if it took place, was probably in 1645 when Lothian's Border Regiment fled south after the battle of Aukdean.
35. JAHM, 'Supplementary Reminiscences of John Scott', *HAST* (1908), pp. 71–2.
36. Quoted by HJRM, Biography.
37. *HA*, 17 Nov. 60, Town Council Proceedings. MP JAHM, Burgess speech.
38. They inherited this trait from their maternal grandfather, Charles Scott, and it passed to two of James' grandsons through his daughters.
39. It may have counted for something that the former Rector of the school, who died the previous year, was another James Murray, a distant kinsman descended from John, brother of Andrew, the Hazel Dog.

Notes to Chapter II

1. MP JAHM, Burgess speech.
2. W. N. Kennedy and Alex Michie, 'Hawick Common Riding', *HAST* (1866), p. 8 sq. For the early history of Hawick see Robert Murray, *History of Hawick from Earliest Times to 1832*, Hawick (1901).
3. MP JAHM, Journal 1866. (Typescript copy.)
4. Information on the conditions in Hawick is found in the files of *HA*, esp. 3 Jan. (housing), 12 Jan. (sanitation), 22 Aug. (lighting), 14 Nov. (cholera scare) 57; 22 May 58 (paving); 27 Oct. 60 (housing).
5. Edgar, pp. 4–5 and 66 sq. *HA*, 19 May 60; 27 Apr. 61.
6. *Border Advertiser*, 5 Oct. 55. *HA*, 18 Dec. 58.
7. *Hawick*, p. 65 sq.
8. Examinations of the Grammar School. *HA*, 5 May 55; 12 Apr. 56; 11 Apr. 57.

9. MP Recollections of former pupils collected by HJRM.
10. *HA*, 26 Sept. 63. This was the highest degree which the Institute could award for attainments in scholarship and success in practical teaching.
11. *HA*, 12 Sept. 57.
12. MP Printed card announcing classes, 12 Oct. 61. *HA*, 26 Oct. 61; 24 Oct. 63.
13. Examinations of the Academy. *HA*, 27 Feb., 31 July 58; 1 Aug. 63.
14. MP M. Melrose McEwen, 'Childhood recollections of Sir James Murray' (1923).
15. MP Sir Thomas Hunter, Town Clerk of Edinburgh, to AAM, 4 Aug. 15.
16. MP JAHM, Burgess speech.
17. MP Examples of material used in connection with the school.
18. MP Andrew Waugh, 'A few reminiscences of the School and Schoolmaster' (1922).
19. Examination of the Academy, *HA*, 30 July 59.
20. GFT, pp. 11–12.
21. MP JAHM, answer to a reviewer of *OED*, Part Crouchmas-Czech (undated draft, 93 or 4).
22. *HA*, 21 June 56.
23. JAHM, Sermons. Job xxii 21.
24. GFT, p. 12.
25. MP Archibald Geikie to JAHM, 27 Oct. 62.
26. GFT, p. 13.
27. MP JAHM, Catalogue of Books to end of 1856.
28. MP M. M. McEwen, 'Childhood Recollections', and A. Waugh, 'Reminiscences'.
29. JAHM to AECRM, 2 Feb. 07.
30. MP Adam Scott to JAHM, 25 Dec. 56.
31. MP COM, 'Reminiscences'.
32. *HA*, 5 July 58.
33. *HA*, 3 Feb. 55; Supplement to *HA*, 15 Sept. 55. MP JAHM notes on cutting from *HA*, 3 Feb. 55.
34. *HA*, 2 Dec. 54.
35. MP JAHM, Burgess speech, cf. *HA*, 29 Sept. 55.
36. *HA*, 3 Sept. 64.
37. On completing his apprenticeship in 1862 at the age of twenty-two, Alexander became Editor of the *Peebles Advertiser*, later of the *Fife Journal*, the *Dumfries Courier*, and finally from 1870 of the *Newcastle Daily Journal*. He died in 1907.
38. MP J. H. Rutherford to JAHM, 29 Aug. 96.
39. MP COM, 'Reminiscences'. Charles learned lithography at the Edinburgh

School of Design and studied at the Royal Scottish Academy. He took up wood engraving, became a book illustrator, and was on the staff of *Punch and Judy*. Later, turning to etching, he was a founder member of the Royal Society of Painter Etchers. He died in 1923.

40. MP C. T. Onions to HJRM, 3 Mar. 26.
41. *HA*, 7 July 60.
42. *HA*, 5 Jan. 56; 12 Jan., 24 Jan. 57; 9 Jan. 58.
43. *HA*, 3 Jan. 57. For Soirées in general see *Hawick*, pp. 31–2.
44. *HA*, 18 Dec. 58.
45. MP JAHM, 'Archaeology. Its Aims and Results'. Paper read to HAS, *HA*, 5 July 58.
46. *HA*, 10 Nov. 60.
47. MP JAHM, untitled lecture.
48. GFT, p. 13.
49. *Hawick*, p. 2 sq.
50. *HA*, 20 Feb. 58.
51. *HA*, 2 May 57; 30 Apr., 14 May 59; 15 Sept. 60; 2 Apr., 23 Apr. 64. MP JAHM, Speech on Garibaldi (printed).
52. Edgar, p. 91 sq., based on files of *HA* which supply more detail. Cf. *HA*, 26 Sept., 31 Oct., 19 Dec. 57; 20 Feb., 17 Apr. 58.
53. *HA*, 29 June 57.
54. *HA*, 17 Apr. 58.
55. *HA*, 8 May 58.
56. *HA*, 12 June 58.
57. *HA*, 26 June 58.
58. *HA*, 27 Nov., 4 Dec., 11 Dec. 58.
59. Edgar, p. 29 sq. and *HA* files.
60. *HA*, 17 Apr. 58.
61. *HA*, 16 May, 30 May, 6 June, 13 Sept. 57; 2 Feb. 61.
62. *HA*, 26 Feb., 5 Mar., 19 Mar. 59.
63. *HA*, 22 Oct. 59.
64. *HA*, 15 Oct. 59.
65. *HA*, 13 Oct. 60.
66. MP JAHM, Burgess speech.
67. Edgar, p. 54.
68. *The Times*, 19 Sept. 06. JAHM speech at HAS Jubilee dinner.

Notes to Chapter III

1. *HA*, 31 May 62.
2. *HA*, 2 Dec. 54; 10 Nov. 55; 2 Feb. 56.
3. MP HAS Minutes (draft). The original Minute books kept by JAHM are in possession of the HAS Secretary.
4. MP HW, Notes.
5. *HA*, 27 Sept. 56.
6. MP JAHM, 'Up the Slitrig'.
7. 'Field Meeting at Hermitage and Ninestane Rig', *HAST* (1864), pp. 28–30.

8. JAHM, 'Antiquarian Ramble' and 'Up the Slitrig'.
9. *HA*, 5 Sept. 63. MP H. McLaughlan to unnamed correspondent, 11 May 64. JAHM, 'Personal researches on the Catrail'.
10. HAS Minutes, 1 Oct. 61.
11. MP JAHM, 'Visit to the Roman Camp at Lyne'. (1862).
12. In 1903 (GFT, p. 12) JAHM said this was when he was 24 (1861), but a testimonial from Bell (MP 5 Nov. 1861) states that he had known JAHM for some years, first as a private pupil and later as 'a most intelligent and talented friend'. Bell's Visible Speech had forty-three signs which he claimed expressed sounds to the eye with the same exactitude with which the mouth forms sounds to the ear, but this is now known to have been based on an erroneous theory of the position of the tongue. *Cf.* S. S. Eustace, 'Meaning of the Palæotype in A. J. Ellis' "On Early English Pronunciation" ', *PST* (1968), pp. 34–5.
13. GFT, p. 12.
14. Henry Scott Riddell (1798–1870), minor poet, was a Selkirkshire shepherd who worked his way to Edinburgh University. His best known poem is 'Scotland Yet'.
15. *Centenary Celebration of the Birth of Henry Scott Riddell*. (Published for HAS, Hawick 1898), p. 13. For JAHM's criticism of Riddell's version see JAHM, 'On the Origin and History of the Scottish Language'. Paper read to HAS, *HA*, 9 Apr. 59.
16. GFT, pp. 13–14.
17. *Ibid.*, p. 14.
18. JAHM, 'Old Method of Preparing Flax'. *HAST* (1863), pp. 62–3; *A Week among the Antiquities of Orkney*, Hawick (1861), p. 46; MP 'Up the Slitrig' (1861); 'On the Origin of the Name of Hawick'. Two papers read to HAS, *HA*, 17 Mar., 7 Apr. 60; 'Personal Names. Their Origin and History'. Paper read to HAS, *HA*, 17 May 62.
19. JAHM, 'On the Origin of the Name of Hawick'. Paper read to HAS, *HA*, 7 Apr. 60.
20. MP JAHM, 'Antiquarian Ramble'.
21. *HA*, 11 May 61; *HAST* (1863), pp. 42, 47.
22. *HA*, 22 Sept. 60. The fragment of the cross is now in the garden of Wilton House Museum, Hawick.
23. *HA*, 11 May, 6 June 61; 5 Apr. 62. MP JAHM, 'Archaeology, Its Aims and Results'. Paper read to HAS, *HA*, 5 July 62.
24. Reports of HAS meetings, *HA*, 22 June, 14 Sept. 61; MP JAHM, Oxford Board of Studies, Lecture 3 (1911), p. 5.

25. GFT, p. 14.

26. *Ibid.*, also MP J. Douglas to JAHM, 12 Oct. 63.

27. MP Letter to Editor from JGE, London, 26 Nov. 60 (newspaper cutting).

28. MP Testimonial (n.d.) to M. Scott on resignation.

29. MP Testimonials to JAHM, Nov. 61.

30. *HA*, 1 Aug. 63.

31. MP M. Miller to JAHM, 28 Sept. 64.

32. MP J. Douglas to JAHM, 8 June 64.

33. *HAST* (1864), pp. 37-8.

34. MP W. Elliot to JAHM, 10 June 63.

35. MP Robert Beveridge to JAHM, 3 Sept. 64.

36. *HAST* (1864), p. 36. sq. *HA*, 3 Sept., 10 Sept. 64.

37. MP J. M. Diener and William Munro to JAHM, 2 Nov. 64.

38. His contributions were 'Scottish Dialects with special reference to that of Teviotdale' (1869); 'Life and writings of Sir David Lyndesay of the Mount' (1871); 'Present extent of Gaelic speaking territory' (1873); 'The Complaynt of Scotlande' (1874); 'The prophecies of Thomas the Rymour of Ersyldoune' (1873); 'The world of words, & its Explorers' (1906).

39. MP Programme, menu, and newspaper cuttings. The clock, the casket, and illuminated address are all in the possession of a great grandson, J. G. Murray.

40. Gwyneth, the youngest, recalled this as happening 'any time after Rugby', but the tradition handed down by Oswyn to his family was 'never before Shap', Lady M., p. 84.

Notes to Chapter IV

1. MP JAHM, British Museum Application [20 Nov. 66] (draft).

2. *HAST* (1866), pp. 31-2.

3. JAHM, Sermons. 'Congregationalism'.

4. MP JAHM, Temperance Address.

5. John Ruthven, *Geological Map of the Lake District* (1855).

6. In possession of Mrs Manning.

7. See JAHM, 'Concerning an old Copy Book', *Leisure Hour* (Jan. 1870), p. 59 sq. and *HAST* (1910), p. 75 sq. The ms. is now in the National Library of Scotland.

8. MP COM, Reminiscences.

9. GFT, pp. 15-16.

10. MP JAHM, Peckham address, and sermon for a Church Anniversary.

11. MP Thomas Murray to JAHM, 1 July 66.

12. MP JAHM to Mamma (Mrs Ruthven), 3 Feb. 67.

13. MP Thomas Murray to JAHM, 11 Mar. 67, and Mary Murray to JAHM, 28 Mar. 67.

14. Bell also helped James to find the wedding ring at a critical moment in the ceremony. MP A. G. Bell to AAM, 26 Aug. 15.

15. MP JAHM to HJRM, 23 June 05.

16. *Ibid.*, 7 Feb. 92.

17. MP JAHM to Ethelbert T. R. Murray, 9 Jan. 10 (Extract copied by R. N. R. Murray).

18. MP W. Elliot to JAHM, 14 June 67.

19. MP W. Ralston to JAHM, 'Friday morning', [Nov. 66.]

20. MP G. Grote to JAHM, 23 Nov. 66.

21. MP W. Ewart to A. D. Murray, 29 Dec. 66 and to JAHM, 3 Jan. 67.

22. MP JAHM, British Museum Application [20 Nov. 66] (draft).

23. MP John Scott to JAHM, 16 Jan. 67.

24. MP W. Ewart to JAHM, 9 Jan. 67 (enclosing letter from the Speaker to Ewart, 9 Jan. 67).

25. MP J. Winter-Jones to JAHM, 1 Feb. 67, and J. Stevenson to JAHM, 20 May 67.

26. MP W. Greenwell to JAHM, 12 Sept. 68.

27. See D. J. Palmer, *The Rise of English Studies* (1965).

28. *Athenaeum* (23 Mar. 67), p. 390.

29. HS, Presidential Address to the PS 1877, *Collected Papers*, ed. H. C. Wyld (1913), p. 90.

30. Palmer, *op. cit.*, pp. 18-19; 29 sq., and 47-8.

31. *DNB*.

32. MP contain many letters from A. J. Ellis as well as letters from JAHM to Ellis which Ellis later returned to him. These and letters from other correspondents contain much information on the research into dialects, only briefly touched on in the present work.

33. MP AJE to JAHM, 29 Aug. 77, 30 Sept. 78.

34. *Ibid.*, 10 Nov. 68, 6 Mar. 71.

35. *Ibid.*, 30 June, 8 July 68.

36. *Ibid.*, 19 Nov. 68.

37. *Ibid.*, 16 Nov. 68.

38. Furnivall Papers. Melville Bell, Pamphlet launching 'Visible Speech', 1864. Both Visible Speech and Palæotype have long been superseded. S. S. Eustace, *loc. cit.*, describes Palæotype as 'incomprehensible' and Visible Speech as 'one of the most inconvenient alphabets ever devised'.

39. MP AJE to JAHM, 26 May 69.

40. JAHM, *Dialect*, p. 90, and p. 98 sq.

41. MP AJE to JAHM, 3 Oct. 75.

42. *Ibid.*, 19 Nov. 77.
43. *Ibid.*, 30 Apr. 77.
44. *Ibid.*, 4 Jan. 74; JAHM to LLB, 28 June 73.
45. MP JAHM to AJE, 'Monday', [August 75].
46. MP AJE to JAHM, 28 Dec. 73.
47. *Ibid.*, 24 Nov. 73.
48. MP JAHM, 'Shakespere's Grammar'. Paper read to PS, 15 Feb. 72. The reference to Hamlet is to Act V. i. 81.
49. MP AJE to JAHM, 22 Feb. 76.
50. MP JAHM, 'Early and Modern English Dialects'. Paper read to PS, 20 Feb. 74. Manuscript note.
51. The *Bulletin*, 28 July 15.
52. MP JAHM to AJE, 'Monday', [Aug. 75], and 15 Sept. 75.
53. MP R. J. Lloyd to JAHM, 7 Feb. 01.
54. MP JAHM, Note, marked Private, to an unnamed correspondent, n.d., [1901].
55. MP HN to JAHM, 25 and 29 Dec. 79.
56. *Ibid.*, 22 May 71, 23 Feb. 73.
57. MP AJE to JAHM, 3 Aug. 74.
58. *Ibid.*, 27 Apr., 30 Apr. 77. See also F. T. Elworthy, *An Outline of the Grammar of the Dialect of West Somerset* (English Dialect Society, 1877), Introduction, pp. 2–3, and p. 112 sq.
59. GFT, p. 16.
60. JAHM, *Dialect*, p. 41.
61. *Ibid.*
62. MP JAHM, unpublished letter to the *Athenaeum*, 19 Apr. 69.
63. MP JAHM to Freeman, n.d. [1872] (draft), and JAHM to AJE, 26 Mar. 75.
64. MP JAHM, 'Early and Modern English Dialects'. 1874.
65. MP JAHM to AJE, 13 July 75.
66. See p. 50 above.
67. MP AJE to JAHM, 26 Jan. 70. A. G. Bell, 'Prehistoric Telephone Days', *Nat. Geographic Magazine*, XLI, pt. 3 (March 1921), pp. 232–3 describes lunch with the Prince.
68. MP JAHM to LLB, 2 July 70.
69. MP JAHM to AJE, 4 Aug. 75.
70. MP AJE to JAHM, 29 Aug. 75; JAHM to AJE, 20 Sept. 75.
71. *Ibid.*, 3 June 68.
72. MP FJF to JAHM, 20 Oct. 68.
73. MP AJE to JAHM, 5 Aug. 69.
74. MP R. Chambers to JAHM, 9 Apr. 69.
75. MP AJE to JAHM, 11 Apr. 69.
76. JAHM, *Dialect*, Preface, p. v.
77. MP JAHM to J. H. Grimrod, 9 July 12. (Typescript copy.)
78. *Athenaeum* (26 July 73), pp. 104–5.

79. *Academy* (1 Aug. 73), p. 297 sq.
80. *Revue Celtique*, II. 2. (Juin 74).
81. W. Skeat, *A Student's Pastime* (1896), Introduction, pp. ix–xxi; xxix.
82. MP WS to JAHM, 6 May 73.
83. *Ibid.*, 8 May 73.
84. OUP JAHM to FH, 11 Nov. 96.
85. *Athenaeum* (3 Apr. 75), pp. 451–3; MP JAHM, 'The Rushworth Glosses' (draft), f. 2.
86. HS, Presidential Address to the PS 1878, *Collected Papers*, p. 128.

Notes to Chapter V

1. For F. J. Furnivall's life and character see *DNB*; W. P. Ker, 'Obituary', *British Academy Proceedings* (1910), p. 375 sq.; *Frederick James Furnivall, A Volume of Personal Record* (1911), from which the following details are drawn. There are many letters included in MP.
2. L. Toulmin Smith to JAHM, 20 Dec. 82.
3. John Munro, 'Biography', in *Personal Record*, p. lxxxii.
4. MP AJE to JAHM, 6 Sept. 73.
5. J. Munro, *loc. cit.*, p. lxxxii.
6. MP B. Dawson to JAHM, 10 July 97.
7. MP E. A. Freeman to JAHM, 27 July 73.
8. *Ibid.*, 22 June 73.
9. J. Munro, *loc. cit.*, pp. lvi–lix.
10. W. P. Ker, 'Obituary', *loc. cit.*, p. 375.
11. Report on the EETS, issued with Extra Series vol cii (1908), p. 5.
12. *Ibid.*, pp. 4 and 2.
13. HS, Presidential Address to the PS, 1877, *Collected Papers*, p. 89, quoting Professor Zupitza. Many of Furnivall's letters to JAHM (MP) support this criticism.
14. MP FJF to JAHM, 11, 24 May 69.
15. JAHM, *The Complaynt of Scotlande 1549 A.D.*, part I and II, EETS Extra Series, vols xvii and xviii (1872–3), Introduction, p. civ.
16. *Ibid.*, pp. lvii, cvii.
17. MP JAHM to AAM, 2 Sept. 70 (quoted by HJRM, Biography).
18. *Athenaeum* (9 Aug. 73), p. 170; *Academy* (1 Oct. 73), pp. 377–8.
19. JAHM, *Complaynt of Scotlande*, Introduction, p. cxix.
20. *Athenaeum* (26 Oct. 67), pp. 532–3.
21. MP FJF to JAHM, 11 May 69.
22. *Ibid.*, 31 Mar., 1 Aug. (on back of Sam Hakett to FJF, 28 July), 6 Sept. 70.
23. *Ibid.*, 26 Mar. 70; H. B. Wheatley to JAHM, 26 Mar. 70; JAHM to H. B. Wheatley, 28 Mar. 70; H. B. Wheatley to JAHM, 28 Mar. 70.

24. MP JAHM to WS, 18 Dec. 88.
25. MP FJF to JAHM, 19 Sept., 8 Nov. 70 (postcard).
26. *Ibid.*, 3 Sept. 70. (There are two letters of this date.)
27. JAHM, *Sir David Lyndesay's Works*, Part V. EETS, vol. 47 (1871), Temporary Introduction.
28. MP FJF to JAHM, 17 Sept., 17 Oct. 69.
29. MP S. W. Kershaw to FJF, 27 Jan. 70 with note by FJF.
30. MP FJF to JAHM, 11 Dec. 73.
31. *Athenaeum* (10 Nov. 66), pp. 606–7.
32. MP FJF to JAHM, 11 Dec. 73.
33. *Ibid.*, 8 Dec. 73.
34. JAHM, *The Romance and Prophecies of Thomas of Erceldoune*, EETS Vol. 61 (1875), Introduction, pp. v, lii.
35. MP FJF to H. Cromie, 3 Jan. 76.
36. MP WS to JAHM, 20 Jan. 69 and n.d. [1869].
37. *Ibid.*, 18 May 70.
38. MP FJF to JAHM, 4, 5 Jan. 70.
39. *Athenaeum* (11 June 70), pp. 765–7; MP T. R. Lumby to FJF, n.d. and to JAHM, 17 Feb. 70.
40. MP FJF to JAHM, 25 Feb. 70.
41. MP WS to JAHM, n.d.
42. MP J. Zupitza to FJF, 25 Aug. 74. See J. Zupitza, *Guy of Warwick*, Part II, EETS, Extra Series, vol. xlix (1887).
43. MP FJF to JAHM, 13 Aug. 74.
44. MP H. Bradshaw to JAHM, 3, 11, 13 Jan., 28 Sept. 75.
45. *Ibid.*, 10 Sept., 20 Oct., 23 Nov. 74.
46. MP W. Greenwell to JAHM, 8 Apr. 76; 23 Jan. 78; JAHM to Dean & Chapter, Durham (undated draft).
47. MP HS to JAHM, 27 July 79; JAHM to 'My Lord', 19 June 80 (draft).
48. MP EA to JAHM, 9 May 73.
49. MP T. S. Baynes to JAHM, 3 Jan. 78.
50. JAHM, Presidential Address, *PST* (1877–9), p. 566.
51. MP T. S. Baynes to JAHM, 14 Mar. 78.

Notes to Chapter VI

1. PSCM, 12 May 69; *PST* (1870–2), Appendix, p. 12 (3 Feb. 71); p. 15 (15 Feb. 72).
2. MP AJE to JAHM, 25 Nov., 30 Nov. 69. These, like many of AJE's letters, are written in simplified spelling and his actual words read: 'bad from everi konseévab'l point ov veu . . . a disgrais too dhi Komiti'.
3. MP AJE to JAHM, 21 Oct. 70.
4. *Ibid.*, 19 Nov. 70 (postcard). D. P. Fry favoured a wholly phonetic system, Ellis a

partial system—his 'Glossic'—to be introduced for concurrent use with existing orthography. *PST* (1880–1), p. 270 sq.
5. JAHM, Presidential Address, *PST* (1880–1), p. 147 sq., p. 270 sq. and pp. 320–1; *PST* (1882–4), p. xiii.
6. *New York Globe*, 27 Aug. 05.
7. MP AJE to JAHM, 1 Nov. 74.
8. MP FJF to JAHM, 7 Sept. 73.
9. MP HW, Notes.
10. H. G. B. James, *History of Mill Hill School*.
11. MP HW, Notes.
12. MP Typescript copies of correspondence between RFW and JAHM, 24 June to 23 July 70.
13. MP JAHM to LLB, 2 July 70 (draft).
14. MP AJE to JAHM, 3 Aug. 70.
15. MP RFW to JAHM, 29 June 70 (typescript).
16. James, p. 17.
17. *Ibid.*, pp. 218, 258; GFT, *Et Virtutem . . . Essays on Mill Hill*, privately printed (1957), p. 37.
18. MP RFW to JAHM, 28, 29 June 70 (typescript).
19. MP JAHM to RFW, 11 July 70 (typescript).
20. Lady M., p. 2.
21. MP RFW to JAHM, 13, 20 July 70; JAHM to Bank, 25 July 70 (typescripts).
22. Lady M., p. 6.
23. MP JAHM, note on word *fray*, n.d. [*c.* 1897].
24. WGRM, p. 53.
25. MP House Agent's advertisement. (The Murrays let the house each year when away for the summer holiday.)
26. JAHM to AECRM, 27 Mar. 03.
27. GFT, p. 17.
28. MP JAHM, Notes for Mill Hill New Foundation Day speech, 23 June 93. *Cf.* H. J. Tucker to JAHM, 11 Nov. 76.
29. James, p. 218.
30. *Mill Hill Magazine*, xiii. i (June, 1885), pp. 14–15.
31. James, p. 254.
32. JAHM to AECRM, 2 Feb. 07.
33. MP J. F. Wintringham to JAHM, n.d. [1886]; J. H. Dallmeyer to JAHM, 6 May 76.
34. MP Alexander Mackennal to Mr Pileness, 2 Dec. 76; J. Milne to JAHM, 4 Dec. 76 (post at Wyggeston Hospital School, Leicestershire); Robert Bruce to JAHM, 9 Jan. 77 (post at Huddersfield College).
35. MP 'Mainly about People', The *Star*, 20 June 89.

36. MP Gurney, Notes (1929).
37. GFT, *Et Virtutem*, p. 35.
38. MP JAHM, Address to Mill Hill Nat. Hist. Soc.
39. James, pp. 231, 254.
40. MP Gurney, Notes.
41. GFT, *Et Virtutem*, p. 35.
42. *Ibid.*, p. 33; James, p. 259.
43. GFT, *Et Virtutem*, pp. 35–6; James, p. 248. *Cf.* MP J. H. Tucker to JAHM, 11 Nov. 76.
44. MP P. H. Pye Smith to JAHM, 18 Mar., 2 Aug. 81.
45. James, pp. 255, 257.
46. Mill Hill Archives, 6. JAHM to T. Scrutton, Apr. 86.
47. James, p. 254.
48. Furnivall Papers. JAHM to FJF, 19 Nov. 78.
49. MP JAHM to WS, 29 May 80. He ends the letter, 'But, really I forgot to whom I was writing!'
50. MP HJRM, Biography.
51. JAHM, Introduction to 1st edition of *Synopsis of Paley's Horae Paulinae*, published by Hodder & Stoughton (1872), and Note to 4th edition, published by William Kent (1879).
52. *OED*, 1st edition, Vol. I, p. vi.
53. MP HN to JAHM, 10 Mar., 18 Mar. 74.
54. MP F. Macmillan to JAHM, 17 Apr. 78; J. R. Green to JAHM, 18 Sept. 78. G. G. Bradley, 1821–1903, was Headmaster of Marlborough, 1858–70, later Master of University College Oxford and Dean of Westminster; F. M. Buss, 1827–94, Headmistress of North London Collegiate School, 1850–94.
55. MP AMcm to JAHM, 18 Jan. 81.
56. James, p. 253.
57. MP AJE to JAHM, 23 Dec. 73; JAHM to AJE, 4 Aug. 75.
58. James, pp. 221, 254.
59. JAHM, Sermons (1 Kings xviii: 21), p. 16.
60. *Ibid.* (John ix: 4), delivered 1871, 1878, 1882, pp. 11, 8.
61. *Ibid.* (Genesis i: 14), p. 12.
62. *Ibid.* (Rom. xv: 30), pp. 21–3.
63. MP FJF to JAHM, 24 Jan. 74.
64. MP HN to AJE, 30 Dec. 74.
65. MP JAHM to Secretary S.E.I. (draft, undated); and W. Kennaly to JAHM, 18 July 70.
66. MP H. Gaidez to JAHM. Postscript to letter written in French: 'What the deuce can F E I S be?' 22 Jan. 74.
67. MP AJE to JAHM, 4 Nov. 73.
68. George Tancred, *Rulewater & its People*, Edinburgh (1907), p. 21 sq.
69. MP W. Elliot to JAHM, 20, 28 Aug. 73.
70. MP Lord Neaves to JAHM, 7 Oct. 73.
71. *Ibid.*, 5 Mar. 74.
72. MP Testimonial from FJF, 26 Mar. 74 (copy by JAHM).
73. MP Testimonials from LLB, 21 Mar. 74; AJE, 24 Mar. 74 (copies by JAHM) and G. G. Latham (copy by AAM).
74. MP JAHM to W. Elliot, 25 Mar. 74.
75. MP W. Elliot to JAHM, 23 Mar. 74.
76. MP A. Grant to W. Elliot, 29 Mar. 74.
77. MP COM to JAHM, 2 Apr. 74 (postcard); FJF to JAHM, 6 Apr. 74; AJE to JAHM, 6 Apr. 74.
78. MP Christie & Kilpatrick to JAHM, 11, 14 Apr. 74.
79. *HA*, 2 May 74.
80. *HA*, 25 Apr. 74.
81. MP Registrar London Univ. to JAHM, 8 Apr. 74; A. Milman (for Registrar) to JAHM, 14 Apr. 74.
82. MP Registrar London Univ. to JAHM, 14 May 74.
83. MP FJF to JAHM, 11 Apr. 76.
84. MP R. Cust to JAHM, 25 Mar. 80.
85. JAHM, Presidential Address, *PST* (1882–4), p. 600.
86. MP S. Tilly, clerk to Hendon Local Board to JAHM, 9 Feb. 80; Robert Hunter to JAHM, 11 Feb. 80.
87. JAHM, 'A Chapter on Names', *Border Magazine* (Aug. 1863), p. 84 sq.; 'Personal Names their origins and History', *HAST* (1862). The gibe at 'wily priests' was omitted in the *Border Magazine*. See also JAHM, 'Saint Cuthbert's Chapel by the Slitrig', *HAST* (1862).
88. JAHM, *Dialect*, pp. 14–15.
89. MP HJRM to AAM, letters Aug. and Sept. 73.
90. MP AAM to HJRM, 7 Feb. 92.
91. MP JAHM to EA, 27 Mar. 05. Oswyn's mature handwriting, rather larger than the characteristic 'family hand', was used as an example of good script in *Handbook for Teachers* (H.M.S.O., 1927) Fig. 1, p. 323.
92. MP HJRM, letters to the family from Chepstow, Apr. 80.
93. *Ibid.*, letters to AAM, 5, 6 Sept. 83.
94. JAHM, Sermons (Ps. cxxi: 1–2), pp. 10–11.
95. MP JAHM to H. I. Jenkinson, 23 Oct. 80.
96. MP JAHM to HJRM, 23 June 08.
97. MP HJRM, 'Diary of our visit to Westmoreland' (1877).

98. WGRM, p. 63 sq. abbreviated from original in possession of Mrs Bergne.

Notes to Chapter VII

1. MP AMcm to JAHM, 3 Apr. 76. JAHM's memory was at fault when he said in 1903, 'Somebody (I never knew who) told them I was the man to edit it.' GFT, p. 17.
2. MP WJ to JAHM, 16 May 76. See R. K. Leavitt, *Noah's Ark. New England Yankees and the Endless Quest: A Short History of the Original Webster Dictionaries* (Springfield, Mass., 1947), p. 69.
3. JAHM, *The Evolution of English Lexicography*. The Romanes Lecture (1900), gives a history of the precursors of the *OED*. See also J. R. Hulbert, *Dictionaries British and American* (1955).
4. Samuel Johnson, *Preface to a Dictionary of the English Language* (1755). *Collected Works* (Oxford, 1825), v: pp. 39–40.
5. See Hans Aarsleff, *The Study of Language in England, 1780–1860* (Princeton University Press, 1967), for a full account of this school, the foundation of the Philological Society, and the idea of an historical dictionary.
6. *PST* (1873–4), pp. 251–2, quoted by Aarsleff, *op. cit.*, p. 230.
7. C. T. Onions, 'Historical Introduction' to *OED Supplement* (1933) and JAHM in *Personal Record*, p. 122 sq. give details of the early history of the *OED*.
8. R. C. Trench. *English Past and Present* (1855), pp. 8–9, and *On the Study of Words* (1851), Vol. I, p. 40, quoted by Aarsleff, *op. cit.*, pp. 245, 240–1.
9. Letter of Herbert Coleridge to Trench, 1860, published as an addendum to the 2nd edition of Trench. *On Some Deficiencies in Our English Dictionaries* (1860), and by George Wheelwright, *Appeal to the English Speaking Public on behalf of a New English Dictionary* (1875). See also Aarsleff, *op. cit.*, pp. 252–3.
10. Trench, *Some Deficiencies in our English Dictionaries*. Paper read to the PS, 5, 19 Nov. 57. Printed as Part II of *PST* (1857).
11. Coleridge to Trench, 1860, *loc. cit.*; JAHM in *Personal Record*, p. 128; MP JAHM, Lecture on Dictionaries (frgt.); W. Tuckwell, *Reminiscences of Oxford* (1900), p. 119.
12. MP FJF, Circular to members of the PS, 9 Nov. 62, pp. 3–4, quoting preliminary notice to the last part of the *Third Period Basis of Comparison*, Apr. 61.

13. D. Hudson, *Man of Two Worlds. The Life and Diaries of A. J. Munby* (1974), pp. 123–4.
14. MP FJF, Circular to Members of the PS, 9 Nov. 62.
15. MP FJF, Circular to Sub-Editors, 15 Sept. 62 and MS note on his specimen of *The Abstract of the Full Articles proposed for the Concise Dictionary* (1862).
16. See Chapter V, above.
17. MP *Proposal for the Publication of a New English Dictionary by the Philological Society* (1859), p. 7. See also *Athenaeum* (2 Feb. 67), p. 158. Half of the Anglo-Saxon and more than half the Early English MSS were unprinted.
18. MP FJF, Circular to members of the PS, 26 Oct. 65, p. 4.
19. MP FJF to JAHM, 3 Dec. 78.
20. MP W. Gee, *The Philological Society New English Dictionary Vocabulary of Words Beginning with the letter B* (1863). List of books to be cut up, including several folios of the sixteenth and seventeenth centuries.
21. *Athenaeum* (16 May 68), p. 698.
22. PSCM, 21 Apr. 71.
23. MP G. Wheelwright, *Appeal to the English Speaking People on behalf of a New English Dictionary*, 5 Mar. 75; G.11021/19.937. G. Wheelwright to HG, 2 Sept. 75.
24. MP FJF to JAHM, 21 Jan. 82.
25. PSCM, 5 Nov. 75; 4 Feb., 18 Feb., 3 Mar. 76.
26. Furnivall Papers, WS to FJF, 17 Nov. 65.
27. MP WS to JAHM, 6 Apr. 76.
28. Hudson, *op. cit.*, pp. 22, 26.
29. MP FJF to JAHM, 21 Jan. 82.
30. *Ibid.*, 6 June 76.
31. *Ibid.*, 9 Oct. 76.
32. MP John Murray to FJF, 12, 13 May 58.
33. MP FJF to JAHM, 6 June 76.
34. MP AJE to JAHM, 14 Nov. 76.
35. MP FJF to JAHM, 11 Oct. 76.
36. *Ibid.*, 6 June 76.
37. *Ibid.*, 18 Nov. 76.
38. *Ibid.*, 23 Nov. 76.
39. MP WJ to JAHM, 10 Oct. 76.
40 MP FJF to JAHM, 9 Oct. 76.
41. MP WJ to JAHM, 10 Oct. 76; GMcm to JAHM, 11 Oct. 76. The proofs prepared are also in MP.
42. PSCM, 3, 17 Nov. 76.
43. PSCM, 2 Oct., 3 Nov., 1 Dec. 76. MP FJF to JAHM, 23 Nov. 76. The firm of H. S. King were not prepared to divert capital but suggested issuing debentures of £50 each to

gentlemen interested in the English language. It was estimated that, after the issue of Part I, 200 debentures would yield 6 per cent.

44. PSCM, 2 Oct. 76. MP WJ to JAHM, 17 Oct., 23 Oct. (two letters), 27 Oct., 19 Nov. 76.

45. MP GMcm to JAHM, 14 Dec. 76, with copy of GMcm to FJF, 14 (Dec.; WJ to JAHM, 18 Dec. 76 with copies of FJF to GMcm, 15 Dec. 76 and GMcm to FJF, 18 Dec. 76. See also PSCM, 15 Dec. 76.

46. MP AMcm to JAHM, 19 Dec. 76.

47. MP WJ to JAHM, 18 Dec. 76.

48. See GMcm in *Personal Record*, p. 105: 'I do not think that we had any reason to regret that the enterprise passed out of our hands into those of the Clarendon Press'.

49. MP WJ to JAHM, 19 Nov. 76; R. Martineau to JAHM, 14 Nov. 76; J. B. Mayor to FJF, 3 Nov. 76 and to JAHM, n.d. [Nov. 76].

50. MP AJE to JAHM, 30 Nov. 76.

51. MP HN to JAHM, 6 Nov. 77.

52. MP WS to JAHM, 2 Mar. [88] and undated letter [Nov. 77].

53. MP FJF to JAHM, 15 Nov. 76.

54. *Ibid.*, 23 Nov. 76.

55. *Ibid.*, 29 Nov. 76.

56. MP JAHM to AJE, 29 Nov. 76.

57. MP AJE to JAHM, 30 Nov. 76.

Notes to Chapter VIII

1. MP FJF to JAHM, 20 Dec. 76.

2. MP WS to JAHM, n.d. [Nov. 77].

3. *Ibid.*, 9 Mar. [77].

4. PSCM, 17 Nov. 76.

5. MP WS to JAHM, 9, 23 and 27 Mar. [77].

6. MP FJF to JAHM, 14 Mar. 92, with marginal note by JAHM; AMcm to JAHM, 14 May 77; HS to BP, 20 Apr. 77 (copy).

7. MP HS to BP, 20 Apr. 77; see Appendix above, p. 342.

8. PSCM, 20 Apr., 4 May 77; *OD*, 11 May 77, p. 366. 8. 1; MP T. Shepherd to FJF, n.d.; HG to FJF, 5 June 77.

9. MP JAHM to BP, 6 Dec. 73. The agreement was not cancelled till 1891. H. Boyd to JAHM, 19 Dec. 91. For criticism of delay see FJF to JAHM, 26 Apr. 77 and BP to JAHM, 28 May 77.

10. PSCM, 18 May 77; OD, 30 Nov. 77, p. 378.7.

11. MP FJF to BP, 1 June 77.

12. *Ibid.*, 5 June 77.

13. MP BP to FJF, 5 June 77.

14. MP AMcm to JAHM, 14 May 77.

15. MP HS to JAHM, 29 June 77.

16. OD, MxM, observations (inset), 10 May 78, p. 395.13:

17. MP HS to FJF, 28 June 77; HS to JAHM, 29 June 77.

18. MP BP to JAHM, 13, 24, 27 Nov. 77.

19. MP MxM to JAHM, 16 Nov. 77; JAHM to AJE, 17 Nov. 77.

20. MP BP to JAHM, 4 Dec. 77; OD, 30 Nov. 77, p. 378.7.

21. OD, 30 Nov. 77, p. 378.5. The book had first come to the Delegates on 14 July 77, *ibid.*, p. 371.4.

22. MP WS to JAHM, n.d. [Nov. 77], 3 letters. By Mar. 78 FJF knew about the book. See MP WS to JAHM, 6 Mar. [78].

23. WS, *Etymological Dictionary* (1882), Preface, p. xi.

24. MP MxM to JAHM, 6 Nov. 77.

25. MP WS to JAHM, 6 Mar. 78.

26. MP FJF to JAHM, 18 Mar. (postcard), 20, 24 Mar. 78; FJF to JAHM, 14 Mar. 92 with note by JAHM.

27. GFT, pp. 18–19 (1903) and MP JAHM draft note, probably to a newspaper reporter, outlining his career [May 1880]. These accounts, one written nearly 30 years and the other 3 years after the events, are not substantiated by the letters and minutes, and it seems that James deliberately dramatised and condensed the facts. It appears, from the evidence, that the time of his actual decision to become Editor was between 18 and 28 March 1878, but in the 1903 account he says Price persuaded him because the Delegates 'had seen me, heard me, knew me', and he did not meet them till April. Nor can one accept his statement, 'I had never asked myself if I was prepared to do this . . . *who* was to do it never crossed my mind.' There had been several occasions when he had been asked, and certainly from April 1877 the Dictionary Committee of the Philological Society conducted negotiations with the Press on the assumption that he would be the Editor. On the other hand there were also times both before and after April 1878 when he had reason to hesitate, and it may be true that it was only when faced with the need to put his signature to an agreement, that he really considered all the implications. He liked a good story, and that he was taken by surprise when he found his editorship assumed was more dramatic than the reality.

28. É. Littré, 'Causerie de 1er mars 1880', printed in the Introduction to the 1956 edition of his *Dictionnaire* and quoted by Stanislas Aquarone, *Life and Works of Émile*

Littré (1958), pp. 76–7.
29. MP FJF to JAHM, 24 Mar. 78.
30. *Ibid.*, 28 Mar. 78.
31. MP WJ to JAHM, 10 Apr. 78.
32. MP BP to JAHM, 26, 29 Mar. 78; JAHM to BP, 27 Mar. 78.
33. MP W. R. Morfill to JAHM, 23 Apr. 78.
34. OD, 26 Apr. 78, p. 393.2.
35. See p. 114 above.
36. MP JAHM to AAM, 24 Apr. 78 (typescript copy). The Congress of Berlin, at which Lord Beaconsfield, British Premier, Prince Gortchakov, Russian Chancellor, Bismark, German Chancellor and Count Andrassy, Austria-Hungarian Foreign Minister, were involved, did not begin till June, but a European conference to resolve the situation arising from the Russo-Turkish war in the Balkans had already been proposed. *Cf.* Ensor, *England 1870–1914* (Oxford, 1939), pp. 48–50.
37. MP MxM to JAHM, 26 Apr., 1 May 78.
38. OD MxM, observations (inset), 10 May 78, p. 395.
39. MP BP to JAHM, 14 May 78.
40. MP JAHM to BP, 16 May 78.
41. PSOM, 17 May 78.
42. MP JAHM to BP, 30 May 78 (draft).
43. PSCM, 21 June 78.
44. MP JAHM to BP, 30 May 78 (draft).
45. MP HS to BP, 20 Apr. 77 (copy).
46. MP FJF to JAHM, memo., n.d. [1878]; FJF to JAHM, 3 Dec. 78. In a further letter on 5 Dec. 78 FJF said, '£150 ... is far too high an estimate I think £40'll pay for Dicty's wants'.
47. MP JAHM to BP, 30 May, 6 June 78 (drafts).
48. PSCM, 20 Dec. 78. Inset letter JAHM to FJF, 14 Dec. 78.
49. PSCM, 5 Dec. 79.
50. MP BP to JAHM, 24 June 78; OD, 21 June 78, p. 399.12, and 20 July 78, p. 400.1.
51. MP HS to JAHM, 7 July 78.
52. MP FJF to JAHM, 9, 15 July 78.
53. MP BP to JAHM, 22 July 78.
54. MP P. Williams to FJF, 27, 29 July, 1, 3 Aug. 78; RFW to HS, 18 Oct. 78.
55. MP JAHM to RFW, undated draft [Oct. 78] and memo by RFW, 17 Oct. 78.
56. The suggestion of 50 per cent was made in MP Sweet to BP, 20 Apr. 77; 40 per cent to be divided equally between the Society and the Editor was proposed by BP in letters to JAHM and FJF, 24 June 78, and accepted by FJF; see FJF to JAHM, 26 June 78.
57. MP BP to FJF, 2 Dec. 78 (copy); BP to JAHM, 2 Dec. 78.

58. MP FJF to JAHM, 5 Dec. 78.
59. PSCM, 20 Dec. 78; OD, 13 Dec. 78, p. 416.2. Nine Delegates were present.
60. PSCM, 20 Dec. 78. Inset letter JAHM to FJF, 14 Dec. 78.
61. OD, 13 Dec. 78, p. 416.3. i & ii.
62. MP BP to JAHM, 29 Mar. 78.
63. OD, 7 Mar. 90, p. 411.17; 18 Sept. 96, p. 221.12.
64. MP F. Pollock to JAHM, 13 Oct. 92.
65. MP W. Osler to JAHM, 3 Feb. 12.
66. MP JAHM, Lecture to Blackpool National Home Reading Union (1889), p. 14.
67. MP JAHM, *ibid.*; EA to JAHM, 29 Nov. 84; White (Royal Society) to JAHM, 28 Dec. 80; WS to JAHM, incomplete, undated [1881], 26 Mar. 89, 13 Sept. 96. The very adequate library provided for the Editor of the Supplement now in preparation includes some books marked as loans to the Dictionary from the library of JAHM.
68. MP FJF to JAHM, 'Brit. Mus. Wed. p.m.' [1878].
69. MP MxM to JAHM, 5 Dec. 78.
70. OD, 4 May, p. 178.7.1; 11 May, p. 179.7; 15 June 1900, p. 187.4. PSCM, 4 May 1900.
71. PSCM, 20 Dec. 78. Inset letter JAHM to FJF, 14 Dec. 78.
72. MP BP to JAHM, 19 Dec. 78.
73. PSCM, 20 Dec. 78.
74. MP FJF to JAHM, 12 Feb. 79.
75. MP BP to JAHM, 19 Dec. 78; 5 Feb. 79; OD, 31 Jan. 79, p. 423.11.
76. PSCM, 24 Jan. 79.
77. GFT, p. 19. *Cf* note 27, p. 363 above.
78. PSCM, 20 Dec. 78.
79. PSCM, 24 Jan. 79. Attached proof of circular letter to members. See also MP corrected proof.
80. PSOM, 7 Feb. 79.
81. MP FJF to JAHM, 12 Feb. 79.
82. MP BP to JAHM, 1 Mar. 79; OD, 14 Mar. 79, p. 428.13. Agreements with the Society and with JAHM had been executed and deposited in the strong room. The Agreement with the Society is printed in *PST* (1877–9), Appendix pp. xlix sq.
83. These figures include the 1933 supplement.
84. MP BP to FJF, 2 Dec. 78 (copy).
85. PSOM, 7 Feb. 79.
86. MP Indenture of agreement between the Clarendon Press and JAHM, 1 Mar. 79.
87. *Periodical*, xiii. 143 (15 Feb. 28), p. 3.
88. PSCM, 20 Dec. 78. Inset letter JAHM to FJF, 14 Dec. 78.
89. Coleridge to Trench, 2 May 60, *loc. cit.*
90. MP FJF Circular letter to members of

the PS (18 Oct. 64), pp. 2–3 and n.

91. JAHM, Dictionary Report, 4 Mar. 92. *PST* (1891–4), p. 269.

92. MP FJF to JAHM, 28 Oct. 92.

93. MP Appeal to the English-speaking and English-reading Public. Apr. 79.

94. OUP, JAHM to FH, 11 Apr. 99.

95. MP FJF to BP, 1 June 77.

96. MP FJF, Circular letter to sub-editors, 15 Sept. 62.

97. MP WS to JAHM, 6 Apr. 76.

98. Furnivall Papers, WS to FJF, 17 Nov. 65.

Notes to Chapter IX

The quotation used for the chapter title is from JAHM, Presidential address, *PST* (1877–9), p. 567.

1. For the Mill Hill Scriptorium and the start of work there, see Jennett Humphreys, 'English: Its Ancestors, Its Progeny', *Fraser's Magazine*, New Series, cliv (Oct. 1882), p. 444 sq.; 'Dictionary Making', *Leisure Hour* (June 1883), pp. 362–6; MP JAHM, Lecture on Dictionaries, given to the London Institute, Nov. 1910.

2. MP FJF to JAHM, 5 Dec. 78.

3. MP FJF to JAHM, 2 Feb. 79 (postcard).

4. *Ibid.*, 19 Aug. 79.

5. MP JAHM to T. Scrutton, 8 Feb. 79, with sketch plan of proposed position of the 'iron house'; Wallis Nash to T. Scrutton, 10 Feb. 79; JAHM to RFW, 10 Feb. 79 (copy); RFW to JAHM, 4 Mar. 79.

6. J. Humphreys, *loc. cit.*, p. 447.

7. MP FJF to JAHM, 27 Mar. 79.

8. *Ibid.*, 29 Mar. 79.

9. MP H. Morgan to FJF, 23 May (postcard), 26 May (postcard), 2 June 77.

10. MP JAHM, Lecture on Dictionaries (1910), p. 19.

11. MP FJF to JAHM, 24 May 77; 28 Mar., 10 May 79.

12. JAHM, Presidential address, *PST* (1877–9), p. 570.

13. Robert Gittings, *Young Thomas Hardy* (1975), p. 37 sq.

14. MP JAHM to FJF, 10 May 79.

15. MP FJF to JAHM, 10 May 79 (2 letters).

16. MP G. P. Marsh to FJF, 4 May 79.

17. MP J. G. Middleton to JAHM, 14 May 79.

18. MP FJF to JAHM, 3 Nov. 80; JAHM, Presidential address, *PST* (1880–1), p. 129 and note.

19. JAHM, Presidential address, *PST* (1877–9), pp. 569–70.

20. JAHM, Dictionary Report, *PST* (1880–1), p. 267.

21. MP Appeal, Apr. 79, with list of books requiring reading: those already taken struck out.

22. MP JAHM, Lecture on Dictionaries (1910), p. 20.

23. JAHM, Presidential address, *PST* (1877–9), pp. 571–2.

24. MP 'Directions to Readers for the Dictionary', Apr. 79.

25. *The Graphic*, 25 June 1921, p. 778.

26. These 'high' rates of pay were only introduced at Oxford. At Mill Hill the standard rate was a penny an hour, and the older members of the family cited the Oxford rates as evidence that the younger children were 'spoilt'.

27. AHJM, 'Memoirs'.

28. These volumes have disappeared. JAHM intended to keep every letter and postcard for reference and for history, saying 'That the whole material on which the Dictionary shall be built shall be here for any after use that may be made of it, is an essential part of my scheme.' J. Humphreys, *loc. cit.*, p. 452.

29. MP FJF to JAHM, 28 Apr. 79.

30. See p. 269 below.

31. MP John Dormer to JAHM, 30 Oct. [95]; see also HW to JAHM, 3 Nov. 99; Edward Parry to JAHM, 9 Jan. 07.

32. MP JAHM to Mrs Constance M. Pott, Dec. 80 (draft); Mrs C. M. Pott to JAHM, 14 Dec. 80. She later became a Dictionary reader, *ibid.*, 17 Aug. 81.

33. MP JAHM to W. J. E. Crane, 25 Oct. 81 (copy); Crane to JAHM, 25 Jan. 81; JAHM to Crane, 5 Nov. 81 (copy); Crane to JAHM, 10 Nov. 81; BP to JAHM, 25 Nov. 81; PSCM, 16 Nov., 2 Dec. 81; OD, 18 Nov. 81, p. 35.11.

34. 'A Literary Workshop', *N & Q*, 6th Ser. ii (2 Oct. 80), p. 262.

35. PSCM, 20 Dec. 78. Inset letter JAHM to FJF, 14 Dec. 78; JAHM, Presidential Address, *PST* (1877–9), pp. 570–1.

36. JAHM, Presidential Address, *PST* (1880–1), pp. 125–6, 129.

37. Corpus Christi College, Melbourne, Australia, JAHM to FJF, 7 July 05.

38. JAHM, Presidential Address, *PST* (1880–1), pp. 123–4.

39. OD, 22 Mar. 80, p. 472.8.

40. MP BP to JAHM, 30 Mar. 80.

41. *Ibid.*, 29 Mar. 81; OD, 20 May 81, p. 12.8.

42. MP Appeal, Apr. 79, p. 3.

43. It was not until later that an attempt was made to include specific American usages to illustrate the development of the language in the United States.

44. JAHM, Presidential Address, *PST* (1880–1), pp. 122–4.

45. MP J. Randall to JAHM, 23 Jan. 84.

46. MP J. T. Fowler to JAHM, 22 Nov. 09.

47. *Periodical*, xiii, 143 (15 Feb. 28), pp. 7–8. There are many letters in MP.

48. MP E. Thompson to Macmillan, 16 Apr. 80; E. Thompson to JAHM, 17 Feb. 93.

49. MP J. E. A. Brown to JAHM, 30 Mar. 82; JAHM to HJRM, 19 Dec. 12.

50. 'A Literary Workshop', *loc. cit.*, p. 263.

51. MP OARM to HJRM, Easter Monday 31.

52. Dictionary Making', *loc. cit.*, p. 364. The name of Professor Child is given in MP, HW Notes.

53. J. Humphreys, *loc. cit.*, p. 454.

54. 'A Literary Workshop', *loc. cit.*, p. 262.

55. When the Dictionary was completed in 1928, out of 240,165 main words treated, 52,464 were obsolete words. *Periodical*, xiii, 143 (15 Feb. 28), p. 21.

56. H. Bradley, review of Part I, *A–Ant*, *Academy* (16 Feb. 84). Reprinted in *Collected Papers*, p. 127 sq.

57. MP JAHM, Lecture on Dictionaries (1910), pp. 33–4.

58. J. Humphreys, *loc. cit.*, p. 454.

59. MP H. Harley, 'The Philological Society's New English Dictionary', *Sweep Papers*, n.d. [1879], p. 7.

60. This often repeated story has been attributed variously, but the family were certain that their father invented it at Mill Hill. A. S. Peak, who repeated the story at a party in 1891 at which JAHM was present, says that Murray said the real end was 'The University of Oxford is a respectable body and ought not to be spoken of with scurrility.' At that date he was anxious not to appear critical of the University. *Cf.* A. S. Peak, *Recollections and Appreciations* (1938), p. 212 (reprinted from *Holborn Review*, Oct. 1924).

Notes to Chapter X

1. JAHM, Dictionary Report, Discussion on methods adopted to indicate pronunciation, 17 Mar. 82. *PST* (1882–4), Abstracts, p. 77.

2. OUP JAHM to unnamed correspondent, 5 Jan. 95.

3. *OED*, Vol. I, Preface, pp. x–xi.

4. MP HS to JAHM, 27 Mar. 82, annotated by JAHM.

5. MP W. R. Evans to JAHM, 12, 21, 23 July 81; Isaac Pitman to JAHM, 29 July 81; J. Lecky to JAHM, 21, 27, 31 July, 27 Nov. 81; 11 Jan., 7 Mar. 82.

6. JAHM, Dictionary Report, 20 May 1881. *PST* (1880–1), p. 268.

7. *Ibid.*, 17 Mar. 82. *PST* (1882–4), Abstracts, p. 77.

8. MP HS to JAHM, 22 Mar. 82.

9. *Ibid.*, 27 Mar. 82, note added by JAHM.

10. MP JAHM to HS, 29 Mar. 82. Sweet continued to urge the omission of indications of pronunciation; see MP HS to JAHM, 3 Apr. 82.

11. MP FJF to JAHM, 30 Mar. 82.

12. JAHM, Presidential Address, *PST* (1877–9), p. 573.

13. Bradley, *Collected Papers*, pp. 136–7.

14. MP JAHM to BP, 19 June 82; FJF to JAHM, 11, 12, 19 June, 7 Aug. 82; JAHM to FJF, 19 June 82.

15. OD, 27 Oct. 82, p. 76.2; 16 Feb. 83, p. 94.10.

16. MP JAHM to AJE, 26 Nov. 76.

17. JAHM, Presidential Address, *PST* (1877–9), p. 582; JAHM, Dictionary Report, 20 May 81. *PST* (1881–4), p. 268.

18. MP JAHM, Lecture to the Ashmolean Natural History Society, p. B 2.

19. *OED*, Vol. I, General Explanations, p. xvii. Also JAHM, Presidential Address, *PST* (1880–1), p. 131, comparing the English language to a spot of colour on a damp surface which shades away imperceptibly into the surrounding colourlessness.

20. *OED*, I, p. xviii.

21. OUP H. Coleridge, Draft Report of the Dictionary Committee [*c.* 1860].

22. *OED, Supplement* (1972), Vol. I, Introduction, p. xv.

23. MP H. Dixon to JAHM, 6 Dec. 88; 17 Feb. 91.

24. MP J. S. Farmer to JAHM, 23 July, 1 Sept. 90; 3 June 91.

25. MP W. G. Henley to JAHM, 8 Jan. 94. See *National Observer*, 30 Dec. 93.

26. MP HG to JAHM, 30 July 82; 14 Mar. 83.

27. H. B. Wheatley, *Literary Blunders* (1893), pp. 3–7.

28. MP JAHM, Lecture on Dictionaries (1910), pp. 10–11.

29. OUP R. Martineau, FJF, and other members of the PS, letters to JAHM, 12 Feb. 93.

30. MP HG to JAHM, 20 July 82.

31. *Ibid.*, 14 Mar. 83.
32. OD, 27 Jan. 82, p. 45.18.
33. Bradley, *Collected Papers*, p. 129.
34. MP Harley, *loc. cit.*, p. 6.
35. MP RFW to AAM, 23 Feb. 80.
36. MP FJF to JAHM, 25 Mar. 80.
37. MP JAHM to AAM, 27 Apr. 80 (on back of letter HJRM to AAM, 27 Apr. 80).
38. JAHM, Presidential Address, *PST* (1880–1), p. 118, *ibid.*, *PST* (1882–4), p. 502.
39. MP JAHM to J. B. Rundell, 15 Mar. 81.
40. MP FJF to JAHM, 11 Dec. 80.
41. JAHM, Dictionary Report, 20 May 81. *PST* (1880–1), p. 266.
42. *Cf.* Furnivall Papers, WS to FJF, 17 Nov. 65.
43. MP JAHM, Dictionary Report, 6 May 1910.
44. JAHM, Dictionary Report, 20 May 81, *PST* (1880–1), p. 261.
45. The completed Dictionary contained 1,827,306 illustrative quotations, but well over 5,000,000 were collected. *Periodical* xiii. 143 (15 Feb. 28), p. 21.
46. JAHM, Presidential Address, *PST* (1882–4), pp. 515–16. *Ibid.*, Dictionary Report, 19 May 82. *PST* (1882–4), p. 6.
47. D. E. Erlebach, 'In the Dictionary Margin'. *The Times*, 25 Oct. 29.
48. MP Tennyson to JAHM, 15 Mar. 85. The word occurs in Tennyson's poem 'The Dirge', used in the mistaken sense of 'tree cricket'. Tennyson used Dalzel's *Analecta Graeca Majora* at school, in which balm-cricket occurs in the notes to Theocritus. JAHM found that it was a corruption of the German *baume-grille*. Earlier etymologists confused this with the French *baume*, and it was anglicised as *balm*. *Cf.* 'How to compile a Great Dictionary'. *Westminster Gazette*, 23 Jan. 93. Tennyson's letter on the subject was one of the treasures exhibited to visitors to the Scriptorium.
49. MP JAHM, Lecture on Dictionaries (1910), pp. 23–4. The text is in AAM's hand and includes some alternative examples added by JAHM, which are included in the quotation.
50. *Ibid.*, pp. 24–5.
51. *The Times*, 6 July 73. The case was lost on a question of law, not fact.
52. JAHM HG to JAHM, 16 Apr. 83. The problem was to define Altar in a way which would not suggest sacrifice when used for the Holy table in dissenting churches.
53. JAHM, Presidential Address, *PST* (1882–4), pp. 509–10.
54. MP JAHM to HG, 12 Feb. 82.
55. MP JAHM to BP, 17 Jan. 84.

Notes to Chapter XI

1. MP HN to JAHM, 29 Dec. 79.
2. *DNB*.
3. MP HG to JAHM, 10 Mar. 79; 27 Nov. 82.
4. G 11021/21. 455, 513. JAHM to HG, 27 May 82; 8 Nov. 83.
5. MP HG to JAHM, 18 Oct. 81.
6. G 11021/21. 404. JAHM to HG, 5 July 81.
7. MP HG to JAHM, 18 Oct. 81.
8. G.11021/21. 421 and Postscript. JAHM to HG, 20 Oct. 81. JAHM first calculated that 'alms' ran to 11 times Webster, but in postscript corrected this to 10 times.
9. OD, 28 Oct. 81, p. 31.24; MP BP to JAHM, 4 Nov. 81.
10. MP JAHM to BP, 4 Feb. 82 (copy); JAHM to FJF, 25 Jan. 82 (copy).
11. G 11021/21. 431. JAHM to HG, 6 Nov. 81, enclosing 432. Copy of BP to JAHM, 4 Nov. 81; MP JAHM to HG, 15 Feb. 82 (copy), but *cf.* PSCM, 19 May 82, when James told the PS that setting the first 12 pages showed that no extension beyond 8400 pages would be needed.
12. MP HG to JAHM, 11 Feb. 82.
13. MP JAHM to HG, 15 Feb., 25 Feb. 82 (copies).
14. The first suggestion was for 15 shillings a page, OD, 10 Feb. 82, p. 48.14. It was fixed at 17 shillings on 17 Mar. 82 (p. 53.7) and the new agreement was signed. OD, 19 May 82, p. 63.23.
15. MP HG to JAHM, 17 Feb. 82.
16. MP AJE to JAHM, 16 July 82.
17. MP JAHM to HG, 12 Feb. 82 (copy).
18. *Ibid.*, 25 Feb. 82 (copy).
19. *Ibid.*, 12 Feb. 82 (copy).
20. He was at this time also helping to support his widowed mother.
21. MP FJF to JAHM, 21 Jan. 82. Furnivall wrote that the Society 'was the fulcrum by which the work was continuously lifted, & the centre round which all the workers gathered … Fellows will do for a Socty. founded for public objects, what they won't do for 1 man who only wants to leave—as they think 5 or 10,000£ to each of his children instead of 500£'; JAHM to FJF, 25 Jan. 82 (copy). James pointed out that the Society had had its reward in the influx of new members attracted by the Dictionary when the Society was 'like to shrivel up into a narrow clique', and in the respect which the Dictionary had won for it.

22. MP JAHM to HG, 25 Feb. 82.

23. MP HG to JAHM, 17 Feb., 30 Apr., 4 May, 1 July 82.

24. MP AJE to JAHM, 16 July 82; HG to JAHM, 1 July 82.

25. MP FJF to JAHM, 23 Feb. 80.

26. MP JAHM to FJF, 25 Jan. 82 (copy).

27. G 11021/20. 547 a. JAHM to HG, 7 Feb. 80.

28. MP 'Dictionary expenses during the 3 Preliminary Years'.

29. MP JAHM to Postmaster, 4 July 79 (copy).

30. MP HG to JAHM, 1 July 82.

31. MP FJF to JAHM, 19 Mar. 82. FJF could not resist a mention of Ruthven's employment, 'of course you had a perfect right to keep him so long as his salary came out of your own pocket, but if an appeal has to be made to outsiders I think Mr R's £100 *must be taken as a payment to you*'.

32. MP AJE to JAHM, 10, 14, 16, 18, 23 July 82.

33. *Ibid.*, 29 July 82.

34. OD, 19 July 82, pp. 69/70.11; 26 July 82, p. 71.1; MP BP to JAHM, 28 July 82.

35. MP AJE to JAHM, 26 July, 1 Aug. 82.

36. *Ibid.*, 23 July 82.

37. *Periodical*, xiii 143 (13 Feb. 28), p. 21.

Notes to Chapter XII

1. *The Oxford University Press 1468–1921* (1922), p. 40.

2. OD, 8 Nov. 78, p. 409. Policy report; 29 Nov. 78, pp. 412–13. Memo. to the University Commissioners; 5 Dec. 79, p. 461.13; 27 Feb. 80, p. 469.16; 24 Jan. 93, p. 20.17. Unremunerative expenditure to be limited and regulated on some fixed principle.

3. MP FJF to JAHM, 9 Mar. 83. 'I think you'll have to scamp the work more as you go along ... let the next ed[ito]r fill in'; WS to FJF, 24 Oct. 83.

4. PSCM, 16 Mar. 83. FJF proposed 4 editors with JAHM in general control; OD, 3 Dec. 80, p. 264.16. Furnivall urged entrusting each volume to a separate editor.

5. OD, 11 May 83, p. 104.7. Negotiations on basis of £1 a page and £300 salary, on condition JAHM resided in Oxford.

6. MP FJF to JAHM, 12 June, 12, 22 Aug. 82. The scandal was hushed up, but did not improve relations with Furnivall, who felt JAHM had been too hard.

7. James, *op. cit.*, p. 260.

8. R. W. Chapman, *Lexicography. James*

Bryce Memorial Lecture (1948), pp. 15, 11–12. I am indebted to R. W. Burchfield for this reference.

9. MP JAHM, Dictionary report, 1906. E. L. Speight, who resigned in 1895, urged that a proper inspection of conditions in the Scriptorium be made, since the number of workers compelled to resign or to take prolonged sick leave was an indication that all was not well. Clarendon Press. Incoming Letters, 25 Nov. 95.

10. MP JAHM to BP, 18 June 84 (draft).

11. *Ibid.*, 9 June 83 (drafts 1 & 2).

12. OD, 15 June 83, p. 110.7; 7 July 83, p. 113.12; MP BP to JAHM, 29 June 83.

13. MP JAHM, note on expenses, 1884.

14. MP BP to JAHM, 27 Feb. 79; OD, 21 Feb. 79, p. 426.20; 27 Jan. 82, p. 45.18.

15. Geoffrey Faber, *Jowett* (1957), pp. 24, 30, 390; E. Abbott and L. Campbell, *Life and Letters of Benjamin Jowett* (1897), vol. ii, pp. 221–3; *Westminster Gazette, Extra Number*, 4 Oct. 93, p. 8.

16. MP BJ to JAHM, 27 July [83]; BP to JAHM, 28 July 83.

17. MP Rough notes by JAHM on events of 1883 [Oct. 83]. There is no entry in the Visitor's book of the Master's Lodge for 30–1 July 83.

18. MP Printed copy of the *Suggestions* with ms. Comments and notes by JAHM; JAHM to BJ, 24 Aug. 83.

19. MP JAHM, Comments on Suggestions.

20. MP J. Dixon to JAHM, 8, 29 Dec. 91.

21. MP JAHM to BJ, 24 Aug. 83 (copy).

22. MP JAHM, Comments on Suggestions.

23. *Ibid.*

24. MP JAHM to BP, 18 Aug. 83 (draft).

25. *Ibid.*

26. *Times Literary Supplement*, 13 Oct., 1972, p. 1226. M. Laski to Editor.

27. JAHM, Presidential address, *PST* (1882–4), p. 524.

28. *Periodical*, vol. xiii. 143 (15 Feb. 1928), p. 30.

29. MP JAHM to BP, 18 Oct. 83 (draft).

30. MP FJF notes, 22 Oct., 25 Oct. 83.

31. MP HG to JAHM, 28 Aug. 83.

32. MP JAHM, Notes on events of 1883.

33. G 11021/29. 13. L. Gibbs to VG, 17 Oct. 83 (letter wrongly dated, should be 18 Oct.); 11021/21 505 a. JAHM to HG, 20 Oct. 83; MP JAHM to BP, 18 Oct. 83 (draft).

34. MP JAHM to BP, 23 Oct. 83; G 11021/21. 507 a. JAHM to HG, n.d. [24? Oct. 83].

35. OD, 19 Oct. 83, p. 121.6 (2).

36. MP JAHM to BP, 23 Oct. 83 (draft).

37. G 11021/21. 508. JAHM to HG, 27 Oct. 83.
38. G 11021/29. 15. HG to VG, 2 Nov. 83.
39. G 11021/29. 17. L. Gibbs to VG, 10–15, Nov. 83; 11021/21 507 (c). Note by HG.
40. MP BJ to JAHM, 2 Nov. 83.
41. MP AJE to JAHM, 8 Nov. 83.
42. MP HG to JAHM, 4 Nov. 83.
43. G 11021/21. 513. JAHM to HG, 8 Nov. 83.
44. G 11021/21. 534 (c). HG to FJF, 10 Nov. 83.
45. MP HG to JAHM, 10 Nov. (2 letters), 12 Nov. 83.
46. G.11021/21. 518. HG to BJ, 10 Nov. 83 (copy).
47. 'meddling'.
48. MP HG to JAHM, 12 Nov. 83.
49. MP FH to JAHM, 10 Nov. 83.
50. G 11021/21. 523. BJ to HG, 11 Nov. 83; 521. H. G. Liddell to HG, 11 Nov. 83.
51. *Ibid.*, 523. BJ to HG, 11 Nov. 83.
52. *Ibid.*, 526. JAHM to HG, 13 Nov. 83.
53. *Ibid.*, 529. HG to BJ, 14 Nov. 83 (copy).
54. *Ibid.*, 534 (e). JAHM to HG, 3 Dec. 83.
55. OD, 19 Oct. 83, p. 121.6.1; 16 Nov. 83, p. 127.8.
56. The original title page was to read *A New English Dictionary on a Historical Basis. Founded mainly on Materials Collected by the Philological Society.* The Delegates wanted an alteration in order to avoid 'on ... basis' and 'founded on'. *Cf.* HG to JAHM, 4 Nov. 83. D. E. Erlebach, in a letter to *The Times* (28 Oct. 29), suggested that the reason for the change was a disagreement as to whether 'on a' or 'on an' Historical Basis is better, but the correspondence does not mention this.
57. G 11021/21. 534 (e). JAHM to HG, 3 Dec. 83.
58. MP FE to JAHM, 19, 21 Nov. 83; WS to JAHM, 28 Feb., 24 Mar. 84.
59. OD, 19 July 82, pp. 69–70.11.1. £100 advanced; 26 July 82, p. 71.1. Sum not exceeding £300 to be paid in respect of Part I; 1 June 83, p. 108.7. Further £100; 19 Oct. 83, p. 121.6 (3). £150 on account to enable payment of urgent needs and (4) payment to be made in respect of Part II, notwithstanding that sum advanced in respect of Part I was in excess of entitlement; 14 Dec. 83, p. 132.7. £150 paid on account of Part II; MP BP to JAHM, 22 Dec. 83.
60. G 11021/21. 536. JAHM to HG, 26 Dec. 83.
61. MP JAHM to BP, 17 Jan. 84 (copy).
62. MP HG to JAHM, 23 July 82; 5 Nov. 83; 28 Dec. 83.
63. MP BP to JAHM, 29 Jan. 84.
64. *Academy* (16 Feb. 84), pp. 105 sq.; (1 Mar. 84), pp. 141 sq. Reprinted in Bradley, *Collected Papers*, pp. 127 sq.
65. MP HB to JAHM, 11 June, 28 July 84.
66. JAHM to AECRM, 9 June 05. 'I have had to work so long without adequate recognition that I have ceased to care for mere empty honours, feeling more satisfied with my own consciousness of doing good work, than either the praise or blame of anyone.'
67. MP JAHM to AAM, 16 Apr. 84. Quoted by HJRM, *Biography.*
68. MP J. R. Lowell to JAHM, 5 Jan. 81. *Cf.* Lowell, *My Study Windows* (1871), p. 232.
69. MP OARM to HJRM, Easter Monday 31.
70. MP H. Seymour to JAHM, 20 Mar. 84. The Delegacy had supported the application. OD, 22 Feb. 84, p. 143.20 (a).
71. MP FJF to JAHM, 24 Mar. 84. Efforts to obtain a pension had begun in 1882, but were postponed till the publication of Part I. *Cf.* MP AJE to JAHM, 30 Dec. 82; HG to AJE, 25 Apr. 85; H. Seymour to JAHM, 20 Jan. 83.
72. MP HG to FJF, 5 Nov. 82. *Cf.* G 11021/21. 546. AJE to FJF, 24 Jan. 84.
73. MP JAHM to W. E. Gladstone, 22 Mar. 81 (draft).
74. In 1892 a pension of £150 was obtained for H. Bradley. OD, 10 June 92, p. 545.20 (1); 18 July 92, p. 549.13.
75. MP BP to JAHM, 22 Mar. 84; JAHM to BJ, 26 Aug. 84 (draft).
76. MP HG to JAHM, 4 Nov. 83; FE to JAHM, 19, 21 Nov. 83, 29 May 84; EA to JAHM, 24 Dec. 84; R. Harley to JAHM, 23 May 84.
77. MP RE to JAHM, 24 Oct. 88, 25 May 91; J. Burnet to JAHM, 8, 27 Oct. 92; A. S. Peake to JAHM, 8 Oct. 92; BJ to JAHM, 14 Feb. 92.
78. MP JAHM, Letter of application [July 95] (draft); JAHM to HW, 4 Jan. 96.
79. MP JAHM to BP, 17, 18 June 84 (drafts). The letter was modified by HG. *Cf.* MP HG to JAHM, 19 June 84. A statement of expenses was attached as follows:

Dr Murray* £250 (Pension) +	£500
3 1st class Assistants	
£300 + £250 + £200	750
3 2nd class Assistants,	
£100 each	300
2 3rd class Assistants,	
£75 + £50	125

Expenses, Postage, Paper, Books,
Carriage of heavy boxes of
materials to volunteer Sub-
Editors & back; lighting, heating _____ 75
£1750

* (Prof. Price will state what Mr Gibbs & I thought would
be fair in the event of the Editor receiving additional
pecuniary help from any source, with a view to relieve the
Press of part of its expenses.)

See OD, 20 June 84, p. 156.9 and attached
letter.
80. G 11021/22. 935. JAHM to HG, 18 June
84.
81. MP HG to JAHM, 19 June 84; G
11021/22. 939. JAHM to HG, 19 June 84.
JAHM agreed to omit 'various *intensive*
words'.
82. MP BP to JAHM, 1 July 84; OD, 20
June 84, p. 156.9; 17 July 84, p. 160.10. The
new clause relating to the two-year term was
not to be communicated to JAHM till HG
was consulted.
83. MP JAHM to BP, 2 July 84.
84. MP JAHM to HG, 3 July 84 (draft).
85. MP FJF to JAHM, 9 July 84.
86. G 11021/22. 426. HG to VG, 26 July 84.
87. MP BJ to JAHM, 24 Aug. 84; OD, 24
July 84, p. 162. 2, 31 July 84, pp. 163–4.5. 1.
88. MP FJF to JAHM, 29 July 84.
89. OD, 17 Oct. 84. 168. 16; 31 Oct. 84, p.
171.10; 28 Nov. 84, p. 179.15; MP BP to
JAHM, 22 Oct. 84.
90. MP BP to FJF, 7 Nov. 82.
91. OD, 22 Feb. 84, p. 143.20 (b); 14 Mar.
84, p. 144.17.
92. MP HG to FJF, 30 Apr. 84; FJF to
JAHM, 28 Apr. 84.
93. MP HG to JAHM, 15 Dec. 89.
94. MP HG to JAHM, 3 Feb. 85; OD, 23
Jan. 85, p. 184.15 (1); 20 Feb. 85, p. 189.13.
95. MP JAHM to BP, 4 Feb. 85; OD, 20
Feb. 85, p. 184.13.
96. OD, 6 Mar. 85, p. 191.10; MP BP to
JAHM, 12 Mar. 85.
97. MP FJF to JAHM, 25 Apr. 85.
98. MP BP to WS, 9 May 85 (copy extract by
WS); WS to JAHM, 19 May [85].
99. PSCM, 6 Nov. 85; see MP AJE to
JAHM, 8 Feb., 12 Feb. (postcard) 85; AJE
to HG, 25 Apr. 85.
100. The purchase was made possible by a
loan from WS. See p. 249 below.
101. MP FJF to JAHM, 6 Jan. 85.
102. MP BP to JAHM, 7 May 85; JAHM to
BP, 6 May 85 (draft).
103. MP FJF to JAHM, 29 Nov. 92.
104. OD, 3 May 89, p. 368.13 (4); 18 Oct. 89,

p. 389.20 (4); MP LG to JAHM, 28 Nov. 89.
105. *The Christian Leader*, 14 July 87.
106. MP JAHM to RFW, 8 June 85 (copy);
also printed 'Letter to Old Boys', 13 June 85.
James, *op. cit.*, pp. 305, 308.
107. MP AAM to JAHM, 10 June 85; J.
Mitchell to JAHM, 13 June 85 (postcard).
108. Faber, *op. cit.*, pp. 37–8.
109. M. Deneke, *Ernest Walker* (1951), p.
30.
110. AHJM, *Memoirs*.
111. Stanley, Dean of Westminster,
1815–81; Clough, poet, 1819–61.
112. GFT, p. 20.

Notes to Chapter XIII

1. OD, 22 May 85, p. 202.17.
2. MP WS to JAHM, 16 Mar. [85].
3. MP HS to JAHM, 4 Apr. 70.
4. J. S. Blackie. *Letters to his Wife*, ed. A. S.
Walker (1909), p. 365 note.
5. N. C. Chaudhuri, *Scholar Extraordinary.
The Life of Professor the Rt. Hon. Frederick
Max Müller* (1974), pp. 211, 218.
6. MP JAHM to BP, 6 May 85.
7. G 11021/513. JAHM to HG, 8 Nov. 83.
Postscript.
8. MP F. Pollock to JAHM. 9 July 83.
9. He did not take an MA degree until 1896.
He could have taken this in lieu of the Hon.
MA in 1885, but it would have cost him £30.
Cf. MP BJ to JAHM, 10 Oct. 85.
10. L. R. Farnell, *An Oxonian Looks Back*
(1934), p. 276.
11. MP JAHM, Farewell speech on retirement of the Rev. J. Robertson.
12. *Oxford Review*, 6 May 85.
13. MP WS to JAHM, 19 Jan. 85; undated
letter [Sept. 85]; 13 Sept. 96.
14. MP FJF to JAHM, 7, 11 Nov. 87; 29
Nov. 92; JAHM to FJF, 5 July 93 (draft);
FJF to JAHM, 11 July 93. FJF insisted that
with £750 *p.a.* James could not be called a
poor man.
15. I. Bywater to JAHM, 10 May 14. 'I had
no idea of there being any trouble of that
kind with you.'
16. MP JAHM to JRM, 14 June 05; JRM to
JAHM, 16 June 05. JAHM estimated that
since coming to Oxford he had spent £1000
in excess of his income, drawn from his
savings, a £50 legacy from his mother, a
legacy to Ada from her father, and a life
insurance repaid at 60. Details of later
financial difficulties are in letters of JAHM
to HJRM, OARM and AHJM, 1912–15. In
1914 the Delegates, learning of these

difficulties, made him an *ex gratia* payment of £25. CC to JAHM, 29 May 14.

17. MP JAHM to BP, 9 June 83.

18. MP L. Toulmin Smith to JAHM, 29 July 85.

19. *Athenaeum* (21 May 87), p. 666; PSCM, 19 Nov. 86. Many booksellers cancelled their orders.

20. *Athenaeum* (9 Feb. 84), pp. 177–8; 2 Dec. 93, p. 766.

21. PS Secretary's Papers, ii, Dictionary accounts, 1 July 85–30 June 86.

22. *Newbery House Magazine*, viii, i. (Jan. 1893), p. 10. The price of the *DNB* was almost double. *Cf.* G 11021/30. 576, CC to H. Boyd, 24 Nov. 02.

23. PSOM, 5 Nov. 97.

24. MP JAHM to BP, 9 June 83 (first draft).

25. PSCM, 19 Feb. 86.

26. MP JAHM to LG, 20 May 86.

27. LG to JAHM, 16 July 85.

28. Clarendon Press. Incoming Letters. JAHM to CED, 13 July 85; JAHM to LG, 17 July 85.

29. OD, 29 Jan. 86, p. 223.12; 12 Mar. 86, p. 233.16.

30. PSCM, 16 Apr. 86; OD, 21 May 86, p. 240.13.

31. MP LG to JAHM and CED to JAHM, 17 May 86.

32. MP LG to JAHM, 23 June 86.

33. MP JAHM to LG, 24 June 86.

34. MP LG to JAHM, 28 Aug. 86.

35. *Ibid.*, 3 Sept. 86. This occurred because HB, working ahead on words for Part II, found that because of the bulk of words in B his section would have to be included with a later part, so he went back to unprepared material. *Cf.* HB to JAHM, 20 Aug., 4 Sept. 86.

36. OD, 22 Oct. 86, p. 256.11.

37. MP LG to JAHM, 16 Nov. 86.

38. *Ibid.*, 31 Jan. 87.

39. OD, 4 Feb. 87, p. 269.5.

40. MP LG to JAHM, 23 Mar. 87.

41. *Ibid.*, 6 June 87.

42. MP A. Erlebach to JAHM, 25 June 86; G. F. H. Sykes to JAHM, 19 June 87.

43. MP WS to JAHM, 24 Mar. 86.

44. MP LG to JAHM, 28 Sept. 87.

45. OUP JAHM to FH, 29 June 94.

46. MP LG to JAHM, 6 June, 8 July 87; OD, 1 July 87, p. 289.11, 21 Oct. 87, p. 244.18.

47. OD, 4 Nov. 87, p. 297.8.

48. MP LG to JAHM, 3 Nov., 30 Nov. 87.

49. *Ibid.*, 14 May, 1 June 96; JAHM to CC (undated draft); OD, 22 May 96, p. 190.14.

50. MP BP to JAHM, 27 Mar. 86.

51. MP WS to JAHM, 2 Jan. 81. Attempts to forecast the time needed for the different letters continued to fail. *Cf.* MP JAHM, Dictionary Report, 1899, p. 6.

52. H. Bradley, Obituary of JAHM, *British Academy Proceedings*, vol. viii (1915), pp. 4–5.

53. MP HB to JAHM, 12 Dec. 92.

54. MP JAHM to BP, 17 Apr. 86.

55. MP JAHM to LG, 16 Nov. 87.

Notes to Chapter XIV'

1. MP HB to JAHM, 3 July 85. 'I find this such slow work that I fear your funds are not likely to enable you to pay what will compensate me for the time I spend over it.'

2. MP JAHM to LG, 24 June 86.

3. OD, 13 June 90, p. 424.18; 31 May 92, p. 542, 18.

4. OD, 11 Mar. 92, p. 527.16; 13 May 92, p. 538.16.2 (c). The rate per page was advanced from 30 shillings to £3. Earlier than this attention had been called to Bradley's failure to achieve the agreed output. OD, 17 Oct. 90, p. 431.14 (b). *Cf.* Bywater's report annexed to OD, 21 Feb. 96, p. 170. He estimated HB's pace at $\frac{1}{3}$ to JAHM's $\frac{2}{3}$.

5. MP LG to FJF, 7 Dec. 92.

6. OD, 23 Oct. 85, p. 213.7; MP HB to JAHM, 12 Dec. 90.

7. Furnivall Papers, JAHM to WS, 20 Apr. 04.

8. G 11021/24 397. JAHM to HG, 6 Nov. 86 and HG note. f. 795. (32). 533 JAHM to HG, 14 Nov. 87.

9. MP HG to JAHM, 12 Nov. 87.

10. G 11021/24 547. HB to HG, 30 Jan. 88.

11. MP HB to JAHM, 1 July 93.

12. Bradley, Obituary of JAHM, *loc. cit.*, p. 5.

13. OUP EP/MURRA/32 JAHM to HB, 2 Apr. 12.

14. G 11021/24, f. 795 (32). HG note to letter 397, JAHM to HG, 6 Nov. 86.

15. OD, 27 Apr. 88, p. 319.10.

16. OD, *ibid.* and 17 Feb. 88, p. 315.12.

17. OD, 27 Apr. 88, p. 319.10.

18. OUP JAHM to FH, 21 Sept. 96, 22 Sept. 98.

19. MP FJF to JAHM, 18, 19 Mar. 90 (postcards).

20. MP FH to JAHM, 17 Sept. 90.

21. MP J. Brown to JAHM, 11 Mar. 83. *Cf.* also letters from E. S. Brandreth, 5 Mar. 90, J. T. Fowler, 5 Mar. 90, E. Thompson, 24 Mar. 90.

22. OUP EP/SIE/2. E. Sievers to JAHM, 24 Feb. 88.

23. J. R. Hulbert, *Dictionaries British and American* (1955), p. 33. This was an encyclopaedic Dictionary which included quotations and definitions. It benefited by the example of *OED* at the start but soon, progressing more rapidly, lost the advantage of drawing upon the larger work.

24. MP FJF to JAHM, 19 Oct., 24 Oct. (postcard), 26 Oct. 89. See also HB to JAHM, 18 Oct. 89; R. Martineau to JAHM, 22 Oct. 89; F. Pollock to JAHM, 20 Oct. 89.

25. *Academy* (10 May 90), pp. 320–1.

26. MP F. A. March to JAHM, 30 May 90.

27. *Ibid.*, 26 Aug. 90.

28. HJRM, Biography.

29. MP JAHM to HMRM, 13 Sept. 90.

30. MP BP to JAHM, 29 Nov. 92.

31. MP LG to FJF, 7 Dec. 92.

32. OD, 21 Feb. 90, p. 409.14; MP LG to FJF, 7 Dec. 92; Copy of resolution of the PS Council, 16 Dec. 92.

33. OD, Printed report of the Dictionary Committee, 4 Feb. 93, insert p. 25, received by Delegacy, 10 Feb. 93, p. 25.14. *Cf.* MP HB to JAHM, 12 Dec. 92.

34. Clarendon Press. Incoming letters. JAHM to CED, 21 Aug. 91 (wrongly filed under 1892).

35. MP LG to JAHM, 11 May 97. In 1968 when the *Supplement* was in preparation, graduates in scientific subjects were added to the staff and a panel of consultants formed to read the proofs of articles on the scientific words. *Cf. OED, Supplement*, vol. i, Introduction, p. xiv.

36. S. Johnson, *Preface to Dictionary of the English Language*, quoted by JAHM, *OED*, vol. i, Preface, p. xi.

37. P. 153 above.

38. Aquarone, *op. cit.*, p. 79; Littré, *Causerie, loc. cit.*, p. 84.

39. OD, 3 Dec. 86, p. 264.16; MP FJF to JAHM, 7 Nov. 87.

40. MP FJF to JAHM, 9 Nov. 87.

41. *Ibid.*, 18 Nov. 87 (2 letters of this date).

42. Clarendon Press. Incoming letters. FJF to LG, 3 Dec. 92.

43. MP LG to FJF, 7 Dec. 92.

44. MP FJF to JAHM, 28 Dec. 92. LG to JAHM, 30 Nov. 87 quotes the PS opinion that the desire for perfection should not be permitted to delay early completion of the work.

45. Information from P. H. Sutcliffe, whose book on the history of the Press is in preparation.

46. MP WS to JAHM, 2 Jan. 93 (wrongly dated 1892).

47. MP Printed report of the Dictionary Committee, 4 Feb. 93; OD, 10 Feb. 93, inset, p. 25.

48. A Sub-Editor, 'A few words about the New English Dictionary', *Newbery House Magazine*, viii, i. (Jan. 93), p. 12.

49. MP LG to JAHM, 6 Mar. 93; OD, 10 Mar. 93, p. 31.16 (2 B).

50. Later it was changed to £16 per page of Webster above a norm of 25 pages. LG to JAHM, 9 July 95; OD, 14 June 95, p. 137.7 (1) and (2).

51. MP JAHM to JRM, 14 June 05.

52. MP F. A. Yockney to JAHM, 23 Dec. 11. Yockney, an assistant, had lost few hours himself, but a drop in bonus left him worse off than the year before. Between 1907 and 1911 his salary rose from £114 to £132 *p.a.* but the bonus fell from £15 to nil, leaving him only £3 better off, and rising costs of living left him in debt.

53. MP CC to JAHM, 12 Dec. 08.

54. Corpus Christi College, Melbourne. JAHM to FJF, 7 July 05.

55. MP H. A. Nesbitt to JAHM, 12 Sept. 09.

56. MP CC to JAHM, 20 Dec. 07; OD, 26 Jan. 06, p. 75.1119.

57. MP JAHM to WS, 29 Mar. 93.

58. MP WS to JAHM, 29 Apr., 24 Mar. 93.

59. MP JAHM to LG, 27 Feb. 93 (draft).

60. PSOM, 24 Jan. 90.

61. MP Doc. IV, JAHM to LG, 5 Mar. 96.

62. OD, 10 Mar. 93, p. 13.17; 12 May 93, p. 37.5 (a); 8 Aug. 94, p. 90.9 (1).

63. MP JAHM to LG, 27 Feb. 93 (draft). *Cf.* CED to JAHM, 19, 26 June 94.

64. MP JAHM to LG, 27 Jan. 96 (copy).

65. MP Doc. I. Delegates' Order, 7 Feb. 96.

66. Ingram Bywater (1840–1914) appreciated good scholarship and gave regular help to the Dictionary on words of Greek origin. Appointed a Delegate in 1879, he continued as a supernumerary after retirement until his death, and was associated with the Dictionary for longer than any other Delegate.

67. OD, 18 Nov. 92, p. 10.2, Resolution (b). They were in a minority in asking that a report of the Finance Committee be referred to arbitration; *ibid.*, 2 Dec. 92, p. 16.13.

68. MP Doc. I. Delegates' Order, 7 Feb. 96.

69. OD, 21 Feb. 96, p. 170. Inset ms. report from Bywater.

70. MP CED to JAHM, 25 Feb. 96. *Cf.* Doc. II. Delegates' Order, 21 Feb. 96.

71. MP Doc. IV. JAHM to LG, 5 Mar. 96; VI. FH to HB, 16 Mar. 96. See also HB to

JAHM, 26 Feb. 96.
72. MP Doc. VII. Delegates' Order, 20 Mar. 96.
73. MP Doc. VIII. Delegates' Order, 27 Mar. 96, quoting resolution of the PS Council, 20 Mar. 96; IX. LG to JAHM and HB, 2 Apr. 96.
74. MP Doc. XI. Resolution of the PS Council, 17 Apr. 96; X. HB to LG, 11 Apr. 96; XII. JAHM to LG, 23 Apr. 96.
75. *Saturday Review*, 18 Apr. 96.
76. MP LG to JAHM, 9 May 96; OD, 18 May 96, p. 185.4.
77. MP LG to JAHM, 18 May 96.
78. MP Doc. XII. JAHM to LG, 23 Apr. 96.
79. MP JAHM to HMRM, 22 Apr. 96.
80. MP JAHM to J. Churton Collins, 9 Feb. 95 (copy).
81. MP JAHM to L. C. Collins, 4 June 10 (copy).

Notes to Chapter XV

1. MP LG to JAHM, 22, 27 Sept. 93; CED to JAHM, 2 Nov. 93; LG to JAHM, 23 Jan. 94.
2. *OED Supplement* 1933, Introduction, pp. xxv–vi gives dates of publication.
3. MP LG to JAHM, 28 Oct. 89; JAHM to LG, 30 Oct. 89. *Cf.* FJF to JAHM, 31 Jan. 88; LG to JAHM, 17 June 89; CED to JAHM, 21 June 89; WS to JAHM, 11 Oct. 98.
4. *Cf.* p. 258 above and MP FH to JAHM, 10 Jan. 88.
5. MP HB to JAHM, 27, 31 May 86.
6. MP HB to LG, quoted by LG to JAHM, 30 Nov. 87; OUP PP/1888/1. LG's printed circular letter to voluntary helpers, dated Feb. 88, stated, 'The Delegates of the Clarendon Press, with the concurrence of Dr Murray and of the Philological Society, have invited Mr Henry Bradley to undertake the preparation of an independent portion of the New English Dictionary with the view of expediting the publication . . .'
7. MP JAHM, Dictionary Report, 1899, f. 11; LG to JAHM, 6, 11, 24 May 97.
8. MP LG to JAHM, 14, 16 June 97.
9. I am indebted to Mr P. H. Sutcliffe for information about Lyttelton Gell.
10. MP JAHM to LG, 15 June 97 (copy).
11. MP LG to JAHM, 21 June 97; JAHM to LG, 22 Oct. 97.
12. MP WS to JAHM, 11, 13 Oct. 98.
13. MP CC to JAHM, 21 Jan. 99. OD, 20 Jan. 99, p. 77.13 (2); 27 Jan. 99, p. 79.6 (2).

14. OD, 8 Feb. 01, p. 233.7.3a; 22 Feb. 01. 10 (2).
15. OD, 21 Jan. 98, p. 415.2 (1) b. MP H. C. Gerrans to JAHM, 21 Jan. 98.
16. For volumes published after JAHM's death, the words 'with the assistance of many scholars and men of science', which he had insisted should follow his name in recognition of his band of volunteer readers, were omitted. His position as Editor-in-chief was continued by placing his name first, but otherwise the four editors were given equal standing, the authors of each part then being given below as before. But on the spine of the first edition from vol. vi (the first to which he made no contribution) Murray's name appears immediately under the title, and the names of the Editors of that particular volume are given below his.
17. G 11021/30. 741. JAHM to HG, 15 Apr. 04 (marked Private).
18. *Periodical*, xix. 173 (15 Mar. 34), p. 4.
    In 32 years JAHM averaged 224 pages a year.
    In 29 years HB averaged 155 pages a year.
    In 27 years WAC averaged 109 pages a year.
    In 16 years CTO averaged 52 pages a year.
19. MP JAHM, 'Proposed Scheme for the Scale and Distribution of future Letters and Volumes of the *OED*,' 12 June 96 (printed); CED to JAHM, 26 June 96; JAHM to CED, 27 June 96 (draft); HB to LG, 13 July 96 (printed) commenting on JAHM's scheme; JAHM to LG, 23 July 96 (incomplete draft) reply to HB's letter.
20. MP CC to JAHM, 29 Mar. 01.
21. MP JAHM to WAC, 10 May 01.
22. MP CC to JAHM, 27 Nov. 02; JAHM to CC, 29 Nov. 02; CC to JAHM, 29 Dec. 02 (WAC's failure to condense sufficiently).
23. MP JAHM to WAC, 10 May 01.
24. MP WAC to JAHM, 6 Dec. 02.
25. MP JAHM to CC, 29 Nov. 02.
26. MP CC to JAHM, 9 Jan. 03 giving the cost for the last section as: compositing £197, corrections £121.
27. MP FJF to JAHM, 7, 14 Mar. 92; JAHM to FJF, 8 Mar. 92.
28. MP HB to JAHM, 8, 14, 16 Mar. 92; B. Dawson to JAHM, 14 Mar. 92.
29. MP FJF to JAHM, 14 Mar. 92.
30. MP E. L. Brandreth to JAHM, 20 Mar. 92; HB to JAHM, 16 Mar. 92; FJF to JAHM, 18 Mar. 92. *Cf.* PSCM, 18 Mar., 1 Apr. 92.

31. MP FJF to JAHM, 14 Mar. 92.

32. MP *Ibid.*, 12 Oct. 97, also 5 Dec. 96.

33. See p. 282 above.

34. MP JAHM to JRM, 14 June 05. FJF accused JAHM of unfairness to Bradley in that, when forced to divide his staff in 1887, G. F. H. Sykes, who had already been warned that he lacked suitability (MP JAHM to Sykes, 24 June 86), was transferred to HB. HB constantly complained of his inefficiency (HB to JAHM, 9 Dec. 93; FJF to JAHM, 29 Nov. 28 Dec. 92). Since JAHM was anxious that the work should not suffer from HB's inexperience, it seems unlikely that he would deliberately hamper him, and he probably set against Sykes' limitations the fact that he was conscientious and, because of his experience, of more value than a newcomer would be for some time, especially in view of the difficulty experienced in finding any suitable assistants. He was also concerned for Sykes, a married man, and spoke of the 'intense pain' with which he contemplated having to dispense with his services. HB himself found no solution and Sykes remained his assistant till 1903.

35. OUP JAHM to WAC, 13 Mar. 13.

36. MP JAHM, note on back of letter H. Kingsford to JAHM, 28 June 99; CC to JAHM, 19 Jan. 01.

37. OUP JAHM to WAC, 25 Apr. 01.

38. I am indebted to R. W. Burchfield for this information from C. T. Onions.

39. C. T. Onions, Obituary of H. Bradley, *English Association Bulletin*, No. 49 (Dec. 1923), p. 23.

40. OUP JAHM to WAC, 3 Dec. 02. WAC accepted the direction given to him unwillingly. *CF.* MP WAC to JAHM, 6 Dec. 02.

41. OUP Proof of part of *P* marked 'Dr M. criticises quotations. 1 Feb. 09'.

42. MP HB to JAHM, 21 Nov. 01; JAHM to HB (undated draft); HB to JAHM, 25 Nov. 01.

43. E.g. MP F. W. Maitland to JAHM, 22 May 94, returning slips on *owner*; WS to JAHM, 21 Nov. 99. Has mislaid slip on *yuga* and warns JAHM not to send him anything unique; Bishop of Salisbury to JAHM, 30 Feb. 08. JAHM has borrowed for him from WAC slips on *Romanensian* and *Romish*.

44. MP JAHM to unnamed correspondent, 13 Aug. 01 (draft).

45. E.g. when Bradley was away for three months. See MP LG to JAHM, 2 June 92.

46. MP WS to JAHM, 29 Mar. 96.

47. Gladstone quoted *OED* for *put up job*, *The Times*, 6 Dec. 93; Joseph Chamberlain consulted JAHM on origin of *patriotism* used in his speech at installation as Rector, Glasgow University, *ibid.*, 4 Nov. 97; MP Inquiry re meaning of *proper* in Licensing Act 1828, G. L. Fenwick, Chief Constable of Cheshire, to JAHM, 28 Sept. 93; Lord Rosebery on *calumny*, used by Premier in debate, *Punch*, 23 Mar. 04; fictitious debate with JAHM in chair, 'Should we not strain every nerve to enlarge the language?' *ibid.*, 25 May 04.

48. MP LG to JAHM, 21 June, 17 Aug. 97. *Periodical*, iv. (Dec. 1897), p. 1. On completion in 1928 the last volume was presented to George V.

49. MP JRM to JAHM, 16 June 05.

50. MP CC to JAHM, 21 Dec. 06, 20 Dec. 07, 18 Mar. 02.

51. MP WS to JAHM, 29 Mar. 96.

52. MP JRM to JAHM, 9 Aug. 97.

53. OUP JAHM to FH, 20 Oct. 97.

54. *Daily Chronicle*, 13 Oct. 97; *Christian World*, 14 Oct. 97.

55. *Periodical*, iv. 4 (Dec. 97), p. 4.

NEW ENGLISH DICTIONARY

Receipts and Expenses for a year and accumulated deficit to March 31, 1902, when about half the book was completed.

	£	s	d	£	s	d
Expenditure to 31 March 1901				81,298	18	5¾
Add for year 1901–2:						
Literary expenses	3,365	7	6			
Printing, Paper, Binding and Plates	2,557	11	5			
Advertising etc. & trade expenses	761	5				
				6,684	3	11
				87,983	2	4¾
Receipts to March 31 1901	26,075	0	11¾			
Receipts for year 1901–2	2,807	11	6¾			
				28,882	12	6¼
31 March 1902						
Actual net deficit not including interest on outlay or warehousing				59,100	9	10¼

56. *The Times*, 14 Oct. 97, quoted in *Periodical, loc. cit.*

57. MP JAHM, Dictionary Report, 1899, p. 10.

58. JAHM, *The Evolution of English Lexicography*, Romanes Lecture, 1900, p. 49.

59. G 11021/30. 779: [see foot of p. 374.]

60. MP HG to JAHM, 14 Apr. 04; Alban Gibbs to JAHM, 21 Jan. 05; HG to JAHM, 8 June 05.

61. MP CC to JAHM, 1 Oct. 08.

62. MP JAHM to Thomas Shaw, 5 June 05 (draft); A. Carnegie to JAHM, 13 July 05.

63. Awarded in 1886, 1896, 1901, 1902, 1905, 1908, 1913 respectively.

64. Correspondence of Miss Jones, Girton College Cambridge. I am indebted to Miss H. I. McMorran, former librarian, for this reference. Glasgow was in fact only his sixth degree.

65. MP JAHM, Lecture to the Ashmolean Natural History Society.

66. Awarded in 1905, 1909, 1913, 1913, 1914, 1907, 1914 and 1909 respectively.

67. JAHM to AECRM, 6 Mar. 03. When the Dictionary was completed in 1928 the British Academy awarded JAHM one of the three first gold medals struck to commemorate preeminent achievement in the field of English scholarship. It was presented to HJRM and is in possession of JAHM's great grandson, J. G. Murray.

68. The mss. of these lectures are in MP.

69. OD, 19 June 14, p. 30.3023.

70. MP JAHM to HMRM, 4 Nov. 14.

71. MP JAHM to HJRM, 11 June 08; also JAHM to OARM, 10 June 08, in possession of Mrs Bergne.

72. MP JAHM to H. H. Asquith, 18 June 08 (copy).

73. JAHM to OARM, 29 June and to AECRM, 2 July 08 (letters in possession of Mrs Bergne and Mrs Manning) and to WGRM, 1913, quoted by WGRM, p. 122.

74. MP JAHM to HMRM, 10 May 10.

75. JAHM to AECRM, 28 Oct. 04, quoted by WGRM, p. 122.

76. Birmingham University Library. EA 148, JAHM to EA, 14 Jan. 1900.

77. OUP JAHM to FH, 31 Dec. 96.

78. MP JAHM to FJF (undated draft [Dec. 96]).

79. JAHM to AECRM, 6 Feb. 13.

80. G. Renwick, 'A Great Dictionary Maker', *Daily Chronicle*, 1 Nov. 13.

81. MP JAHM to AAM, 18 May 14.

82. MP JAHM to Kate M. Murray, 10 Oct. 12.

83. P. J. Philip, 'In the Scriptorium', *Daily News*, 28 July 15. The 'skull-cap' was his Edinburgh 'Knox' cap.

84. MP JAHM, Second lecture to the Oxford English School (1911), p. 23.

85. The letter from George Elio at Girton College, Cambridge. That from R. L. Stevenson is MP RLS to JAHM [Jan. 87].

86. MP A. Brandl to JAHM, 13 Oct. 11.

87. MP JAHM to HW, 23 June 1900.

88. MP R. H. Humes, Birmingham Book Club, to JAHM, 1 May 06, note by JAHM.

89. MP JAHM to FJF, 1 Dec. 96; FJF to JAHM, 10 Apr. 07.

90. MP JAHM, Dictionary Report, 1906. JAHM to AECRM, 8 June 06.

91. JAHM to AECRM, May day 03.

92. MP JAHM to HMRM, 18 Mar. 08.

93. 'A Dictionary in the Making', *Morning Post*, 25 Feb. 13.

94. MP JAHM to the President, Imperial Academy of Science, Vienna, undated draft [05].

95. Birmingham University Library. EA 149. JAHM to EA, 24 Dec. 04.

96. MP JAHM, Dictionary Report, 1906.

Notes to Chapter XVI

1. MP JAHM, Dictionary Report, 1908.

2. MP FJF to JAHM, 15 Apr. 10.

3. MP JAHM to HMRM, 17 Apr. 10.

4. Corpus Christi College Melbourne, JAHM to FJF, 17 Apr. 10.

5. *DNB*. The correspondence between JAHM and FH is divided between MP and OUP. K. M. Wales wrote on the OUP letters in *N & Q*, vol. ccxix (Dec. 1974), pp. 463–6. For dispute with the PS see PSCM, 19 Feb. 69 and OUP JAHM to FH, 11 Apr., 4 May 99.

6. MP FH to JAHM, 18 Nov. 92, 3 May 97, 12 May, 7 Aug., 1900; R. D. Hall to JAHM, 15 Feb. 01; OUP JAHM to R. D. Hall, 17 Feb. 01.

7. MP S. D. Saunders to JAHM, 27 Aug. 06; FH to JAHM, 18 Nov. 92. FH's son R. D. Hall wrote warmly of his father: R. D. Hall to JAHM, 15 Feb. 01.

8. *OED*, JAHM prefaces to vols. i, p. xiii, ii, p. vii, iii, p. vii, v, pp. vi–vii; OUP JAHM to FH, 13 Nov. 95.

9. OUP JAHM to WAC, 25 Apr. 01, 28 Oct. 02.

10. OUP JAHM to R. D. Hall, 17 Feb. 01; JAHM to FH, 7 Dec. 93.

11. MP Doc. VI. FH to HB, 16 Mar. 96; FH to JAHM, 19 Mar., 17 Sept. 90.

12. See Hayden Church, 'The Strange Case of Dr Minor', *Strand Magazine* (Sept. 1915), p. 251 sq.; *Lloyd's Weekly News*, 24 Oct. 15. Interest was revived when a stone lion, all that remained of the Brewery after enemy action, was restored for the South Bank Festival of Britain exhibition.

13. OUP JAHM to WAC, 28 July 01. When Minor gave up work he handed JAHM his more important books and indices. *Cf.* OUP JAHM to J. J. Thompson, 3 Oct. 02.

14. MP C. W. Minor to JAHM, 25 July 05.

15. Francis H. Brown of Boston. He was visiting Oxford with a party of librarians. See MP F. H. Brown to JAHM (undated) and JAHM to HMRM, 8 Apr. 10.

16. See MP William Platt, *James Platt the Younger* (privately printed, London, n.d.).

17. *PST* (1882–4), Abstracts 17 Nov. 82, pp. i–ii; PSCM, 16 Feb., 2 Mar. 83; MP HS to JAHM, 9 Feb. 83.

18. MP JAHM to J. Platt, 23 June 99 (draft); J. Platt to JAHM, 28 June 99.

19. MP JAHM to Mrs Platt, [n.d.] (draft); Mrs Platt to JAHM, 29 Mar. 10.

20. MP JAHM, Dictionary Report, 1899.

21. JAHM to AECRM, 14 Dec. 06.

22. MP JAHM to WS, 22 July 12.

23. JAHM to AECRM, 2 May 13.

24. Corpus Christi College Melbourne, JAHM to FJF, 17 Apr. 10.

25. JAHM to AECRM, 25 Nov. 04.

26. JAHM to AHJM, 22 May 14.

27. Harvey Cushing, *Life of Sir William Osler* (1925), ii, p. 199 n.

28. JAHM to AHJM, 3 Jan. 15.

29. MP JAHM to HW, 26 Apr. 15.

30. WGRM, pp. 124–5.

31. *Periodical*, v. lxxxiii (Sept. 1915), p. 201.

32. *Times Literary Supplement*, 13 Oct. 1972, p. 1211. The writer cites as defects the intentional exclusion of recent dialect words and forms, specialist technical terms and taboo obscene words. In a few instances the sense analyses require re-doing. The normal limitation of one quotation per century is inadequate. In the same issue, p. 1226, Miss Marghanita Laski takes this criticism further in a plea for the need of a perpetual trust to revise the *OED* continuously, and says, 'The *OED* is still — just — a working tool that is deservedly a world-famous glory of English culture. Soon now it will be a magnificent fossil.'

33. *Periodical*, xiii. 143 (19 Feb. 28), p. 1.

34. OD, 22 Oct. 15, p. 72; MP Printed copy.

Notes to Chapter XVII

1. See p. 228 *supra*.

2. MP JAHM to HJRM, 23 June 08.

3. Only the youngest, Gwyneth, felt her father to be a remote being, immersed in his work. In her case there was a very wide age gap: James was 51 when she was born. She missed the memorable family holidays in the Lake District.

4. JAHM to AECRM, 5 Aug. 04.

5. JAHM to AHJM, 24 Feb., 13 June 11; JAHM to AECRM, 27 Apr. 06.

6. 'How to compile a Great Dictionary.' *Westminster Gazette*, 23 Jan. 93.

7. JAHM to AECRM, 5 Dec. 02.

8. JAHM to AHJM, 24 July, 3 Aug. 09; JAHM to AECRM, 5 Aug. 04, 23 Mar. 12 (postcard).

9. JAHM to AECRM, 1 May 03.

10. Birmingham University Library. Letter EA 153, JAHM to EA, 27 Mar. 05.

11. MP AAM to JAHM, 15 Apr. 90.

12. Lady M., p. 120.

13. Obituary in *The Christian*, 19 Aug. 15.

14. The Association of Total Abstainers wore a small strip of blue ribbon as a badge.

15. JAHM to AECRM, 18 July 13.

16. C. E. M. Joad, *The Pleasure of Being Oneself*, New York (1951), p. 13 sq. I am indebted to Mrs Thomas Ballard for this reference.

17. JAHM to AHJM, 5 Nov. 09.

18. Lady M., pp. 13–14, 16.

19. JAHM to AECRM, 17 Aug. 02.

20. By letting Sunnyside the cost of the holiday was covered. In 1880 they rented a house at Keswick for £5 including gas, fire, and attendance. In 1892 full board at Ilfracombe was 3 shillings and sixpence per day each for rooms and 3 shillings and threepence each for all meals. *Cf.* MP G. Storey to JAHM, 16 June 80 and AAM to HJRM, 31 Aug. 92.

21. MP JAHM to HJRM, 1 Aug. 91; *cf.* also JAHM to Railway 23 July 91 (draft).

22. Robinson Ellis used to contribute a regular £10 or £20 towards the Murray family holidays. At his death he left James a legacy of £200, which was used towards paying off the mortgage on the house, and £50 each to three of the girls; but James shared with the University the regret that the old man had evidently no idea what he was worth. He always spoke as if badly off, made no bequest to the University, and his considerable fortune passed to the husband of a remote cousin. See JAHM to AHJM, 24

Oct. 13 and G. B. Grundy, *Fifty-Five Years at Oxford* (1945), p. 112.

23. MP JAHM to JRM, 14 June 05; CC to JAHM, 17 June 05.

24. C. Oman, *Memories of Victorian Oxford* (1941), p. 203; Grundy, *op. cit.*, p. 111 sq.

25. MP JAHM to HMRM, 26 Aug. 04; and JAHM to Ethelwyn Murray, 16 Sept. 04 (in possession of Mrs Manning).

26. Lady M, p. 120. At a Royal Academy Banquet, 1 May 99, the portrait painter Herkomer could not take his eyes off JAHM and thought he had the finest head and presence of anyone present. MP OARM to HJRM, Easter Monday 31.

27. MP FJF to JAHM, 10 Nov. 85.

28. Sidney Walton, 'A Dictionary Maker', *Christian World*, 27 Feb. 13.

29. JAHM to AECRM, 19 Sept., 31 Oct. 02; 9 Oct. 03.

30. Lady M, p. 78.

31. JAHM to AHJM, 24 Oct. 13. JAHM to AECRM, 5 Aug. 04.

32. JAHM to AECRM, 30 Apr. 09, also 24 Mar. 05, 13 Dec. 07.

33. *Ibid.*, 31 July 03.

34. MP JAHM to HJRM, 7 Feb. 92.

35. MP AAM to HJRM, 22 Oct. 91; JAHM to AAM, 24 May 14; JAHM to Mr Thorpe, 11 Sept. 02 (copy).

36. MP JAHM to HMRM, 17 July 97.

37. MP JAHM to Sir Richard Tangye, 22–9 Sept. 95 (copy); JAHM to HW, [Jan. 11] (draft).

38. MP AAM to HMRM, 25 July 99.

39. JAHM to AHJM, 17 Jan., 21 Jan. 10; 23 Sept. 13. JAHM to AECRM, 24 Mar. 05. MP JAHM to HMRM, 31 Jan. 10.

40. MP AAM to HJRM, 2 Mar. 93. JAHM to AHJM, 24 July, 3 Aug., 27 Oct. 09; 10 May, 7 June 10.

41. MP AAM to HJRM, 7 Feb. 92.

42. A. Graham Bell, 'Prehistoric Telephone Days', *National Geographic Magazine*, xli. 3 (Mar. 22), p. 231.

43. MP J. Wright to JAHM, 29 Jan. 96. E. M. Wright, *Life of Joseph Wright* (1932), ii, pp. 447–8.

44. JAHM to AHJM, 6 Dec. 10.

45. MP JAHM, 'Remarkable Meteoric Appearance', 2 Sept. 95 (draft letter).

46. JAHM to AECRM, 2 July 08.

47. JAHM to AHJM, 23 Sept. 13.

48. JAHM to AECRM, 31 July, 9 Oct. 03. See also Birmingham University Library, Letter EA 148, JAHM to EA, 14 Jan. 1900. MP R. H. Jenkin to JAHM, 17 May 84; JAHM to AHJM, 20 Oct. 09. WGRM, pp. 12–15.

49. JAHM to AECRM, 24 Dec. 09. JAHM to AHJM, 17, 21 Jan., 17 Feb., 6 Dec. 10. For other references to his political views, see JAHM to AECRM, 13 Dec. 07, 8 May 08, 1 Apr. 10; JAHM to AHJM, 3 Sept., 27 Oct., 5, 17 Nov. 09.

50. N. Mitchison, *Small Talk. Memories of an Edwardian Childhood* (1973), p. 90. She was not allowed to play with the Gilbert Murray children because they were Liberals.

51. JAHM to AECRM, 15 Apr. 10. MP JAHM address, 'Why we are Congregationalists'. He was strongly against the proposal to erect a statue to Cardinal Newman near the Martyrs' Memorial in Oxford: AAM to HJRM, 26 Jan. 92.

52. G 11021/24. 375. JAHM to HG, 19 Aug. 86.

53. JAHM to AHJM, 31 Dec. 11, 3 Jan. 15, 21 Jan. 10.

54. MP JAHM to AAM, 27 May 14.

55. MP JAHM to HMRM, 27 Mar. 15.

56. JAHM to AHJM, 26 Apr. 10.

57. JAHM to AECRM, 14 Dec. 06.

58. *Ibid.*, 2 Feb. 07, 17 Nov. 05, 18 May 06.

59. *The Times* Obituary, 11 July 36.

60. *Periodical*, xiii. 143 (15 Feb. 28), p. 30.

61. GFT, pp. 20–1.

INDEX

(1897), 290; Balliol College, JAHM a member of, 243–4, attends Gaudy (1908), 294; Exeter, Merton and Trinity Colleges, JAHM hopes for fellowship at, 237

Palæotype phonetic system, 74
Palmer, Mr, Dictionary voluntary sub-editor, 176
——Canon Edwin, 156
Palmerston, Lord, Conspiracy to Murder Bill of, 41
Parlane, the Rev. James, congregational minister, Hawick, 120
Passow, Franz, lexicographer, 135
Pattison, Mark, Rector Exeter College, 156, 207, 220, 226
Pauli, Dr Reinhold, 119; *Life of Alfred the Great*, 51
Peckham, London: Beaufort Terrace, Nunhead Lane, 60, 68; Nunhead Cemetery, 65
Peden, Alexander, covenanter, 20
Penn, Mrs, of Innerleithen, 19
Philip, P. J., *OED* assistant, 298
Philips, Professor G. M., University of Lewisburg, 184
Phillips, Dr Henry of Philadelphia, 184
Philological Society, London, 78–9, 86, 98, 259; F. J. Furnivall, Secretary, 87, 89, 172; Proposal for a New English Dictionary (1857), 100, 132 sq., 195; concise version proposed by Furnivall, 138, 141, 143; committee to search for Editor, 139; JAHM named editor, 140, 142; negotiations with Macmillan to use Philological Society's materials, 133, 140–7; approach to Delegates of Oxford University Press, 140, 143, and to Cambridge University Press Syndics, 148; committee to re-open negotiations with Oxford names JAHM as Editor, 149 and Appendix I; for subsequent history of negotiations, *see OED*; Society registers as Company for purpose of agreement with Press, 158; special meeting to confirm agreement, 166–7; agreement later cancelled, 164–5; responsibility for appointment of editors, 226–7, 239, 286
——JAHM contacts with membership of, 50, 73, 81, 87, 117, 119, 122, 173; threatened resignation, 286; President of, *see* Murray, J. A. H. M.; presidential address, 199; reports to on *OED*, 177, 180, 192, 199, 223, 274, 283, 291, 302, 303; disappointed by lack of help from members, 183, 190; supported by Society in controversy with Jowett, 224, 229; disagrees with Society on policy, 217, 269, 270, 273; special meetings on *OED* policy, (1883), 224, (1892), 268, (1896), 276–8
——Interest of in spelling reform, 101–2
——Hall suspended by, 305; Platt censured by, 307

Phonetic systems, use in recording dialects, 74–6, 85; views of Delegates of Oxford University Press on, 157–8; possible use in indicating pronunciation in *OED*, 190–1
Pierson, the Rev. J. of Michigan, 184
Pitman, Isaac, 74, 190
Platt, James, junior, *OED* voluntary reader, 307–8
Pollock, Sir Frederick, 163
Postmaster General, 212–13
Powell, Professor Frederick York, 275, 278, 282
Price, Bartholomew, Secretary to Delegates of Oxford University Press, 149–52, 156–7, 160, 162–3, 165–6, 167, 183–4, 192, 199, 207–8, 210, 213, 220–1, 226, 228, 231–2, 234, 237, 239, 240, 246–7, 250, 260, 267, 271, 275, 278

Ralston, William, sub-librarian, British Museum, 69
Randall, John, *OED* voluntary reader, 184
Rask, R. C., *Anglo Saxon Grammar*, 55
Religious Tract Society, *The Visitor or Monthly Instuctor*, 22
Revue Celtique, 83
Rhys, Professor Sir John, 256
Richardson, Charles, *New English Dictionary*, 133–4, 148, 207
Riddell, Henry Scott, minor poet, 50–1
Romic phonetic system, 77
Rothenstein, Sir William, *Oxford Characters. A Series of Lithographs*, 293
Royal Asiatic Society, 122
——Society, loan of books to Scriptorium, 164
Ruskin, John, 306
Rutherford, Catherine, teacher at Cavers School, 13
Ruthven, Ada Agnes, *see* Murray, Ada Agnes *née* Ruthven
——George, father-in-law of JAHM (1816–71), 62, 66, 68, 316
——Emily (*née* Groom), mother-in-law of JAHM, 63, 67
——Herbert, brother-in-law of JAHM, *OED* assistant, 172, 173, 174, 182, 212, 218

Saffi, Signor, 41, 235
St Andrews University, 118, 119, 282
Saturday Review, quoted, 278
Scotland, course of Reformation in, 8
Scott, Miss, *OED* assistant, 175
——Adam, cousin of JAHM (1826–81), 10, 35, 43
——Charlie o' the Crescent, grandfather of JAHM (1759–1840), 5–6
——Charles, uncle of JAHM (1794–1861), 27, 28
——George, master of Denholm Parish School, 15–17, 21, 25, 30
——James, great-uncle of JAHM (b. 1768), 5
——Johnnie, schoolfellow of JAHM, 23